ExtREMely MORoNiC MAD

ALSO AVAILABLE FROM MAD BOOKS

Insanely Awesome MAD

Epic MAD

Amazingly Stupid MAD

Spy vs. Spy Omnibus

MAD About Super Heroes Vol. 2

Spy vs. Spy: The Top Secret Files!

PLUS

Planet Tad (HarperCollins)

MAD's Greatest Artists: Sergio Aragonés (Running Press)

MAD's Greatest Artists: Mort Drucker (Running Press)

The MAD Fold-In Collection 1964–2010 (Chronicle Books)

Spy vs. Spy 2: The Joke and Dagger Files (Watson-Guptill Publications)

MAD About *Star Wars* (Ballantine Books - Del Rey)

MAD Archives Volume 3 (DC Comics)

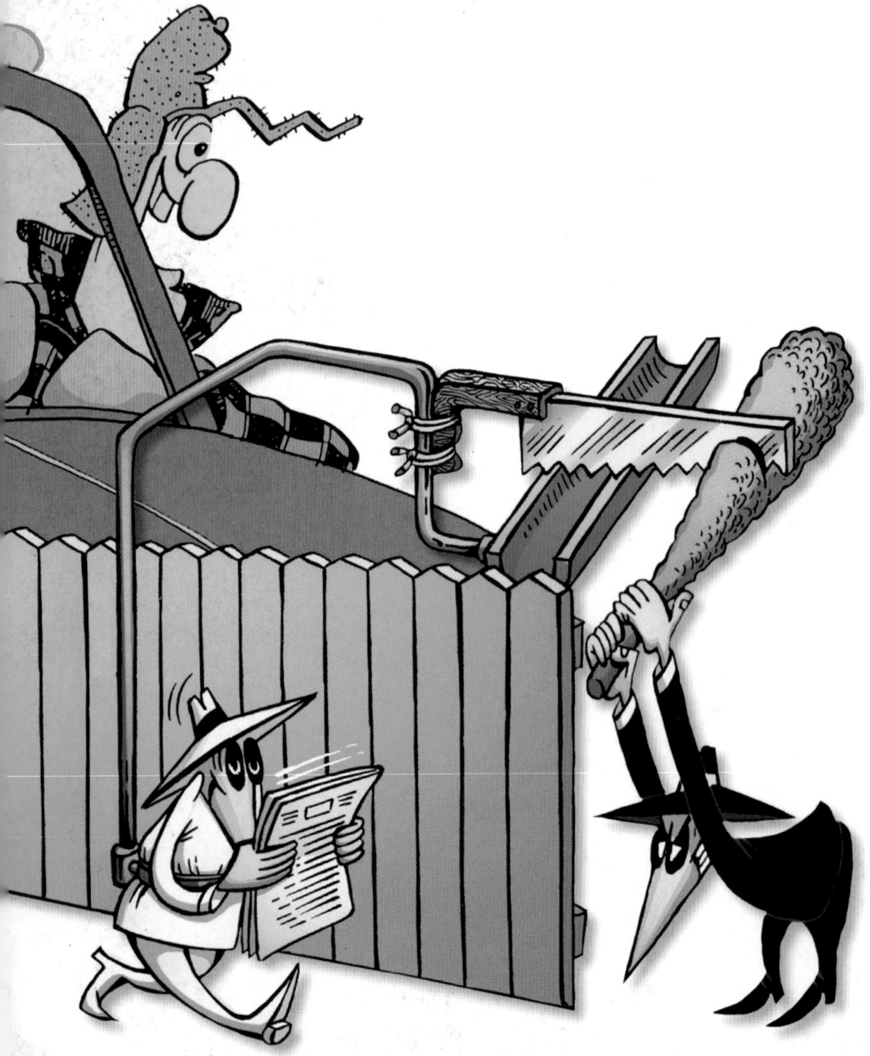

Extremely MORONIC MAD

BY
"THE USUAL GANG OF IDIOTS"

MAD
NEW YORK
BOOKS™

MAD BOOKS

William Gaines **FOUNDER**

John Ficarra **EDITOR**

Charlie Kadau, Joe Raiola **SENIOR EDITORS**

Dave Croatto, Jacob Lambert **ASSOCIATE EDITORS**

Sam Viviano **ART DIRECTOR**

Ryan Flanders **ASSISTANT ART DIRECTOR**

Doug Thomson **PRODUCTION ARTIST**

CONTRIBUTING WRITERS AND ARTISTS:
"The Usual Gang of Idiots"

ADMINISTRATION

Diane Nelson **PRESIDENT**
Dan DiDio and Jim Lee **CO-PUBLISHERS**
Geoff Johns **CHIEF CREATIVE OFFICER**
John Rood **EXECUTIVE VP – SALES, MARKETING AND BUSINESS DEVELOPMENT**
Amy Genkins **SENIOR VP – BUSINESS AND LEGAL AFFAIRS**
Nairi Gardiner **SENIOR VP – FINANCE**
Jeff Boison **VP – PUBLISHING OPERATIONS**
John Cunningham **VP – MARKETING**
Terri Cunningham **VP – TALENT RELATIONS AND SERVICES**
Anne DePies **VP – STRATEGY PLANNING AND REPORTING**
Amit Desai **SENIOR VP – FRANCHISE MANAGEMENT**
Alison Gill **SENIOR VP – MANUFACTURING AND OPERATIONS**
Bob Harras **VP – EDITOR-IN-CHIEF**
Jason James **VP – INTERACTIVE MARKETING**
Hank Kanalz **SENIOR VP – DIGITAL**
Jay Kogan **VP – BUSINESS AND LEGAL AFFAIRS, PUBLISHING**
Jack Mahan **VP – BUSINESS AFFAIRS, TALENT**
Nick Napolitano **VP – MANUFACTURING ADMINISTRATION**
Rich Palermo **VP – BUSINESS AFFAIRS, MEDIA**
Sue Pohja **VP – BOOK SALES**
Courtney Simmons **SENIOR VP – PUBLICITY**
Bob Wayne **SENIOR VP – SALES**

VISIT MAD ONLINE AT: WWW.MADMAGAZINE.COM

Though Alfred E. Neuman wasn't the first to say
"a fool and his money are soon parted," here's
your chance to prove the old adage right —
subscribe to MAD! Simply call 1-800-4-MADMAG
and mention code AWFMDIA. Operators are
standing by (the water cooler).

SUSTAINABLE FORESTRY INITIATIVE
Certified Chain of Custody
At Least 25% Certified Forest Content
www.sfiprogram.org
SFI-01042
APPLIES TO TEXT STOCK ONLY

"Drawn Out Dramas" Throughout By Sergio Aragonés

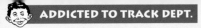

YOU'RE AN OFFICIAL OVER-THE-TOP, NO-LIFE, W NASCAR

As much as we hate to admit it, NASCAR (don't ask us what it stands for) is big and getting bigger. And if it was a *real* sport it would be even more popular! But as faux-sports go, NASCAR, aside from golf, badminton and Chinese checkers, is the absolute, undisputed tops, loved by fans from coast to coast. Problem is, some fans love it a bit too much. Could you be one of them? It's quite simple:

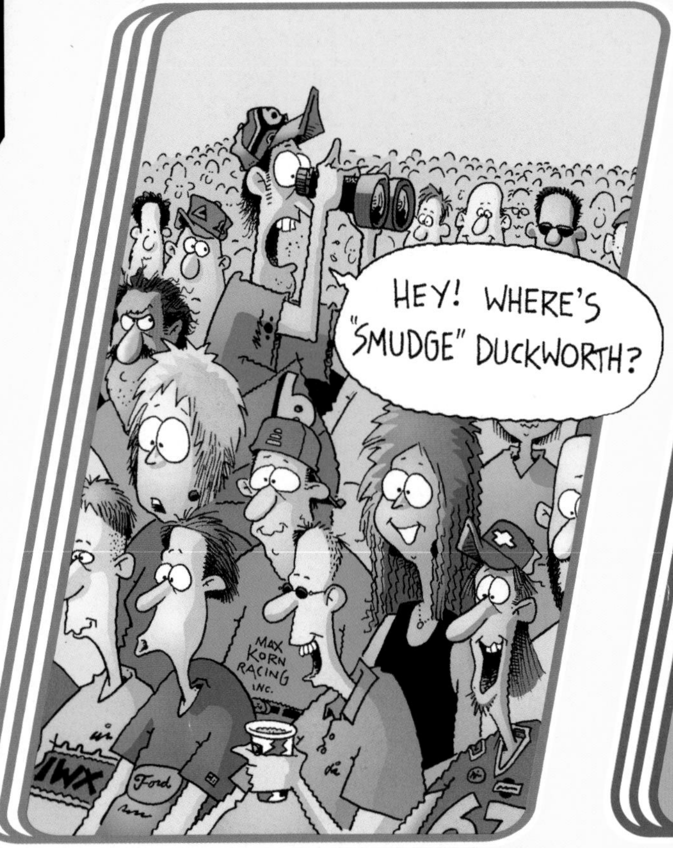
HEY! WHERE'S "SMUDGE" DUCKWORTH?
MAX KORN RACING INC.

You're the only one in the grandstand (or the press box for that matter) who's aware that the 71 car is using a back-up gas can guy.

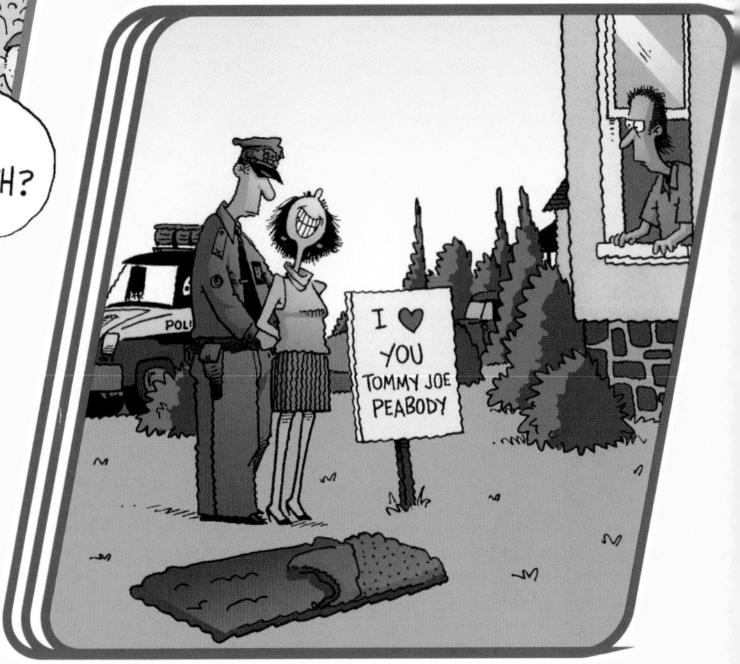
I ♥ YOU TOMMY JOE PEABODY

A number of right rear tire-changers from several pit crews have restraining orders against you.

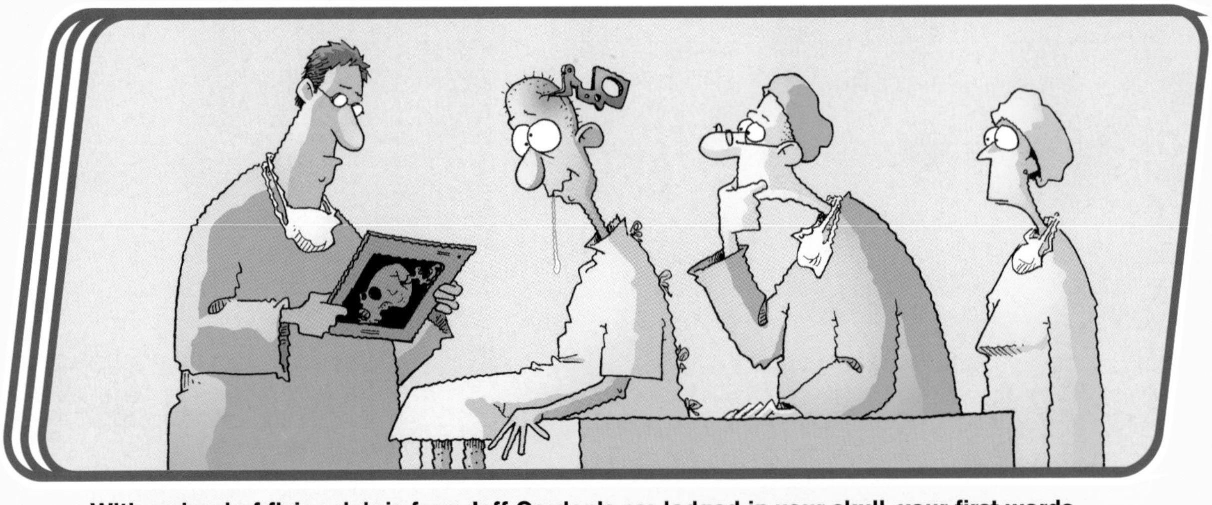

With a shard of flying debris from Jeff Gordon's car lodged in your skull, your first words upon coming to are to threaten a malpractice suit if the doctor tries to remove it.

CARD-CARRYING, HACK-JOB FANATIC IF...

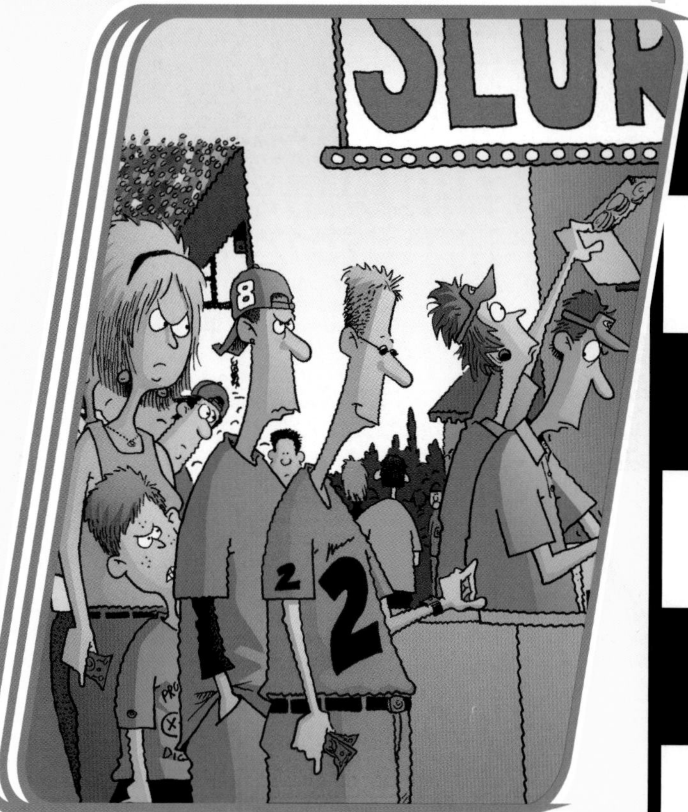

You have no qualms about holding up a Slurpee line for 20 minutes while they try to locate the crummy Hut Stricklin commemorative cup you're missing from your collection.

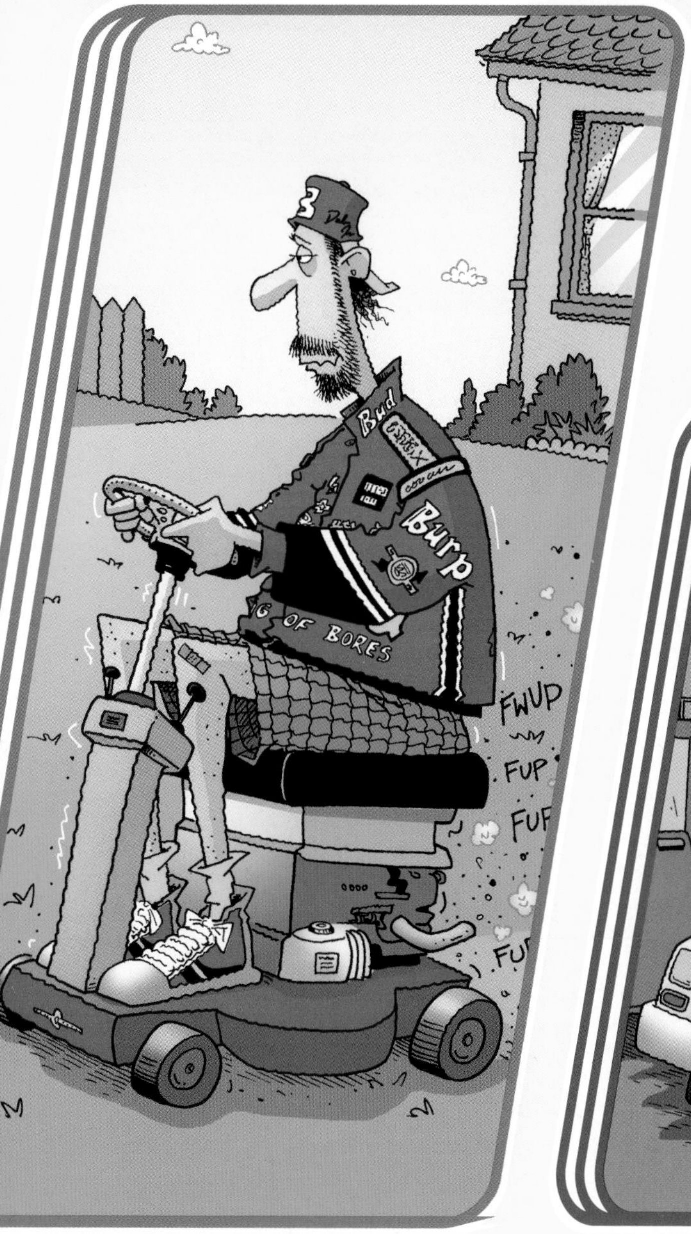

Bud
Burp
OF BORES
FWUP
FUP

You spend $175 to wear the same fireproof team jacket that Dale Jr. wears... to mow your lawn.

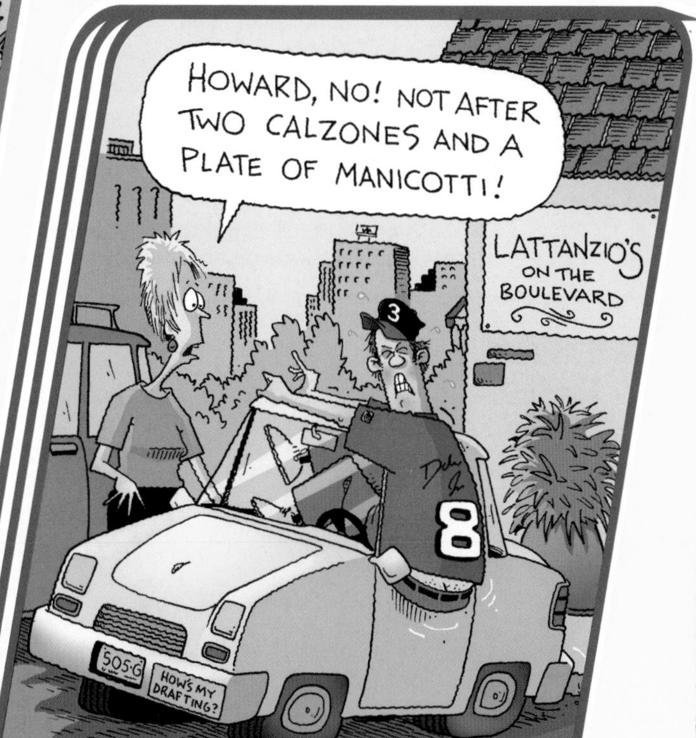

HOWARD, NO! NOT AFTER TWO CALZONES AND A PLATE OF MANICOTTI!
LATTANZIO'S ON THE BOULEVARD
505-G
HOW'S MY DRAFTING?

You haven't used your car doors in three years.

ARTIST AND WRITER: JOHN CALDWELL

YOU'RE AN OFFICIAL OVER-THE-TOP, CARD-CARRYING, NO-LIFE, WHACK-JOB NASCAR FANATIC IF...

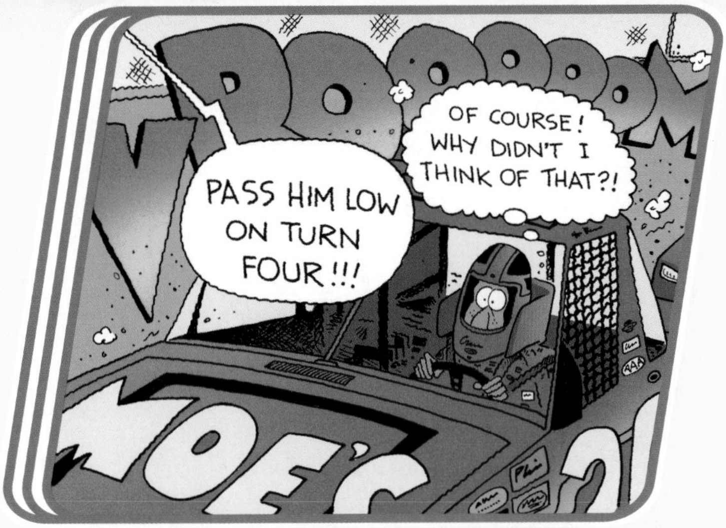

PASS HIM LOW ON TURN FOUR!!!
OF COURSE! WHY DIDN'T I THINK OF THAT?!

You're dead certain that, despite the mega-decibel din of a NASCAR event, your guy can actually hear you screaming driving instructions.

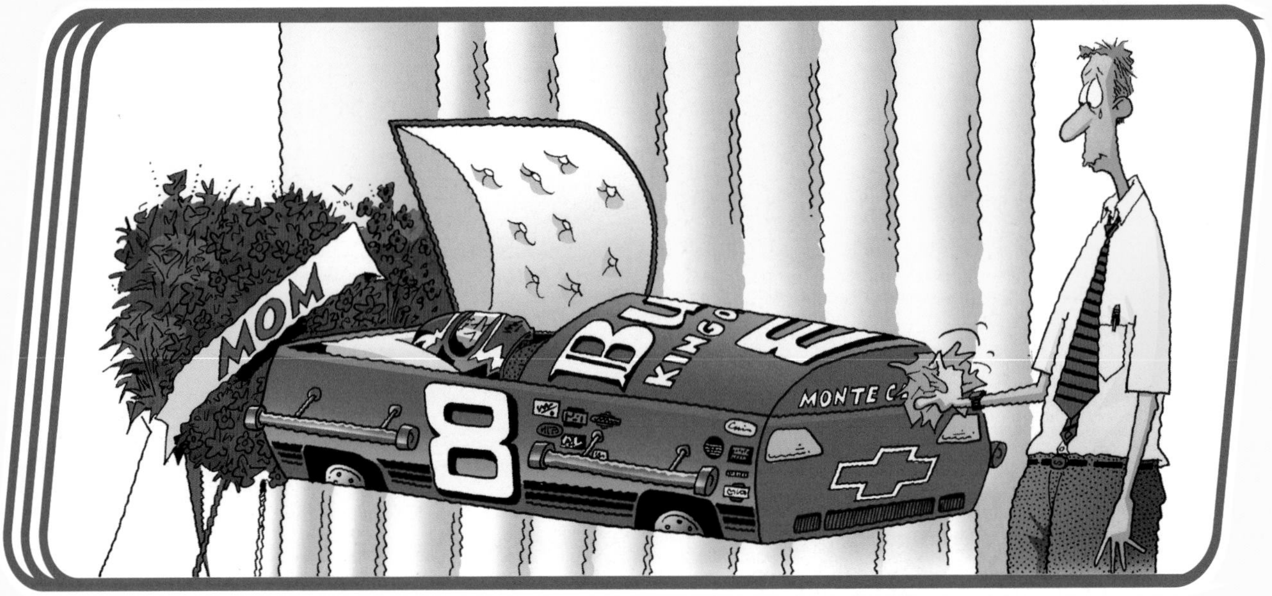

MOM
8

When the time came to choose a casket for your mother, settling on a Budweiser/Chevy paint scheme was a no-brainer.

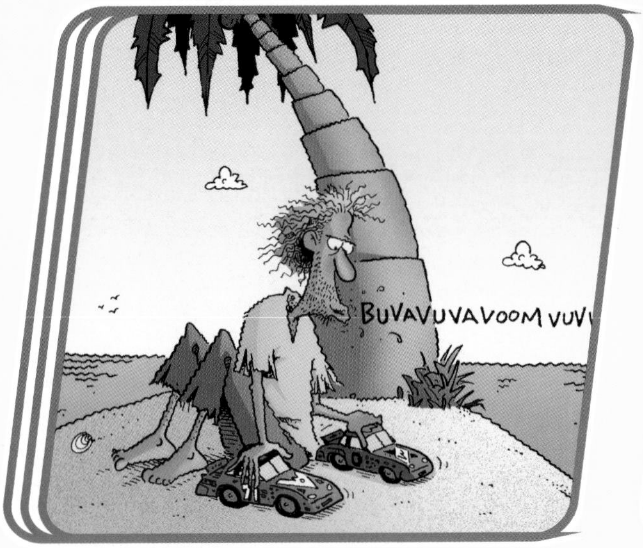

BUVAVUVAVOOM

When asked what two things you'd want with you if you were stranded on a desert island, both would be die-cast collectibles.

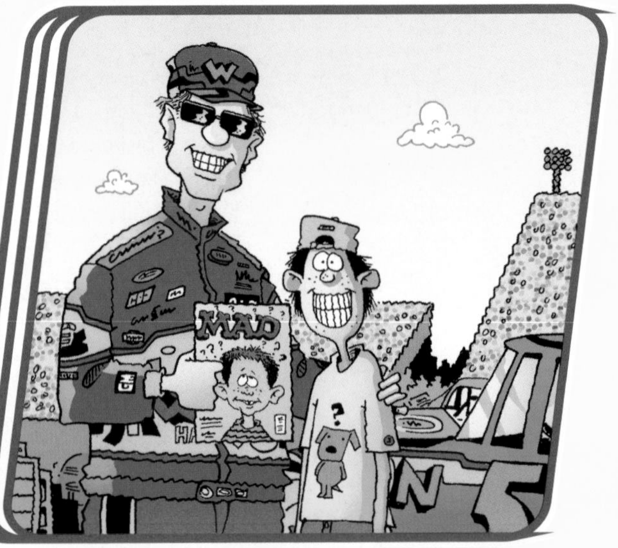

MAD

You actually believe that a photo of you and some guy named Wally Dallenbach qualifies as a "Celebrity Snap" that will net you a free subscription to MAD.

15 REASONS TO HATE SCHOOL

1

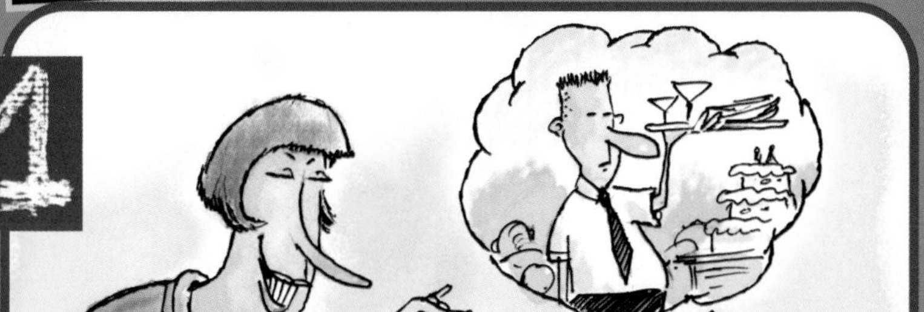

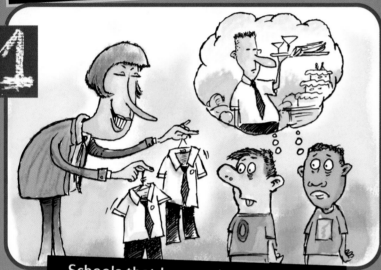

Schools that have strict dress codes, because they think students learn better when they're dressed like someone who cleans tables at weddings.

2

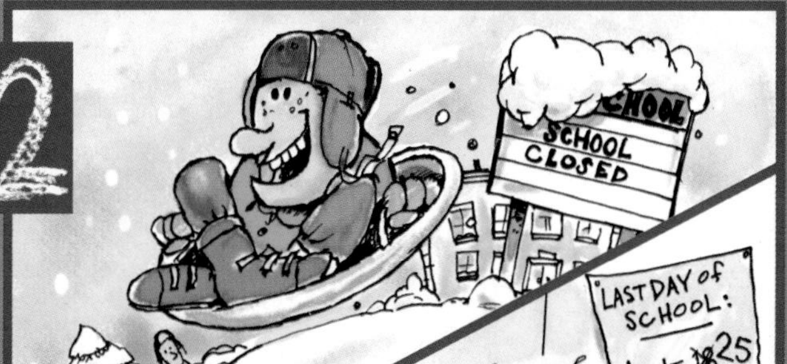
SCHOOL CLOSED
LAST DAY of SCHOOL: JUNE ~~18~~ 25
TEST

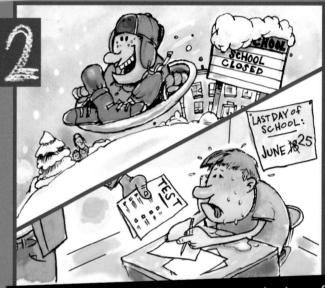

Giant snowstorms, which result in the joy of all classes being cancelled — but then stick you with school make-up days just when you're itching to start summer vacation.

3

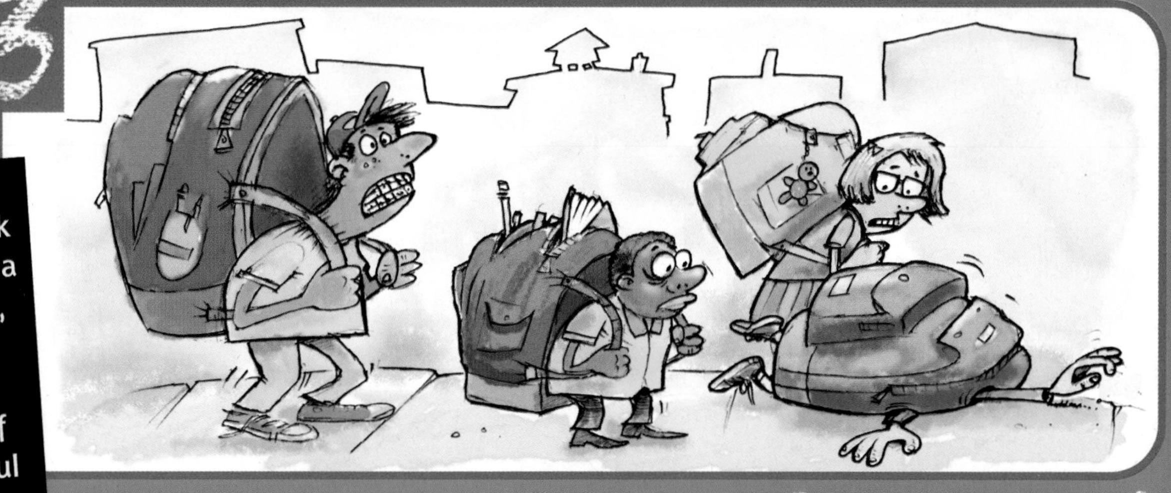

Having to drag around a backpack jammed with half a ton of textbooks, which contain a combined four ounces worth of interesting, useful information.

WRITER: JACOB LAMBERT ARTIST: RICH POWELL

CONTINUED ON THE NEXT PAGE

← CONTINUED FROM PAGE 9

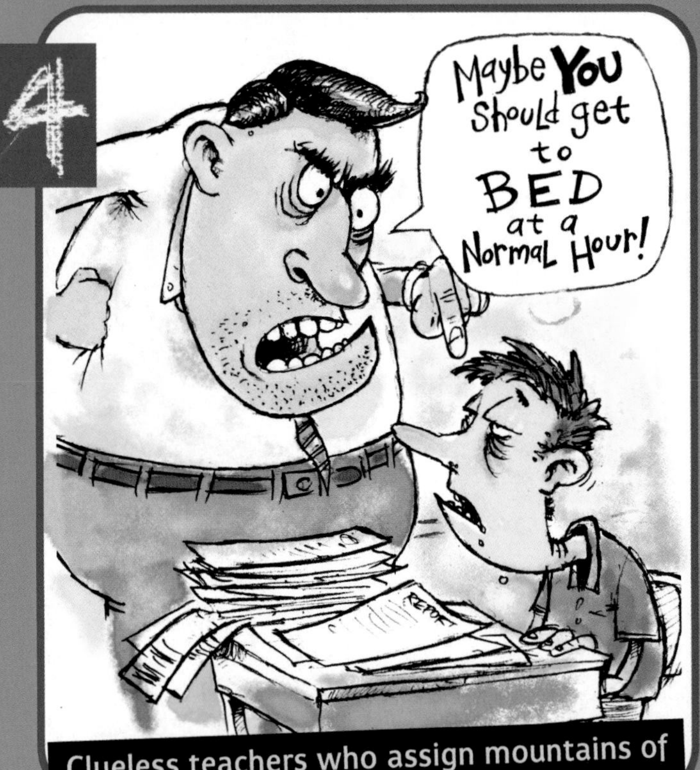
4
Maybe YOU Should get to BED at a Normal Hour!

Clueless teachers who assign mountains of homework every day, and then can't figure out why you always fall asleep in class.

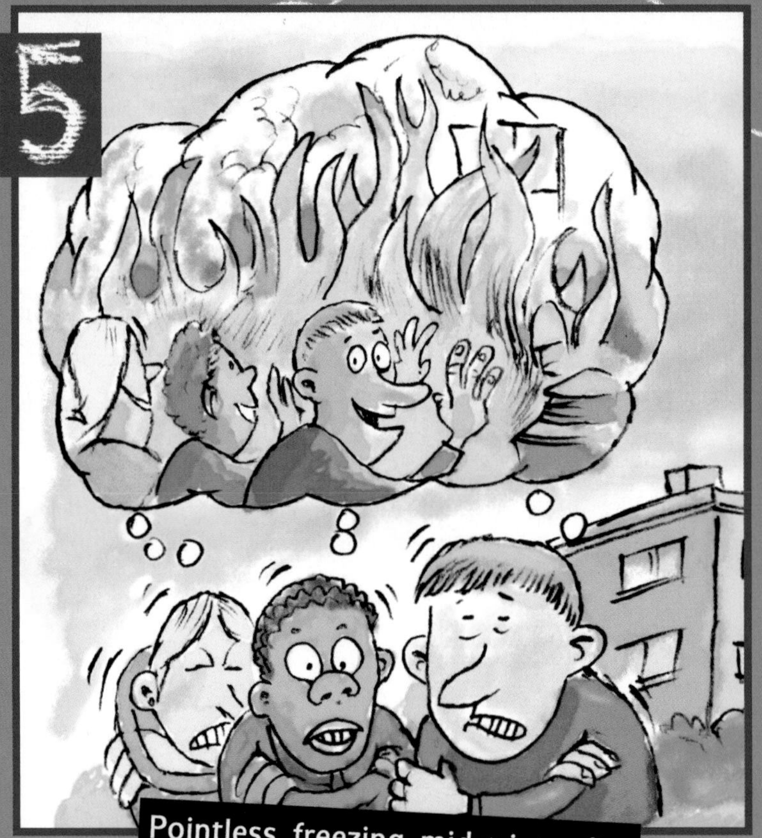
5

Pointless, freezing, mid-winter fire drills that make being roasted alive seem like a better choice.

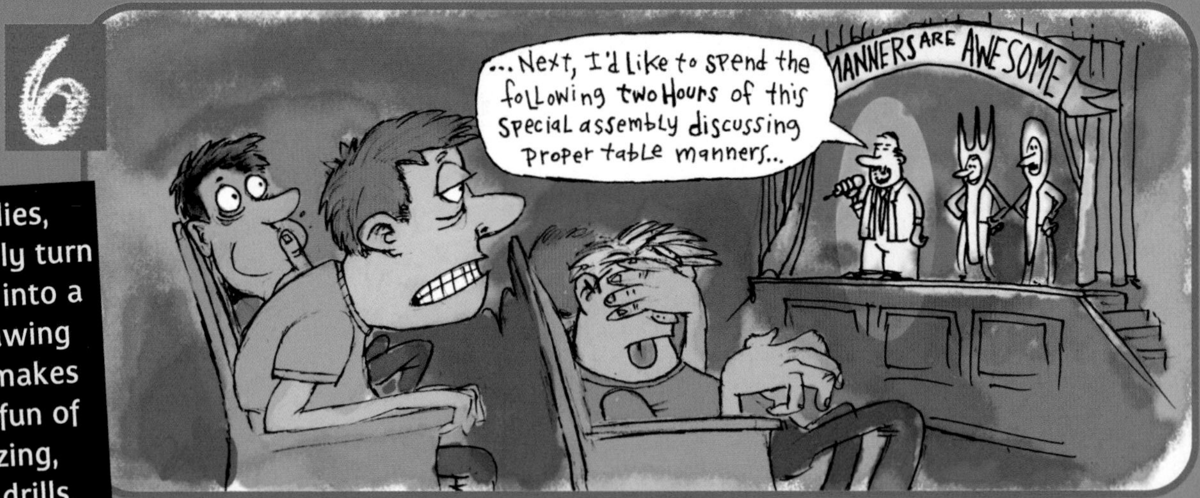
6
...Next, I'd like to spend the following two Hours of this special assembly discussing proper table manners...
MANNERS ARE AWESOME

School Assemblies, which can magically turn a dull school day into a dreadful, eye-clawing nightmare that makes you beg for the fun of pointless, freezing, mid-winter fire drills.

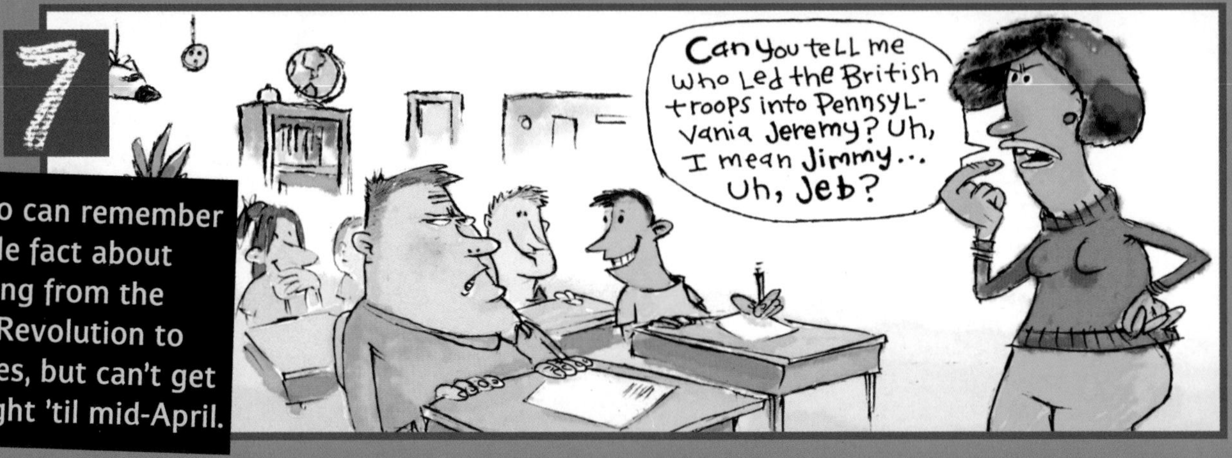
7
Can you tell me who Led the British troops into PennsyLvania Jeremy? Uh, I mean Jimmy... Uh, Jeb?

Teachers who can remember every little fact about everything from the American Revolution to grammar rules, but can't get your name right 'til mid-April.

8

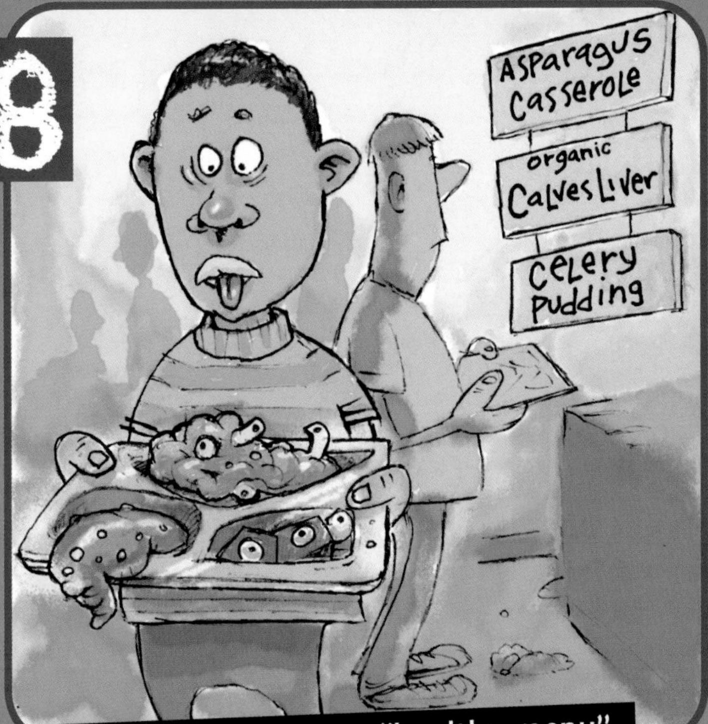
Asparagus Casserole
organic Calves Liver
celery pudding

The new, bad-tasting "healthy menu" cafeteria food that actually makes you miss the *old*, bad tasting cafeteria food

9

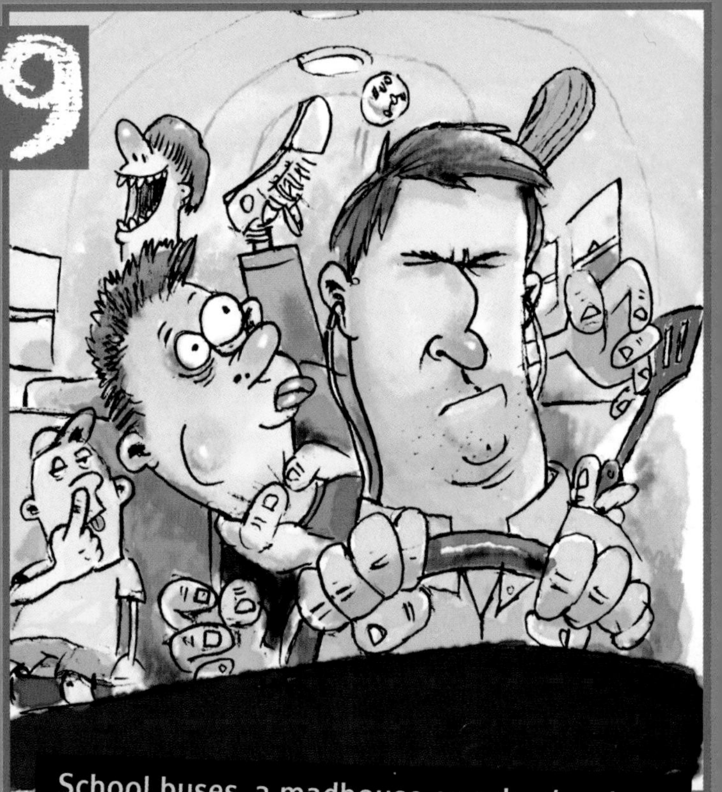

School buses, a madhouse on wheels where there's only slightly less politeness and good manners than at a WWE Raw match.

10

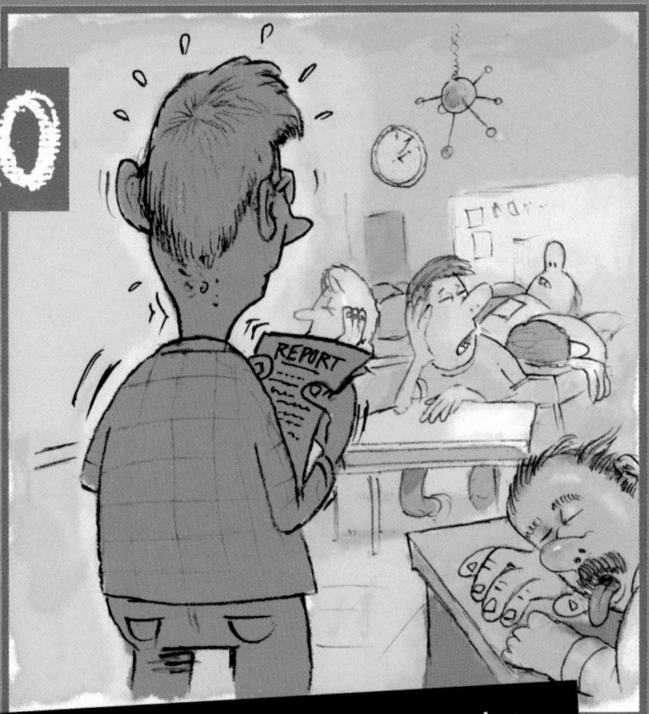
REPORT

Having to speak in front of the class, which always makes you sweat, get a stomach ache and shake — even though your teacher and classmates never actually listen to a word you're saying.

11

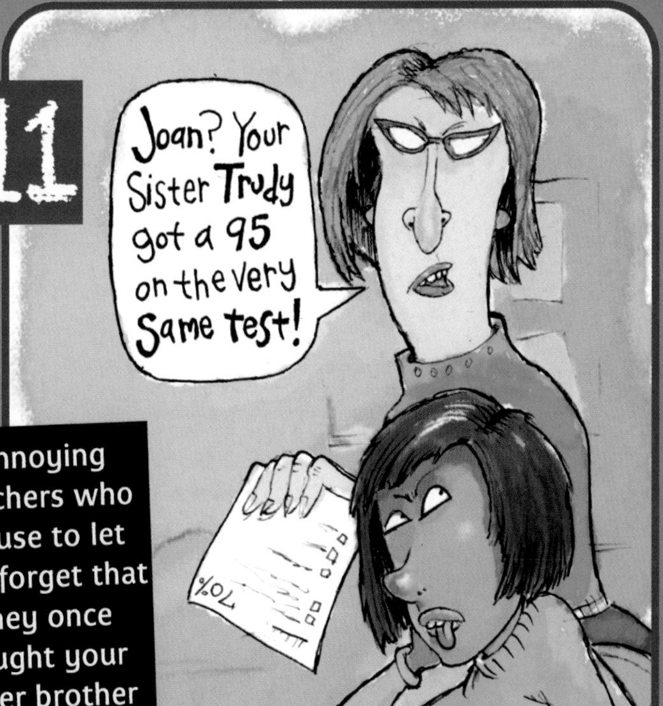
Joan? Your Sister Trudy got a 95 on the very Same test!
70%

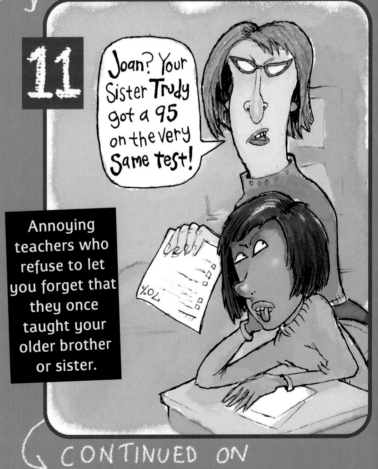

Annoying teachers who refuse to let you forget that they once taught your older brother or sister.

CONTINUED ON PAGE 12

CONTINUED FROM PAGE 12

12

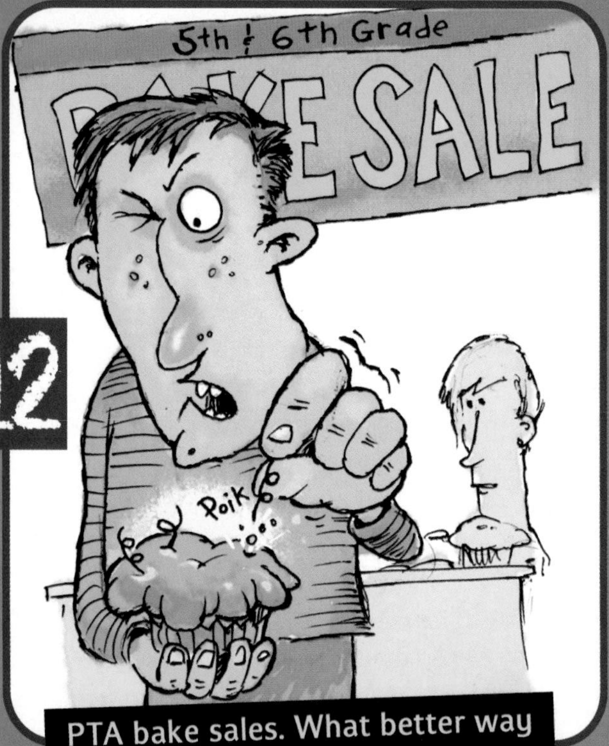
5th & 6th Grade
SALE
Poik

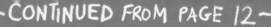

PTA bake sales. What better way to blow your allowance than to buy gross, hair-filled cupcakes.

13

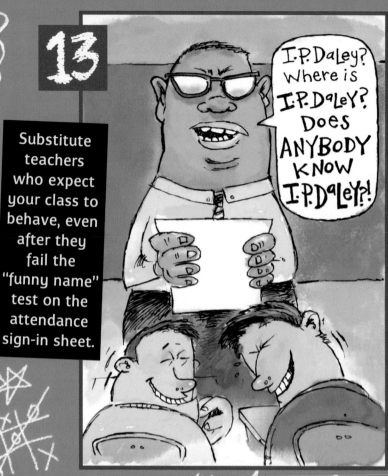

Substitute teachers who expect your class to behave, even after they fail the "funny name" test on the attendance sign-in sheet.

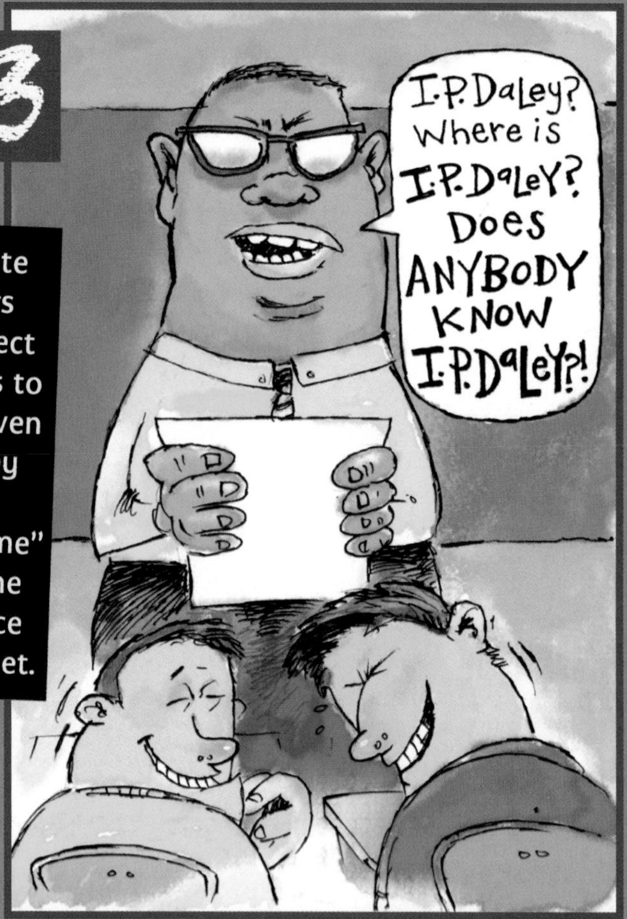
I.P. Daley? Where is I.P. Daley? Does ANYBODY KNOW I.P. Daley?!

14

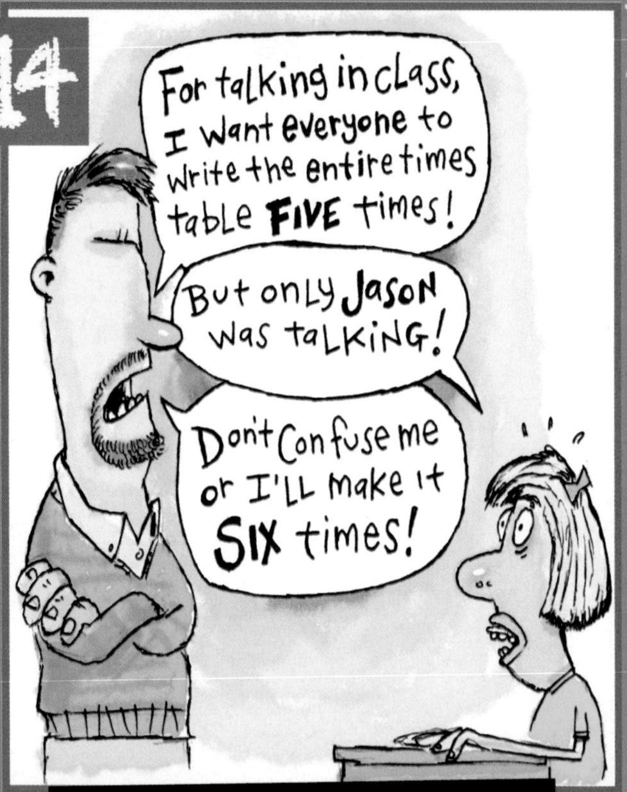
For talking in class, I want everyone to write the entire times table FIVE times!
But only JASON was talking!
Don't confuse me or I'LL make it SIX times!

When the whole class gets punished for something only one kid did. So how come the whole class never gets a good grade when only one kid passes the test?

15

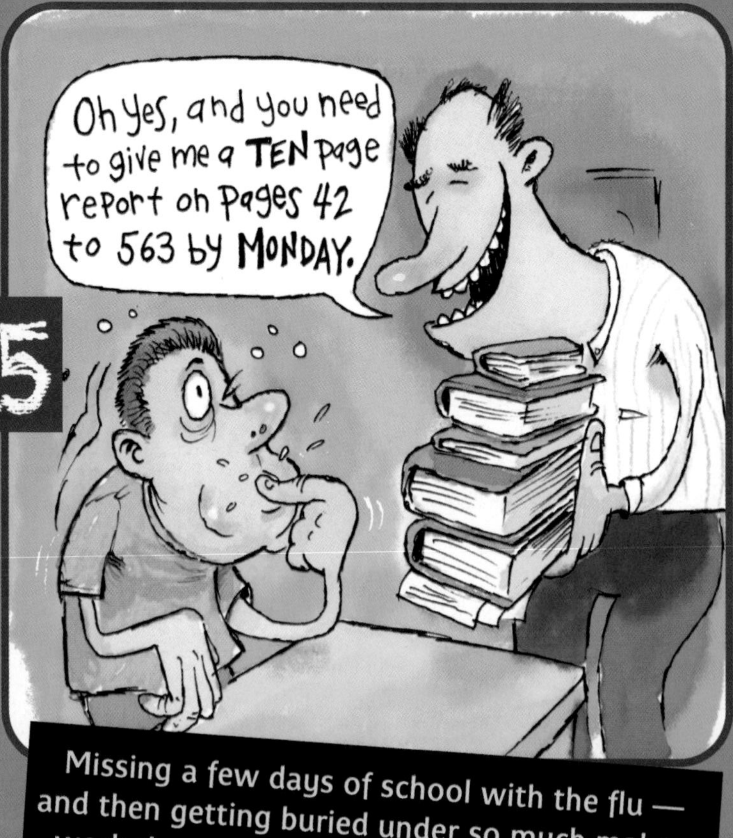
Oh yes, and you need to give me a TEN page report on pages 42 to 563 by MONDAY.

Missing a few days of school with the flu — and then getting buried under so much makeup work that you feel like puking all over again.

JOKE AND DAGGER DEPT.

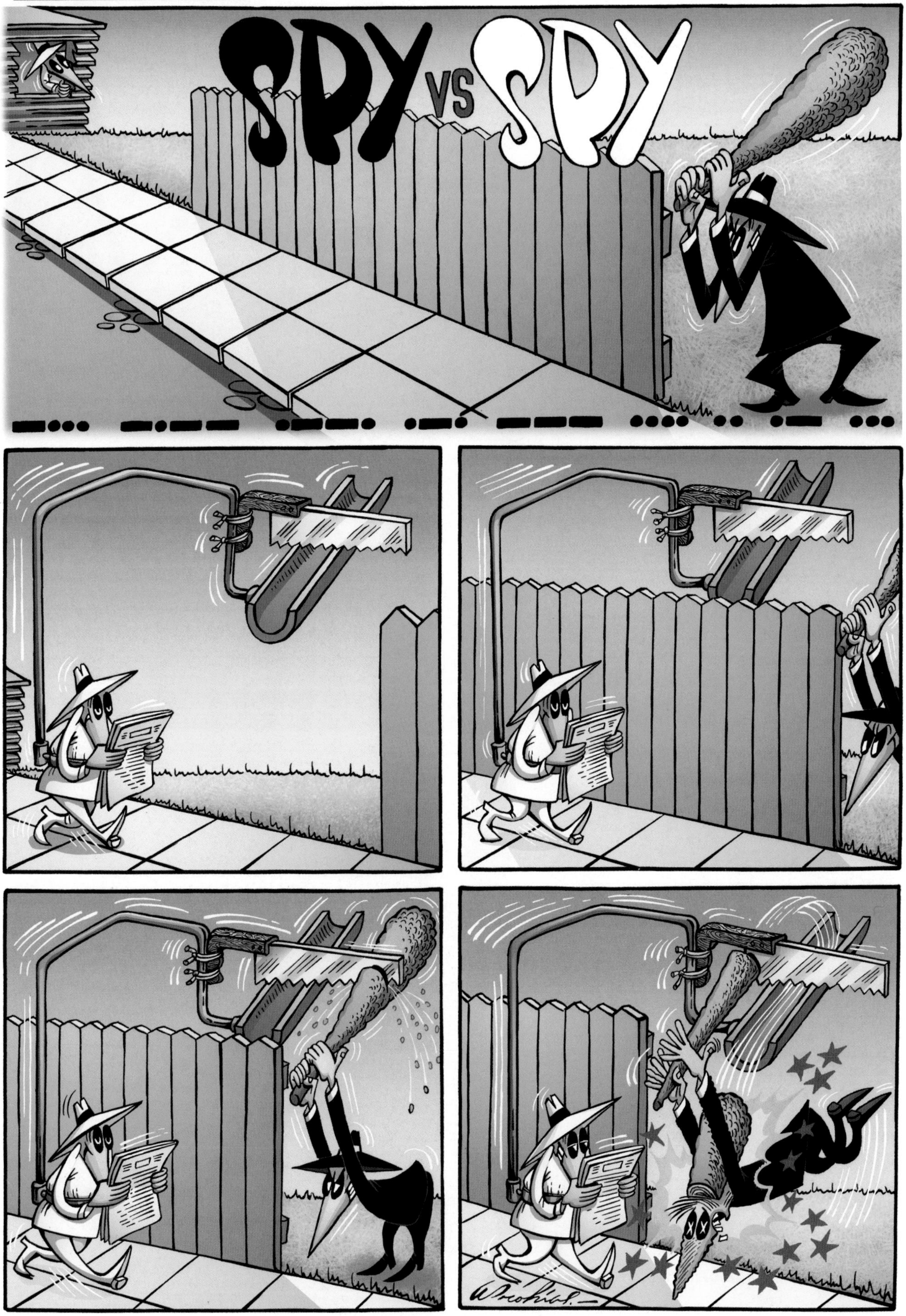
SPY VS SPY

WRITER AND ARTIST: ANTONIO PROHIAS   COLORIST: CARRIE STRACHAN

THINGS TO DO HOME

EAR WAX SCULPTING

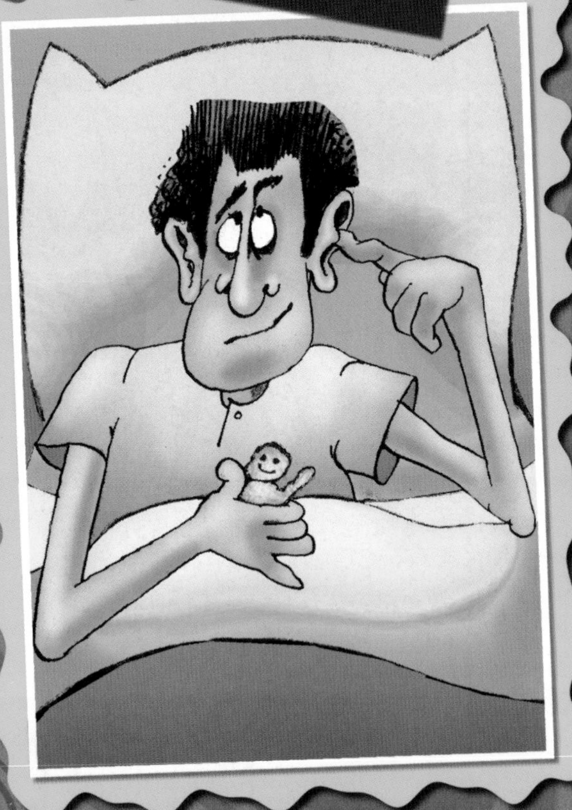

COTTON BALL GOLF

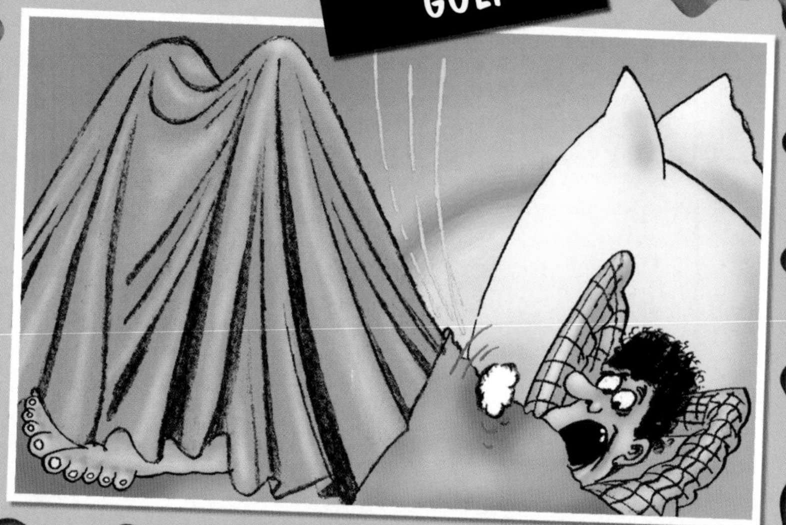

TOE PUPPETS

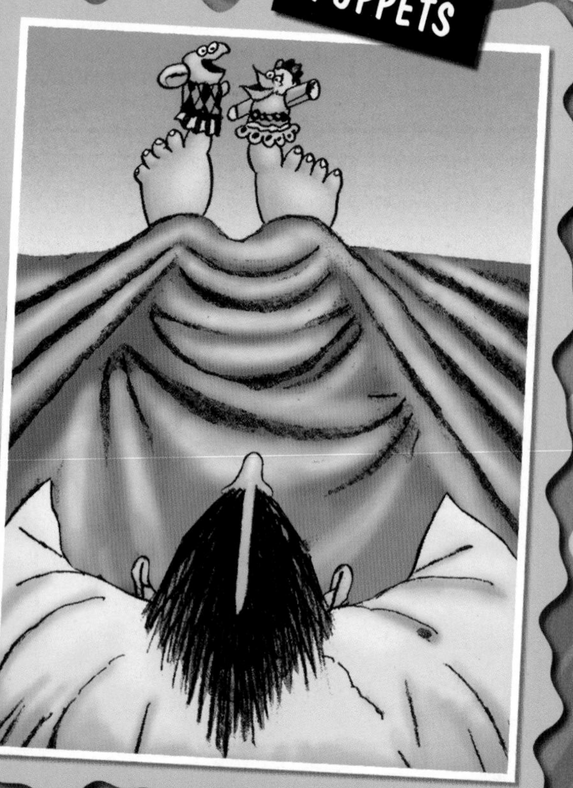

CHICKEN SOUP BLIND MAN'S BLUFF

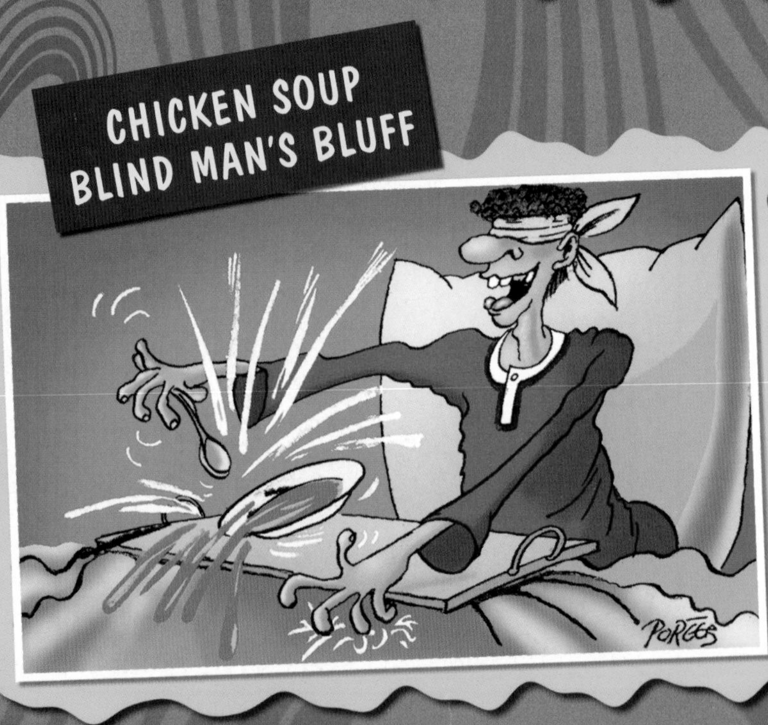
PORGES

WRITER AND ARTIST: PAUL PETER PORGES

WHEN YOU'RE SICK

SUGAR CUBE TIDDLYWINKS

USED TISSUE BASKETBALL

UNDER-THE-BED DUSTBUNNY SAILING RACES

BREAKFAST TRAY LIMBO

CAR SICK DEPT.

Hey, gang! Here we go with another MAD "Hate Book," those little literary gems calculated to help you feel better by

THE MAD CAR-OWN

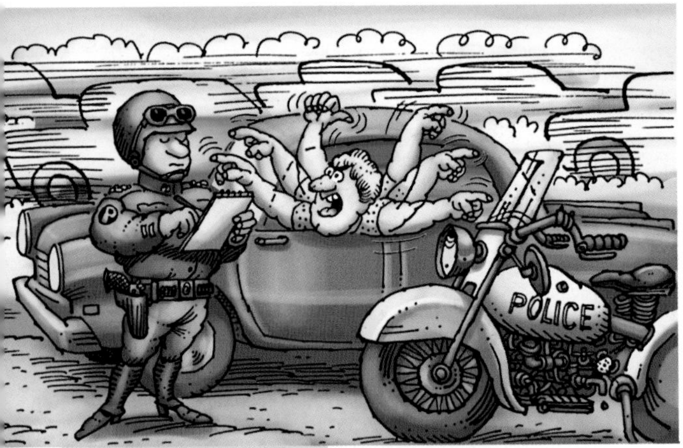
POLICE

DON'T YOU HATE...
. . . being the only one caught speeding when you were just going as fast as everyone else.

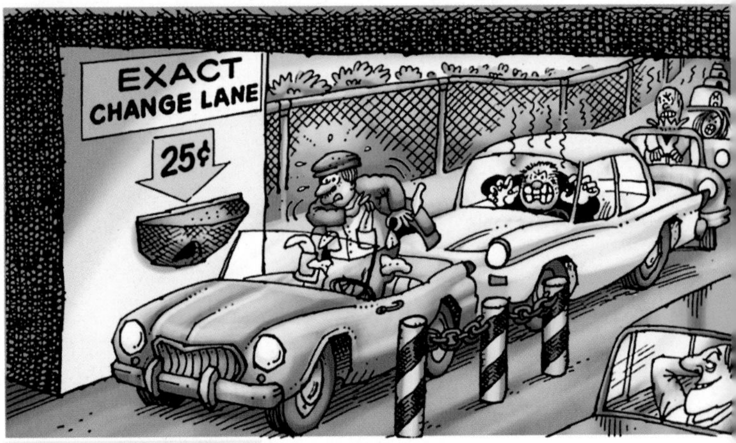
EXACT
CHANGE LANE
25¢

DON'T YOU HATE...
. . . getting into the "Exact Change Only" lane, and ending up behind a guy who finds he hasn't got the exact change.

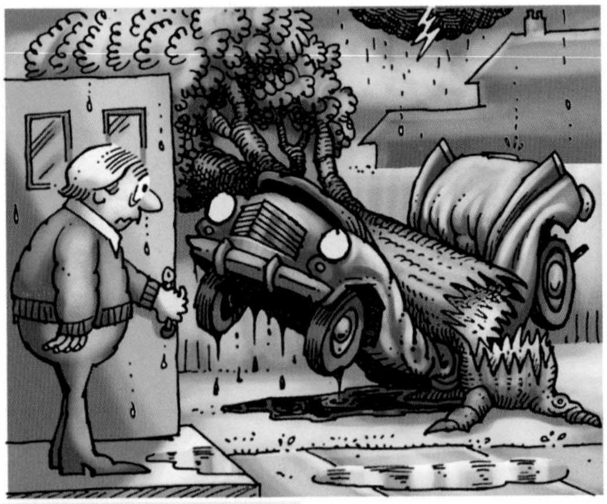

DON'T YOU HATE...
. . . when something happens the day after you let your comprehensive insurance expire.

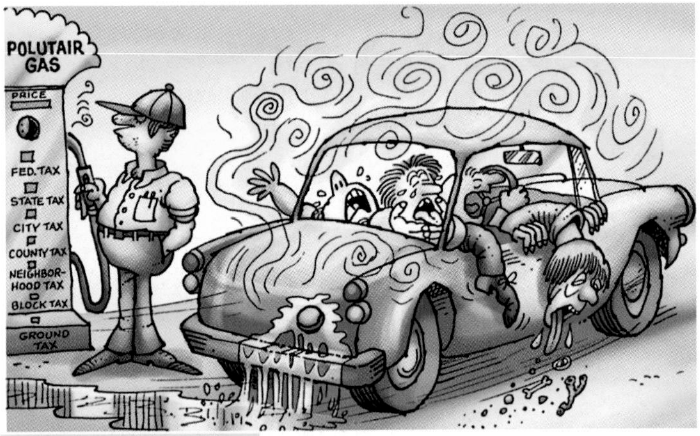
POLUTAIR GAS
PRICE
FED. TAX
STATE TAX
CITY TAX
COUNTY TAX
NEIGHBOR-HOOD TAX
BLOCK TAX
GROUND TAX

DON'T YOU HATE...
...the nauseating smell of gasoline that wafts forward to tell you that they've over-filled your tank again.

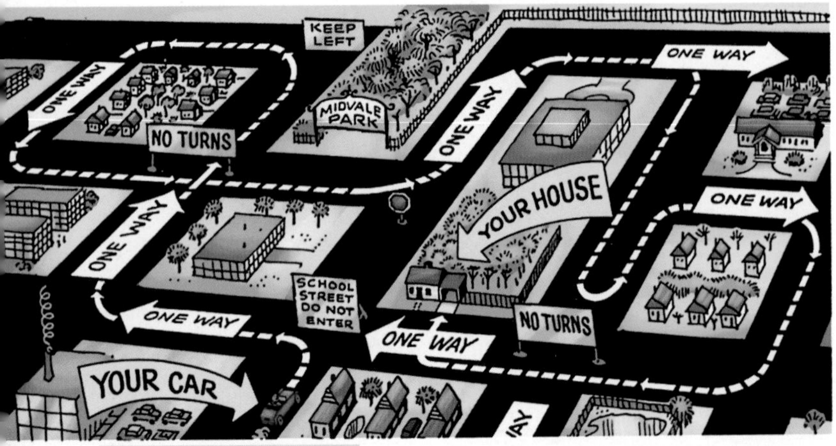
KEEP LEFT
ONE WAY
ONE WAY
MIDVALE PARK
NO TURNS
ONE WAY
YOUR HOUSE
ONE WAY
ONE WAY
SCHOOL STREET DO NOT ENTER
ONE WAY
ONE WAY
NO TURNS
YOUR CAR

DON'T YOU HATE...
. . . "One Way" and "No Turn" signs that take you miles out of your way.

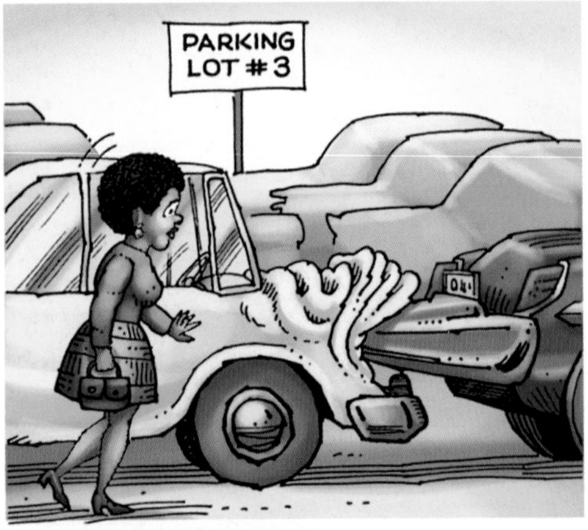
PARKING
LOT #3

DON'T YOU HATE...
. . . bumpers that are higher than yours.

blowing off steam about your pet hates. This one is for the relief of all you car-owners out there, and is called . . .

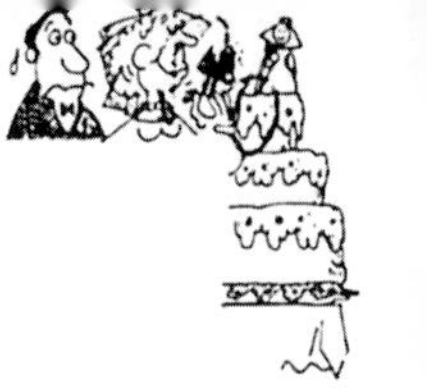

ERS HATE BOOK

WRITER AND ARTIST: AL JAFFEE
COLORIST: CARRIE STRACHAN

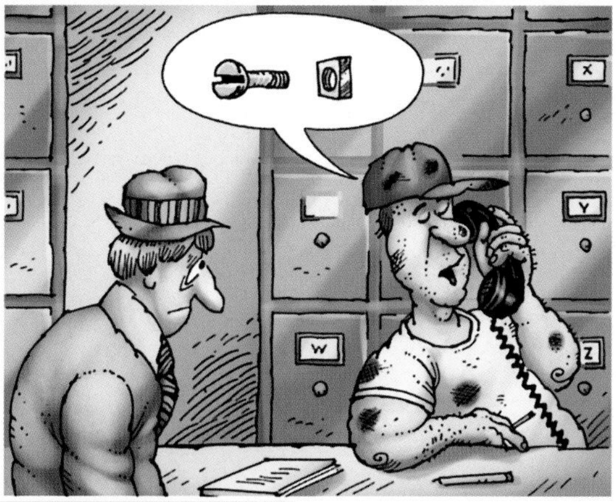

DON'T YOU HATE . . .
. . . repair shops that always have to *order* the part you desperately need.

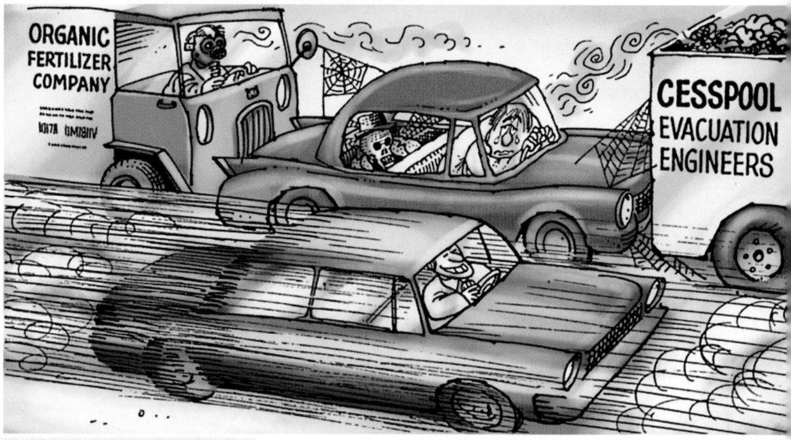

ORGANIC FERTILIZER COMPANY
CESSPOOL EVACUATION ENGINEERS

DON'T YOU HATE . . .
. . . finally getting into that moving lane only to find that it abruptly stops . . . and your old one moves from then on.

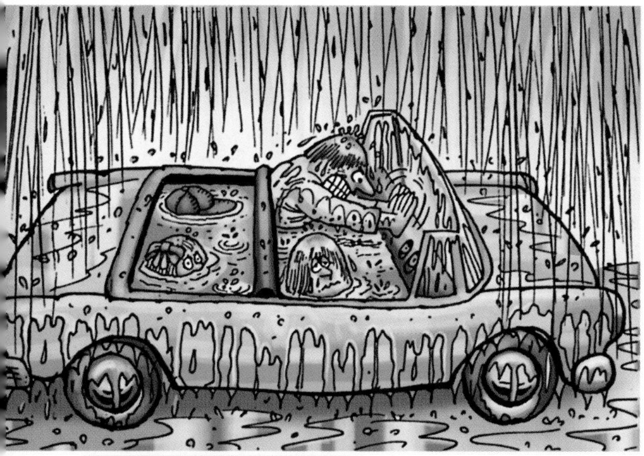

DON'T YOU HATE . . .
. . . a convertible top that invariably fails to operate whenever there's a sudden cloudburst.

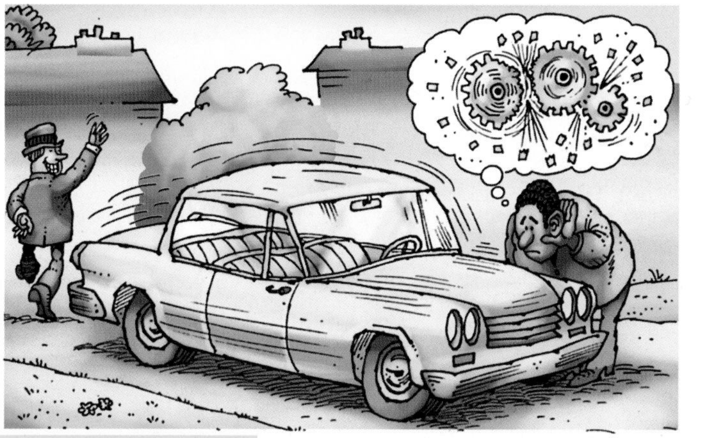

DON'T YOU HATE . . .
. . . lending your car to someone . . . and after it's returned, the engine makes a strange sound you've never heard before.

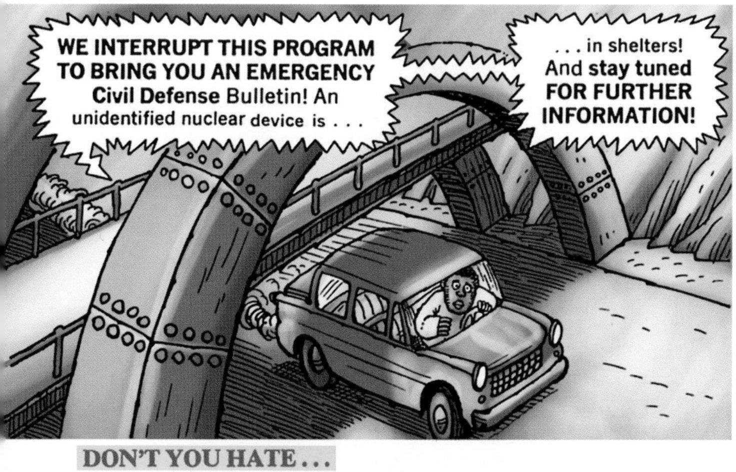

WE INTERRUPT THIS PROGRAM TO BRING YOU AN EMERGENCY Civil Defense Bulletin! An unidentified nuclear device is . . .
. . . in shelters! And stay tuned FOR FURTHER INFORMATION!

DON'T YOU HATE . . .
. . . car radios that fade out at critical moments.

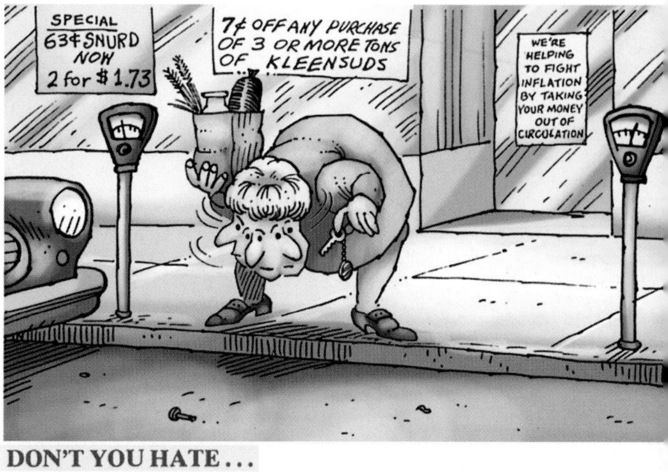

SPECIAL 63¢ SNURD NOW 2 for $1.73
7¢ OFF ANY PURCHASE OF 3 OR MORE TONS OF KLEENSUDS
WE'RE HELPING TO FIGHT INFLATION BY TAKING YOUR MONEY OUT OF CIRCULATION

DON'T YOU HATE . . .
. . . finding a vacant space where you parked your car.

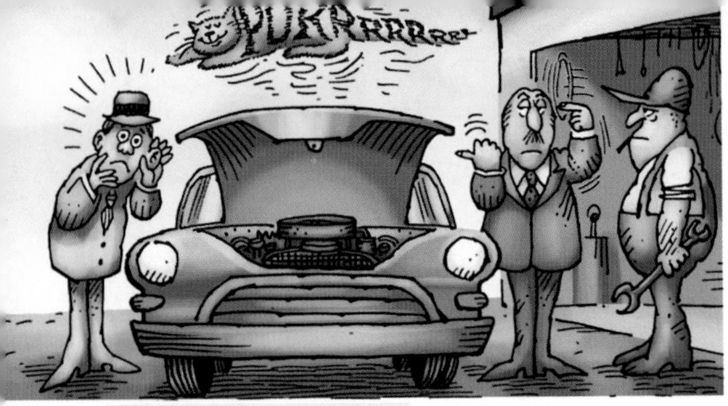
YUKRRRRRrrr

DON'T YOU HATE . . .
. . . strange noises that always disappear the minute you take your new car back to the dealer . . . and re-appear again right after you leave!

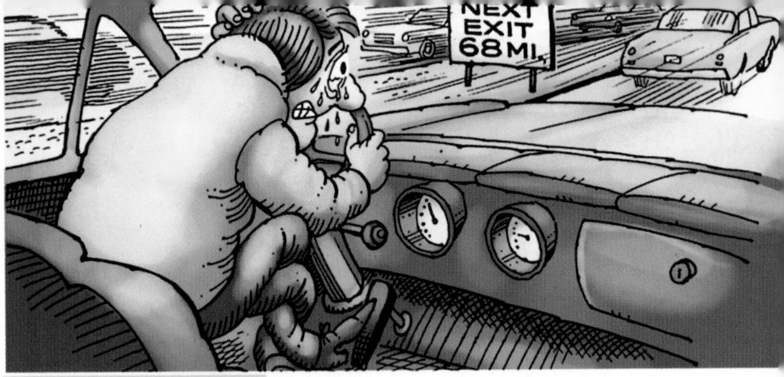
NEXT EXIT 68 MI.

DON'T YOU HATE . . .
. . . having to go to the bathroom on one of those new treeless, bushless, exitless super-highways.

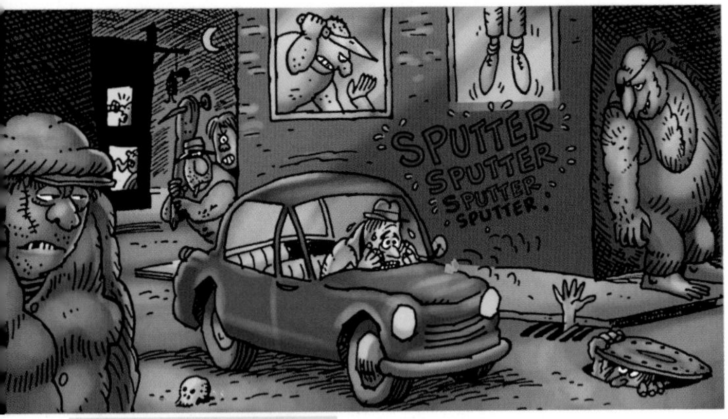
SPUTTER
SPUTTER
SPUTTER
SPUTTER

DON'T YOU HATE . . .
. . . hearing the unmistakable sound of a failing engine when you're right smack in the middle of the worst section of town.

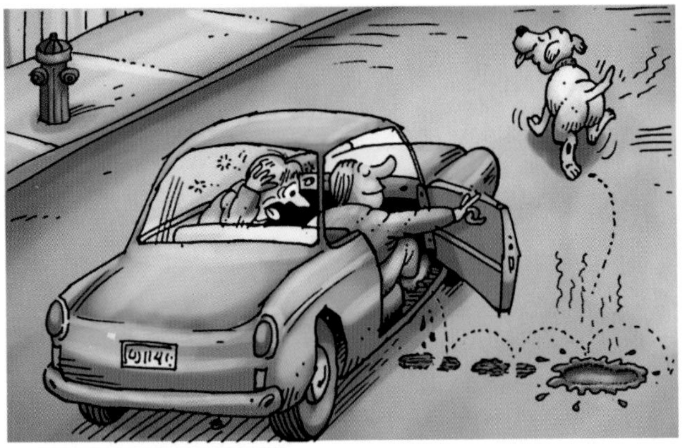

DON'T YOU HATE . . .
. . . people who carelessly track whatever they stepped into right into your brand new car.

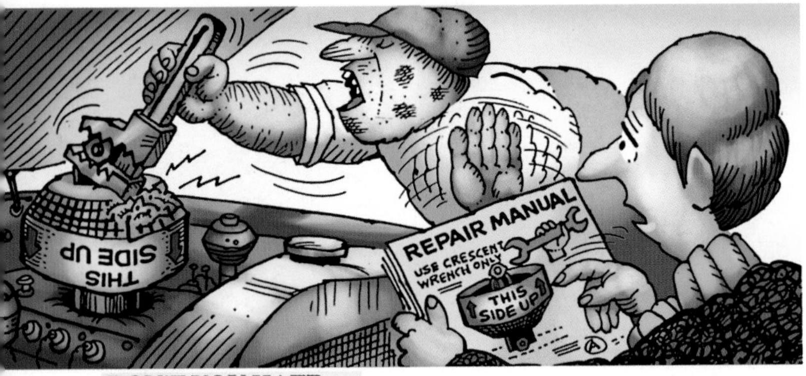
THIS SIDE UP
REPAIR MANUAL
USE CRESCENT WRENCH ONLY
THIS SIDE UP

DON'T YOU HATE . . .
. . . know-it-all mechanics who insist that it's perfectly okay to do exactly the opposite—or use other parts—than what the manufacturer of your car specifically recommends.

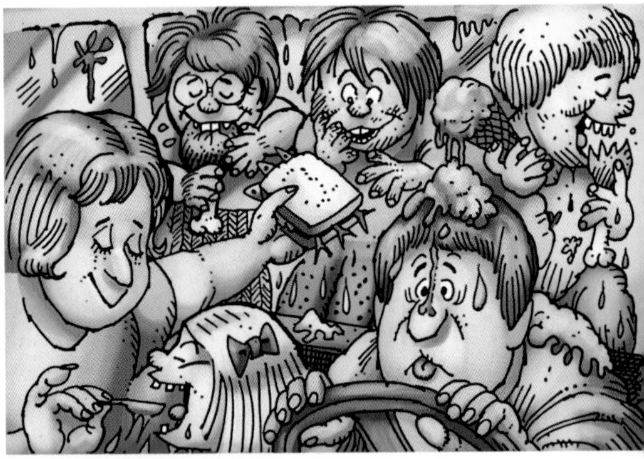

DON'T YOU HATE . . .
. . . people who let kids eat in your new car.

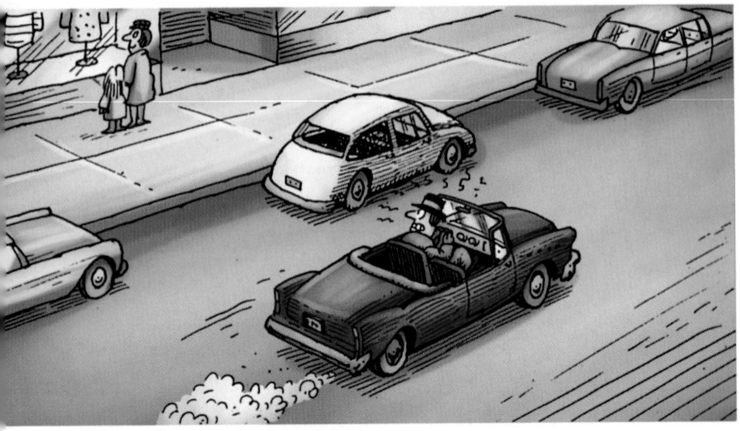

DON'T YOU HATE . . .
. . . two cars that take up three parking spaces.

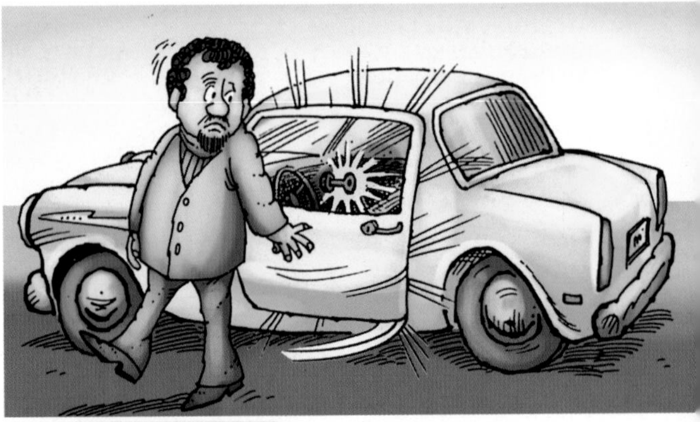

DON'T YOU HATE . . .
. . . glimpsing your car keys in the ignition just as you're slamming the locked car door.

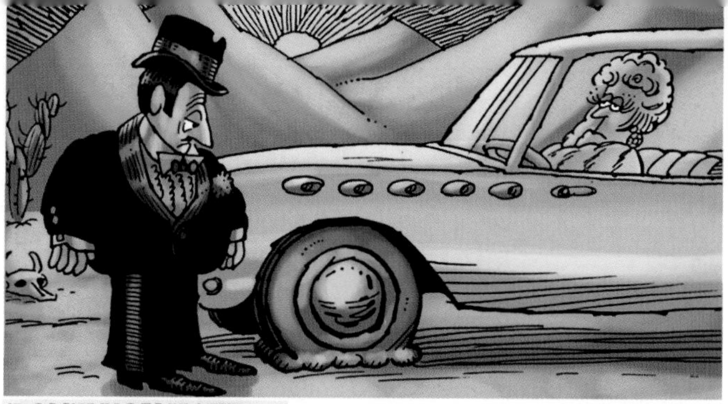

DON'T YOU HATE . . .
. . . getting a flat tire in the middle of nowhere when you're dressed to the hilt.

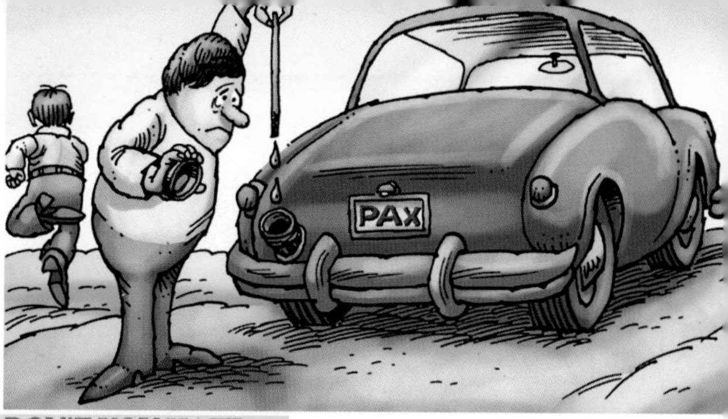
PAX

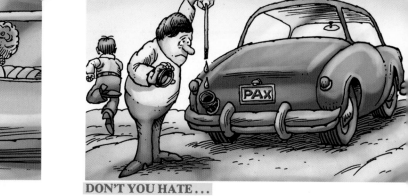

DON'T YOU HATE . . .
. . . lending someone your car with a full tank of gas —and having it returned with exactly two drops left.

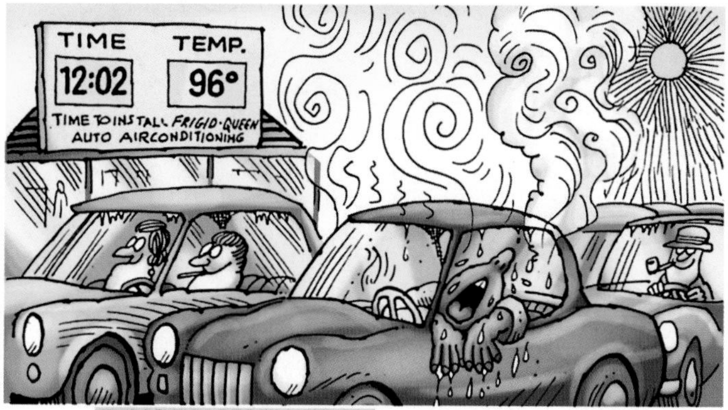
TIME
TEMP.
12:02
96°
TIME TO INSTALL FRIGID-QUEEN AUTO AIRCONDITIONING

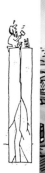

DON'T YOU HATE . . .
. . . your new car's air conditioner that conks out during the first heat wave . . . reminding you of how the heater conked out during the first cold wave.

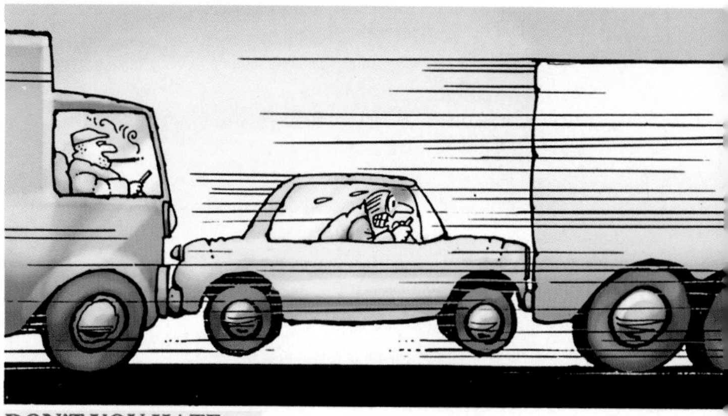

DON'T YOU HATE . . .
. . . being trapped between two huge trucks . . . and having to go miles beyond your turn-off.

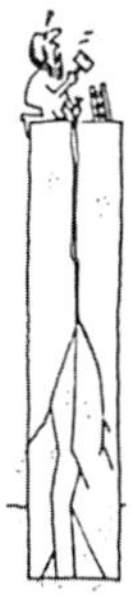

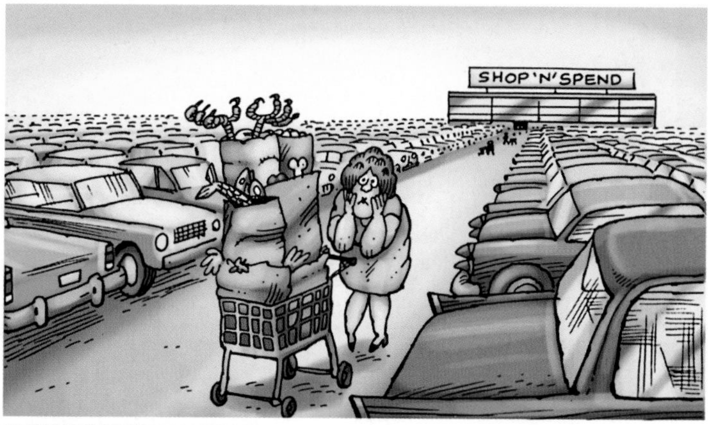
SHOP 'N' SPEND

DON'T YOU HATE . . .
. . . forgetting where you parked your car in a 10,000 car parking lot.

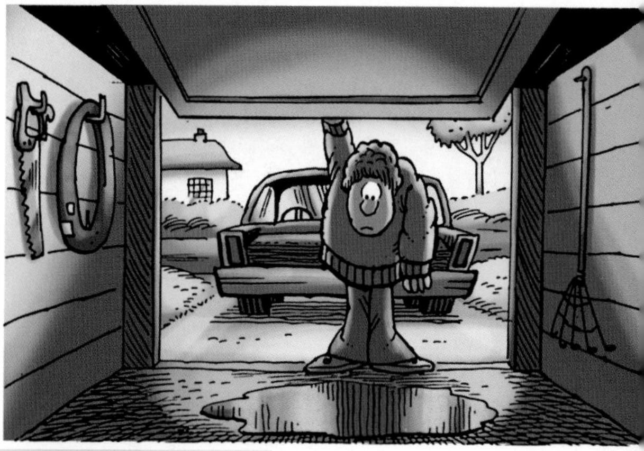

DON'T YOU HATE . . .
. . . finding a strange new puddle in your garage.

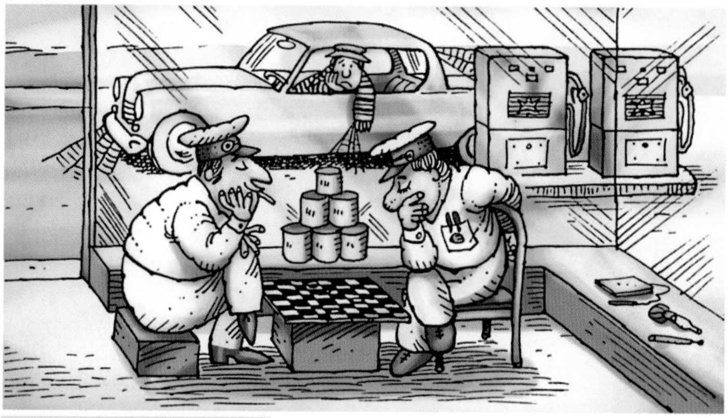

DON'T YOU HATE . . .
. . . gas station attendants who act like they're doing you the biggest favor in the world when they finally get to you.

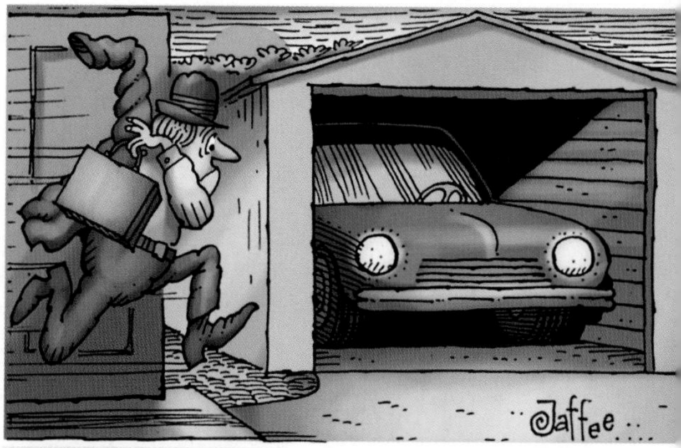
Jaffee

DON'T YOU HATE . . .
. . . returning to your car the next morning just as the last faint glimmer of light fades from your headlights.

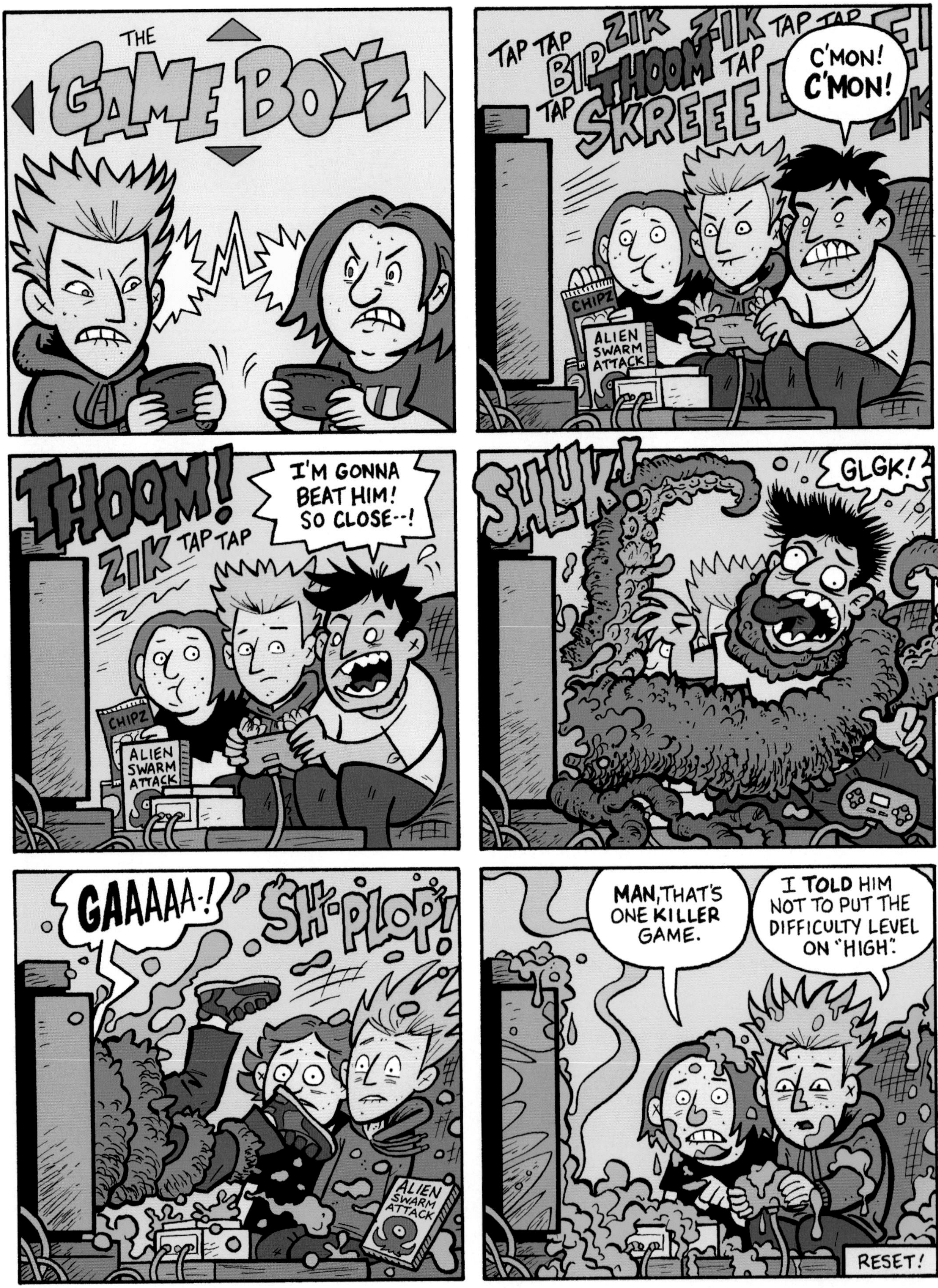
THE
GAME BOYZ
TAP TAP
BIP
ZIK
TAP
THOOM
ZIK
TAP
TAP TAP
SKREEE
C'MON! C'MON!
CHIPZ
ALIEN SWARM ATTACK
THOOM!
ZIK
TAP TAP
I'M GONNA BEAT HIM! SO CLOSE--!
CHIPZ
ALIEN SWARM ATTACK
SHLUK!
GLGK!
GAAAAA-!
SH-PLOP!
ALIEN SWARM ATTACK
MAN, THAT'S ONE KILLER GAME.
I TOLD HIM NOT TO PUT THE DIFFICULTY LEVEL ON "HIGH".
RESET!

WRITER AND ARTIST: EVAN DORKIN COLORIST: SARAH DYER

MERELY 99¢ STORE

Where Lower Quality Means Lower Prices

WE ACCEPT

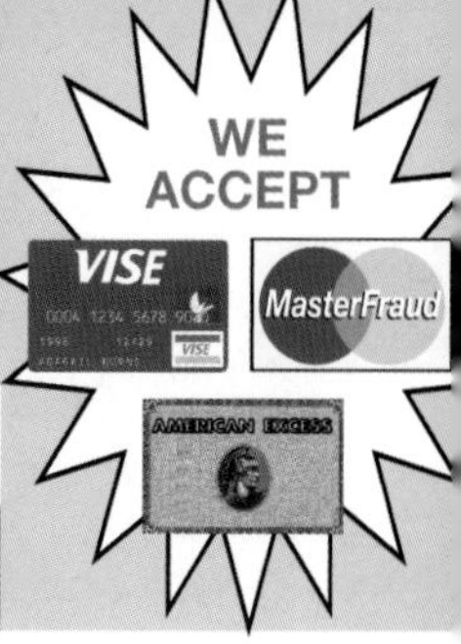
VISE
MasterFraud
AMERICAN EXPRESS

When It Comes To Kids, MERELY 99¢ IS YOUR BUY IT AND BREAK IT HEADQUARTERS!

Toys!

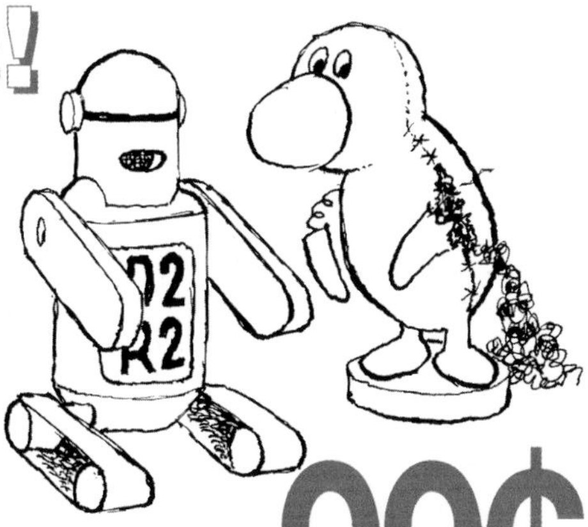
D2
R2

Visit Our Toy Aisle For The Latest In Cheap Copies Of The Toys Kids Really Want!!

Large Selection Of Toys You Won't Mind Lending To Friends Who Never Return Things!

Your Choice merely 99¢

Slightly Irregular

Underpants

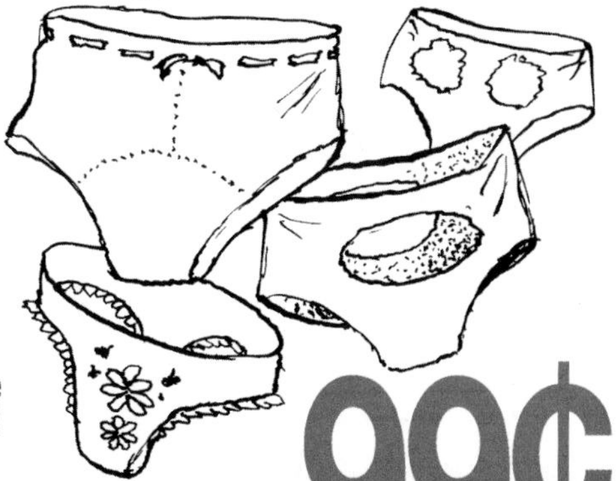

Root Through Our Large Selection Of Loose Underwear In Our Loose Underwear Bin!

Many Surprises!
Too Many Holes!
Not Enough Holes!
Holes Where They Shouldn't Be!

Perfect For Anyone On A Tight Budget!

3 Pairs For merely 99¢

All-Natural Welcome Mats

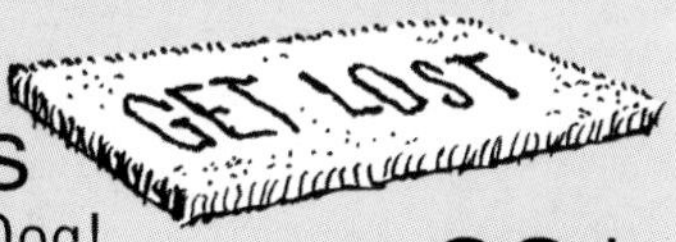
GET LOST

Smells Just Like A Wet Dog!

2 for ....merely 99¢

Brittle Ice Trays

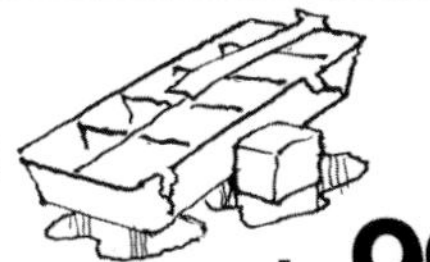

Withstands Temperatures As Low As 40 Degrees!

2 for ....merely 99¢

Calendars

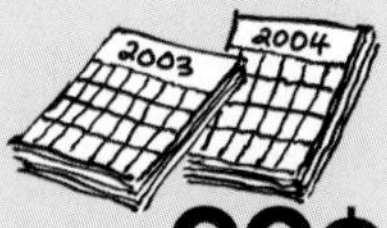
2003
2004

2003 Calendar Accurate Again In 2014
2004 Calendar Accurate Again In 2032
Stock Up Now!

10 for..merely 99¢

32-Piece Colored Marker Set

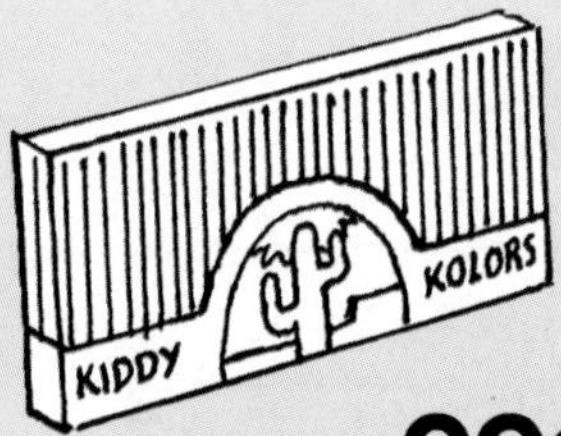
KIDDY
KOLORS

All The Colors Of The Rainbow In Various Stages Of Drying Out

..merely 99¢

McFlimsy 1/4-Ply Toilet Paper

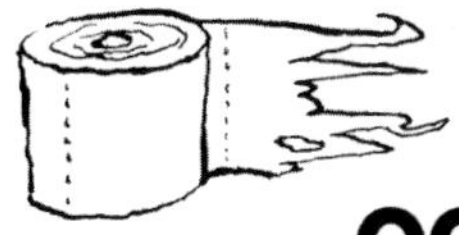

4-Roll Pack....................................merely 99¢

"Melts in your hand, not in the can!"

Toilet Bowl Deodorizers

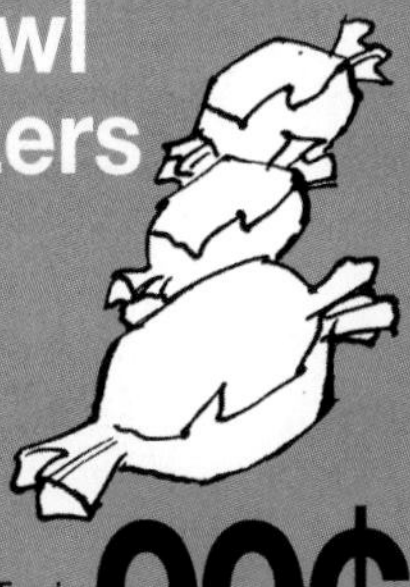

The Kind No One Has Used Since The 1960s • Wrapped In Bright, Multi-Colored Cellophane • Often Mistaken For Candy By Children • Highly Toxic

5 For merely 99¢

Eyeglasses

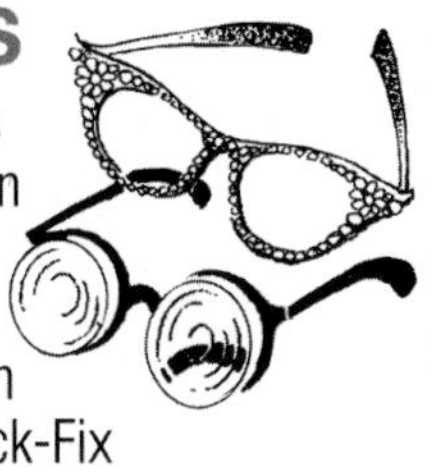

Why Spend Hundreds Of Dollars Going To An Optometrist To Have A Dangerous Eye Condition Cured When You Can Buy Our Quick-Fix For Under A Buck?

merely 99¢

Flat, Oversized Soda

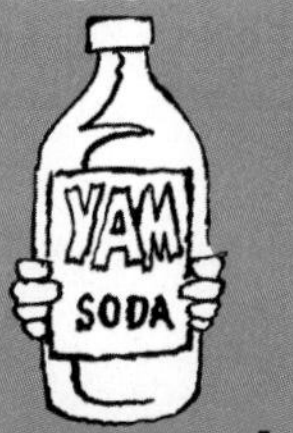
YAM
SODA

Choose From Many Flavors Regular Stores Will Not Stock Due To Lack Of Sales

Grapefruit • Yam • Pine • Peanut Butter • Tapioca

Unwieldy 3 Liter Bottles merely 99¢

WRITER: SCOTT MAIKO
ARTIST: BOB CLARKE

MERELY 99¢ STORE

Where Style Takes A Vacation

Overruns Of Enormous Plastic Cups From Convenience Stores

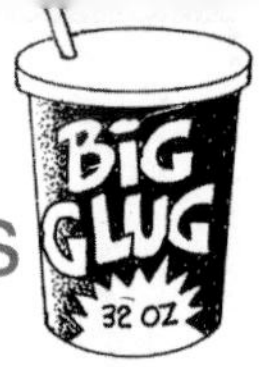
BIG GLUG
32 OZ

Giving Them To Us To Sell Was Cheaper Than Paying Expensive Landfill Fees!

6 For....................merely 99¢

Seasonal Candy

Whatever The Occasion, We've Got Delicious Treats For The Holiday That Was Over Just Three Months Ago!

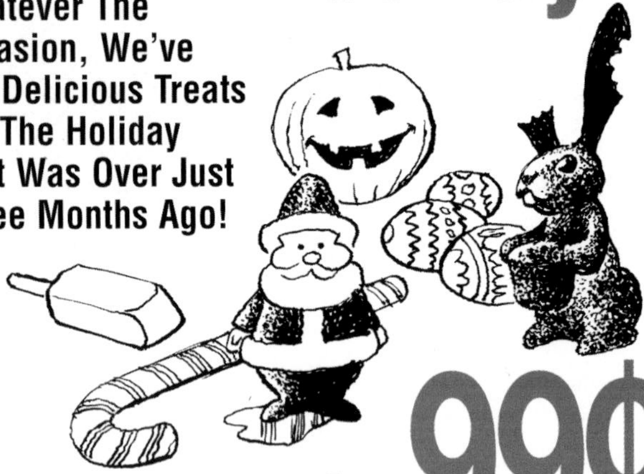

Your Choice merely 99¢

Eighth Generation Brand 60 Classic Cartoons

Over 6 Hours Of Ancient, Badly-Transferred Animated Cartoons On A Low-Grade VHS Tape

Not Considered Funny Or Interesting Since 1948, These Cartoons Fell Into Public Domain Due To Lack Of Interest From The Original Copyright Holders

The Same Cartoons You Can See Much Clearer On Any Number Of Local Television Stations If You Were At All Interested In Watching Them In The First Place!

Poorly-Drawn Box Art Barely Resembles The Characters On The Tape, Thus Releasing The Manufacturer From Copyright Infringements

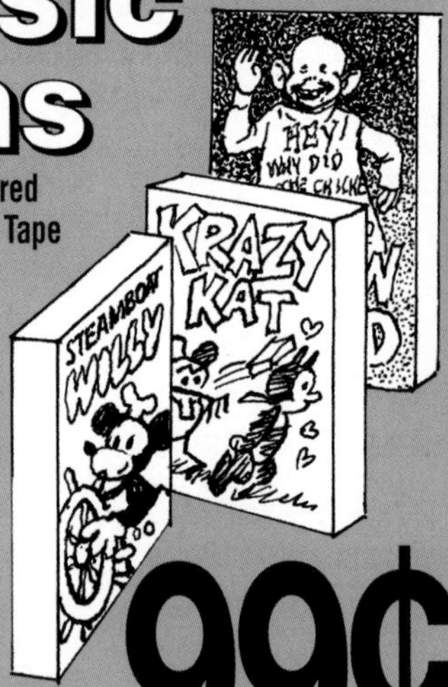
STEAMBOAT WILLY
KRAZY KAT

Great Stocking Stuffers! merely 99¢

MERELY 99¢ *The Only Difference Is The Quality!* **MERELY 99¢** *Home Of The Open And Abandoned Box Of Cookies!* **MERELY 99¢**

Shabbily-Bound© Paint Brushes

No Need To Clean—All The Bristles Are Gone Before You Finish Painting!

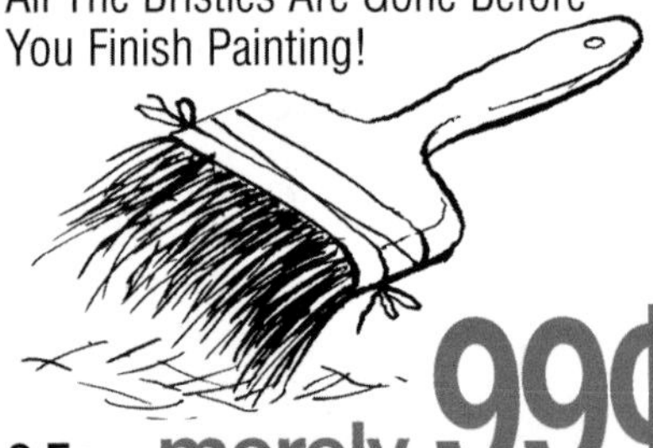

2 For merely 99¢

Misnomer© Cling Wrap

It Doesn't Cling To Anything!

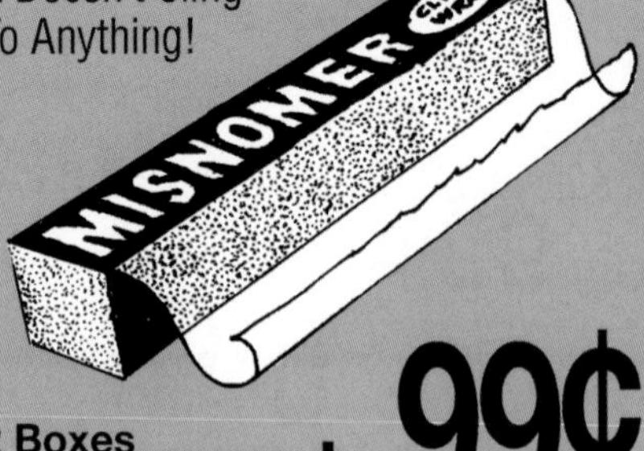
MISNOMER
CLING WRAP

2 Boxes For merely 99¢

Potted Meat Food Product

Have Fun Guessing What It Is!

We Have No Idea Either!

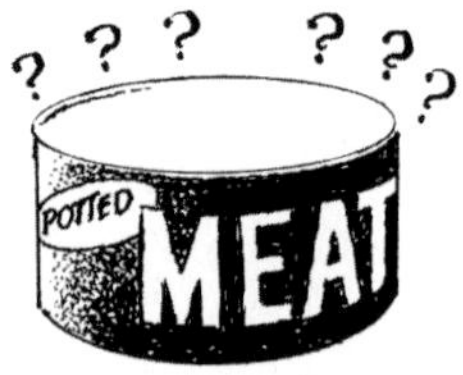
POTTED
MEAT

2 For merely 99¢

Handy Peel & Stick Hooks

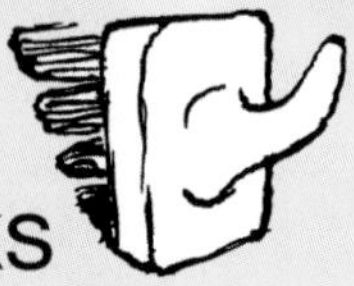

Sturdy Adhesive Backing Remains Attached To Wall Or Refrigerator Long After Plastic Hook Portion Has Snapped Off!

3-Pack....................merely 99¢

Loose-Headed Hammers

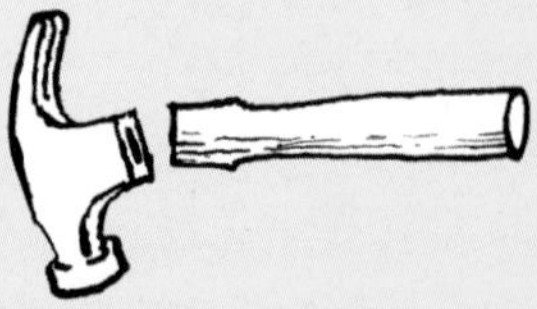

Each....................merely 99¢

Sure To Fly Off And Injure A Bystander!

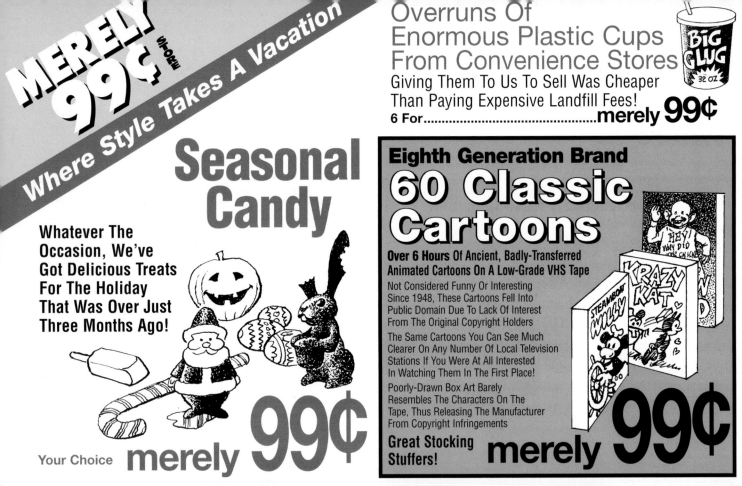

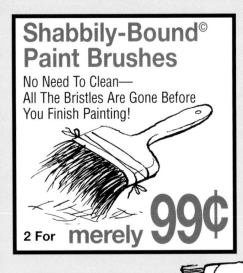

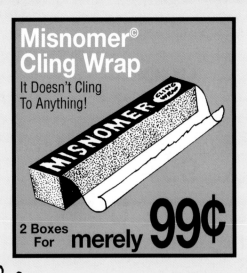

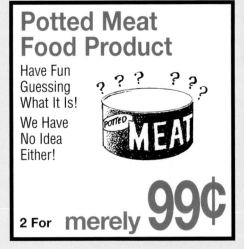

Yes! We Have Rows Of The Identical, Tacky, Badly-Painted Ceramic Knickknacks You Love!

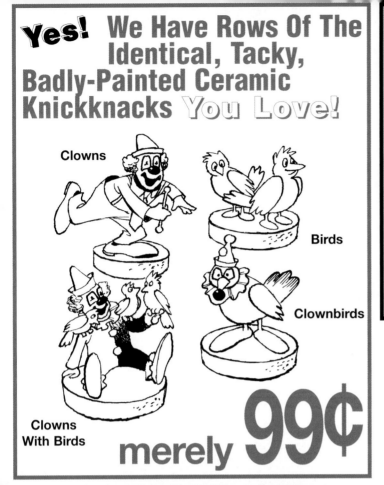

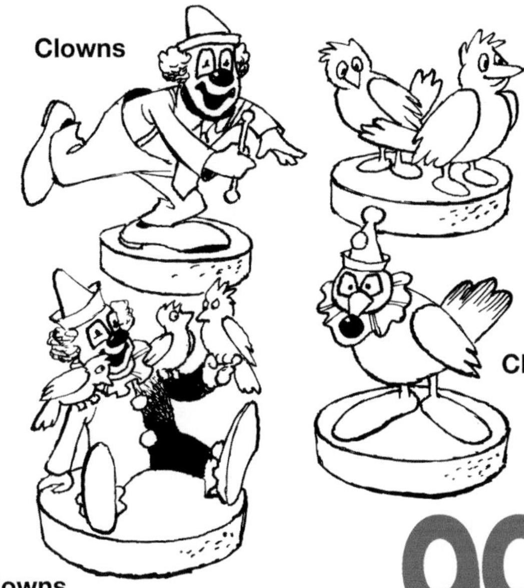
Clowns
Birds
Clownbirds
Clowns With Birds

merely 99¢

Fashion Jewelry! Earrings

Low-Grade Tin Sprayed With A Thin, Scratch-Off Lottery-Ticket-Type Gold Coating

Many Unpopular Styles To Choose From

May Cause Slight Infection In Some Users. If Gangrene Develops, Cut Off Affected Ear(s), And Discontinue Use.

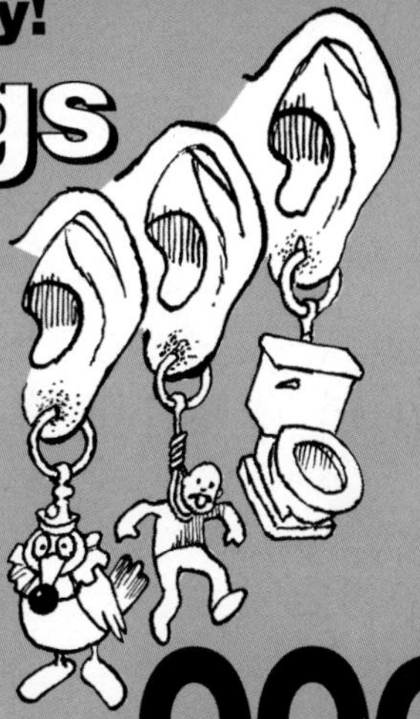

2 Pairs For merely 99¢

Plastic Bowls

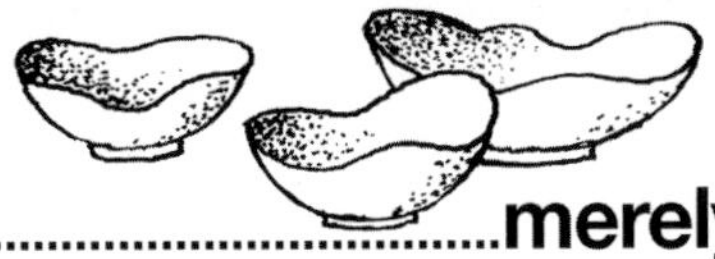

3 for .... merely 99¢

Retains Bowl-Like Shape At Temperatures Up To 85 Degrees

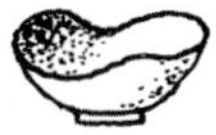

Perfect For Non-Liquid Food Items That Are Not Intended For Human Consumption

Where The Line Always Backs Up Into Our Already Over-Crowded, Narrow Aisles! **MERELY 99¢** ***Things You'd Find In A Dollar Store – But For A Penny Less!*** **MERELY 99¢**

Party Supplies

All Featuring The Hottest Characters From 5 To 12 Years Ago!

Save Big By Decorating Your Event With Favors Picturing Characters No One Cares About Any More!

- Smurfs
- The Addams Family
- Judge Dredd
- He-Man and She-Ra
- Fraggle Rock
- Inspector Gadget
- Mighty Morphin Power Rangers
- MORE!

Cups, Plates, Napkins, Tablecloths

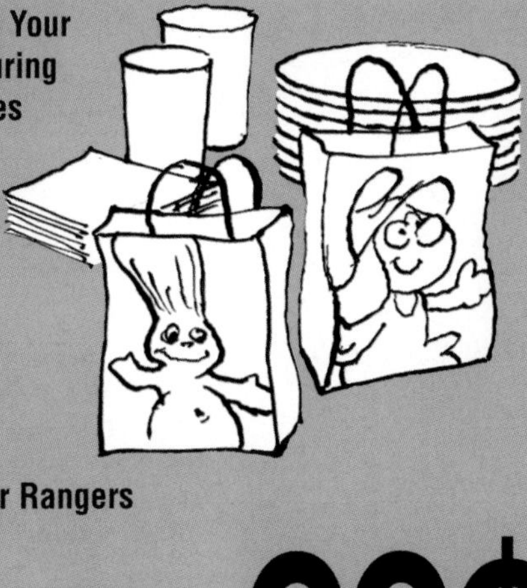

.... merely 99¢

Inaccurate Plastic Measuring Cups With Smudged, Crooked Printing

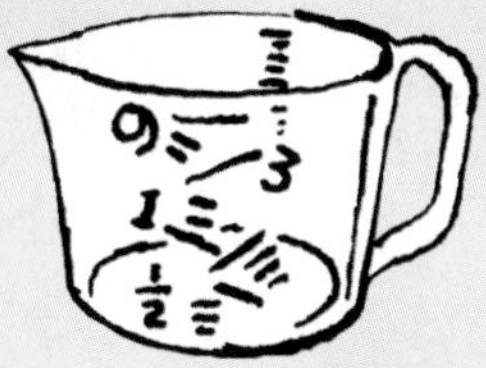

2 for .... merely 99¢

About-To-Expire Cold Cuts

Bargains Galore In Our Lukewarm Soda Case!

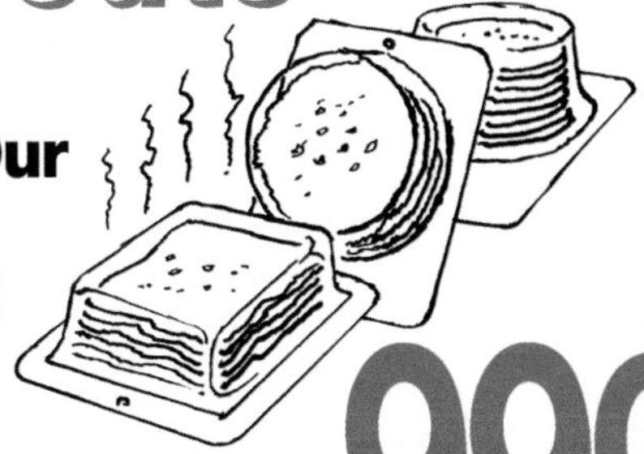

3 Packs For...... merely 99¢

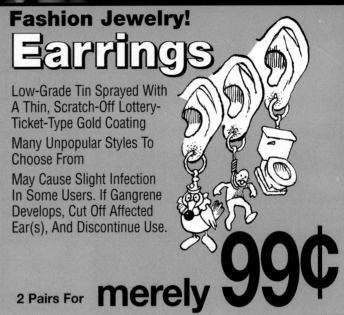

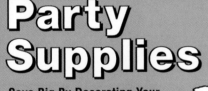

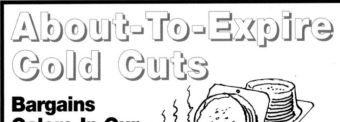

A MAD LOOK AT THE

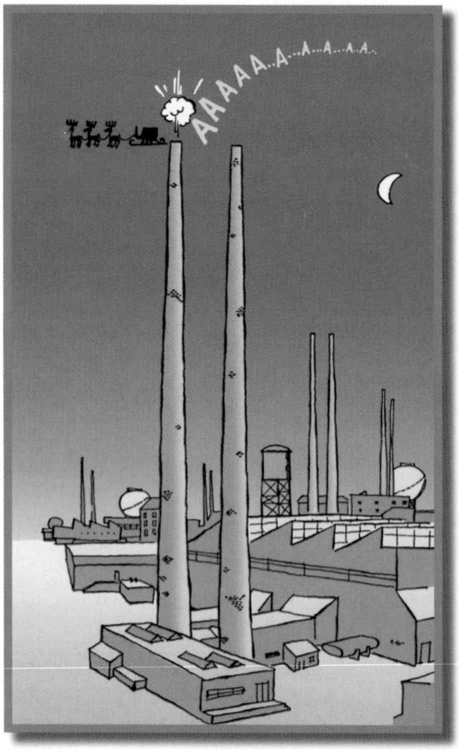

AAAAA..A...A...A...A..

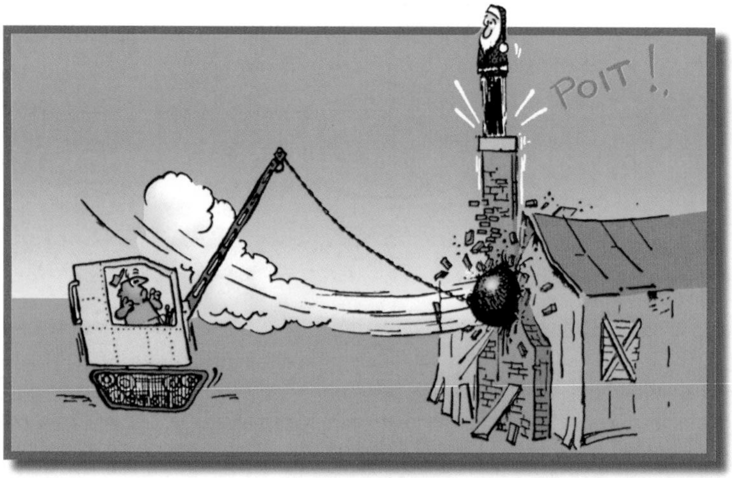

POIT!

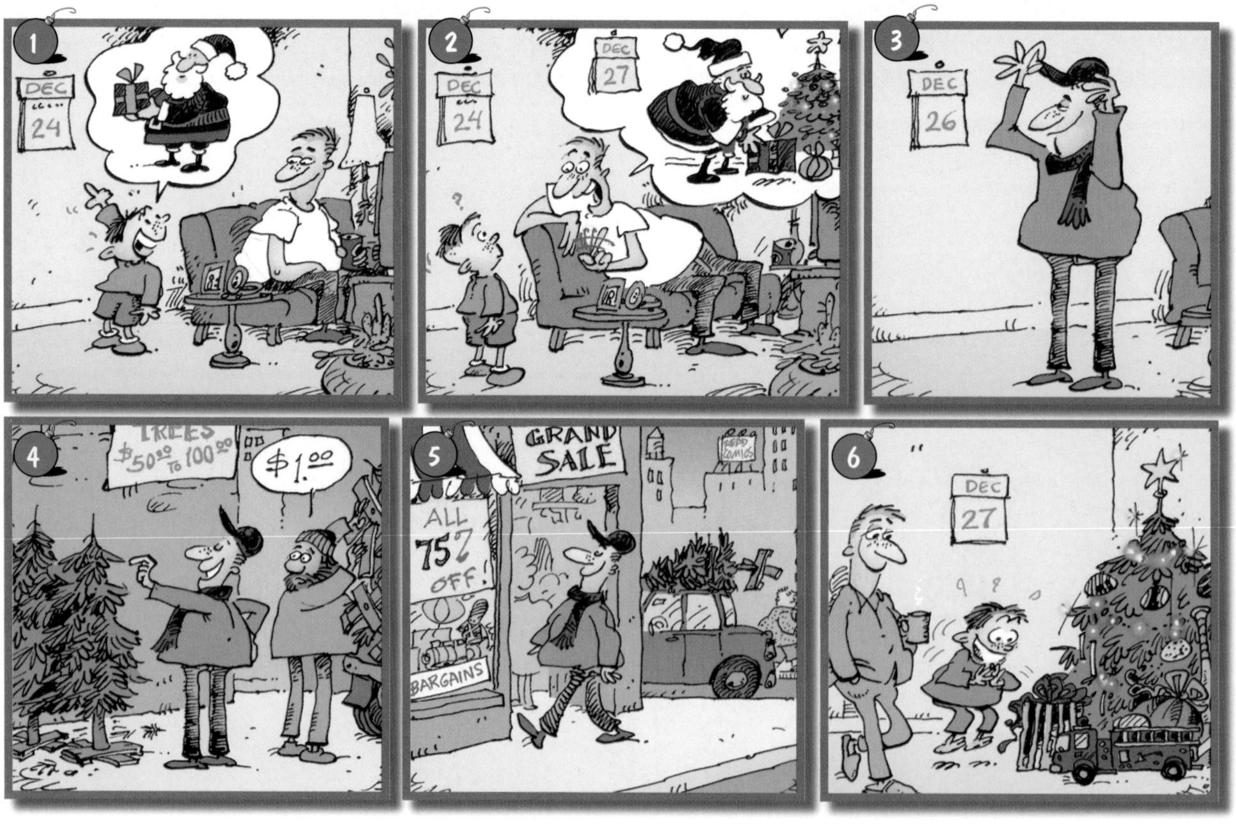

1
DEC 24
2
DEC 24
DEC 27
3
DEC 26
4
TREES $50.00 TO 100.00
$1.00
5
GRAND SALE
ALL 75% OFF
BARGAINS
6
DEC 27

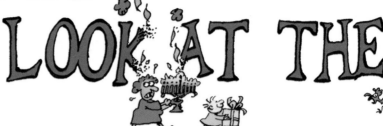

HOLIDAYS

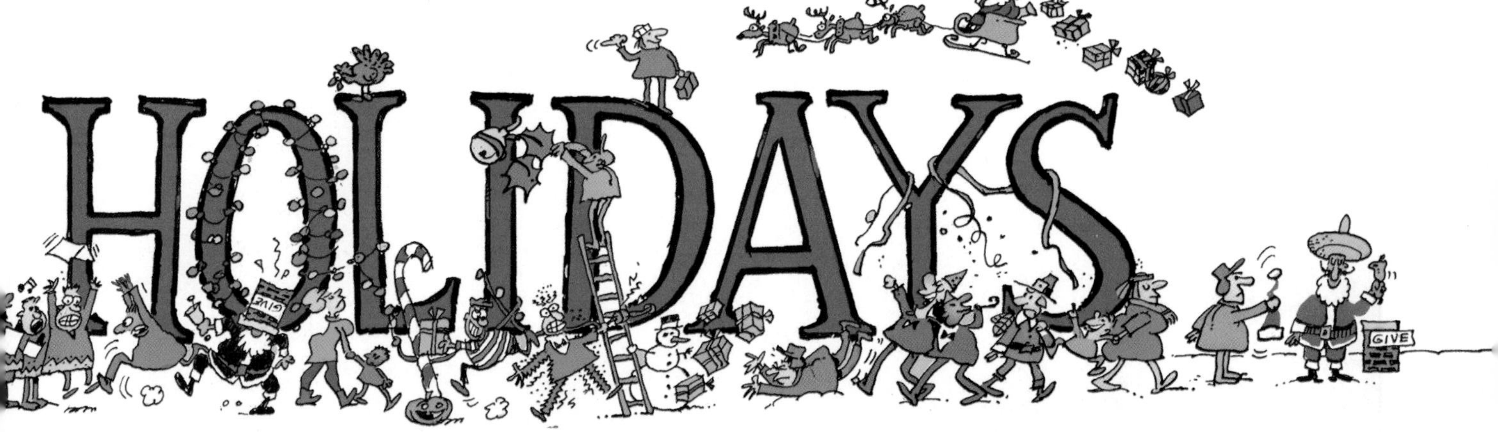

HOLIDAYS
GIVE

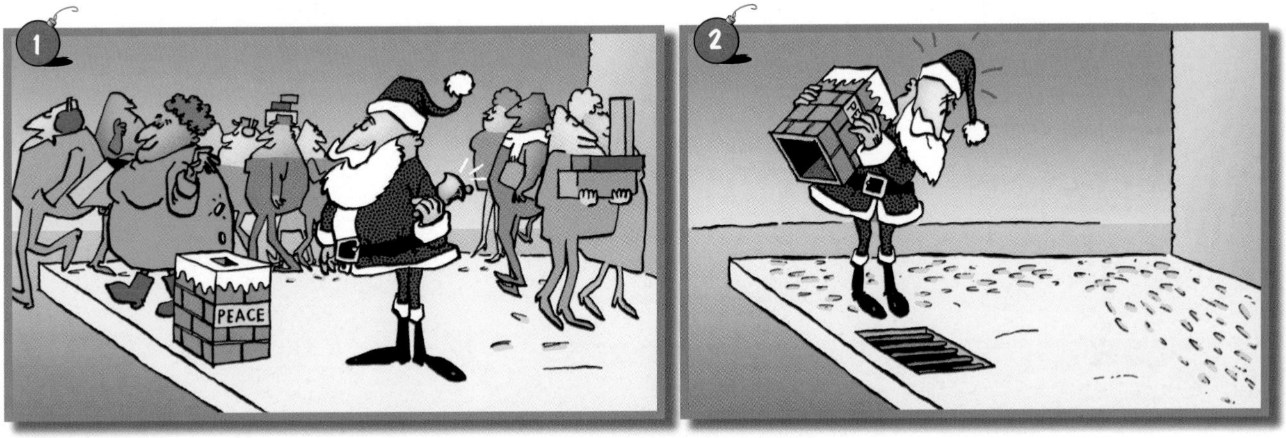

PEACE

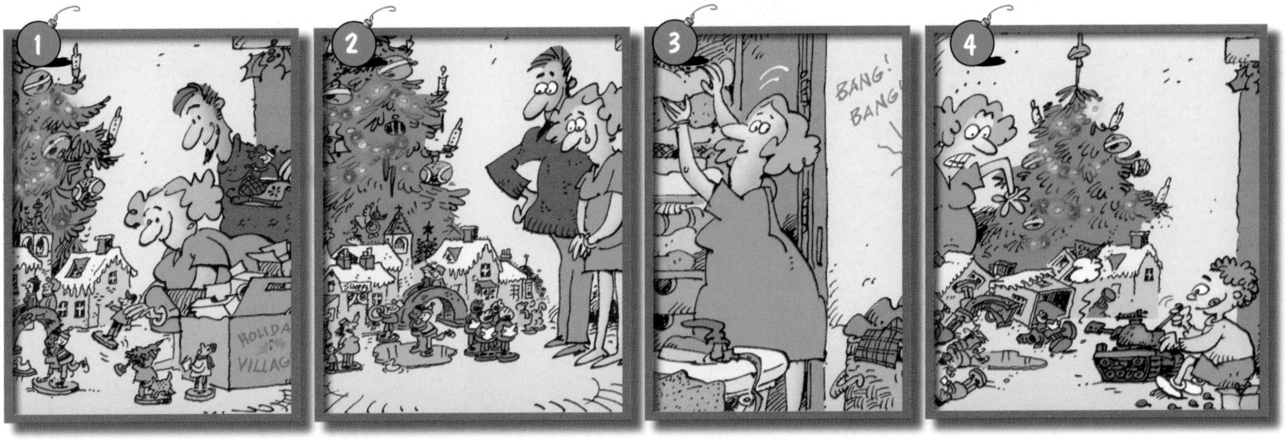

BANG!
BANG!

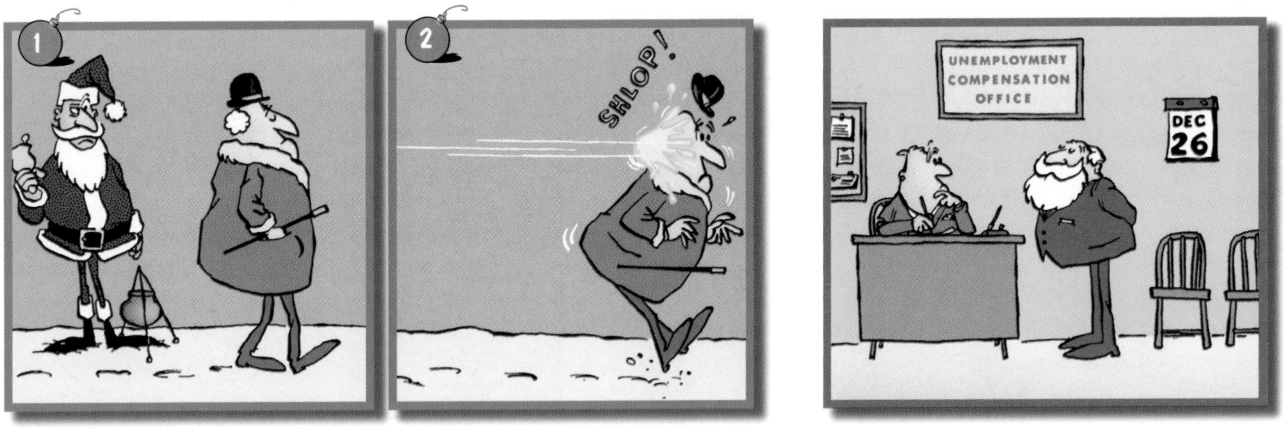

SHLOP!
UNEMPLOYMENT
COMPENSATION
OFFICE
DEC
26

WRITER AND ARTIST: SERGIO ARAGONES

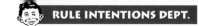

When California Governor and former tibia-snapper Arnold Schwarzenegger signed a bill that outlawed the sale or rental of violent video games to California teenagers, he sent a powerful message to the rest of the country: "I amm a meatt-brained, heepocritical putz!" What he should've *endorsed were...*

VIDEO GA
THAT AMERICA

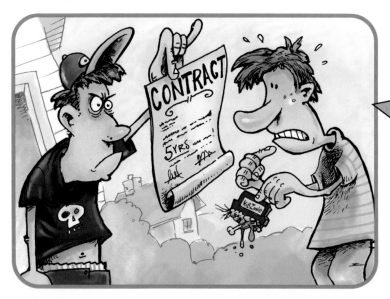

1 Any friend who borrows a game must sign a legally binding contract assuring its return within two weeks, in its original case, and completely free of peanut-butter fingerprints; failure to comply will result in a minimum five-year borrowing ban.

CONTRACT
5YRS
KILLZONE

2 Before giving anti-game-violence speeches, all blowhard politicians will be required to play one hour of *Grand Theft Auto IV*, just to see how fun it is to make a guy's head explode like a rotten orange.

Ms.Clinton, You're on in Forty Seconds!
PLenty of Time for me to PoP this Sucka!

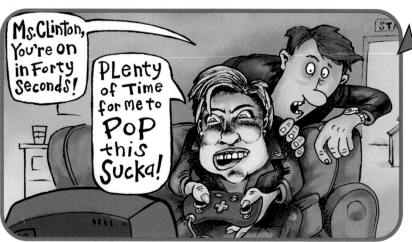

3 Any gamer who finds that his anti-gaming dad spent over eighty percent of his youth playing *Asteroids* in a dingy pizzeria will have all game-related time restrictions permanently lifted.

1979
ROIDS
HIGH SCORE

4 Dismal video game adaptations of box-office flops must be affixed with consumer warning labels similar to those on packs of cigarettes.

NEW!
WARNING. Movie Tie-in intended as a QUICK CASH Grab! NOT intended for entertainment PURPOSES!

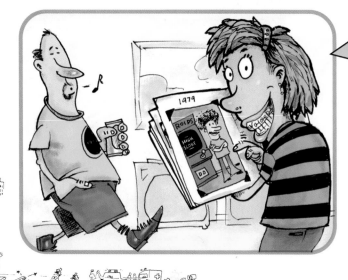

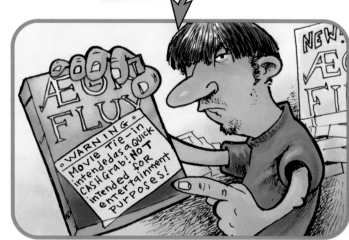

ME LAWS
ACTUALLY *NEEDS*

5 Parents may not complain that their gamer children spend too much time in front of the TV without first being able to explain what benefits said parent reaps from watching the entire CBS Wednesday night lineup.

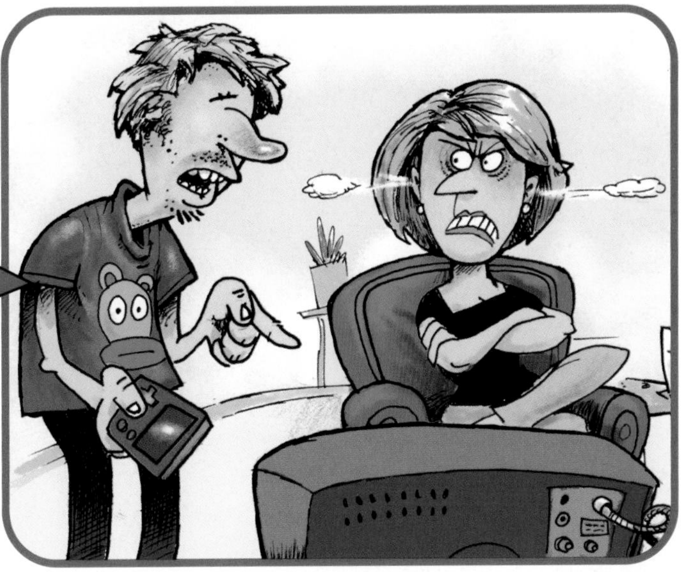

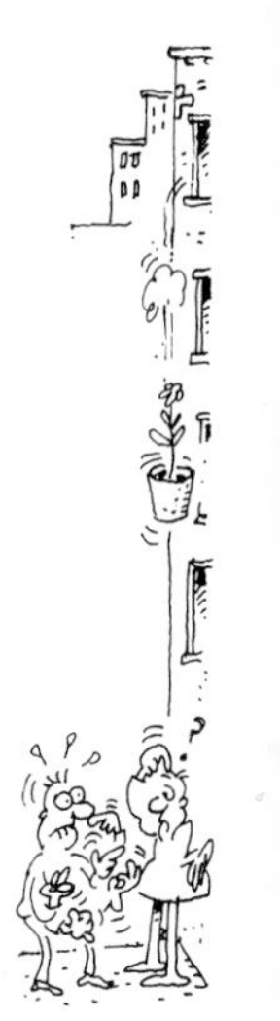

6 Cheapskate parents may not purchase a price-slashed, almost-obsolete system for their children within two months of "next generation" console's release; failure to comply will result in the forcible purchase of "new" console and fifteen new games.

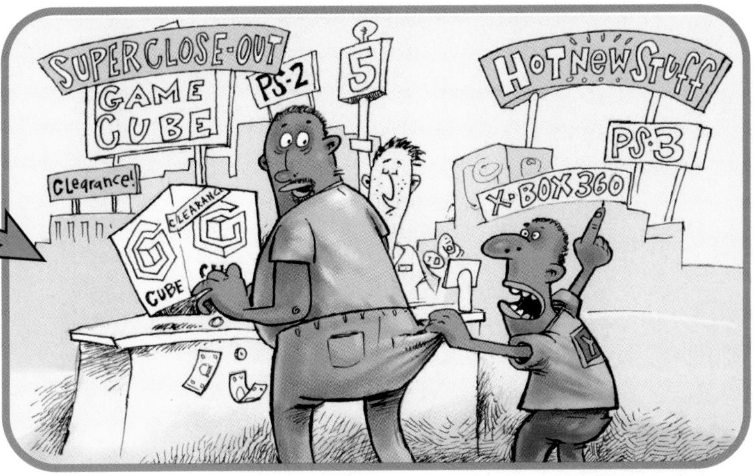
SUPER CLOSE-OUT
GAME CUBE
PS-2
5
Clearance!
CLEARANCE
CUBE
HOT NEW STUFF
PS-3
X-BOX 360

7 Any gamer who brags that his proficiency in *Call of Duty MW3* makes him a fearless warrior will be immediately deployed to downtown Baghdad to see how quickly he pee-pees his fatigues.

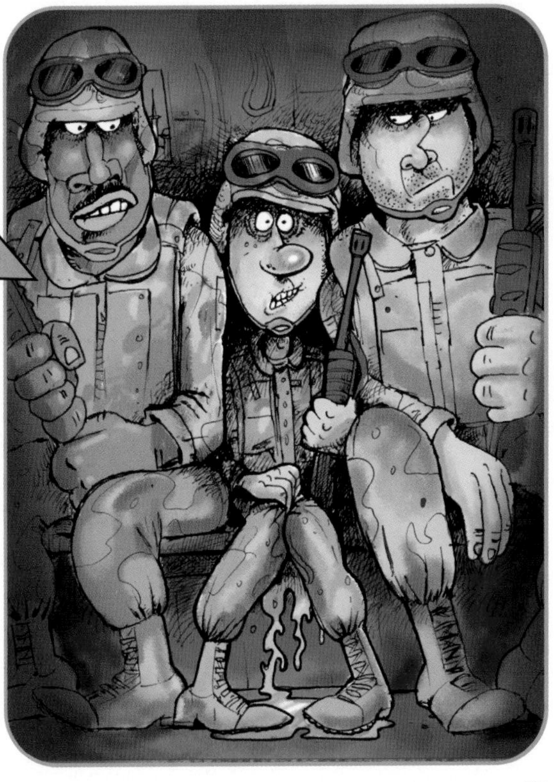

8 Know-it-all game shop clerks must be reminded on a monthly basis that it's actually incredibly depressing, not cool, to know the entire development history of *Final Fantasy XIV.*

WRITER: JACOB LAMBERT

ARTIST: RICH POWELL

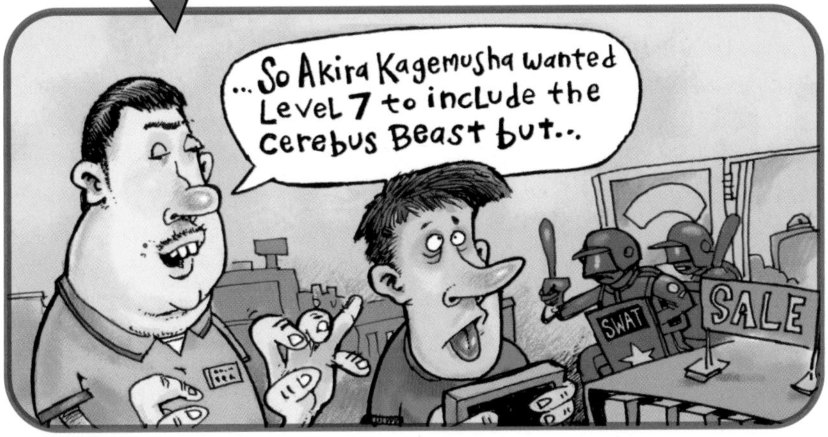
...So Akira Kagemusha wanted Level 7 to include the Cerebus Beast but...
SWAT
SALE

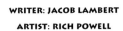

9 Blowhard teachers who confiscate portable systems during class must first sit through an endless, mind-numbing lecture with a PSP in their pocket, just to see how long *they* last.

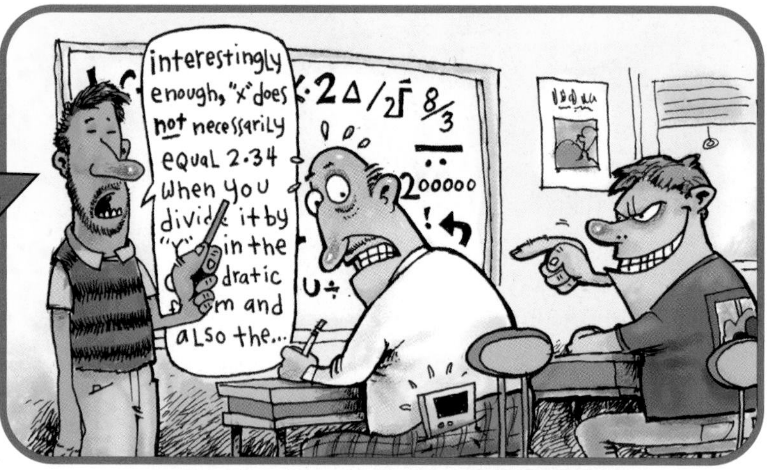
interestingly enough, "x" does not necessarily equal 2.34 when you divide it by
in the
dratic
m and
also the...

10 Any misguided spaz who attends a video game convention "in character" will immediately be ejected for giving normal gamers a bad name.

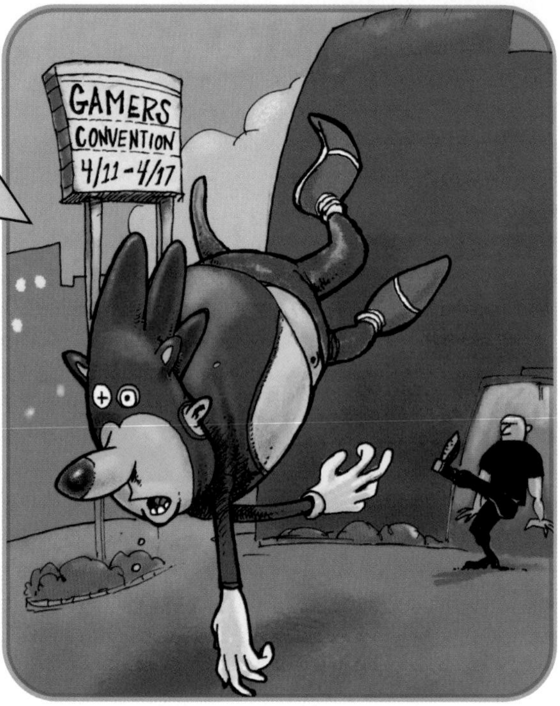
GAMERS
CONVENTION
4/11-4/17

11 Any TV talking head brainless enough to blame a high school shooting on a video game will immediately be demoted to covering traffic jams, bake sales, and waterskiing-animal stories.

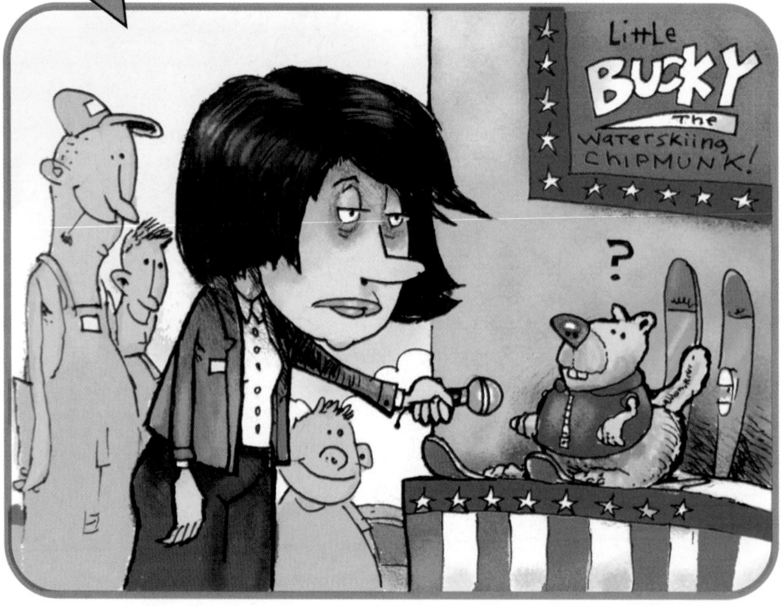
Little
BUCKY
The
Waterskiing
CHIPMUNK!

12 Spoiled brats who don't play 99% of the games their wealthy parents buy for them must donate their entire collections to not-so-rich classmates, who'd actually enjoy them.

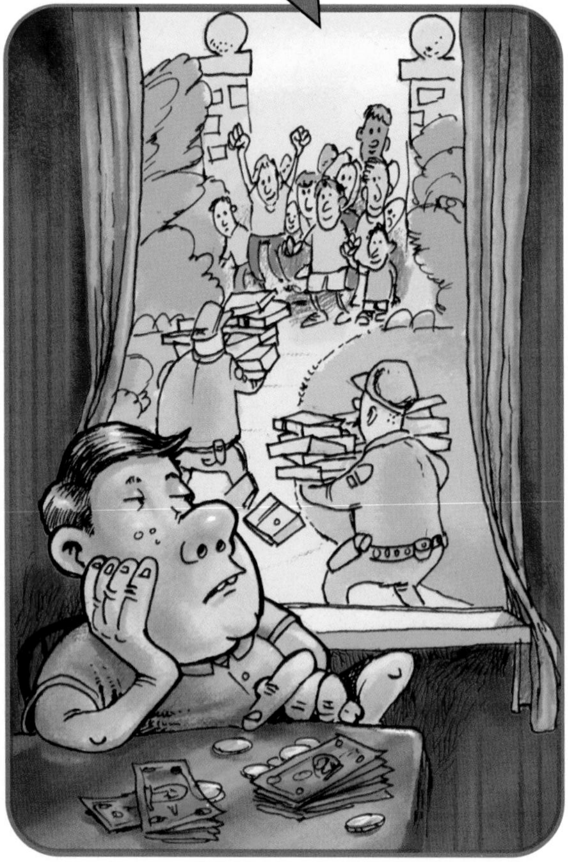

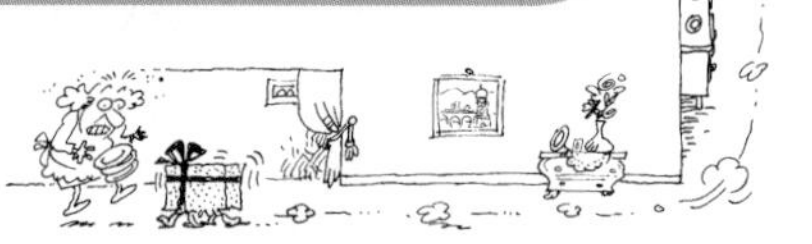

JOKE AND DAGGER DEPT.

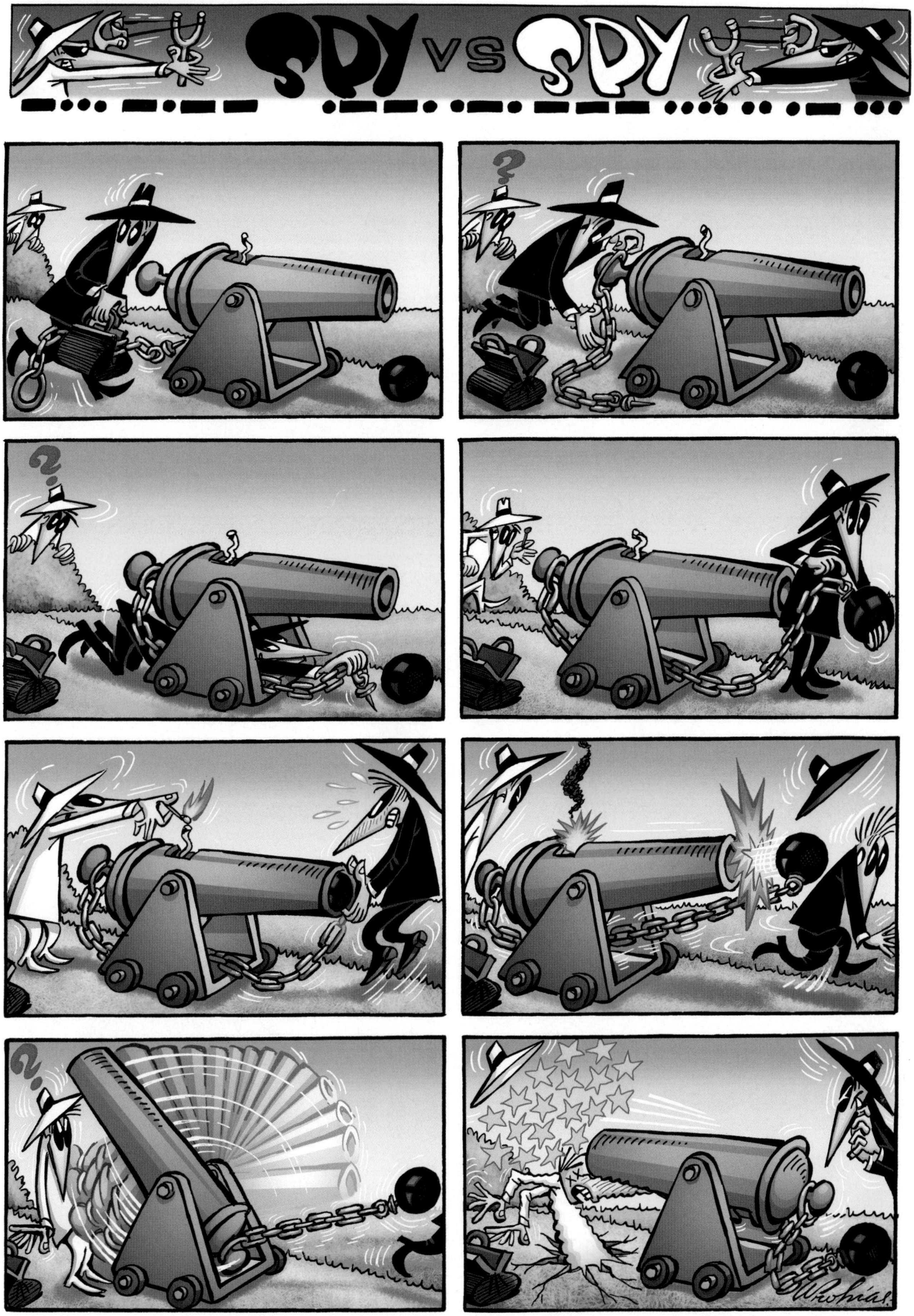
SPY vs SPY
Prohias

WRITER AND ARTIST: ANTONIO PROHIAS COLORIST: CARRIE STRACHAN

There's an old saying that kids in school are taught The Three "R"s of learning...

Readin'! 'Ritin'! 'Rithmetic!

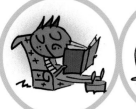

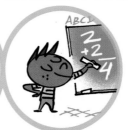

This seems crazy, since any kid spelling those words that way would get a zero!

We wondered if there were more, so we checked and found six more groups of rules that start with...

THE THREE...

The Three B's
of Little League...

DOIK
PLOOP

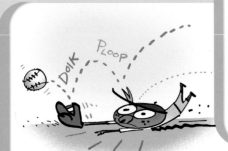

...Bobbling

...Benching

POW!

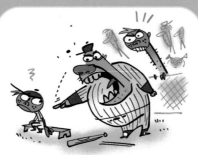

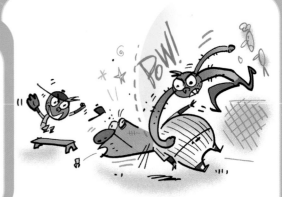

...Brawling!

The Three S's
of Disney World...

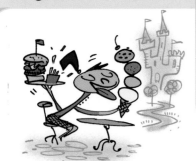

...Snacking

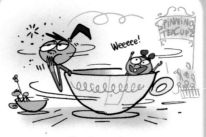

Weeeee!
SPINNING TEACUPZ

...Spinning

SLORP!

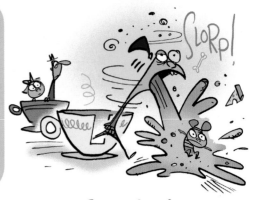

...Spewing!

WRITER: ANDREW J. SCHWARTZBERG   ARTIST: BOB STAKE

The Three P's
of Video Games...

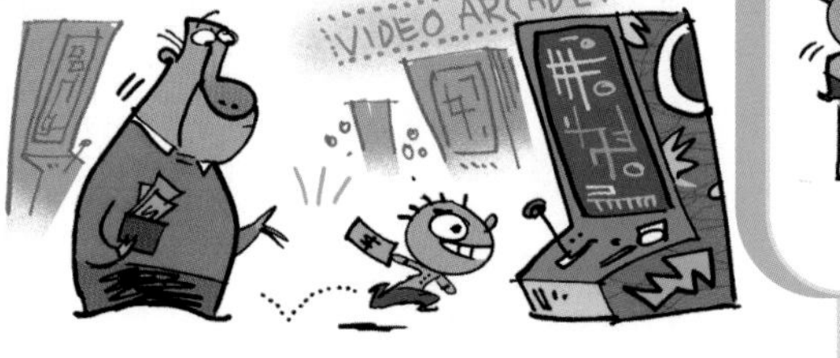
VIDEO ARCADE
...Paying

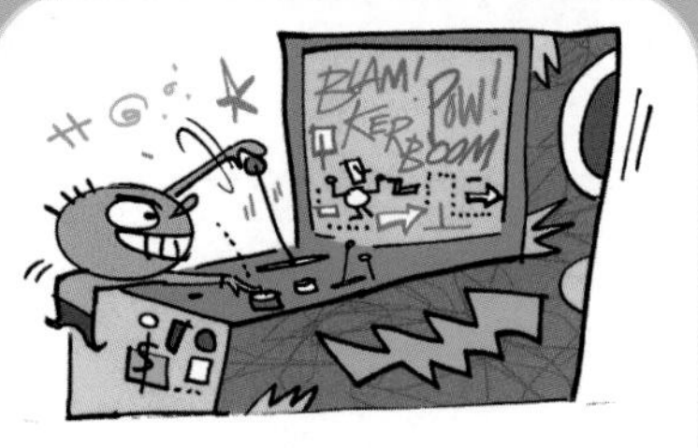
BLAM!
POW!
KER BOOM
...Playing

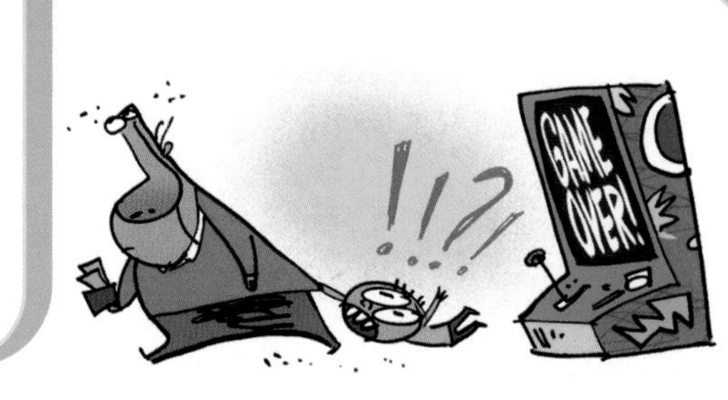
GAME OVER!
...Pleading!

The Three F's
of Report Cards...

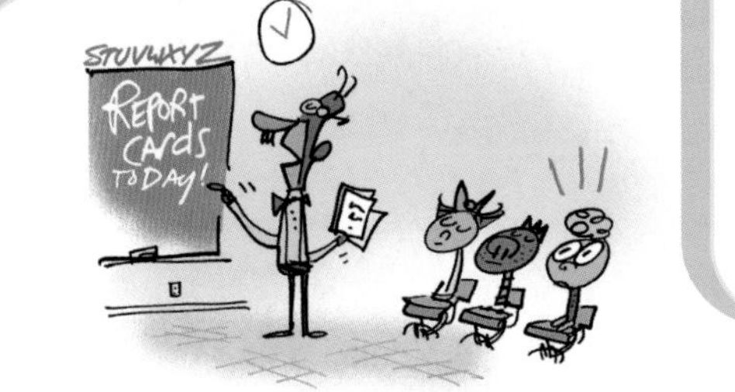
STUVWXYZ
REPORT CARDS TODAY!
...Fearing

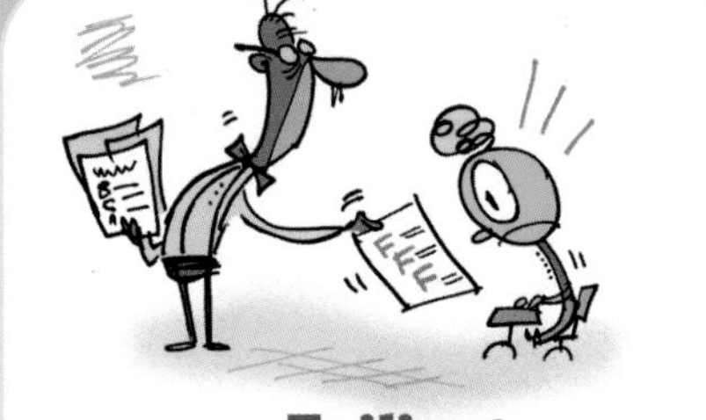
...Failing

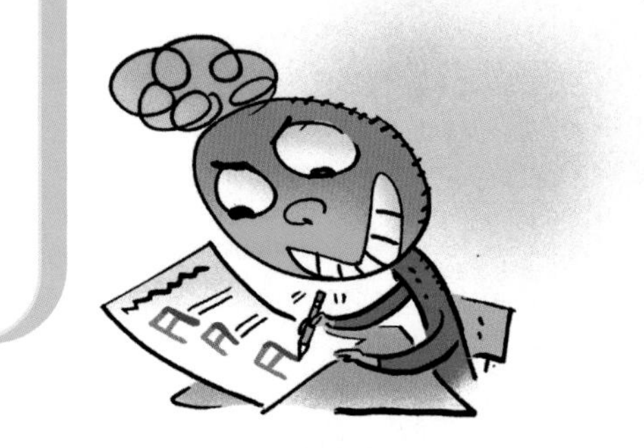
...Forging!

The Three M's
of Thanksgiving...

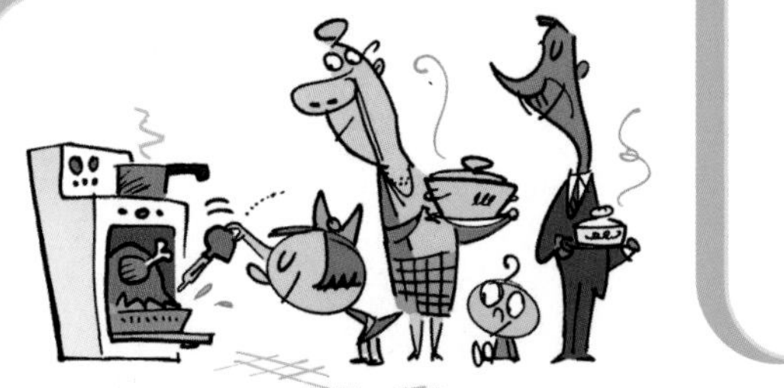
...Making

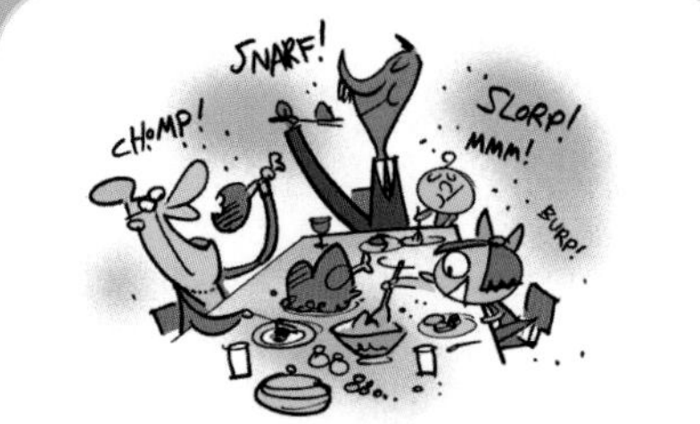
SNARF!
CHOMP!
SLORP!
MMM!
BURP!
...Munching

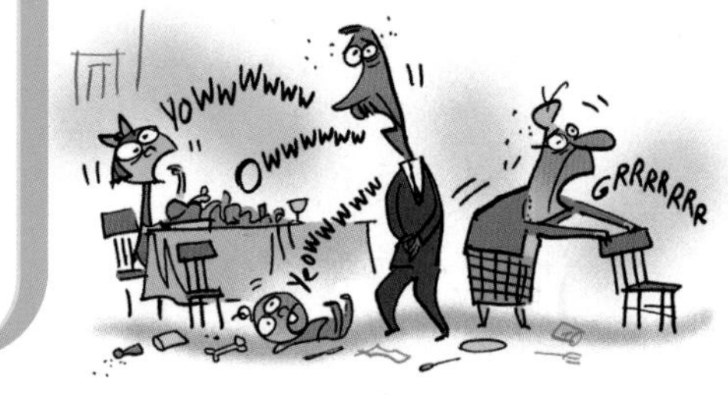
YOWWWWWW
OWWWWWWW
YOWWWWW
GRRRRRRR
...Moaning!

The Three N's
of Dogs...

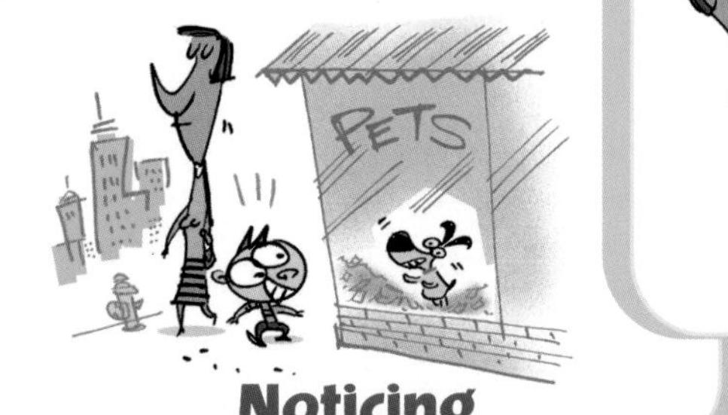
PETS
...Noticing

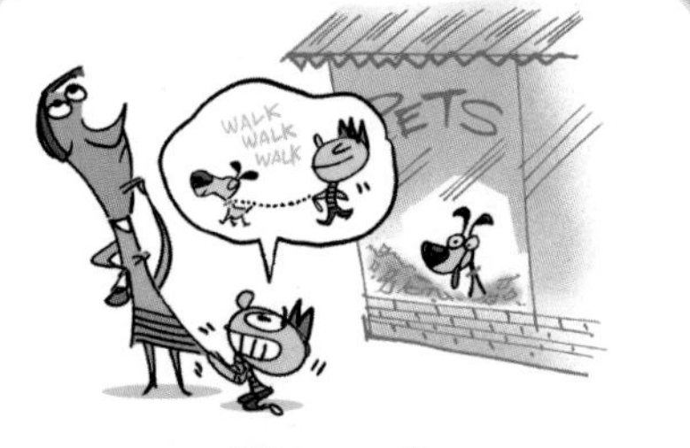
WALK WALK WALK
PETS
...Nagging

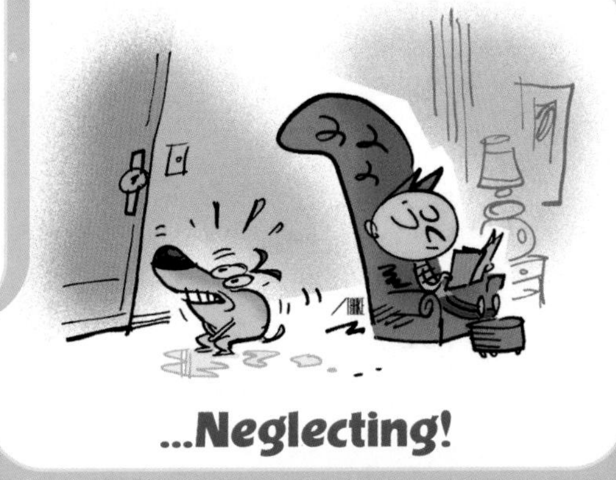
...Neglecting!

THE DWAYNE CHRONICLES

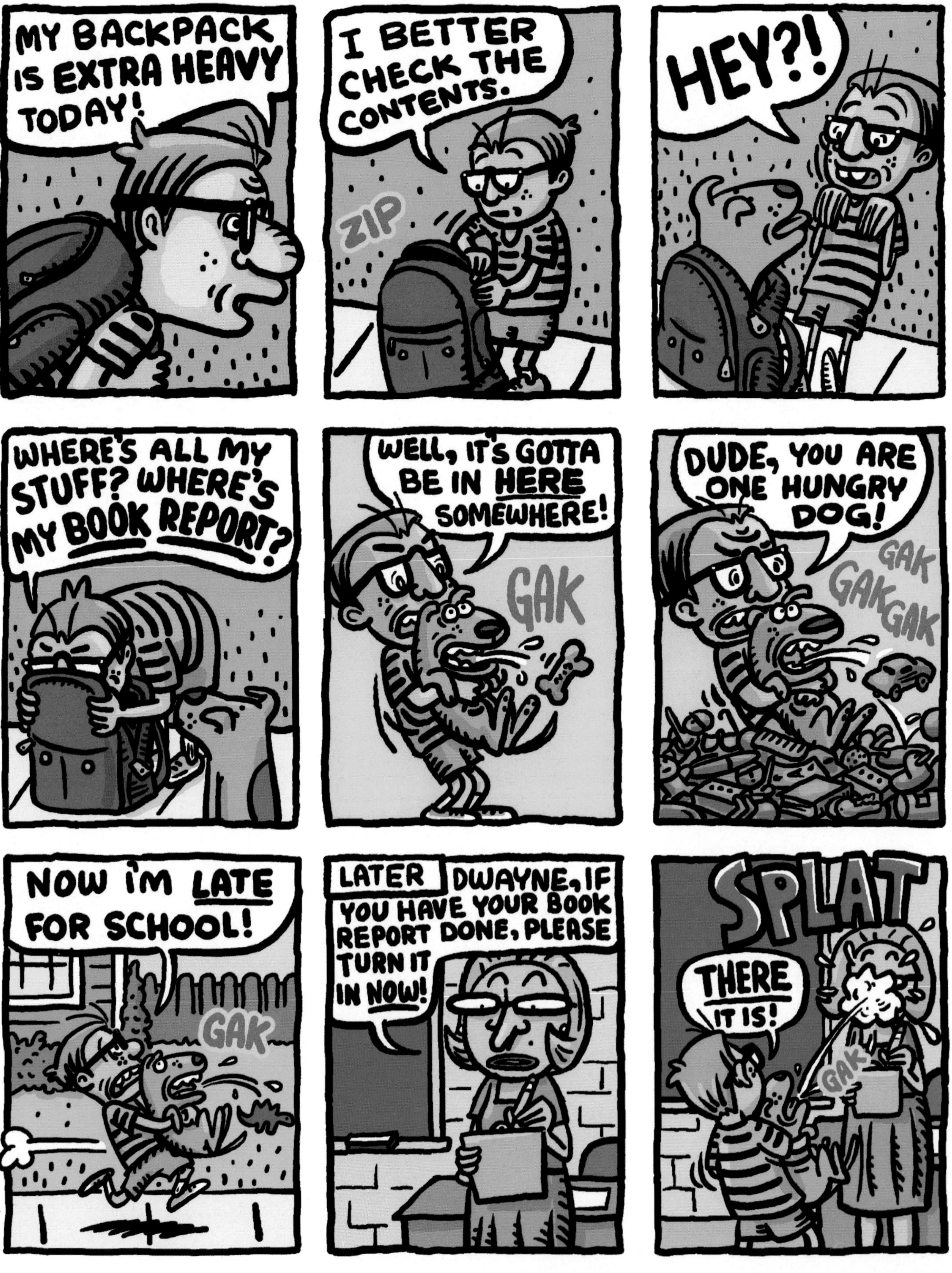

MY BACKPACK IS EXTRA HEAVY TODAY!
I BETTER CHECK THE CONTENTS.
ZIP
HEY?!
WHERE'S ALL MY STUFF? WHERE'S MY BOOK REPORT?
WELL, IT'S GOTTA BE IN HERE SOMEWHERE!
GAK
DUDE, YOU ARE ONE HUNGRY DOG!
GAK GAK GAK
NOW I'M LATE FOR SCHOOL!
GAK
LATER
DWAYNE, IF YOU HAVE YOUR BOOK REPORT DONE, PLEASE TURN IT IN NOW!
SPLAT
THERE IT IS!
GAK

WRITER AND ARTIST: ERIC SCOTT

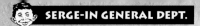

Sergio Aragonés Presents A MAD Look at Pirates

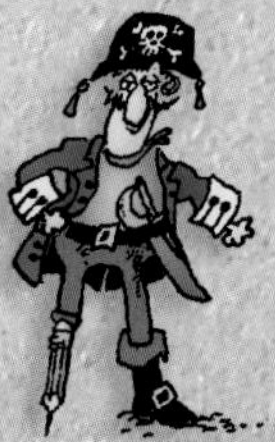

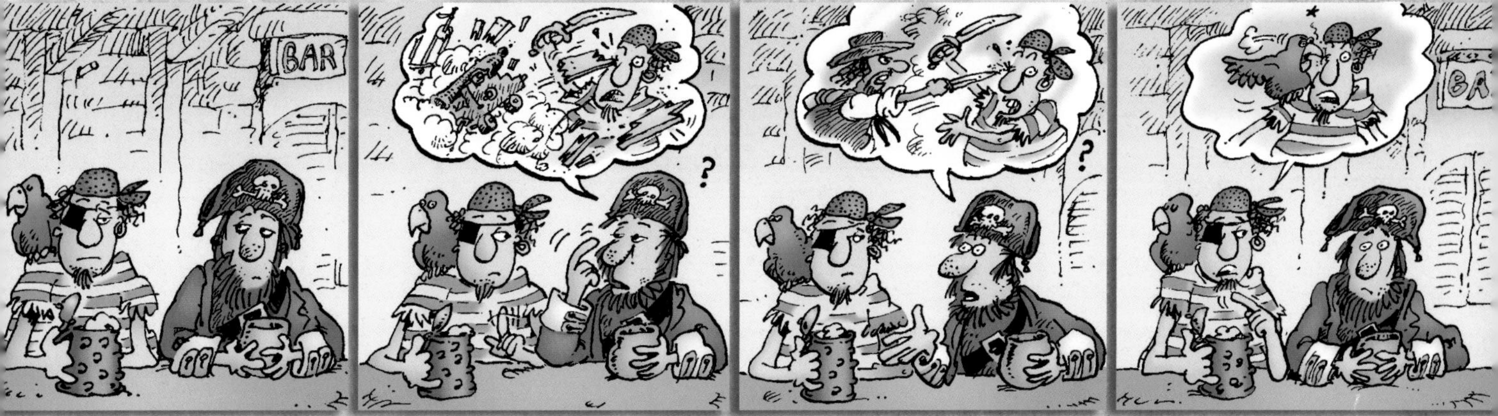
BAR
?
?
BA

WRITER AND ARTIST: SERGIO ARAGONES COLORIST: TOM LUTH

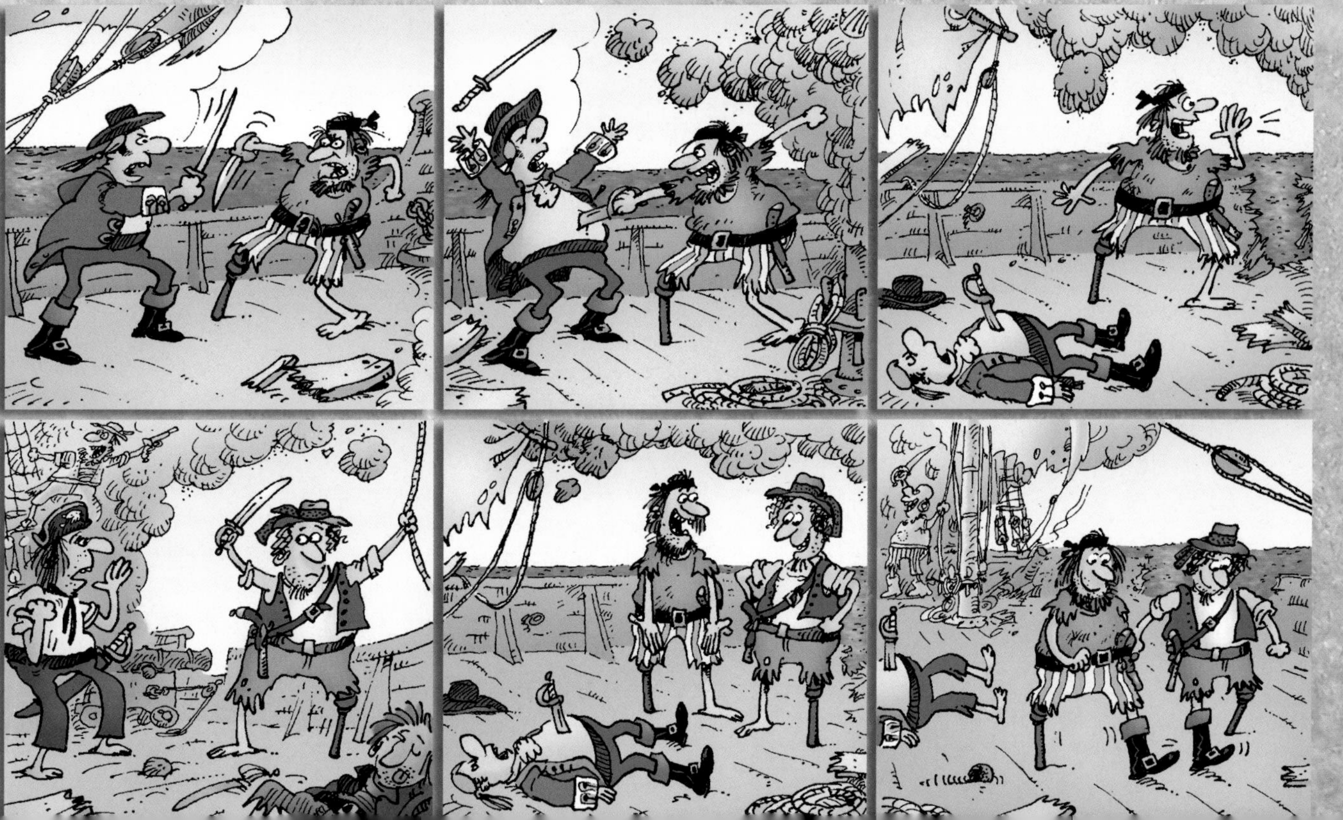

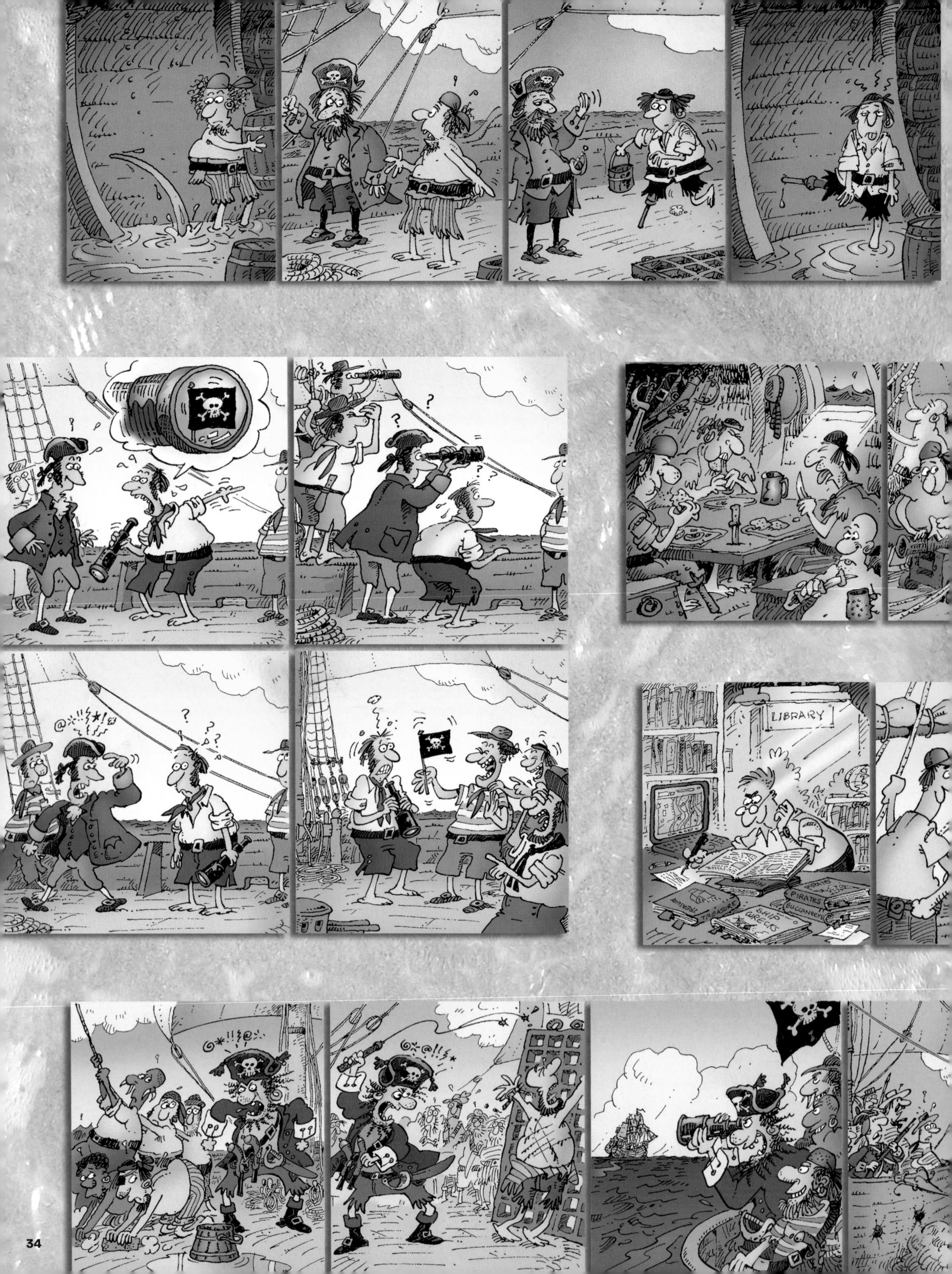
LIBRARY
TREASURE
PIRATES
BUCCANEERS
SHIP WRECKS

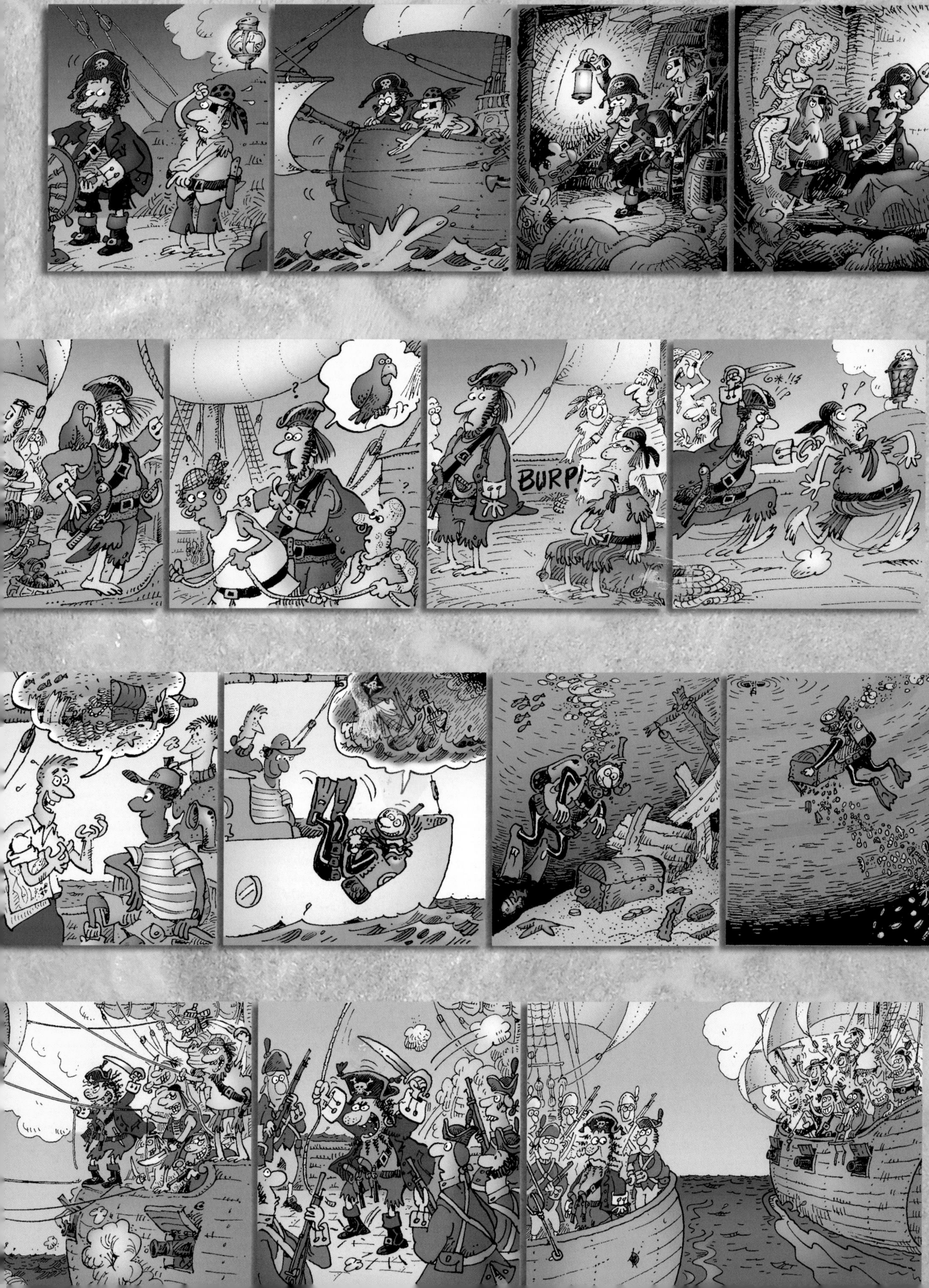
BURP!

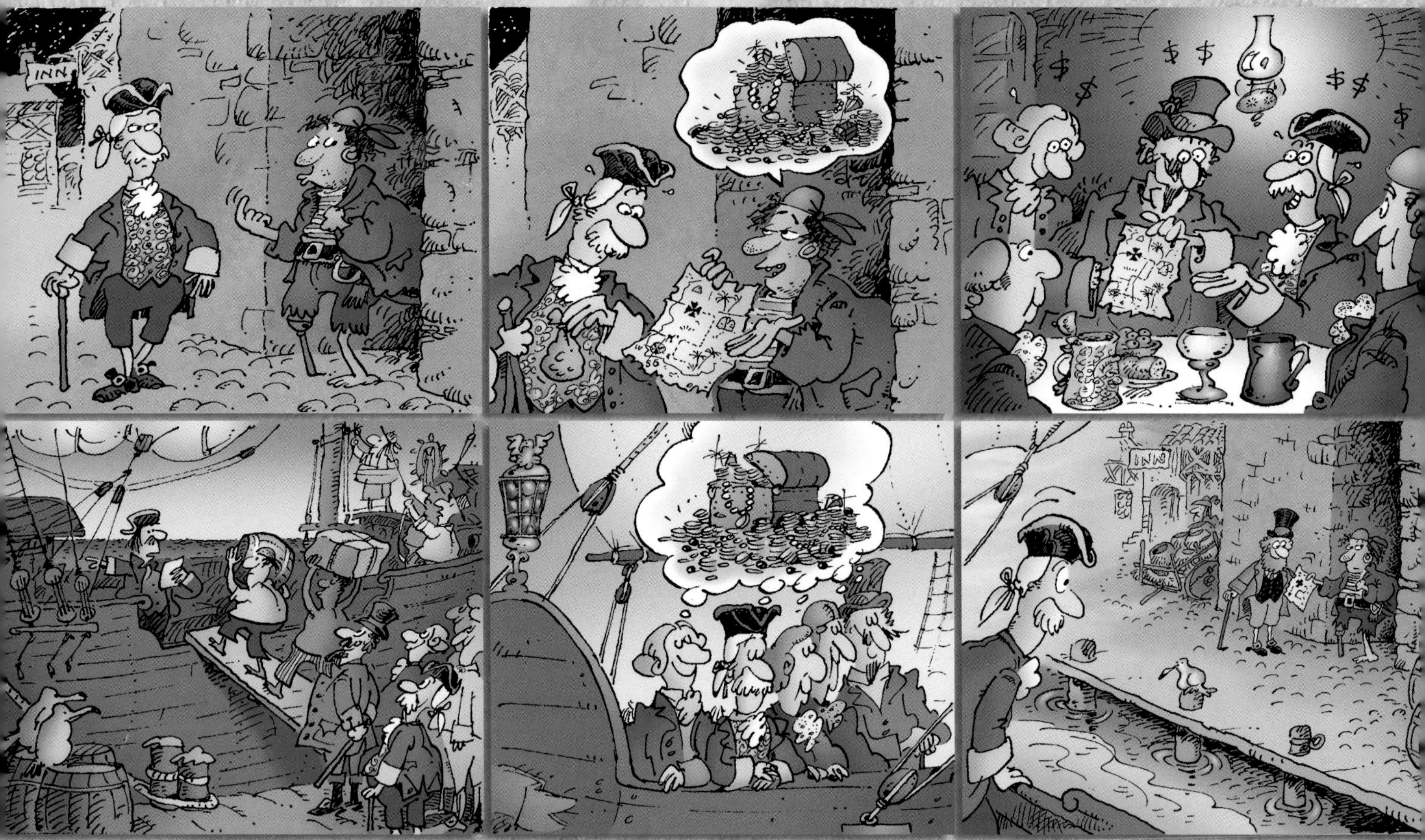
INN
$ $
$ $
$ $
INN

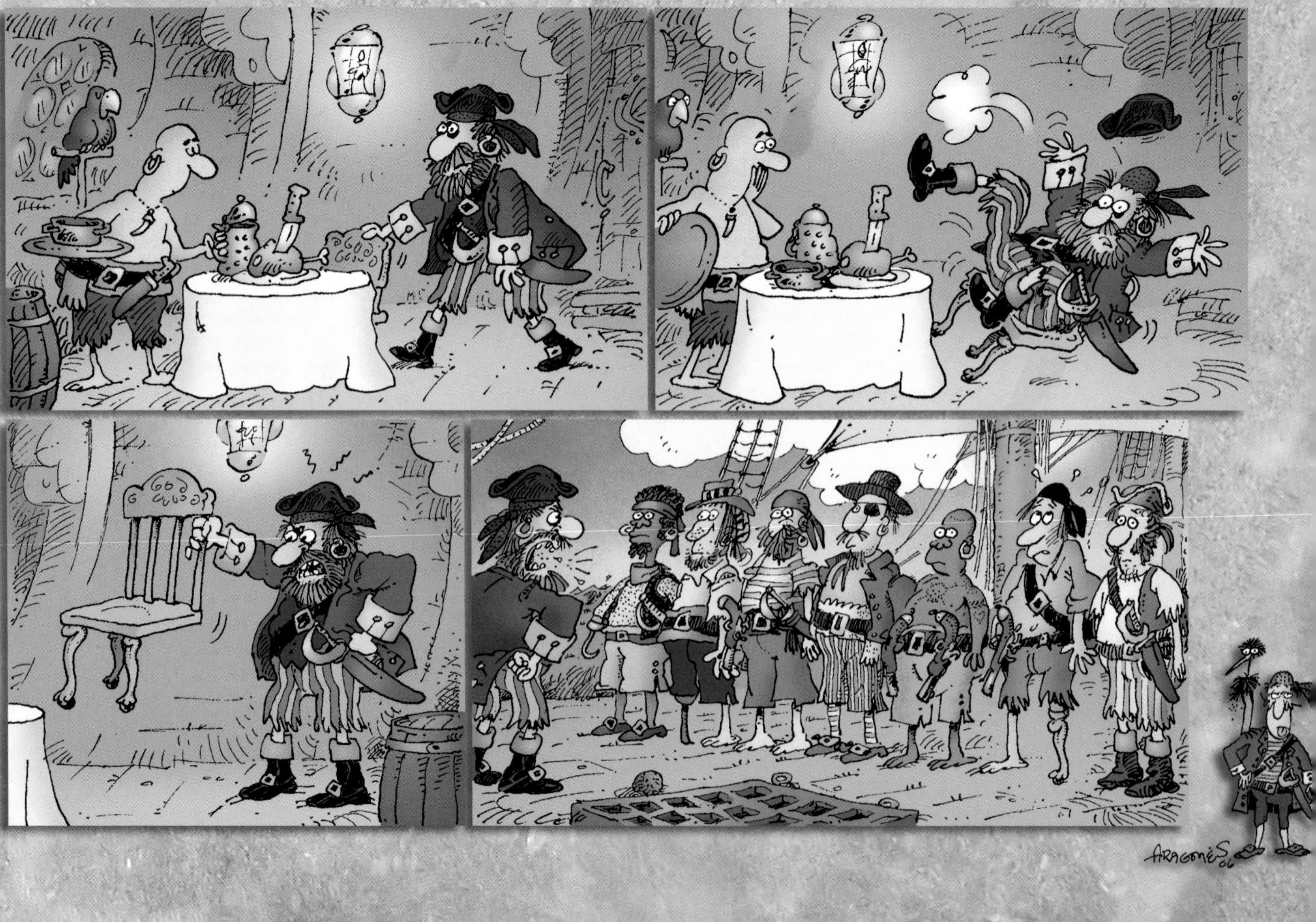
ARAGONÉS 06

IN A SPECIALIST'S OFFICE

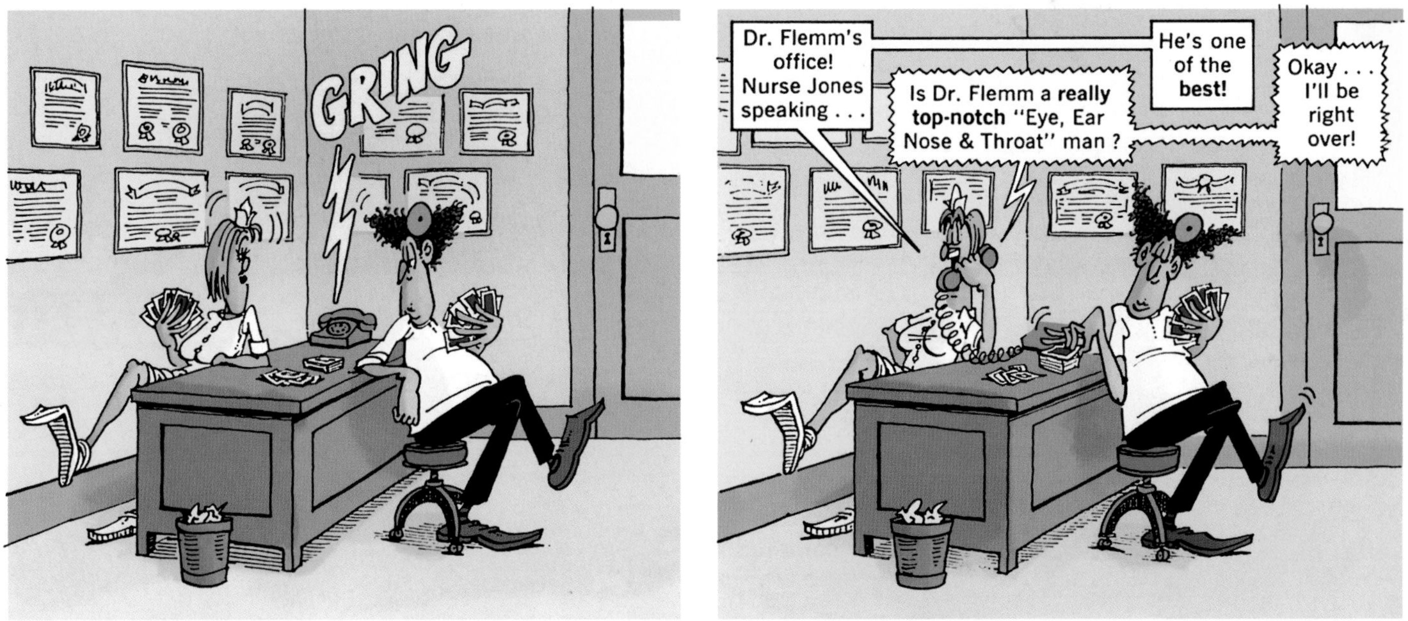

GRING
Dr. Flemm's office! Nurse Jones speaking . . .
Is Dr. Flemm a **really top-notch** "Eye, Ear Nose & Throat" man ?
He's one of the **best!**
Okay . . . I'll be right over!

WRITER AND ARTIST: DON MARTIN **COLORIST: CARL PETERSON**

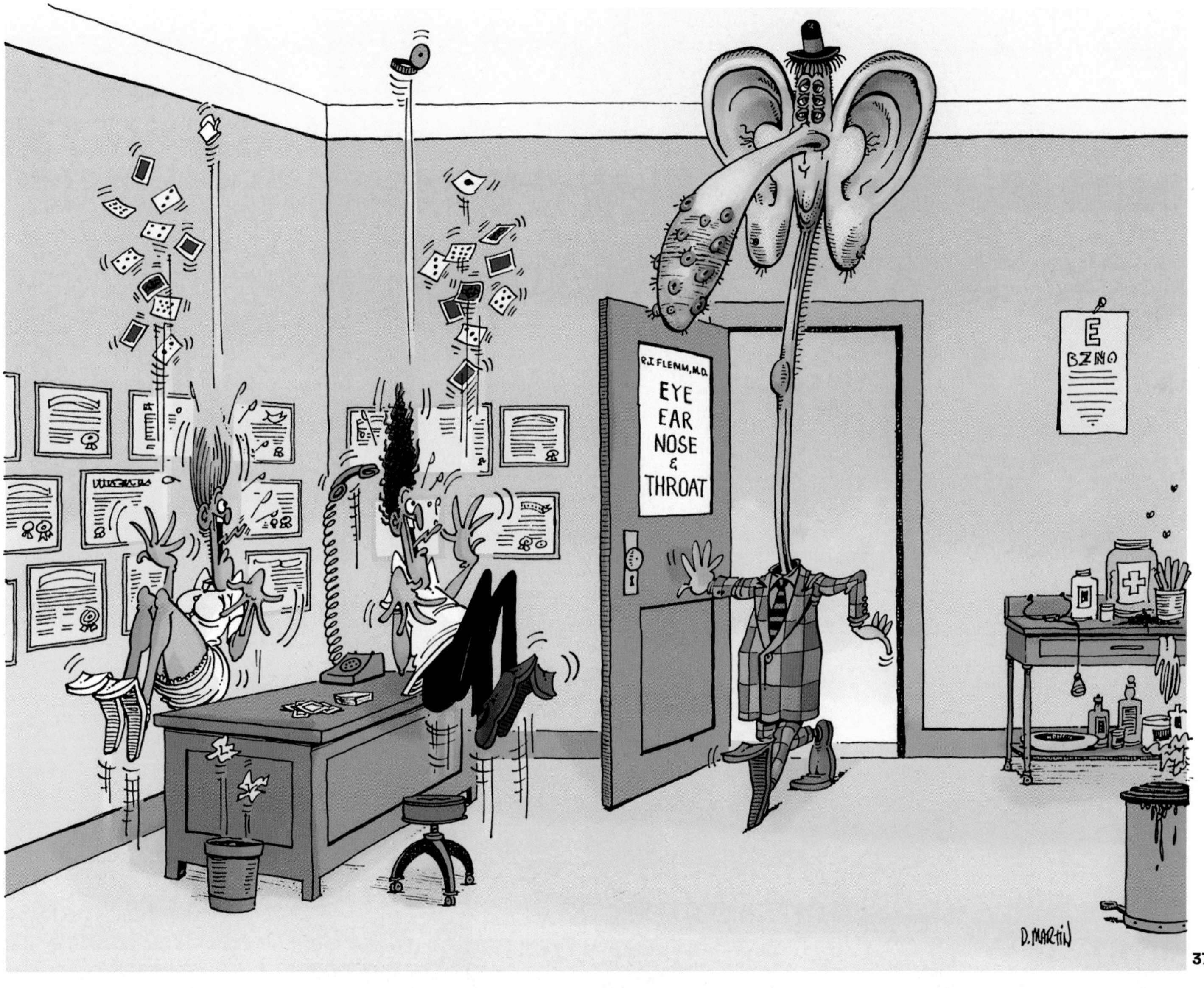

R.I. FLEMM, M.D.
EYE
EAR
NOSE
&
THROAT
E
BZNQ
D. MARTIN

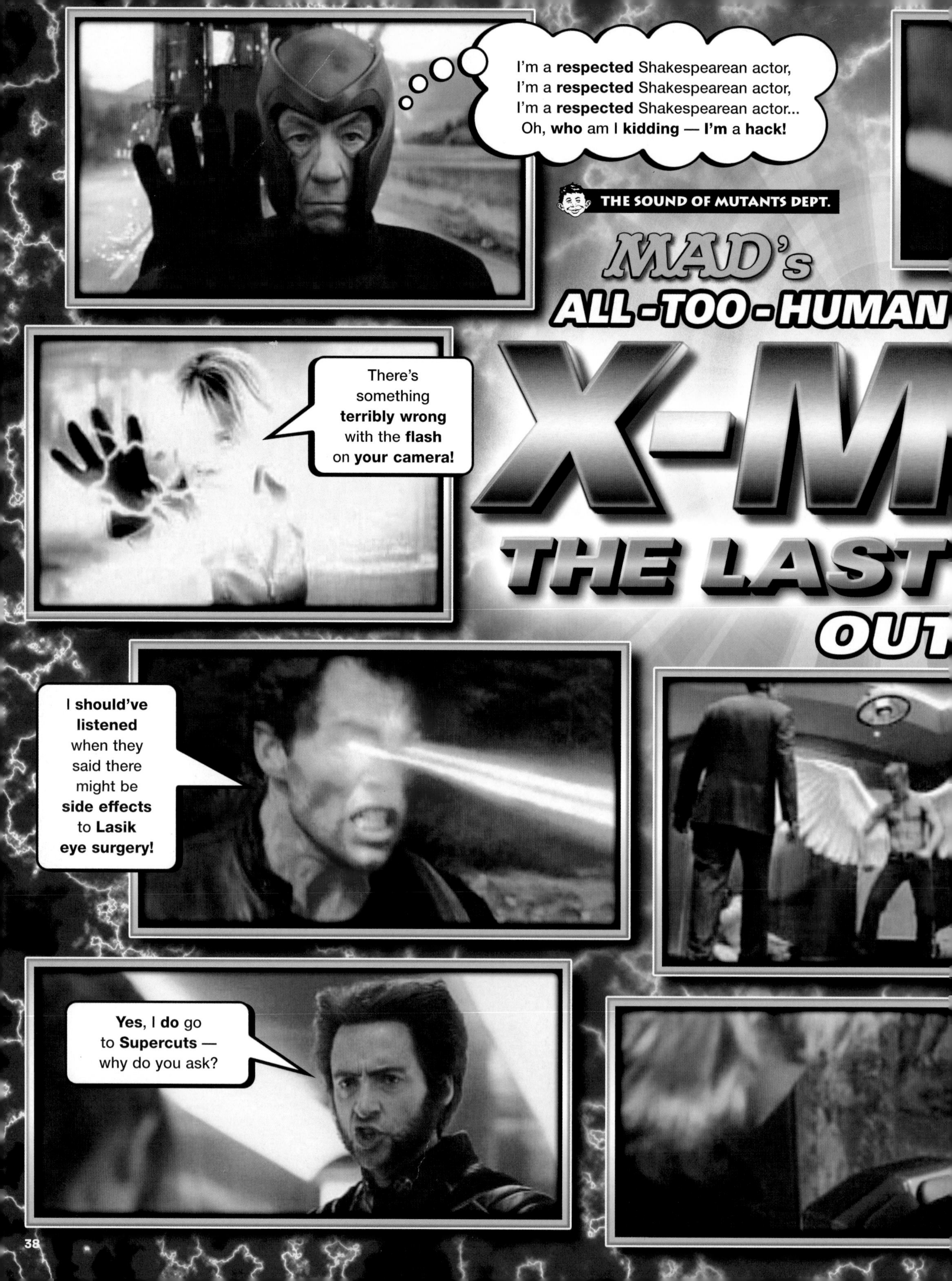
I'm a respected Shakespearean actor,
I'm a respected Shakespearean actor,
I'm a respected Shakespearean actor...
Oh, who am I kidding — I'm a hack!
THE SOUND OF MUTANTS DEPT.
MAD's
ALL-TOO-HUMAN
X-M
THE LAST
OUT
There's something terribly wrong with the flash on your camera!
I should've listened when they said there might be side effects to Lasik eye surgery!
Yes, I do go to Supercuts — why do you ask?

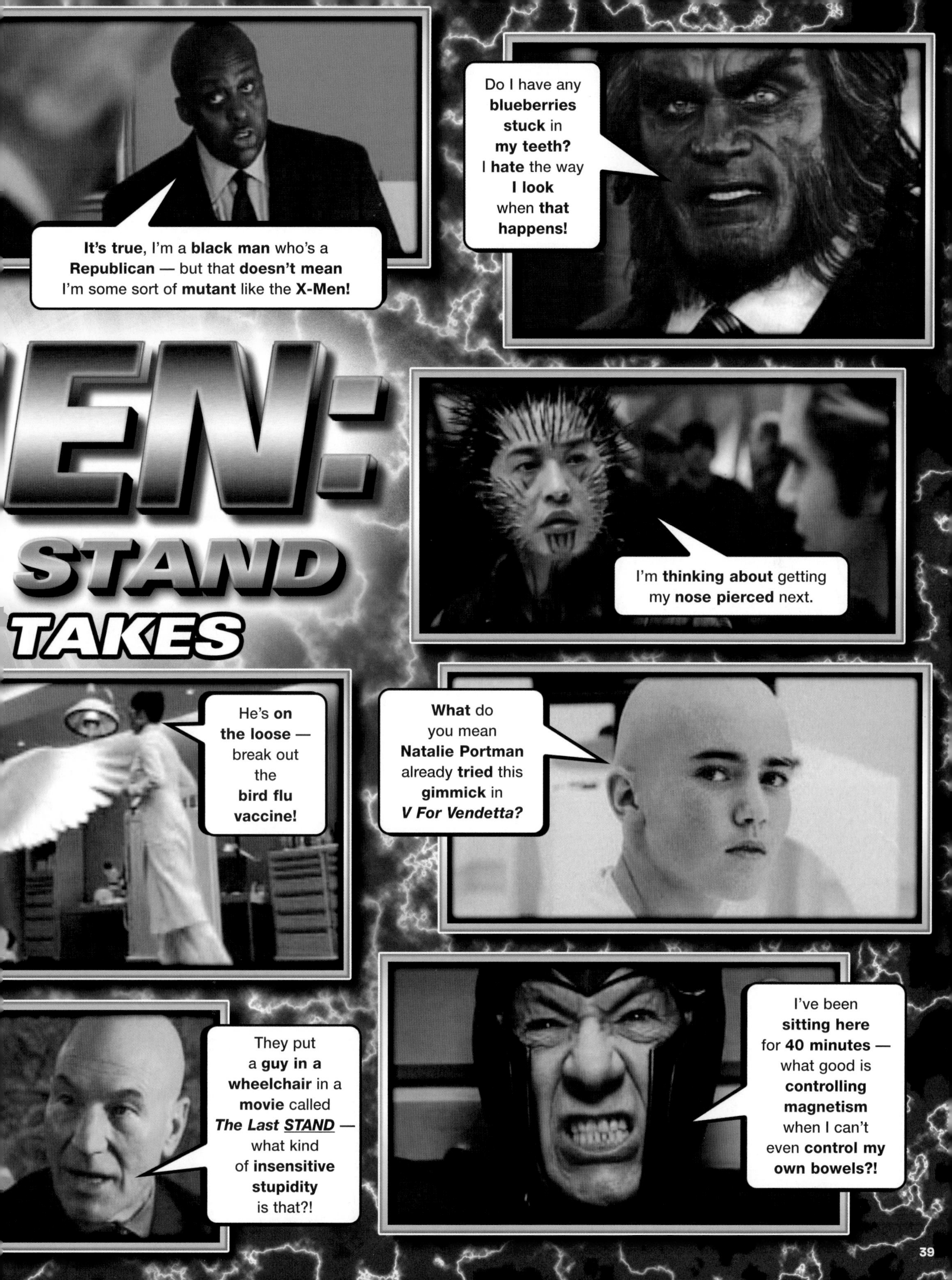
It's true, I'm a black man who's a Republican — but that doesn't mean I'm some sort of mutant like the X-Men!
Do I have any blueberries stuck in my teeth? I hate the way I look when that happens!
EN:
STAND
TAKES
I'm thinking about getting my nose pierced next.
He's on the loose — break out the bird flu vaccine!
What do you mean Natalie Portman already tried this gimmick in V For Vendetta?
They put a guy in a wheelchair in a movie called The Last STAND — what kind of insensitive stupidity is that?!
I've been sitting here for 40 minutes — what good is controlling magnetism when I can't even control my own bowels?!

Sure, you like the presents and the time off from school, but aren't you bothered by

The 10 WORST THINGS about Christmas

1

Grandma Got Run Over By A Reindeer:
Oh yeah, it's really funny to constantly play a "funny" song about a helpless old lady who gets stomped by a 200-pound hoofed animal.

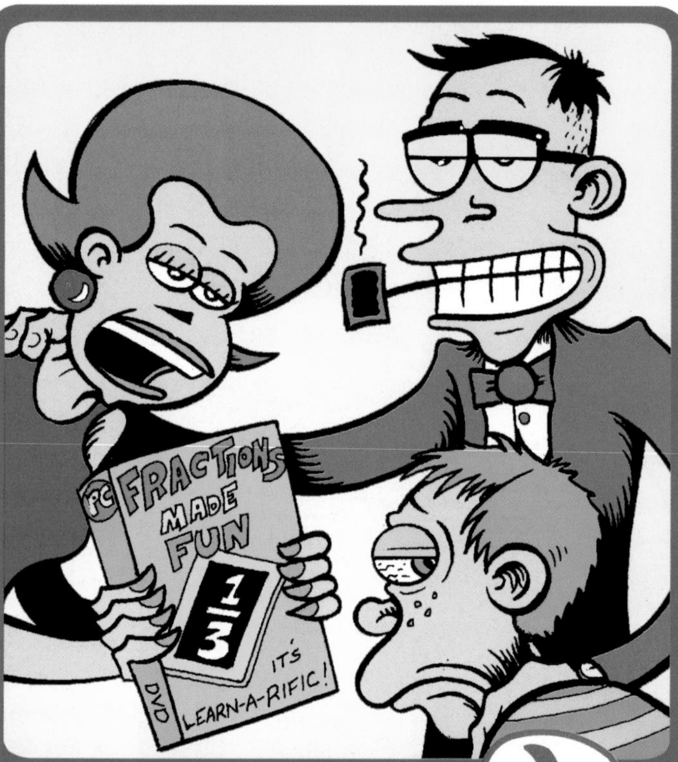
FC
FRACTIONS MADE FUN
1/3
IT'S LEARN-A-RIFIC!
DVD

2

Parents who don't understand that the words "educational" and "toy" rarely go together.

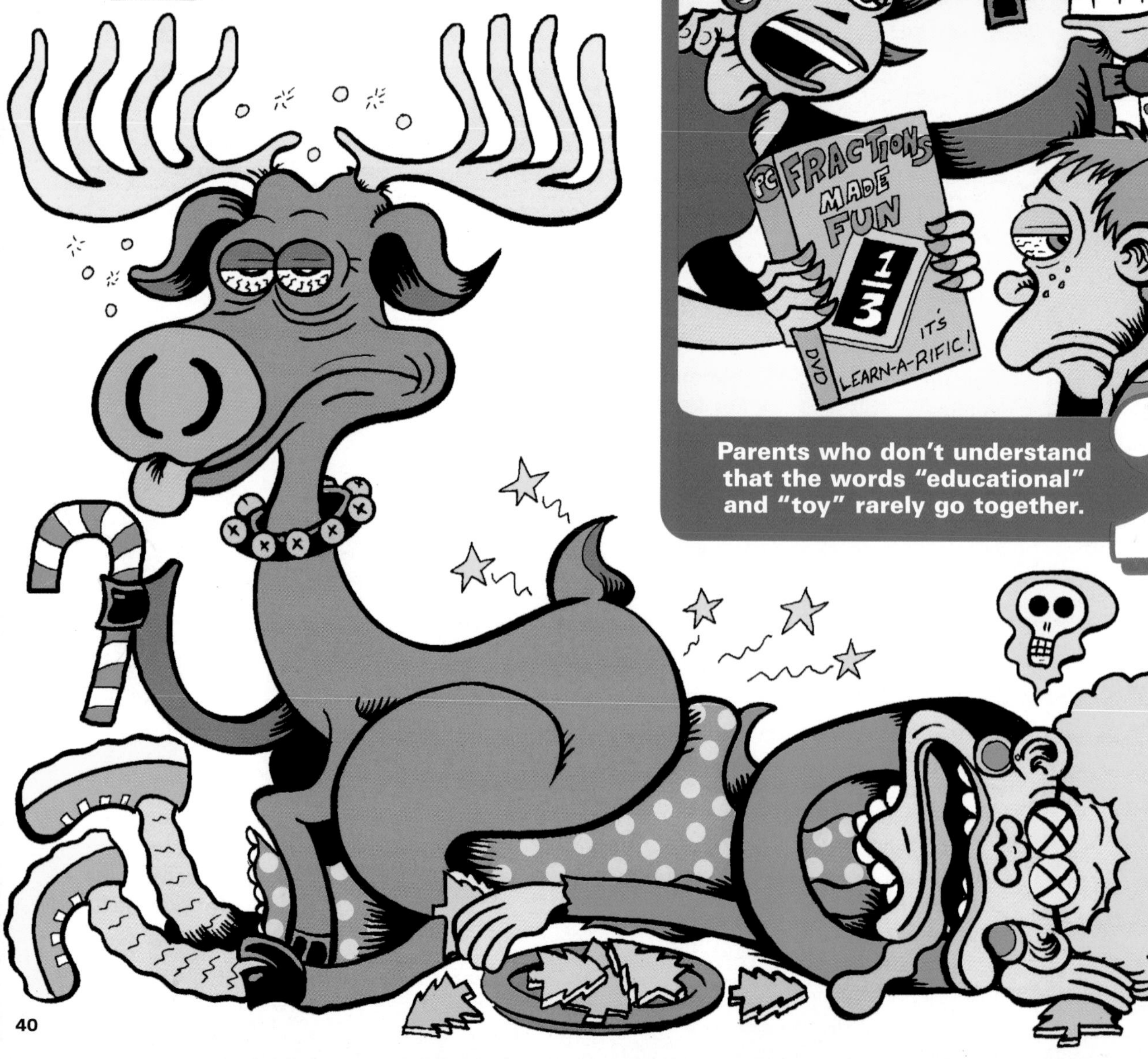

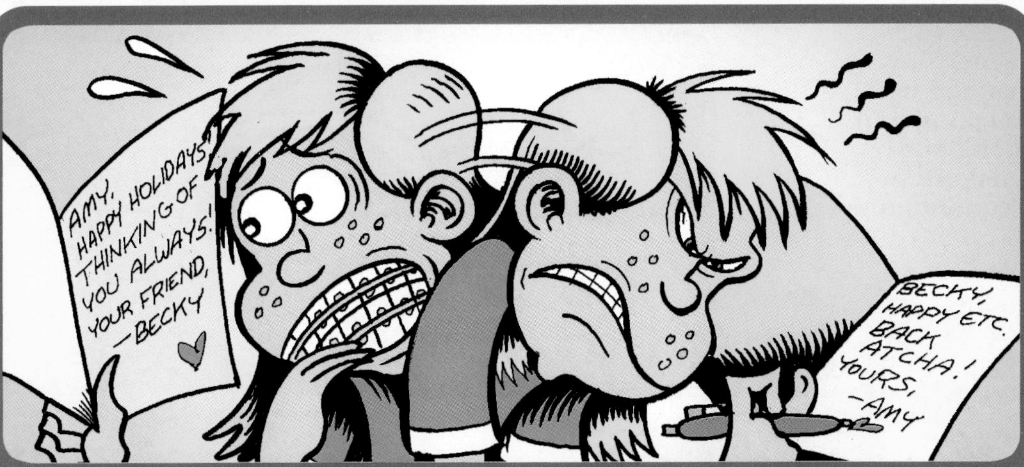
AMY,
HAPPY HOLIDAYS!
THINKING OF
YOU ALWAYS!
YOUR FRIEND,
—BECKY
BECKY,
HAPPY ETC.
BACK
ATCHA!
YOURS,
—AMY

3

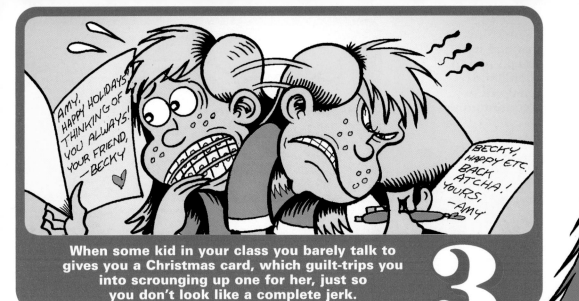

When some kid in your class you barely talk to gives you a Christmas card, which guilt-trips you into scrounging up one for her, just so you don't look like a complete jerk.

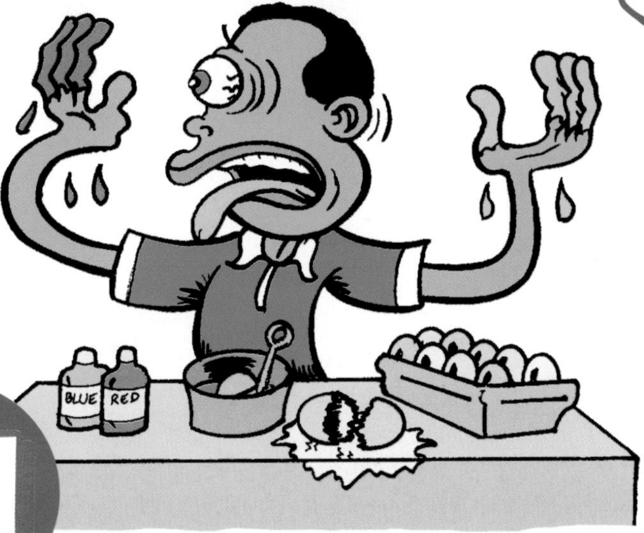
BLUE
RED

4

Getting egg dye all over your hands when...wait,hold on. Wrong holiday. (But it still stinks.)

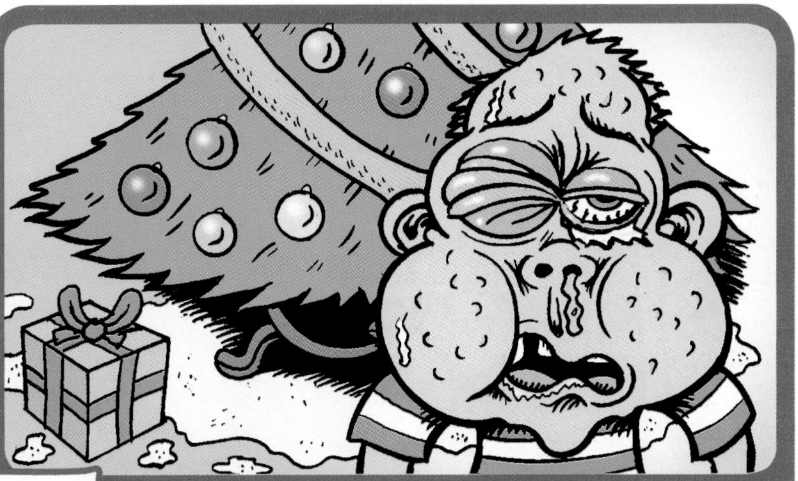

5

That worthless fake "snow" under the tree, the sole purpose of which appears to be causing allergic reactions and skin rashes in your little brother.

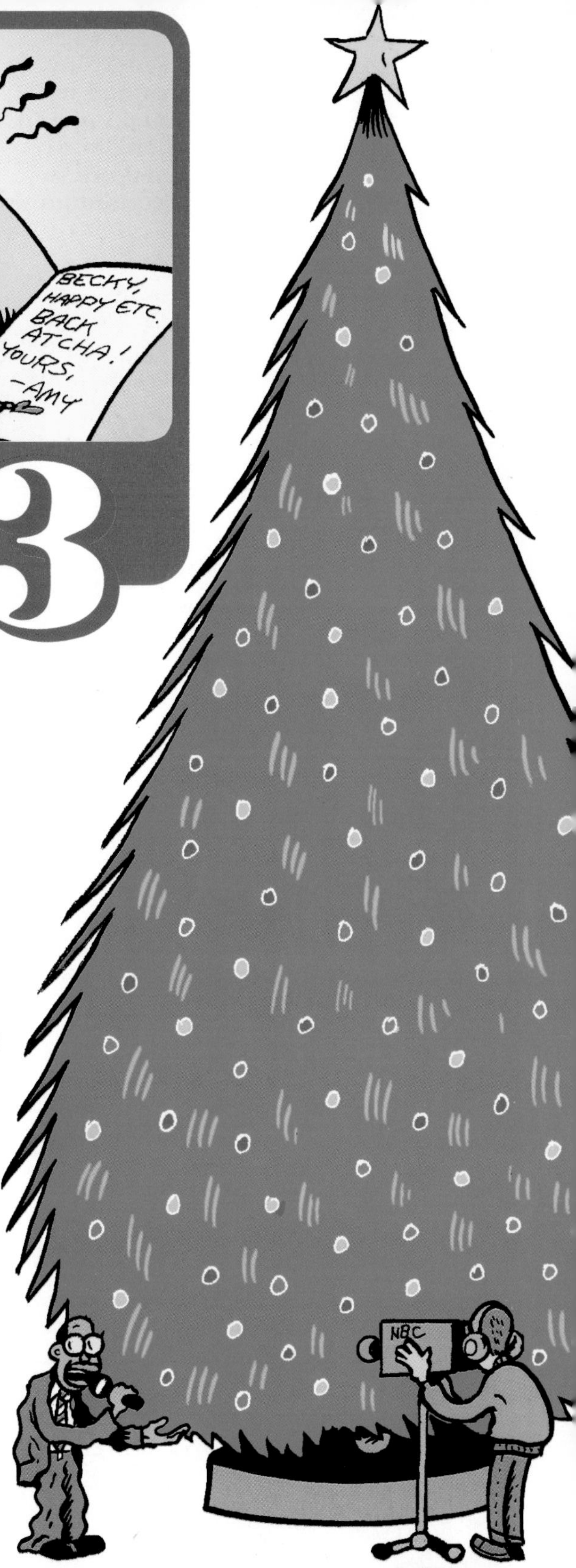
NBC

6

The endless fuss over the annual Rockefeller Center Christmas tree lighting. If Al Roker hadn't dropped 200 pounds, NBC could show the same special from 1995 and no one would be any the wiser.

7 When your Christmas vacation is ruined by Professor Snape giving you extra spells and potions homework (Hogwarts students only).

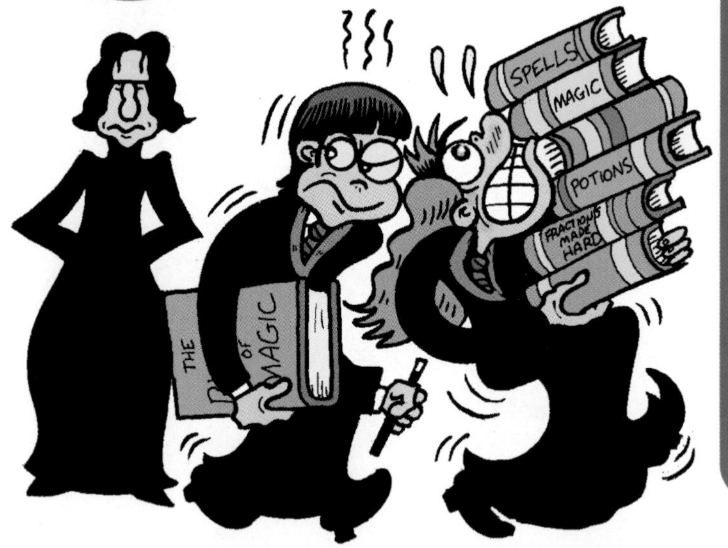
SPELLS
MAGIC
POTIONS
FRACTIONS MADE HARD
THE
OF MAGIC

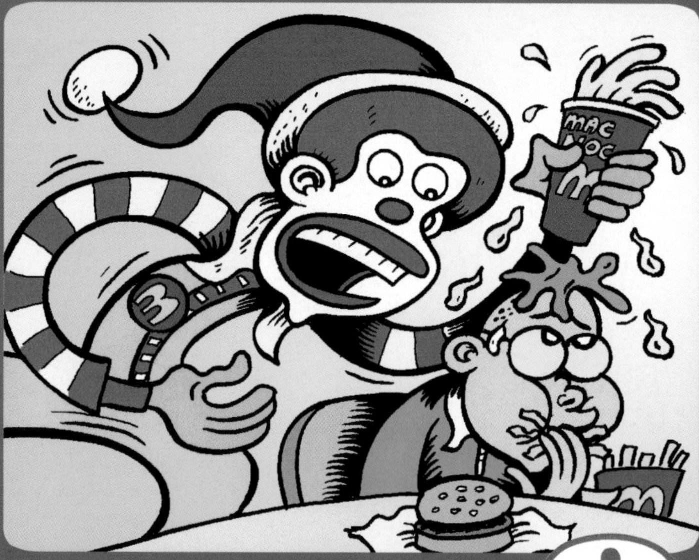

8 Fast food places that get all excited over the fact that they've managed to add artificial eggnog flavor to their shake machines. Big McDeal!

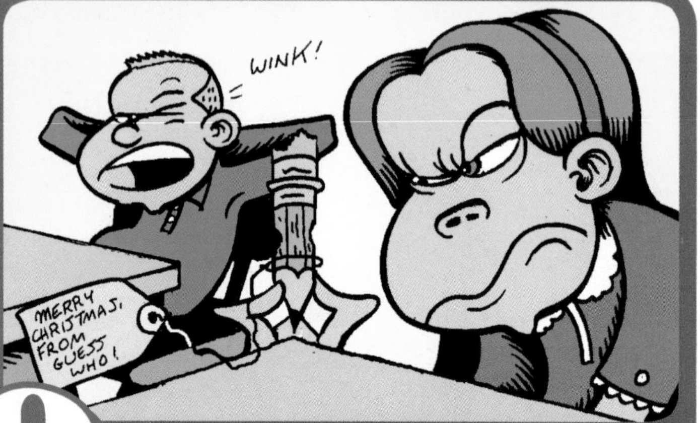
WINK!
MERRY CHRISTMAS, FROM GUESS WHO!

9 When the laziest kid in your class is assigned to be your Secret Santa.

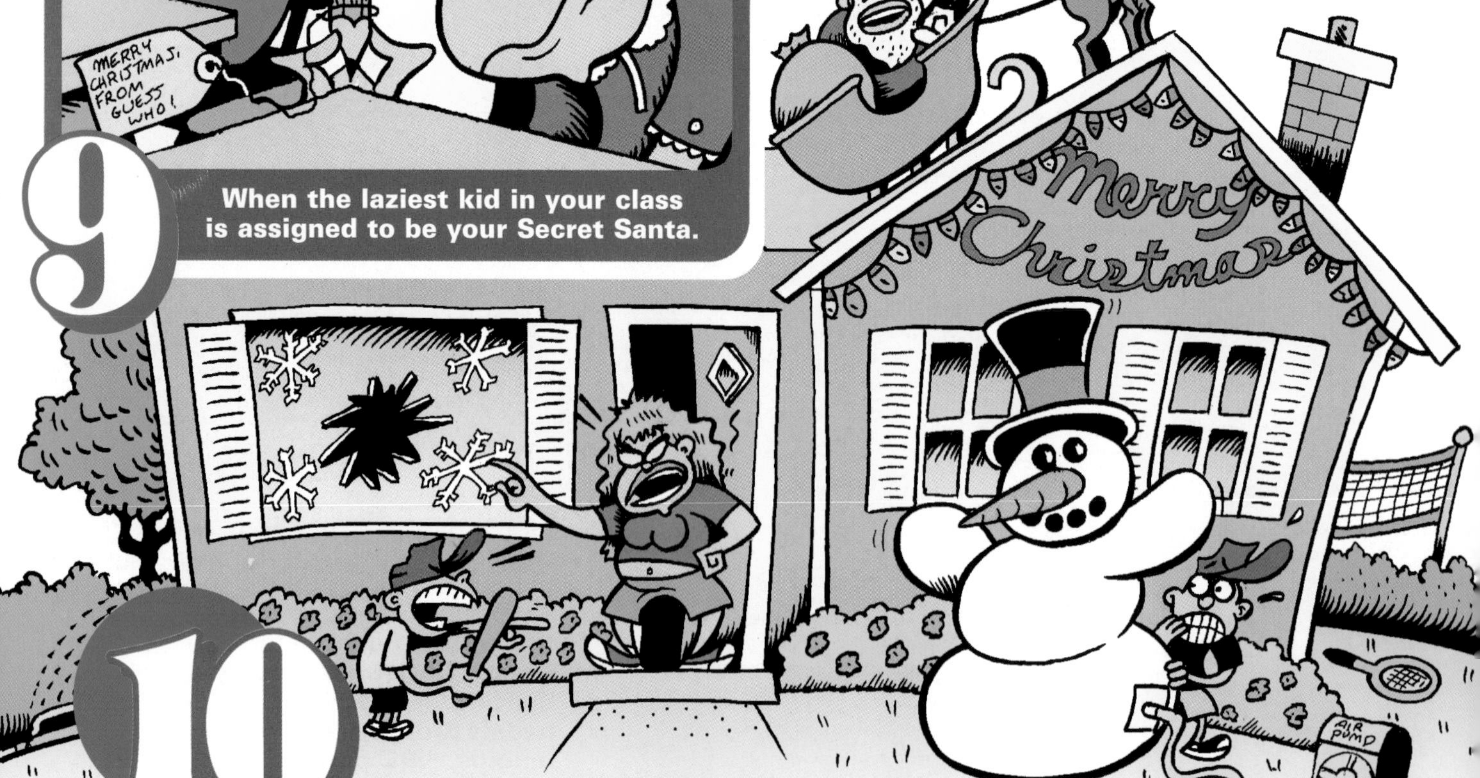
Merry Christmas
AIR PUMP

10 Lazy neighbors who don't take down their cheesy Christmas decorations until around the time when their cheesy 4th of July decorations are shoved down everyone's throat.

ALL IN A DAY'S WORK

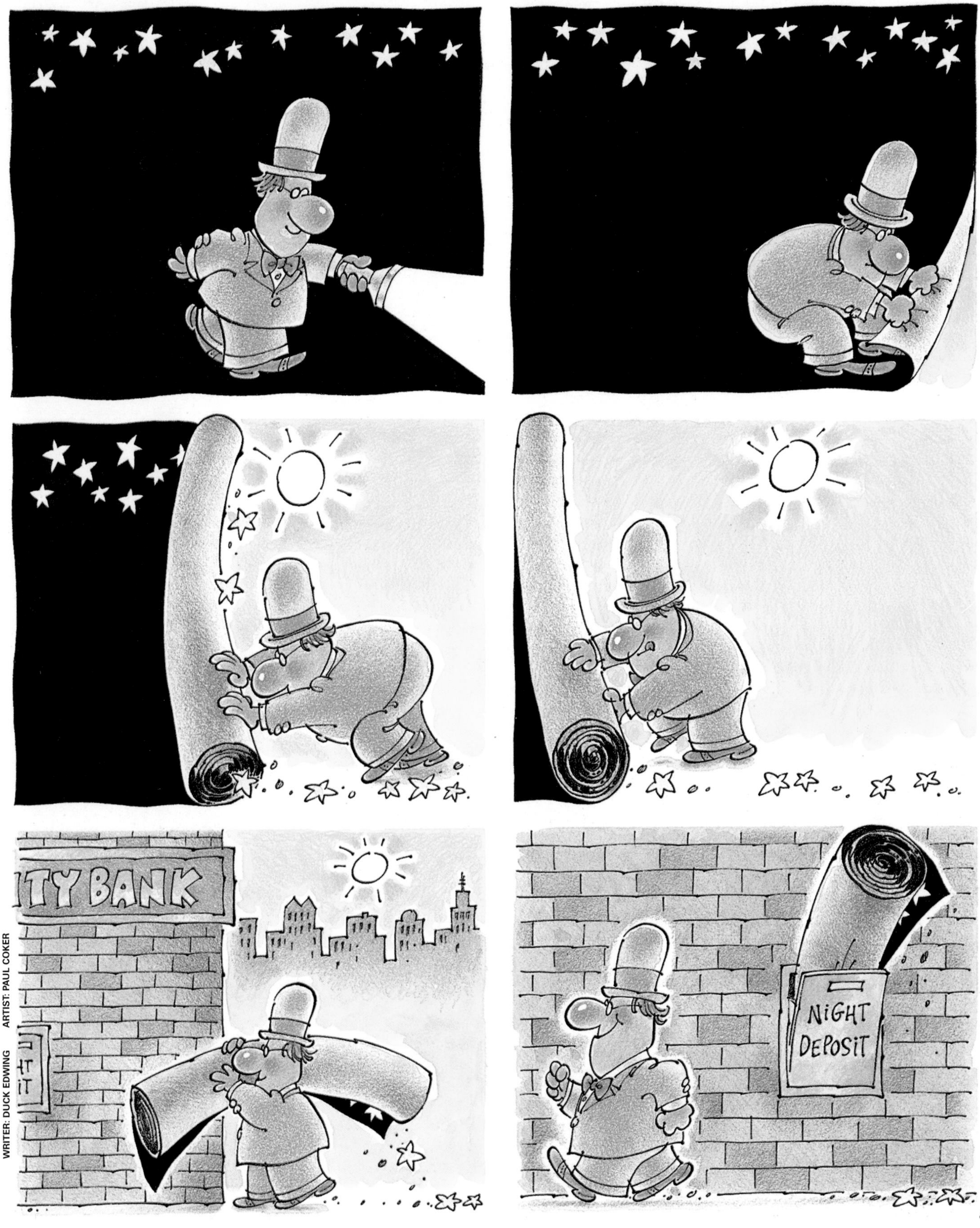

TY BANK
HT
IT
NIGHT DEPOSIT

WRITER: DUCK EDWING ARTIST: PAUL COKER

Planet TAD!!!!!

http://www.galaxyo'blogs.com/planettad

Planet TAD!!!!!

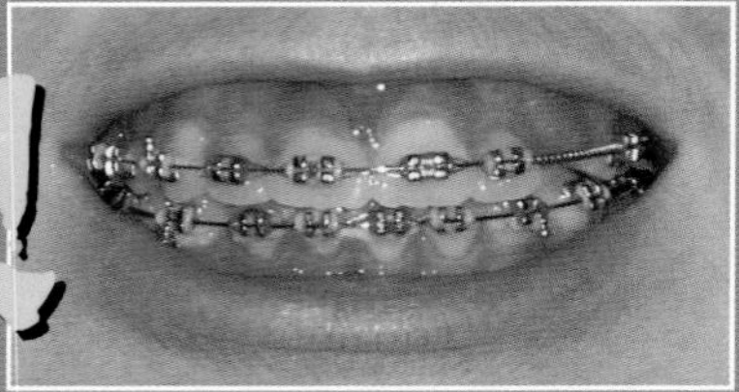

[About Me]

[Name|Tad]
[Grade|9]
[Favorite Name for a
First Lady|Mamie Eisenhower]

[09 March|05:47pm]

This Saturday is my little sister Sophie's 8th birthday. She's having a Barbie-themed party. That was her third choice. Her first choice was to have a princess-themed party, but then my mom told her that if that was the theme of the party, it couldn't just be HER being a princess — she had to let the other girls be princesses, too. Her second choice was a Christina Aguilera-themed party, and both my mom and dad told her absolutely not. So it's a Barbie-themed party. I'm going to try to be out of the house as long as I can.

[11 March|11:23pm]

[mood|  jealous]

Well, today was Sophie's party. I went to the mall and managed to miss almost the whole thing — only one of Sophie's friends was still there when I got home, Brenda Winters, who was waiting for her mom to pick her up. She'd had too much cake and ice cream and kept saying, over and over, "I think I'm gonna throw up!" My mom looked really nervous, because Brenda was sitting on the couch that's not Scotchgarded.

Anyway, for her birthday, my parents got Sophie a guinea pig, which is totally unfair, because they never let me have a pet. This is what her guinea pig looks like:

His name is Thunderclaw. Sophie calls him "Mr. Squeakers," but he and I both know his name is Thunderclaw.

[15 March|08:37pm]

[mood|  evil]

My friend Chet came over today and we sneaked into Sophie's room when she was out at her oboe lesson to play with Thunderclaw. I think he's a really smart guinea pig, because Chet made a little maze out of Legos, and Thunderclaw figured out how to get through it in no time. Chet's coming over on Thursday, when Sophie and my parents are at her recital, and we're going to build a little obstacle course to test Thunderclaw's strength and agility.

44

[19 March|**07:23pm**]

[**mood**| anxious]

Oh, man. Today was a long day. Chet and I were putting Thunderclaw through the obstacle course, and he'd already finished the swimming portion in the bathroom sink, and the ice skating portion inside a carton of sherbet we found in the back of the freezer, but then, during the Road Rally, when we had him in my radio-controlled car, Chet took a turn too hard and it slammed into the coffee table. Thunderclaw went flying off somewhere in the direction of the sofa, and we couldn't find him, despite spending a long time diagramming where he could have landed:

SOFA?
RECLINER?
T.V. CABINET?

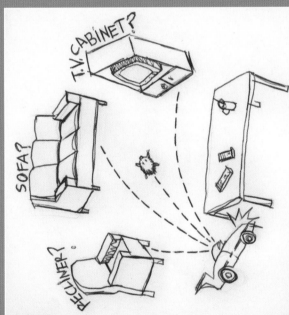

Ultimately, we gave up on finding him. Chet remembered that something sort of like this happened in "Meet the Parents," and so we used a solution that worked pretty well there: We ran down to Pets-a-Million to find a replacement for Thunderclaw before Sophie got home. I think the one we found looks a lot like him, especially after we added some spots with a brown magic marker:

Gotta go — I hear Sophie and my folks getting home.

[20 March|**08:17pm**]

[**mood**| relieved]

Good news! Sophie thinks Thunderclaw II is her original guinea pig! Although she did tell Mom and Dad that Mr. Squeakers is suddenly "a whole lot bitey-er".

[22 March|**07:53pm**]

[**mood**| guilty]

Um. Well. Today brought good news and bad news. The good news is, we found Thunderclaw I. The bad news is, he was in my mom's Special K.

I guess, after we lost him, he ran into the kitchen and climbed into the cereal box for some food, and then he couldn't climb out again. So this morning Mom was pouring herself some cereal, and suddenly she screamed, because there in the bowl, with his four tiny paws in the air, was the lifeless body of Thunderclaw I. Sophie started crying and ran to her room, and then a minute later, she came back down to tell us that it couldn't be her guinea pig, because he was still in his cage. And mom said, "Well, how did a guinea pig that looks just like him wind up in my cereal?" I tried to suggest that maybe it was a prize — like, they were giving away one free dead guinea pig in every box of Special K.

Mom stared at me for a really long time, and then she asked, "Is there something you want to tell us?"

And I answered honestly: No. There was absolutely nothing I wanted to tell her.

WRITER: TIM CARVELL **ARTIST: BRIAN DURNIAK**

ONE DAY ON MOUNT NEVER-REST

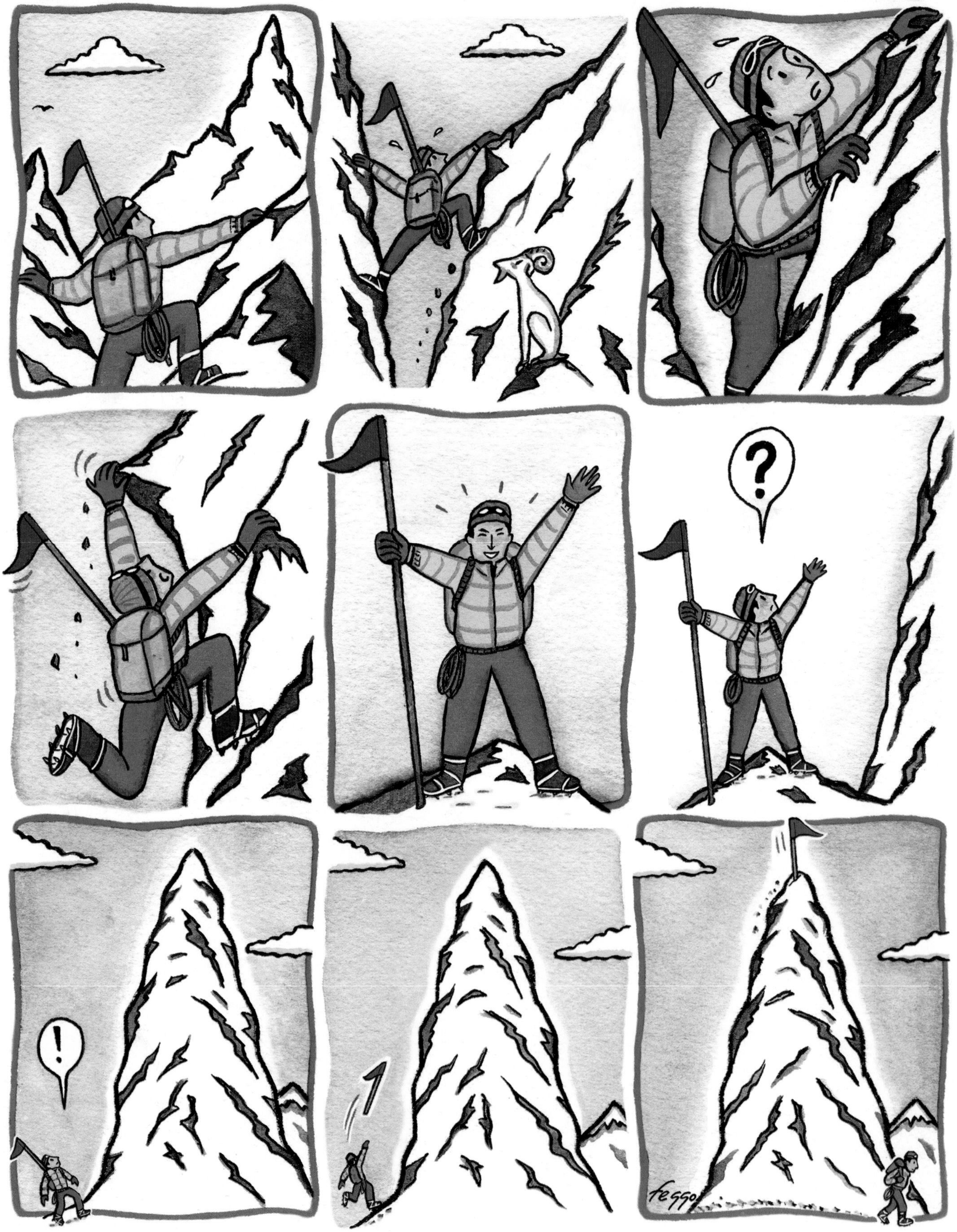

?
!
fego

WRITER AND ARTIST: FELIPE GALINDO

On the bestseller lists, the *Diary of a Wimpy Kid* books are always #1. Here, if you'll pardon the expression...is #2!

DIARRHEA ~~DIARY~~ of a Wimpy Kid

WRITER: DAVE CROATTO

Sunday

Tonight my family went to "Olé!" the local Mexican restaurant. I don't like it very much - there's this really annoying Mexican band there that walks around and plays at the tables. You're always right in the middle of a burrito when all of a sudden some maraca player sneaks up and scares the guacamole out of you.

GAAH!

About half-way through the meal, my brother Rodrick and I got into a pepper-eating contest. They serve these peppers there

1

that are super-hot. But I just swallowed them whole so I wouldn't have to chew them. Rodrick wasn't even blinking an eye, so I just kept wolfing them down.

Then, after the 10th one, Rodrick started laughing like a lunatic. I wasn't sure what was so funny, but then he showed me a bunch of peppers in his napkin. He hadn't actually eaten any, he'd just been hiding them in his hand and putting them on his lap when I wasn't looking.

RODRICK'S NAPKIN

2

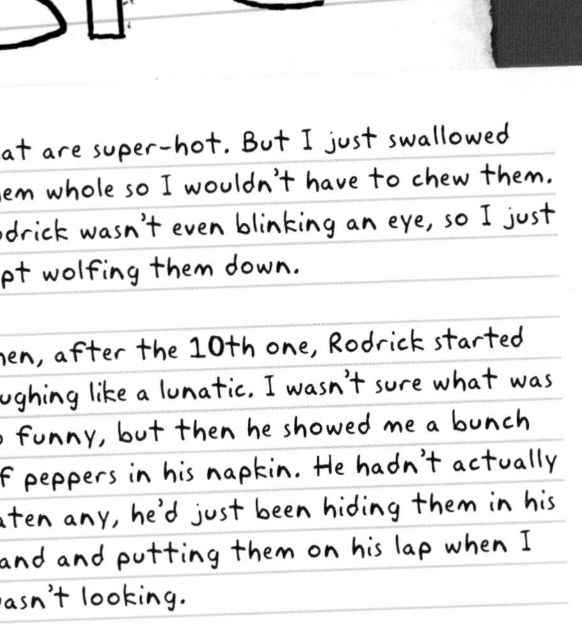

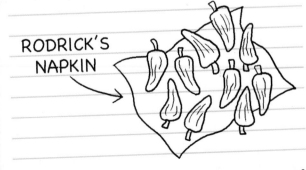

To make matters worse, the band was playing a song that had terrible, grumbling noises in it. To make matters worse YET, when I looked over, I saw that the band was on a break and all those noises were coming from my stomach.

MY STOMACH →

I learned two things that night:
1) never EVER trust Rodrick
2) the Spanish word for bathroom is "baño," while "armario" means closet.

MY SPANISH IS A LITTLE RUSTY...

Bano   Armario

Monday

My stomach was still in bad shape when I went to bed last night, but eventually I fell asleep. I had this dream that my parents took me to Willy Wonka's chocolate factory. I was riding down that chocolate river and all of the Oompa Loompas were singing "Now it's time to make some fudge!" over and over again.

The song kept getting louder and louder, until I woke up and realized what my brain was trying to tell me. I had to sprint to the bathroom before I had another butt-splosion.

THIS SONG MAKES ME FEEL LIKE THERE'S SOMETHING I NEED TO DO...

Tuesday

Even though I didn't get much sleep last night, I was finally feeling a little bit better today. I was even starting to feel hungry for the first time since we went to "Olé!" When I got to the cafeteria, everyone was grossed out that the lunch that day was 5-Bean Salad and Cabbage Casserole, but I was so hungry I didn't care.

LUNCH

After two days of my Poop-apalooza, I was starving, so I wolfed down the whole thing. Rowley didn't want to eat any of his, so I ate his as well. Almost no one in the whole cafeteria was eating theirs, so they were pretty amazed when I had seconds!

I told them that I was starving and the food wasn't really that bad. They seemed pretty impressed by that, and soon other people started offering me their lunches. I wasn't really hungry anymore, but everyone was getting really into it and chanting my name, trying to get me to eat more. I didn't want to disappoint the crowd, so I ate 5 lunches before the bell rang.

I know that sounds like a recipe for disaster, but for whatever reason, I thought that my bout with Tush Mush was like the chicken pox - once I had it, I couldn't get it again.

It didn't take me long to figure out that's not true.

The next period I was in the middle of a pop quiz when all of a sudden I was in the middle of "a poop quiz."

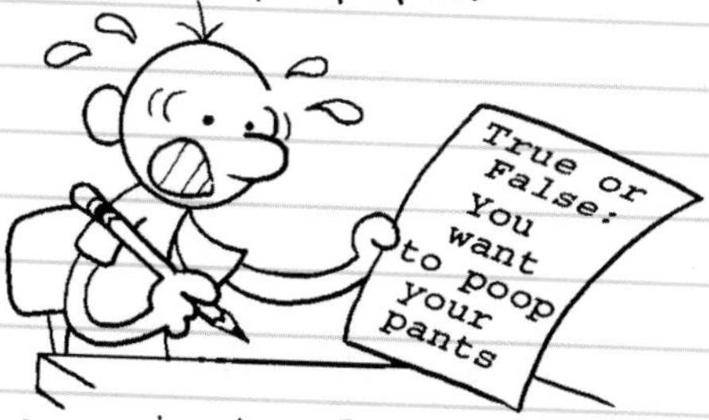
True or False: You want to poop your pants

It was one quiz where I was sure about the right answer.

I left the classroom as quickly as I could, but just as I was getting to the boy's room, one of the Safety Patrol grabbed me. I would've outrun him, but I had to go so bad by then, I could barely walk.

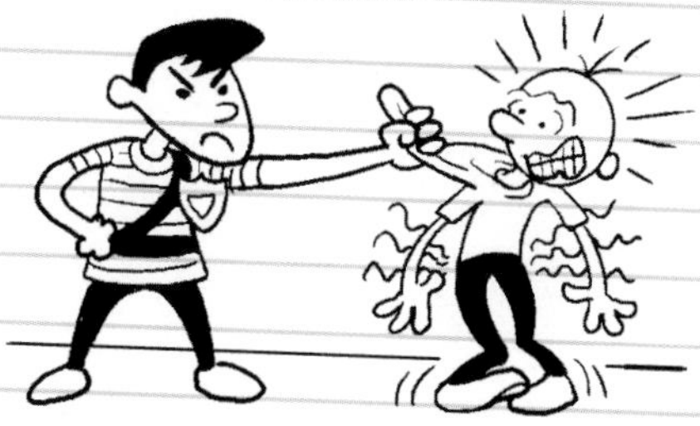

Anyway, he was yelling at me about not having a hall pass, so I couldn't even explain. Finally I just couldn't hold it in anymore. Before I knew it, I felt an awful gut-grind and suddenly we were in the Foam Zone. I dropped a gravy bomb right in the middle of the hall.

The school janitor, Mr. Kochman, came and cleaned it up. He was really nice and said "Accidents happen." Sure seems like they're happening to me a lot lately.

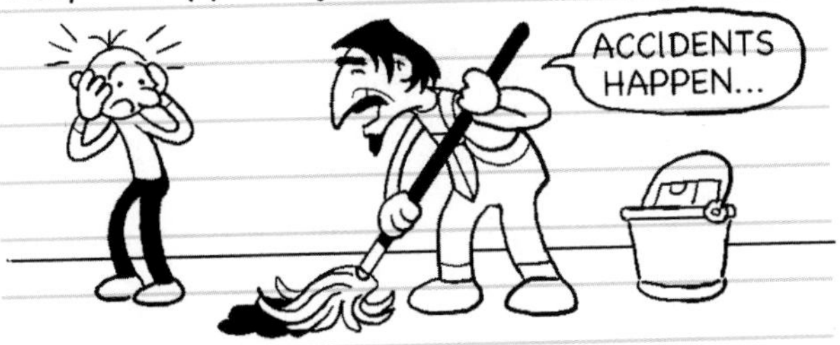
ACCIDENTS HAPPEN...

I was pretty shaken up, but I guess Danny Aguayo, the Safety Patrol kid who busted me, was feeling worse. He turned in his badge the next morning.

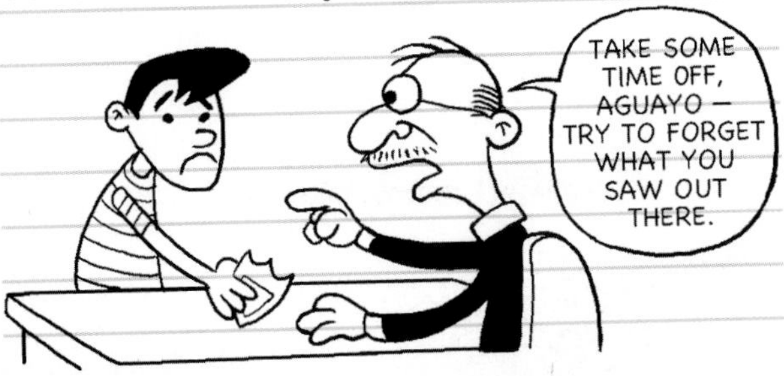
TAKE SOME TIME OFF, AGUAYO — TRY TO FORGET WHAT YOU SAW OUT THERE.

Wednesday

Not a good day. I was still butt-puking from yesterday's five lunches - and when we got to gym, coach said that we were starting our wrestling unit. I told him that I wasn't feeling good, but he just said that taking a few laps would make me feel better. Just what I need in my life - MORE runs!

I managed to keep it together during the warm-up, but once we got to the actual wrestling, it didn't go so well. I got paired up with Fegley, who had invented this new hold he called "The Ab Grab."

The longer he held on, the harder it was for me to hold it in. There was a battle royal going on in my gut and before I knew it, we were in the middle of

Mess-tlemania - and I was the "Stain Event". It was pretty embarrassing, but if I ever become a professional wrestler, at least I know I'll have a gimmick.

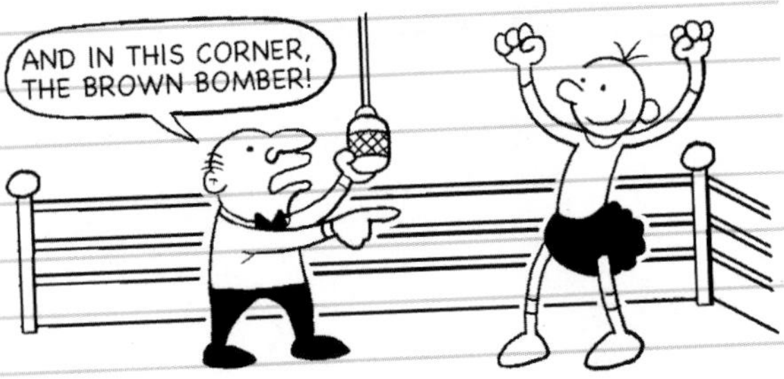
AND IN THIS CORNER, THE BROWN BOMBER!

Long story short, they had to call Mr. Kochman in to throw out the wrestling mat I was using. This time, he wasn't as friendly and didn't say anything about how "accidents happen."

On the upside, Fegley ending up forfeiting, so at least I won the match.

Thursday

Last night, mom and dad took us to the Indian Buffet - they have Indian food, but also other stuff like soft-serve yogurt, French fries and pizza. I wound up having the spicy curry chicken, deep-fried kidney beans and tons of onion rings.

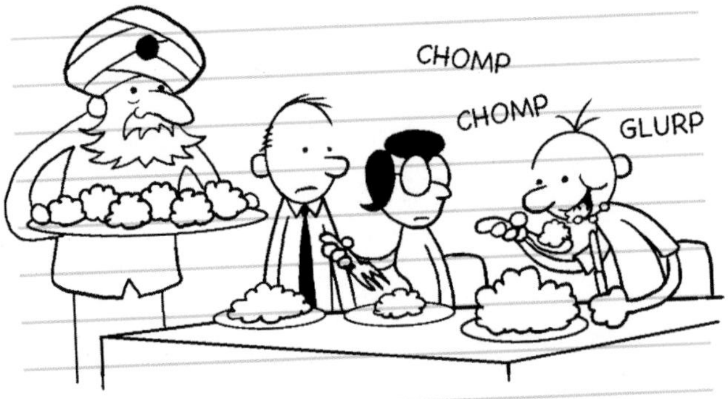
CHOMP
CHOMP
GLURP

They should really put warnings on menus, because I was on my way to first period this morning when I felt a new poo-nami storming up inside me.

I ran to the bathroom and sprinted right by a group of Safety Patrol kids - except now if they see me running, they know they should just let me get to wherever I'm going.

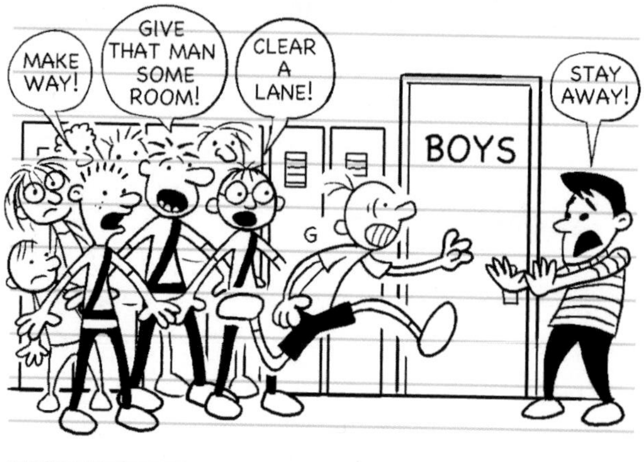
MAKE WAY!
GIVE THAT MAN SOME ROOM!
CLEAR A LANE!
STAY AWAY!
BOYS

I made it to the bathroom just fine this time - the only problem was, when I finished up, I realized there wasn't any toilet paper in the stall.

I had my book bag with me, so I started looking for something I could use - but the only thing I had was my history report, which was due next period. When all was said and done, I didn't even have a bibliography to hand in.

Still, it could've been worse, I could've only had my metal shop project in my bag.

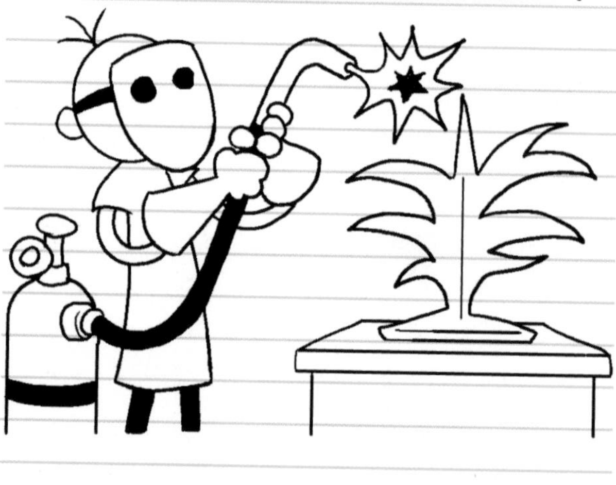

Tuesday

I'm feeling much much better. Part of the reason is that my stomach finally calmed down and I'm not mud-slinging anymore. But I also got Rodrick back for his little pepper prank. Everytime he finishes his band practice, he's always sweaty and comes upstairs to drink a bunch of grape juice right from the bottle.

Well, today, when he was down in the basement, I swapped the grape juice with 100% prune juice.

PRUNE JUICE

15

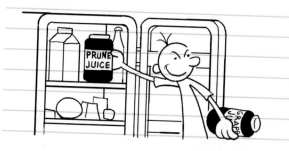

I got a good seat at the kitchen table and watched as he chugged about half a gallon of it. Then he stopped drinking it and I thought I was busted.

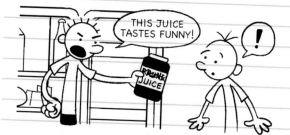

THIS JUICE TASTES FUNNY!
!
JUICE

Luckily, I was quick on my feet.

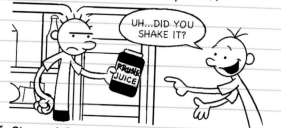

UH...DID YOU SHAKE IT?
JUICE

I figured I was in for it, but he just shrugged and drank the rest of it!

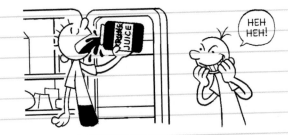

16

HEH HEH!
JUICE

I'm glad he didn't realize that he's never had to shake grape juice the 50 billion other times he drank it.

Rodrick's band is supposed to play a show tomorrow night, but I've got a feeling that he's going to have to sit that one out.

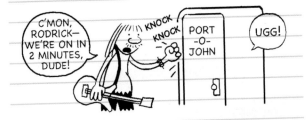

C'MON, RODRICK— WE'RE ON IN 2 MINUTES, DUDE!
KNOCK KNOCK
PORT -O- JOHN
UGG!

THE END

17

Coming Soon!

DIARRHEA
DIARY
of a
Wimpy Kid
RODRICK'S RUNS

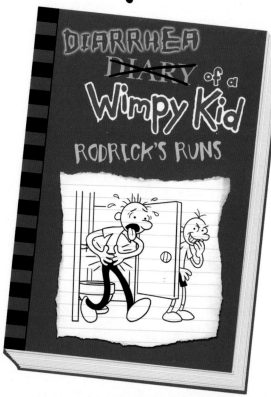

MAD PRESENTS

THE INCREDIBLE HU

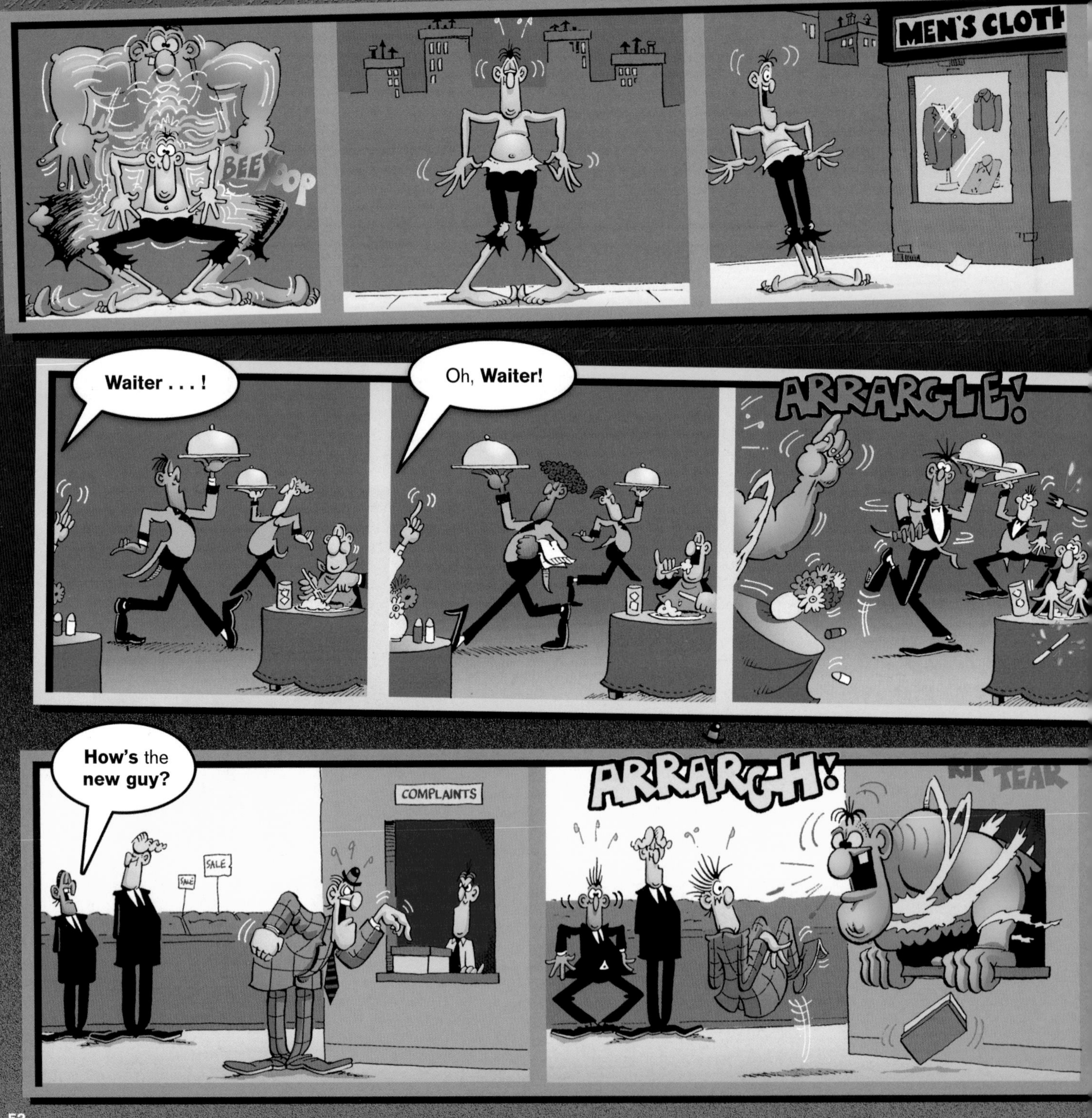

BEEYOOP
MEN'S CLOTH
Waiter . . . !
Oh, Waiter!
ARRARGLE!
How's the new guy?
SALE
SALE
COMPLAINTS
ARRARGH!
TEAR

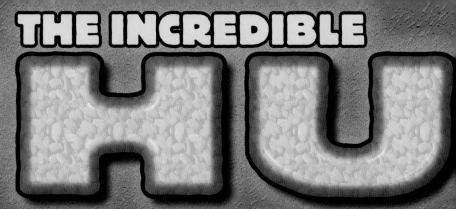

LK FUNNIES

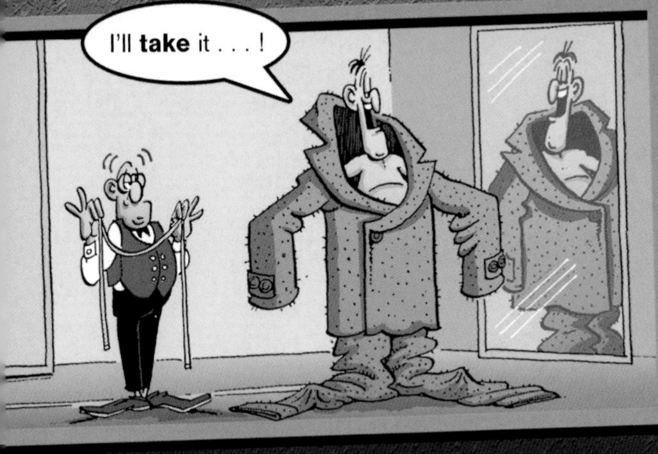

I'll **take** it . . . !

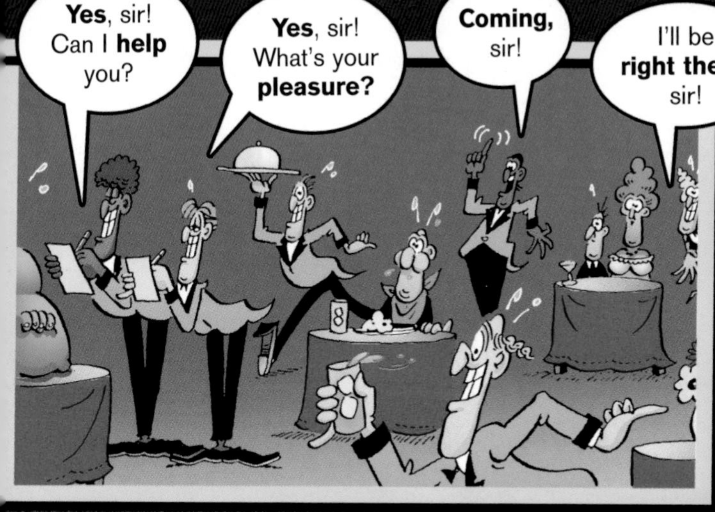

Yes, sir! Can I **help** you?
Yes, sir! What's your **pleasure?**
Coming, sir!
I'll be **right there**, sir!
8

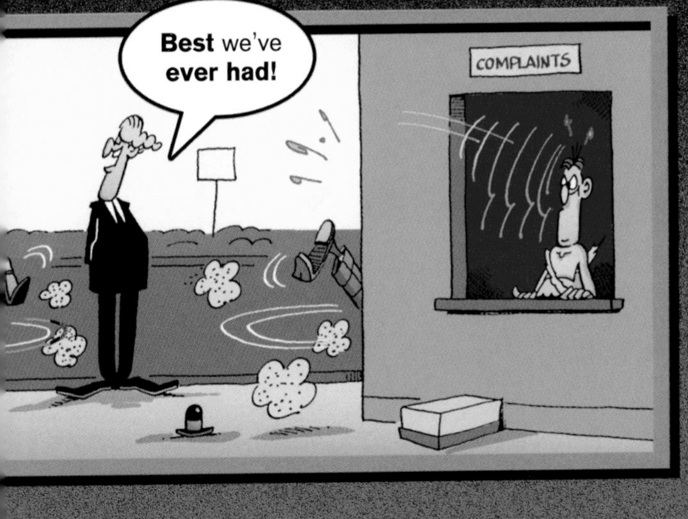

Best we've **ever had!**
COMPLAINTS

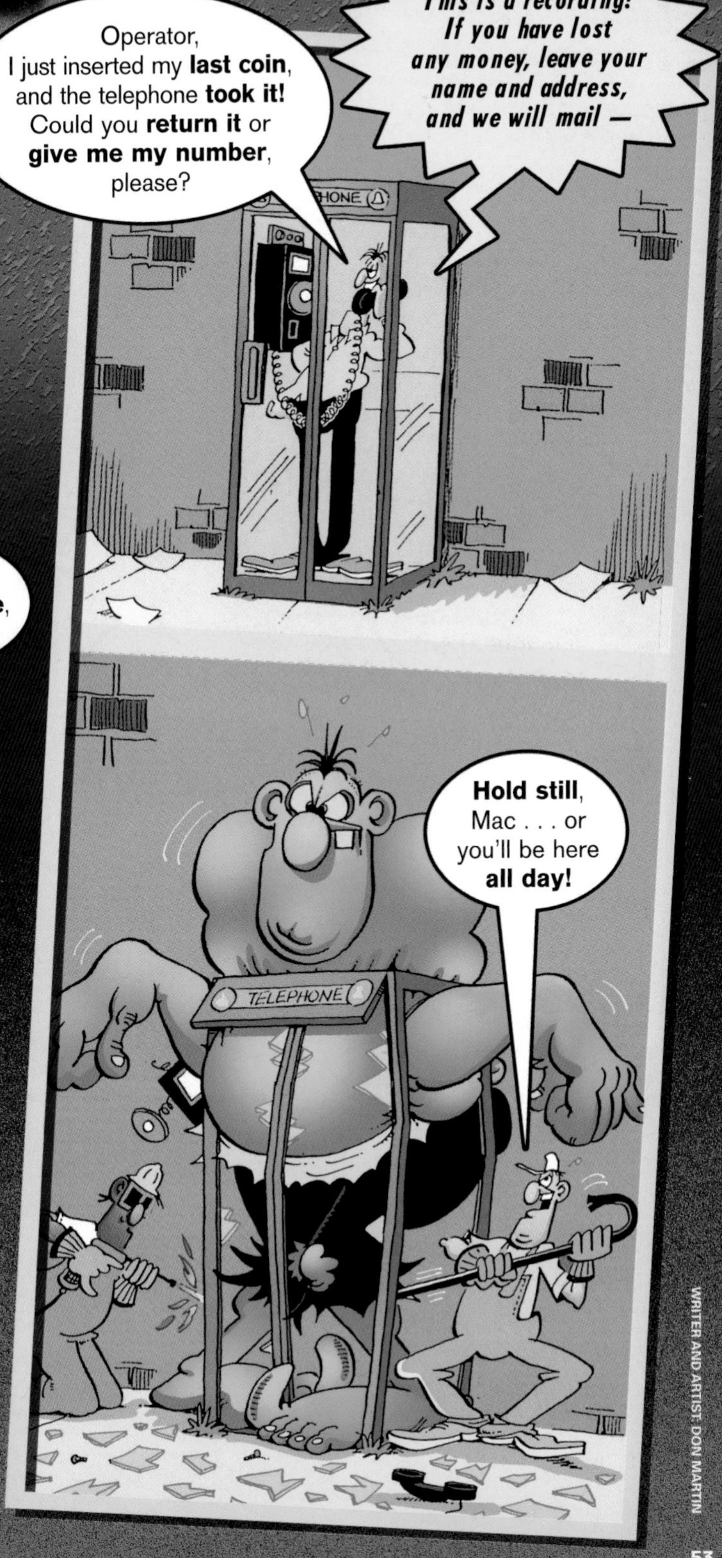

Operator, I just inserted my **last coin**, and the telephone **took it!** Could you **return it** or **give me my number**, please?
This is a recording! If you have lost any money, leave your name and address, and we will mail —
TELEPHONE
Hold still, Mac . . . or you'll be here **all day!**

WRITER AND ARTIST DON MARTIN

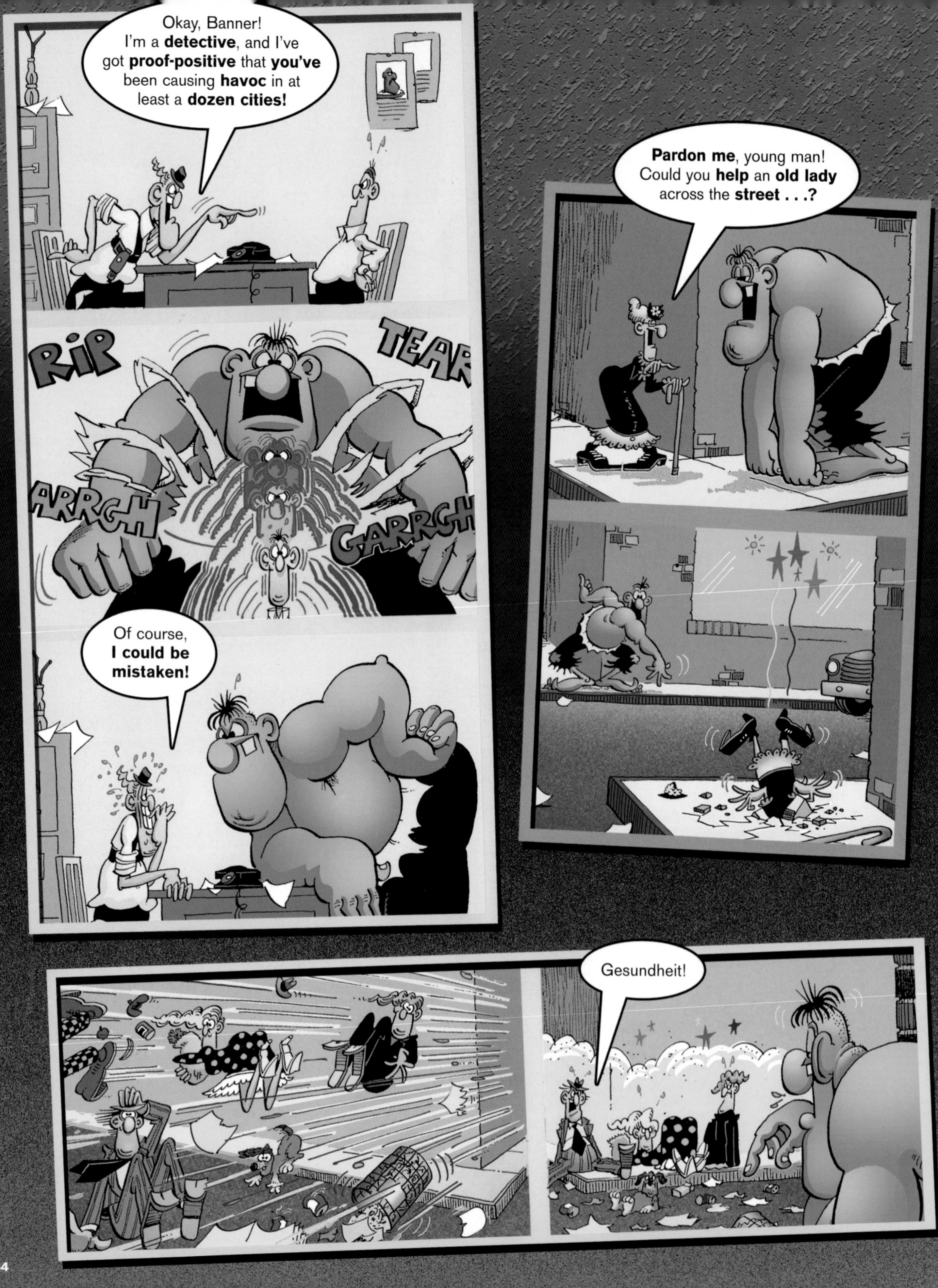
Okay, Banner! I'm a **detective**, and I've got **proof-positive** that **you've** been causing **havoc** in at least a **dozen cities!**
RIP
TEAR
ARRGH
GARRGH
Of course, **I could be mistaken!**
Pardon me, young man! Could you **help** an **old lady** across the **street . . .?**
Gesundheit!

THE COCKROACH

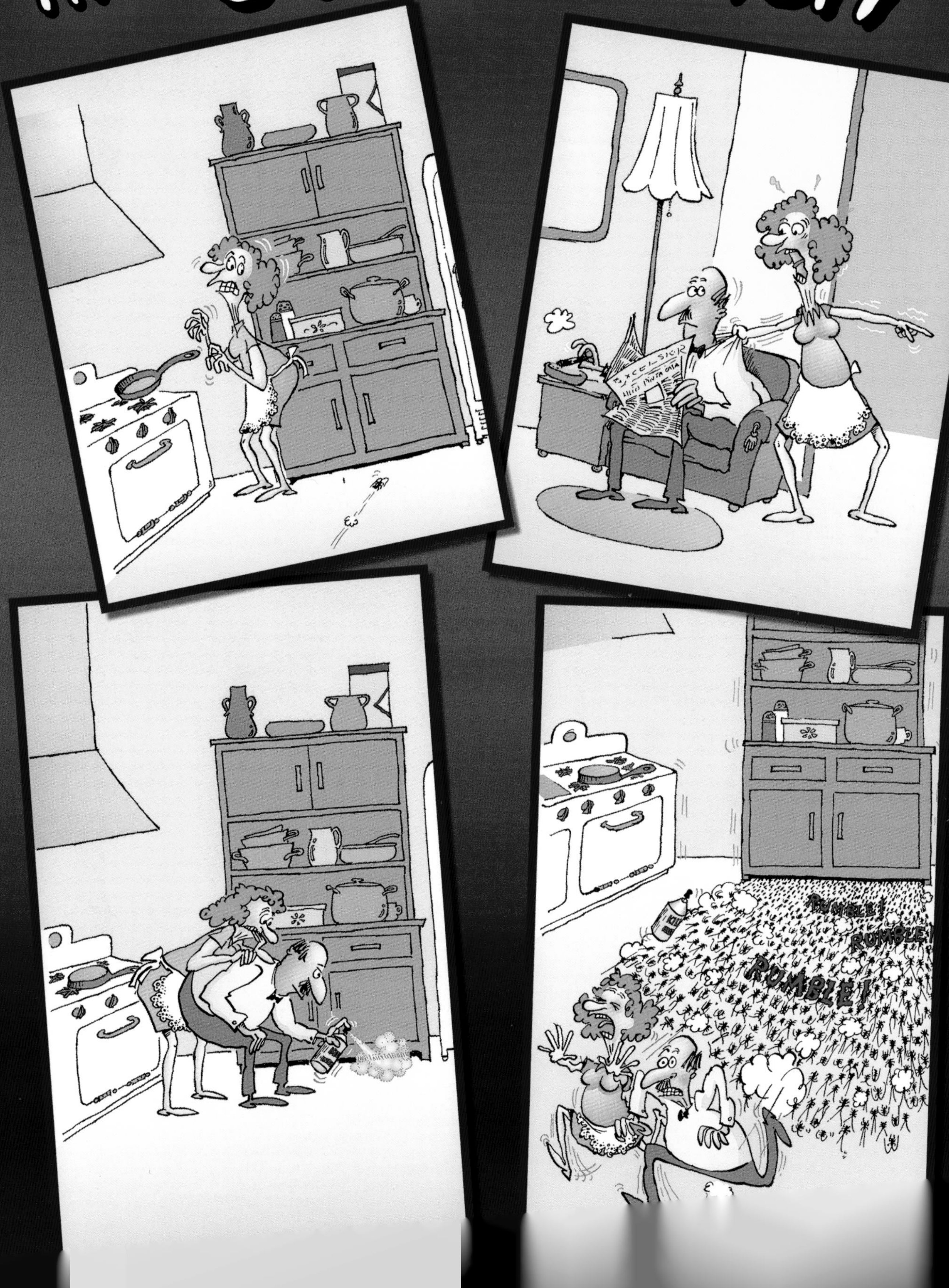
RUMBLE!
RUMBLE!
RUMBLE!

WRITER AND ARTIST: SERGIO ARAG

MAD's Do-It-Yourself "Djingle Bells"

Tired of the same old holiday songs? You don't have to be! Just pick a different line when you come to each of the lists below and you'll sing a new song every time!

IN A ONE-HORSE OPEN SLEIGH:

In a stolen Chevrolet;

Sculpting Rugrats out of clay;

With my basset hound José;

With the Gameboy that I play;

In a wig bought on eBay;

With a SWAT Team on the way;

On my cell phone the whole way;

SNOW

DASHING THROUGH THE

Pants all stuffed with

Buried under

Gulping globs of

Surfing on the

Making yellow

Freezing in the

Throwing balls of

BELLS ON BOBTAIL RING.

Wearing tons of bling,

Here's my pal Yao Ming,

Neopets that sing,

You're a ding-a-ling,

Frodo and his ring,

There's the Burger King,

Elves with static-cling,

ALL THE WAY.

LAUGHING

Crawling

Fighting

Barfing

Rapping

Farting

Oozing

Scratching

WE GO

O'ER THE FIELDS

To the mall

Pigging-out

'Round the block

Hypnotized

Underground

Sick as dogs

Through the swamp

!

A SLEIGHING SONG

In Neverland
With Donald Trump
In Middle Earth
With aliens
While kissing pigs
With Spider-Man
At Boy Scout camp

TO RIDE AND SING

To cut the cheese
To download songs
To pick your nose
When werewolves howl
To scream in pain
In Batman's cape
To belch on-key

WHAT FUN IT IS

MAKING SPIRITS BRIGHT;

Pizza don't taste right;
Wearing pants too tight;
Via satellite;
Itching for a fight;
Sneaking out at night;
Made of Kryptonite;
Getting sloshed on Sprite;

IN A ONE-HORSE OPEN SLEIGH

when Your sneeze lets out a spray
My new braces hurt all day
Now my Gameboy doesn't play
A new zit is on the way
Boy, the teacher's mad today
Saying "can" when you mean "may"
Dyeing all your gym socks gray

IT IS TO RIDE

To lose your lunch
To spread the flu
To suck your toes
To self-destruct
To use The Force
To clone J-Lo
To cast a spell

JINGLE BELLS! JINGLE BELLS! JINGLE ALL THE WAY! OH, WHAT FUN

IN A ONE-HORSE OPEN SLEIGH

Nuts, I spilled my whole lunch tray
When your teeth start to decay
With Fat Albert – Hey Hey Hey
Even though it's only May
As Amanda Bynes cheers "yay"
When you scratch your butt all day
There's a dead horse in my sleigh

IT IS TO RIDE

To belly flop
It is online
To play a prank
To housebreak ants
Your parents have
To kiss a moose
To shave a peach

JINGLE BELLS! JINGLE BELLS! JINGLE ALL THE WAY! OH, WHAT FUN

THE CONTINUING ADVENTURES OF WILLY NILLY

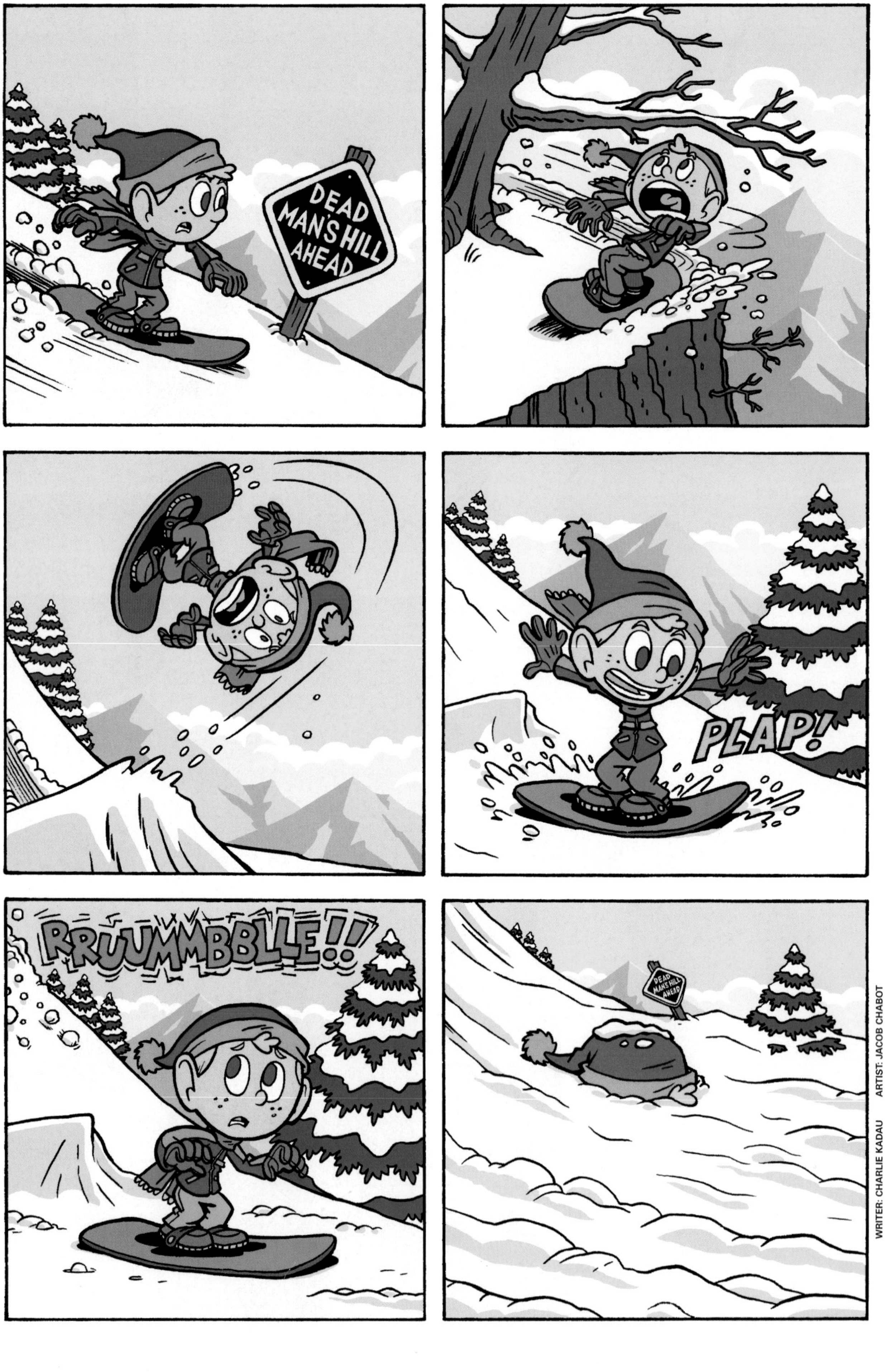
DEAD MAN'S HILL AHEAD
PLAP!
RRUUMMBBLLE!!
DEAD MAN'S HILL AHEAD

WRITER: CHARLIE KADAU ARTIST: JACOB CHABOT

Cents-Less Coupons

Your money-saving circular

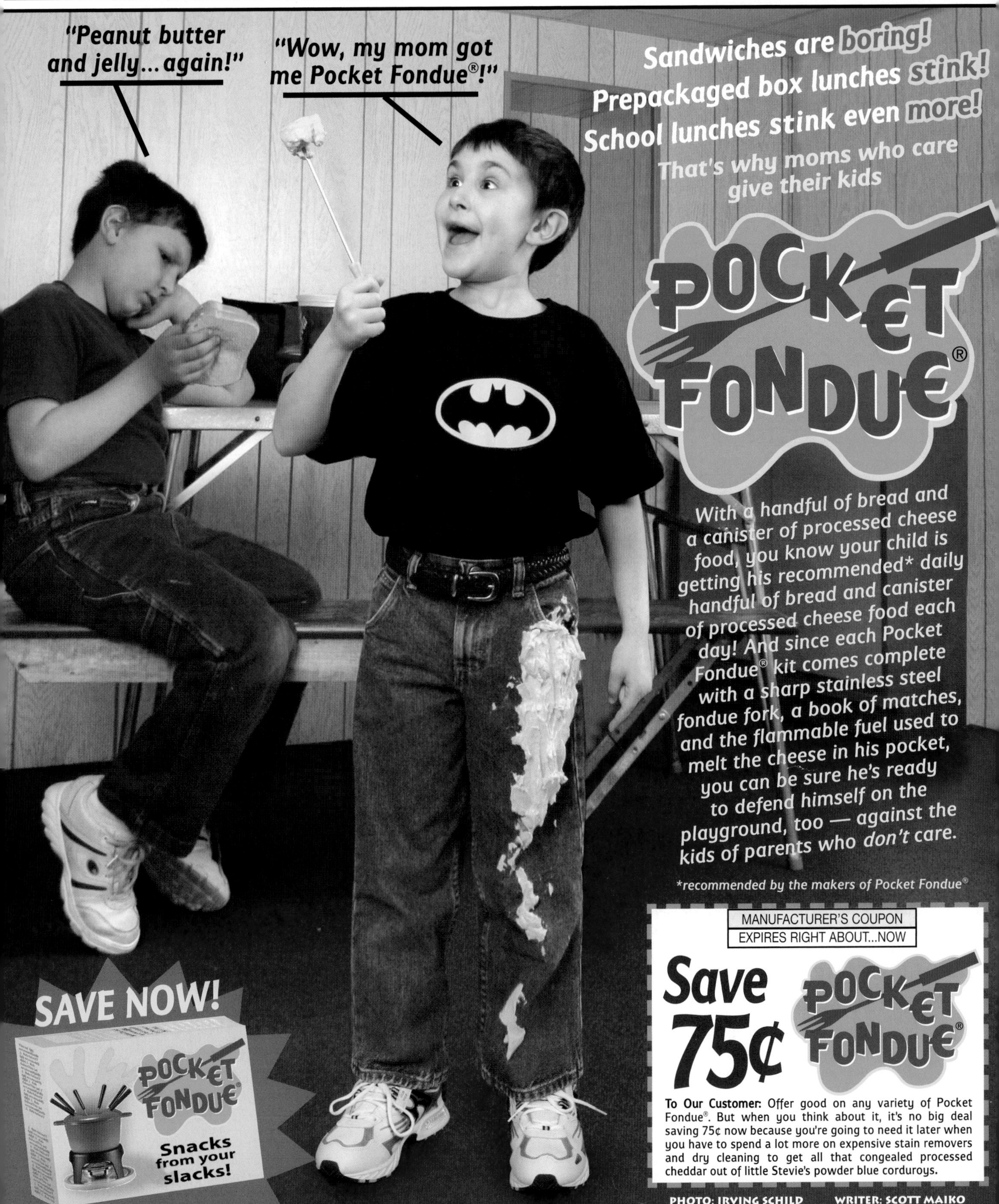
"Peanut butter and jelly...again!"
"Wow, my mom got me Pocket Fondue®!"
Sandwiches are boring!
Prepackaged box lunches stink!
School lunches stink even more!
That's why moms who care give their kids
POCKET FONDUE®
With a handful of bread and a canister of processed cheese food, you know your child is getting his recommended* daily handful of bread and canister of processed cheese food each day! And since each Pocket Fondue® kit comes complete with a sharp stainless steel fondue fork, a book of matches, and the flammable fuel used to melt the cheese in his pocket, you can be sure he's ready to defend himself on the playground, too — against the kids of parents who *don't* care.
*recommended by the makers of Pocket Fondue®
MANUFACTURER'S COUPON
EXPIRES RIGHT ABOUT...NOW
Save 75¢
POCKET FONDUE®
To Our Customer: Offer good on any variety of Pocket Fondue®. But when you think about it, it's no big deal saving 75¢ now because you're going to need it later when you have to spend a lot more on expensive stain removers and dry cleaning to get all that congealed processed cheddar out of little Stevie's powder blue corduroys.
SAVE NOW!
POCKET FONDUE®
Snacks from your slacks!

PHOTO: IRVING SCHILD WRITER: SCOTT MAIKO

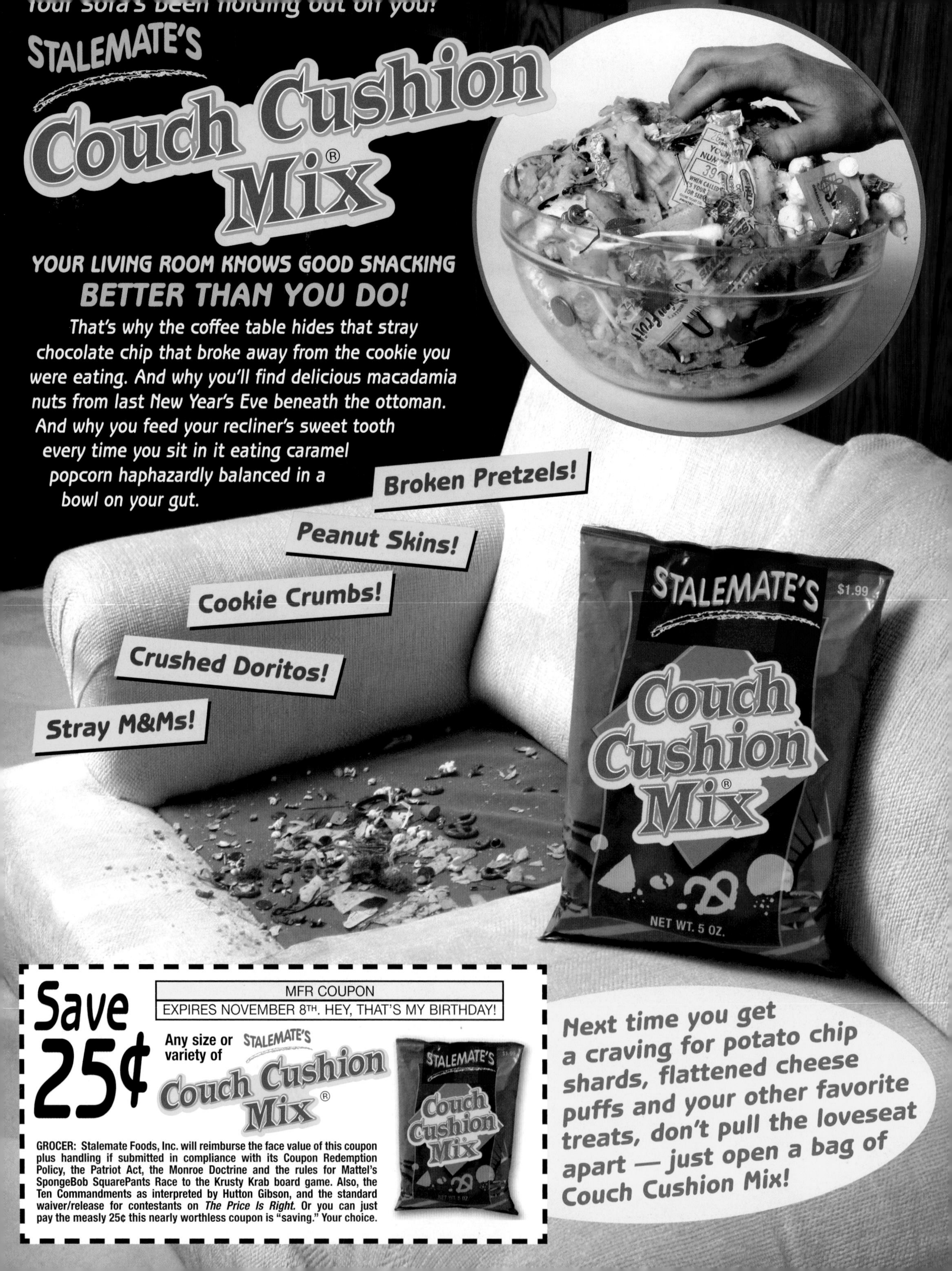

Your Sofa's been holding out on you!
STALEMATE'S
Couch Cushion Mix®
YOUR LIVING ROOM KNOWS GOOD SNACKING
BETTER THAN YOU DO!
That's why the coffee table hides that stray chocolate chip that broke away from the cookie you were eating. And why you'll find delicious macadamia nuts from last New Year's Eve beneath the ottoman. And why you feed your recliner's sweet tooth every time you sit in it eating caramel popcorn haphazardly balanced in a bowl on your gut.
Broken Pretzels!
Peanut Skins!
Cookie Crumbs!
Crushed Doritos!
Stray M&Ms!
STALEMATE'S
$1.99
Couch Cushion Mix®
NET WT. 5 OZ.
Save 25¢
MFR COUPON
EXPIRES NOVEMBER 8TH. HEY, THAT'S MY BIRTHDAY!
Any size or variety of STALEMATE'S Couch Cushion Mix®
GROCER: Stalemate Foods, Inc. will reimburse the face value of this coupon plus handling if submitted in compliance with its Coupon Redemption Policy, the Patriot Act, the Monroe Doctrine and the rules for Mattel's SpongeBob SquarePants Race to the Krusty Krab board game. Also, the Ten Commandments as interpreted by Hutton Gibson, and the standard waiver/release for contestants on The Price Is Right. Or you can just pay the measly 25¢ this nearly worthless coupon is "saving." Your choice.
Next time you get a craving for potato chip shards, flattened cheese puffs and your other favorite treats, don't pull the loveseat apart — just open a bag of Couch Cushion Mix!

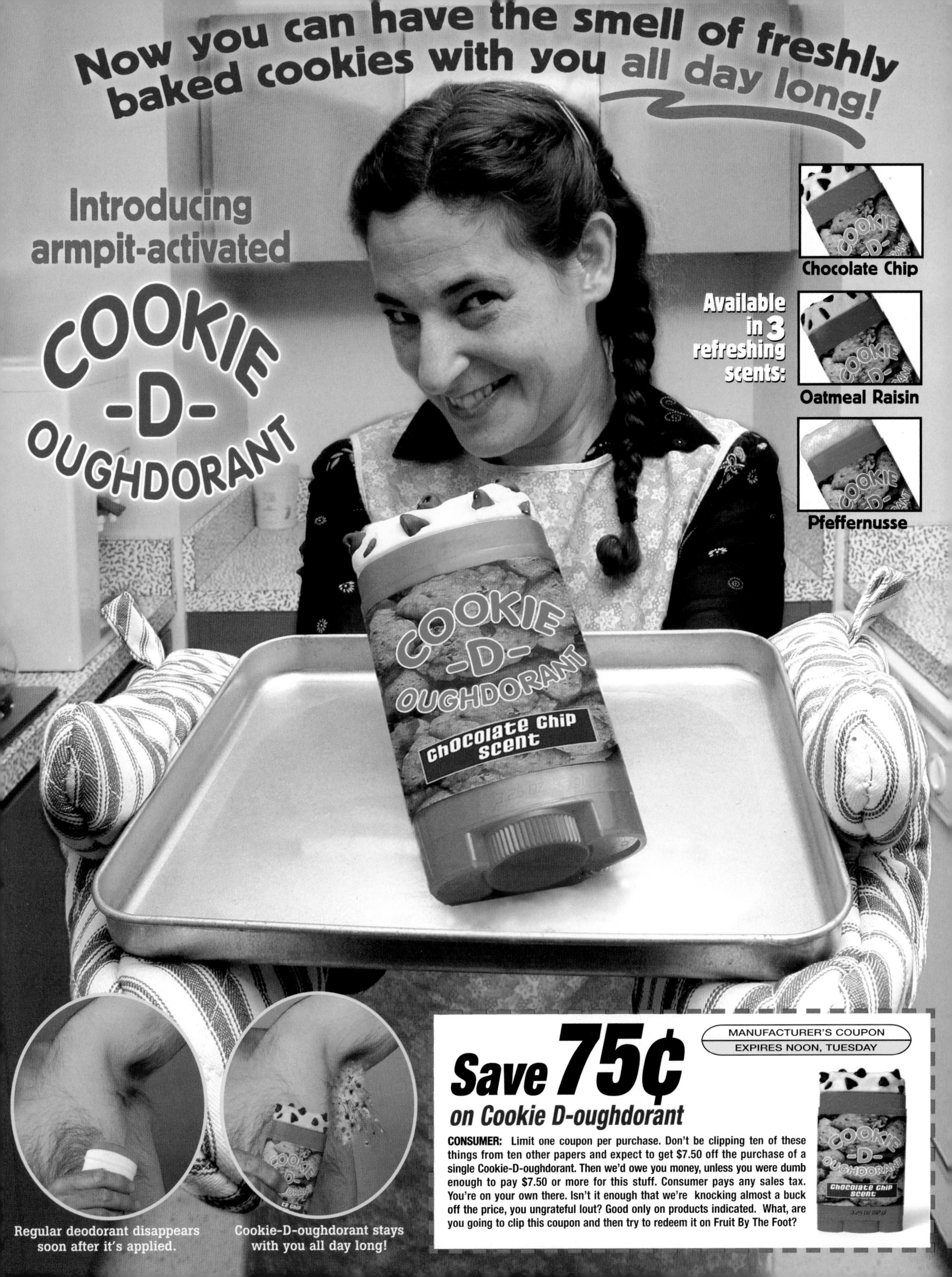

Now you can have the smell of freshly baked cookies with you all day long!
Introducing armpit-activated
COOKIE -D- OUGHDORANT
Chocolate Chip
Available in 3 refreshing scents:
Oatmeal Raisin
Pfeffernusse
COOKIE -D- OUGHDORANT
Chocolate Chip scent
Regular deodorant disappears soon after it's applied.
Cookie-D-oughdorant stays with you all day long!
MANUFACTURER'S COUPON
EXPIRES NOON, TUESDAY
Save 75¢
on Cookie D-oughdorant
CONSUMER: Limit one coupon per purchase. Don't be clipping ten of these things from ten other papers and expect to get $7.50 off the purchase of a single Cookie-D-oughdorant. Then we'd owe you money, unless you were dumb enough to pay $7.50 or more for this stuff. Consumer pays any sales tax. You're on your own there. Isn't it enough that we're knocking almost a buck off the price, you ungrateful lout? Good only on products indicated. What, are you going to clip this coupon and then try to redeem it on Fruit By The Foot?
COOKIE -D- OUGHDORANT
Chocolate Chip scent

How's that? You really think voters can size up candidates fairly, without the slightest touch of bias? Not bloody likely, dude, as you'll see when you check out the differences between...

YOUR CANDIDATE

YOUR CANDIDATE flip-flops on the issues.

MY CANDIDATE has redefined his position.

YOUR CANDIDATE panders to lunatic fringe groups.

MY CANDIDATE reaches out to disenfranchised voters.

YOUR CANDIDATE shamelessly takes contributions from lobbyists and favor-seeking corporations.

MY CANDIDATE believes all Americans have a right to participate in the political process.

YOUR CANDIDATE surrounds himself with bootlicking toadies.

MY CANDIDATE puts together a team that shares his dream for a better America.

YOUR CANDIDATE mumbles weasel-like rationalizations when confronted with his drinking and womanizing in the past.

MY CANDIDATE admits to "youthful indiscretions."

ARTIST: PETER KUPER   WRITER: FRANK JACOBS

AND MY CANDIDATE

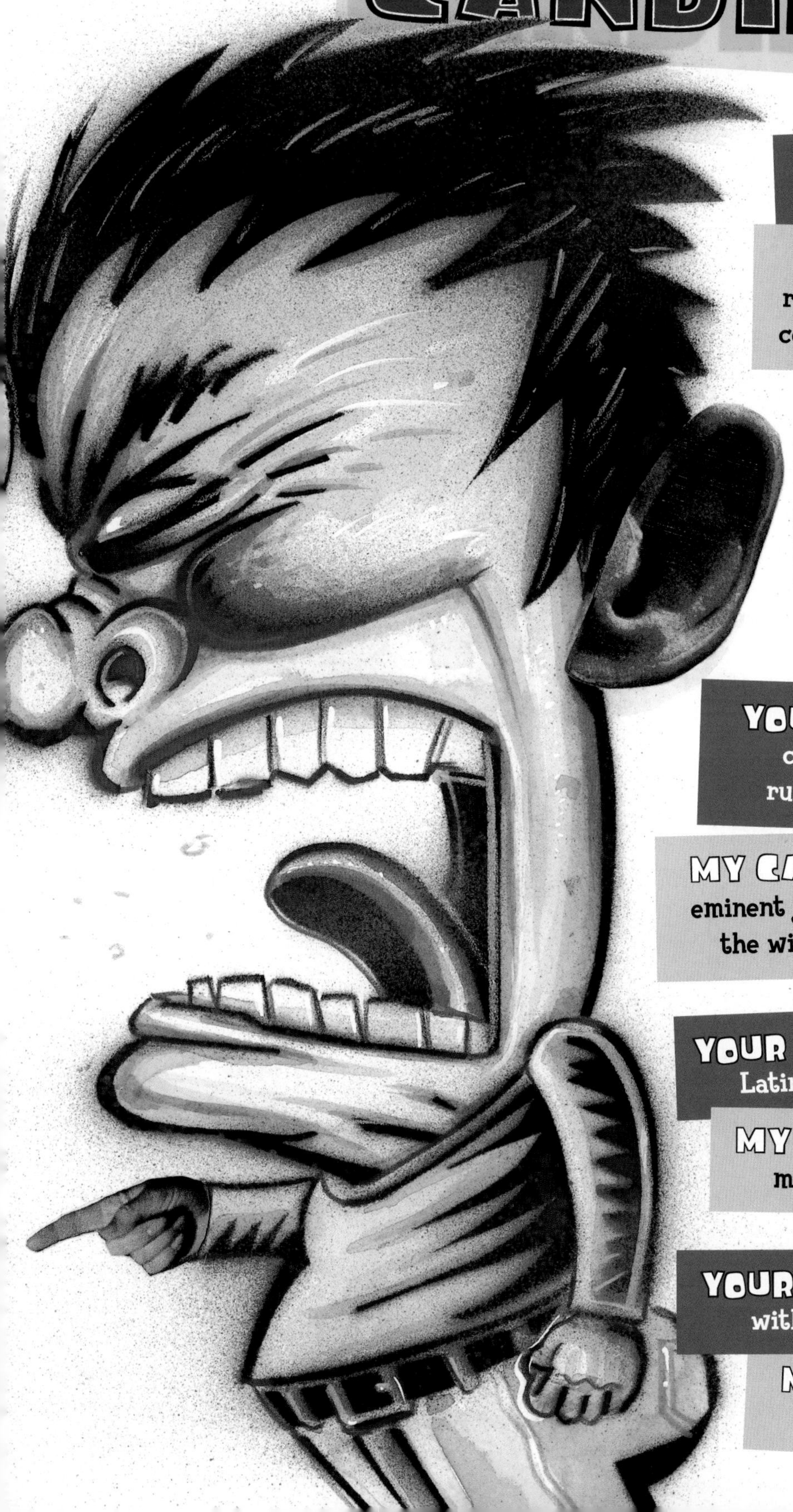

YOUR CANDIDATE stonewalls the press.

MY CANDIDATE reserves the right not to disclose information that could jeopardize the national interest.

YOUR CANDIDATE waffles on the issues.

MY CANDIDATE sees the merits of both sides of the argument.

YOUR CANDIDATE will pack the courts with judicial hacks who'll rubberstamp his extremist agenda.

MY CANDIDATE will handpick eminent jurists whose rulings reflect the will of the American people.

YOUR CANDIDATE sucks up to blacks, Latinos and Asians to get their votes.

MY CANDIDATE works to bring minorities into the mainstream.

YOUR CANDIDATE smears his opponent with vicious lies and personal attacks.

MY CANDIDATE simply wants to set the record straight.

ONE COLD AFTERNOON OUTSIDE BUFFALO

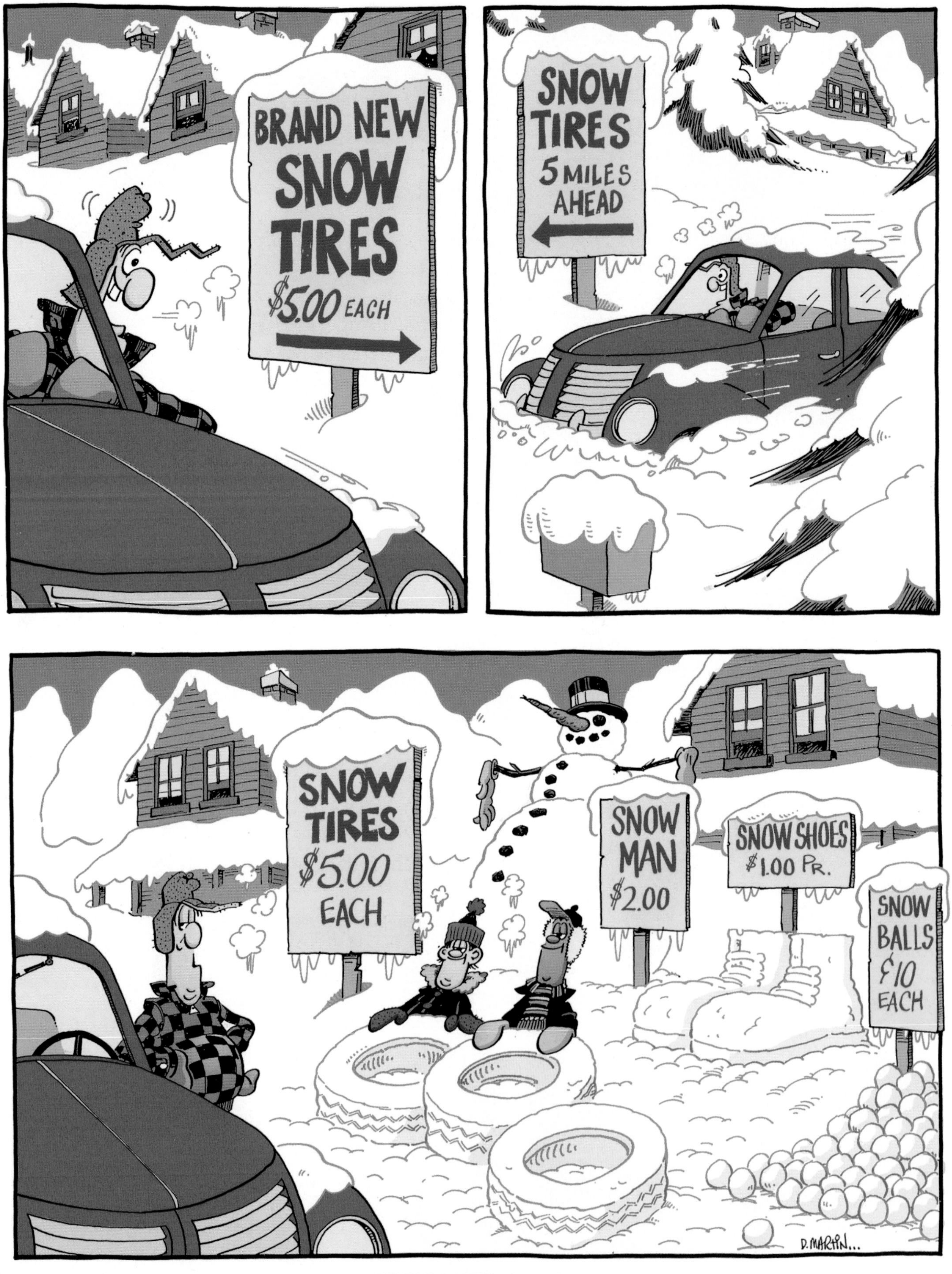
BRAND NEW SNOW TIRES $5.00 EACH
SNOW TIRES 5 MILES AHEAD
SNOW TIRES $5.00 EACH
SNOW MAN $2.00
SNOW SHOES $1.00 PR.
SNOW BALLS ¢10 EACH
D. MARTIN...

WRITER AND ARTIST: DON MARTIN

The practice of embedding one's flesh with permanent dyes has been with us for centuries. Indeed, Queen Nefertitti is said to have had the message "Hecky 4-Ever" placed on her left shin just before the great Egyptian husk famine in the 17th century B.C. In subsequent years, many more practical uses for these permanent skin stains have been discovered...

LAW ENFORCEMENT

Since the Supreme Court's landmark Miranda decision, police officers everywhere found themselves fumbling with little laminated cards at the worst times when advising alleged perpetrators of their rights. Tattoos to the rescue! Located between the wrist and elbow, cops no longer faced the dilemma of having to either release or shoot their detainees on the spot simply because they forgot to recite a few words like "right," "remain" or "silent." There is ample room on their other arm for donut shop hours and overtime pay tables.

SUMMER FUN

A common predicament facing nudists is: not enough nude beaches. Tattoos to the rescue! An easy-to-apply bikini or speedo pattern turns any public beach, swimming pool or open hydrant into a clothing-optional one, insuring the freedom to sun worship unencumbered without facing disapproving stares from conservative bathers, intervention by strong-arm lifeguards and arrest by cops with the Miranda rights tattooed on their arms.

HUNTING

Likewise, hunters found that heavy, non-breatheable surplus camouflage gear rendered the summertime stalking of game impossible. Tattoos to the rescue! The greens, grays and browns of wild foliage randomly and permanently etched into the epidermis now allow sportsmen to be almost as bare as the defenseless prey they relentlessly pursue — and no longer break a sweat.

And yet, with all these ingenious and practical applications for tattoos, the vast, vast majority of people still use them to display messages like "Hecky 4-Ever"! The problem? When Hecky leaves your life, the tattoo remains. Sure, there are removal techniques such as laser treatment, but they're expensive and time consuming. If you're in a hurry or on a budget, we recommend choosing an easy "do-it-yourself" method from...

A MAD GUIDE TO...

THE HIGH-SPEED PLUNGER POP

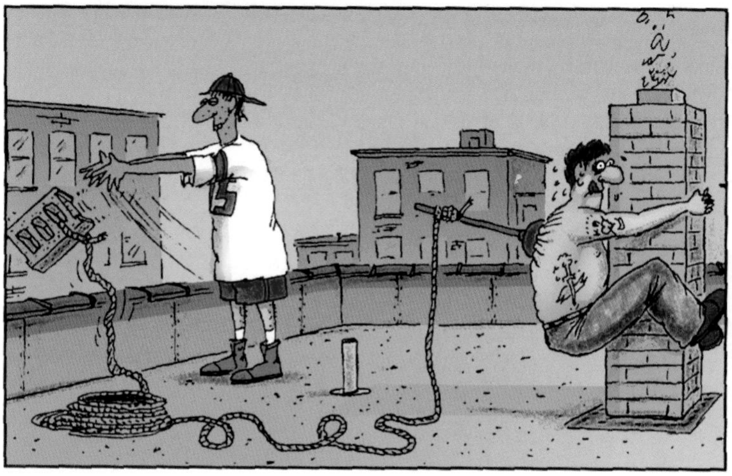

THE ROLLERBLADE RUB-OUT

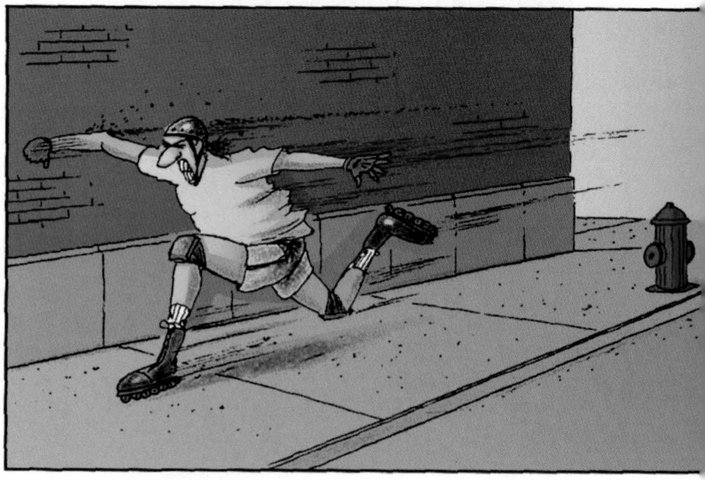

THE LEECH LUNCH-LIFT

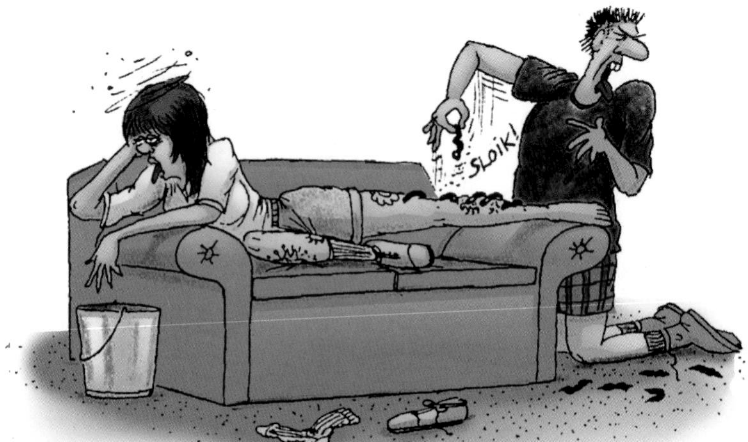
SLOIK!

THE HOT WIRE WELD-OFF

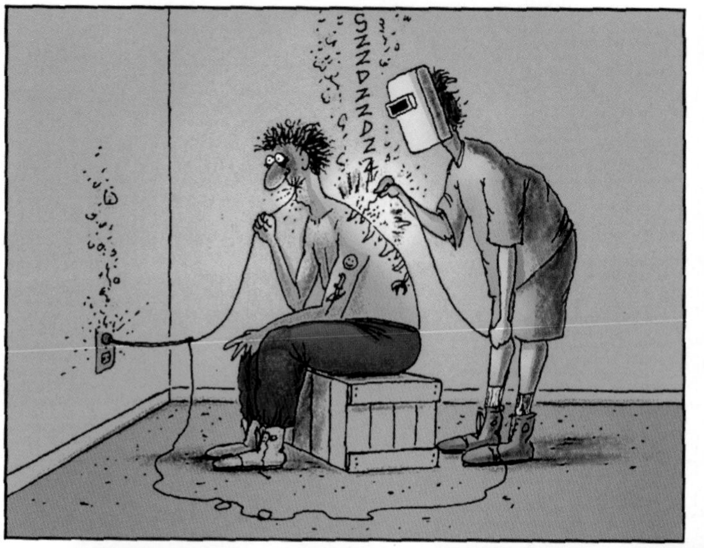

THE POISON IVY SCRATCH-AWAY

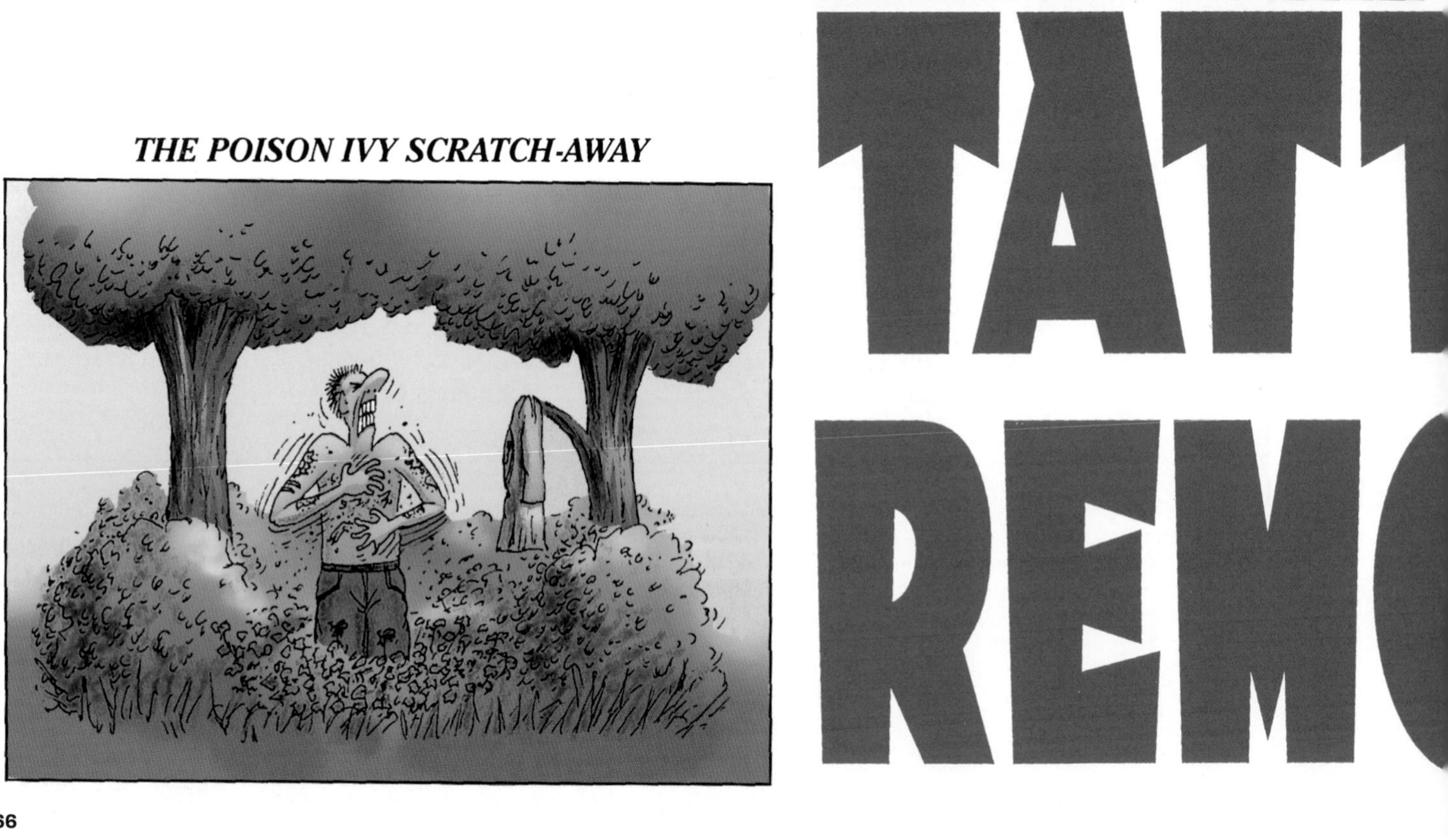

TATT
REMO

THE DUCT TAPE POWER-PEEL

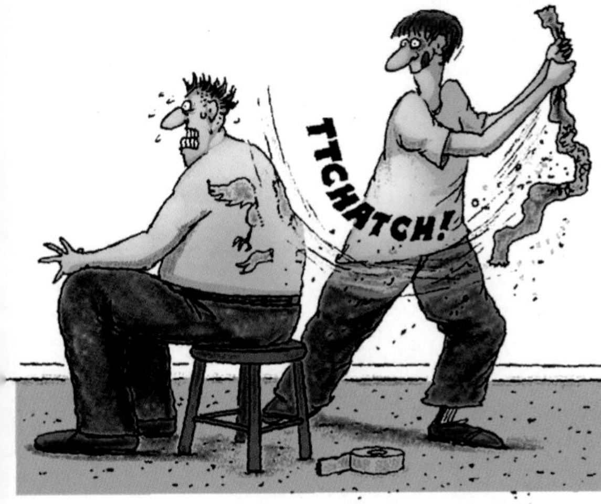
TTCHATCH!

THE COLD LAMPPOST LICK, STICK AND PULL

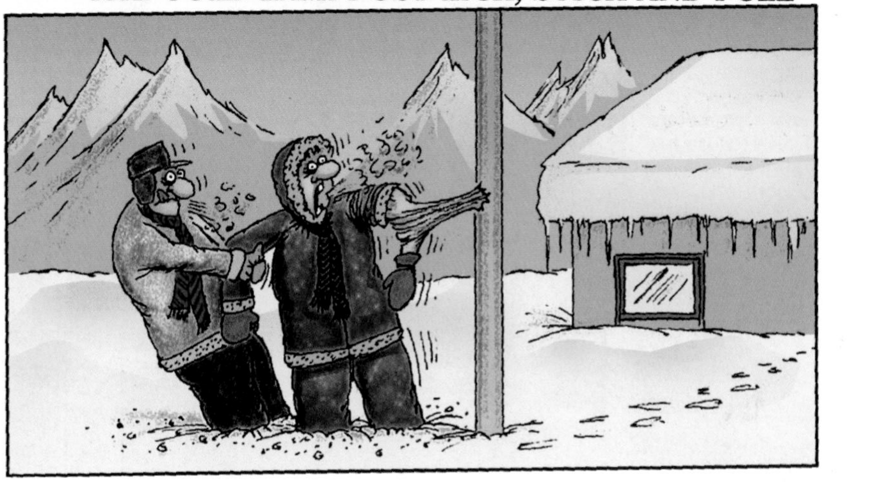

THE MALIBU BAKE-AWAY

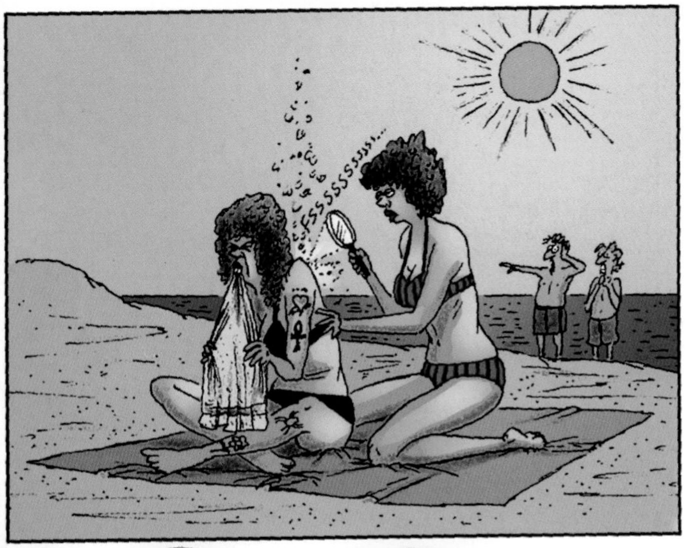

THE HIGH-IMPACT PLANK AND TAR TRANSFER

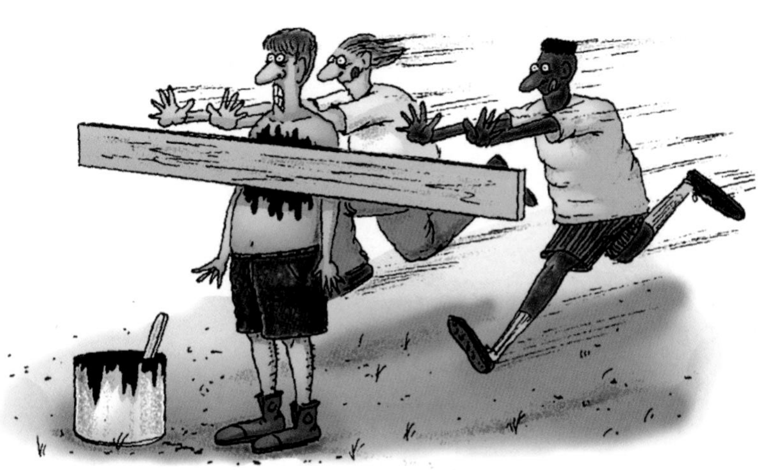

TOO
VAL

THE GUARD DOG GULP 'N' GONE

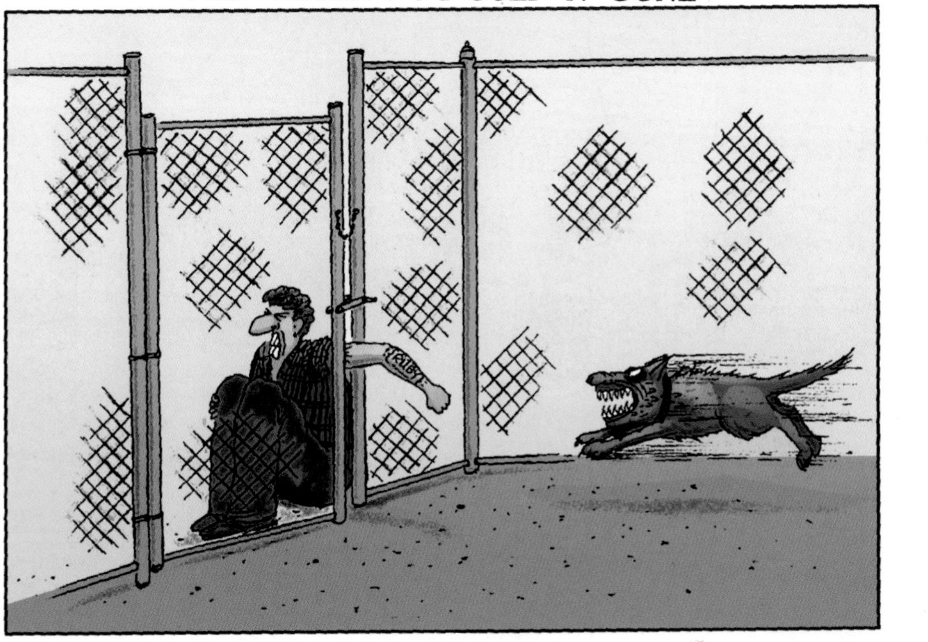

ARTIST AND WRITER: TOM CHENEY

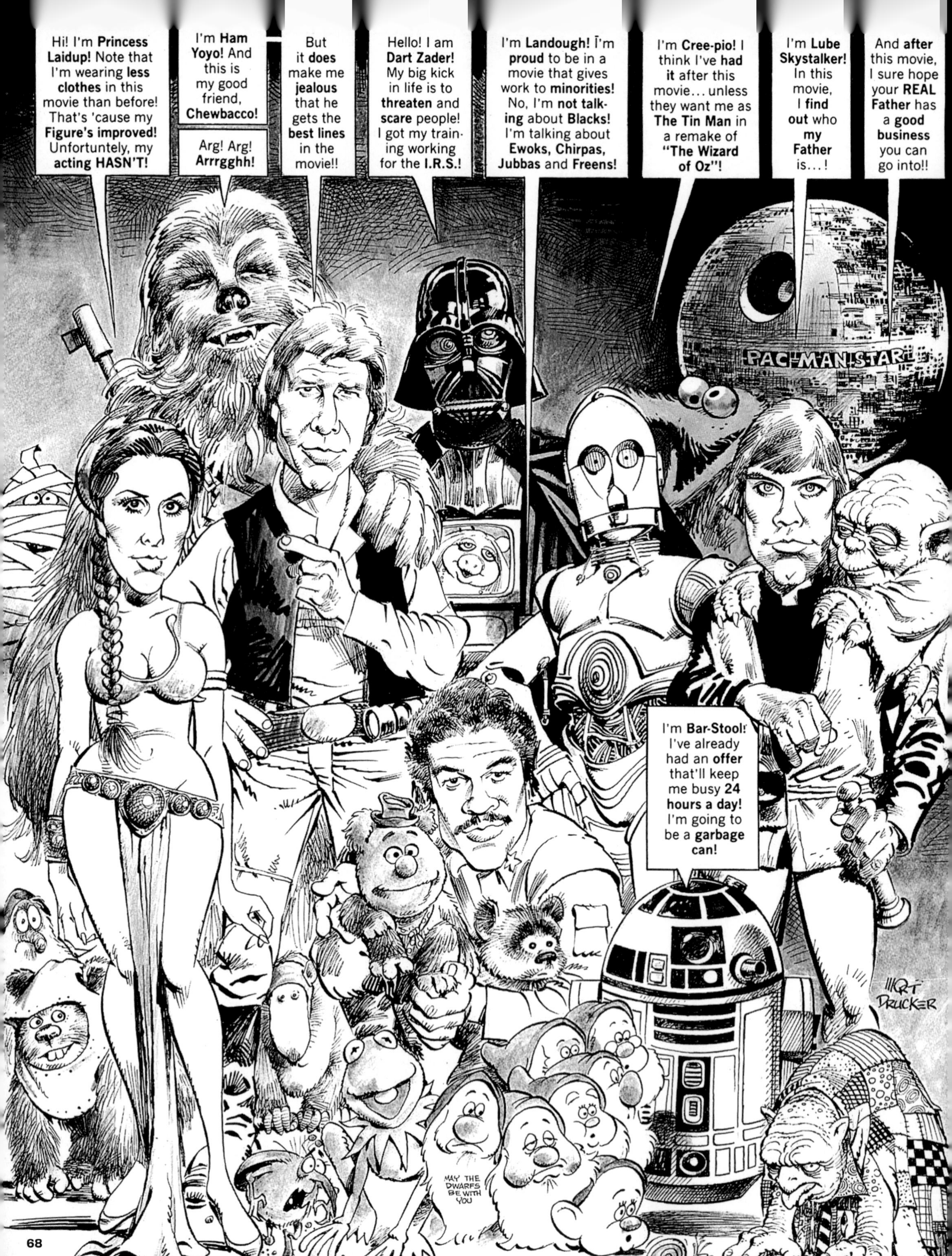
Hi! I'm **Princess Laidup!** Note that I'm wearing **less clothes** in this movie than before! That's 'cause my **Figure's improved!** Unfortuntely, my **acting HASN'T!**
I'm **Ham Yoyo!** And this is my good friend, **Chewbacco!**
Arg! Arg! **Arrrgghh!**
But it **does** make me **jealous** that he gets the **best lines** in the movie!!
Hello! I am **Dart Zader!** My big kick in life is to **threaten** and **scare** people! I got my training working for the **I.R.S.**!
I'm **Landough!** I'm **proud** to be in a movie that gives work to **minorities!** No, I'm **not talking** about **Blacks!** I'm talking about **Ewoks, Chirpas, Jubbas** and **Freens!**
I'm **Cree-pio!** I think I've **had it** after this movie... unless they want me as **The Tin Man** in a remake of **"The Wizard of Oz"**!
I'm **Lube Skystalker!** In this movie, I **find out** who **my Father** is...!
And **after** this movie, I sure hope your **REAL Father** has a **good business** you can go into!!
PAC-MAN STAR
I'm **Bar-Stool!** I've already had an **offer** that'll keep me busy **24 hours a day!** I'm going to be a **garbage can!**
MAY THE DWARFS BE WITH YOU
MORT DRUCKER

STAR BORES

RE-HASH OF THE JETI

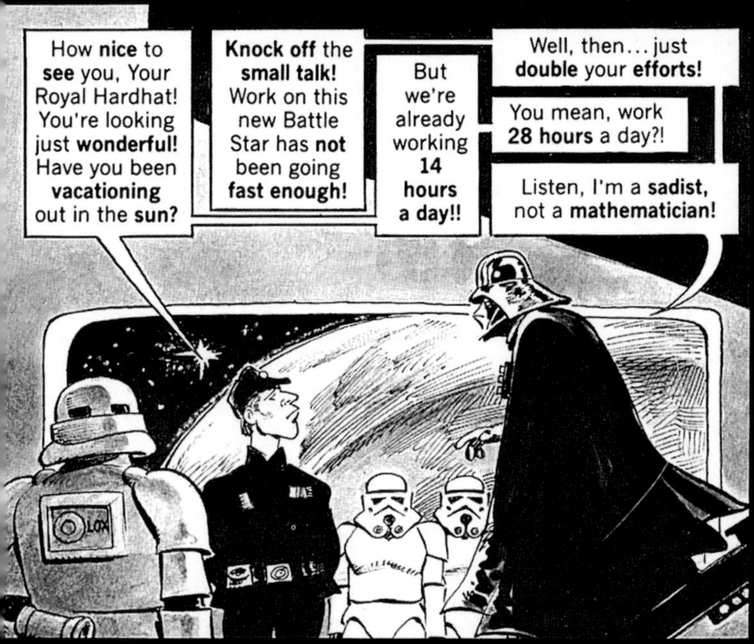
How nice to see you, Your Royal Hardhat! You're looking just wonderful! Have you been vacationing out in the sun?
Knock off the small talk! Work on this new Battle Star has not been going fast enough!
But we're already working 14 hours a day!!
Well, then... just double your efforts!
You mean, work 28 hours a day?!
Listen, I'm a sadist, not a mathematician!
LOX

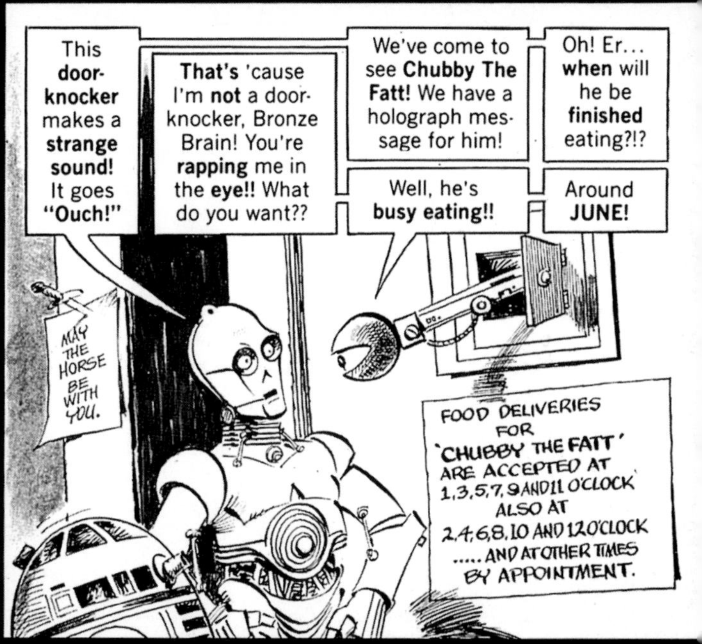
This door-knocker makes a strange sound! It goes "Ouch!"
That's 'cause I'm not a door-knocker, Bronze Brain! You're rapping me in the eye!! What do you want??
We've come to see Chubby The Fatt! We have a holograph message for him!
Well, he's busy eating!!
Oh! Er... when will he be finished eating?!?
Around JUNE!
MAY THE HORSE BE WITH YOU.
FOOD DELIVERIES FOR 'CHUBBY THE FATT' ARE ACCEPTED AT 1,3,5,7,9 AND 11 O'CLOCK ALSO AT 2,4,6,8,10 AND 12 O'CLOCK ..... AND AT OTHER TIMES BY APPOINTMENT.

ARTIST: MORT DRUCKER WRITER: DICK DE BARTOLO

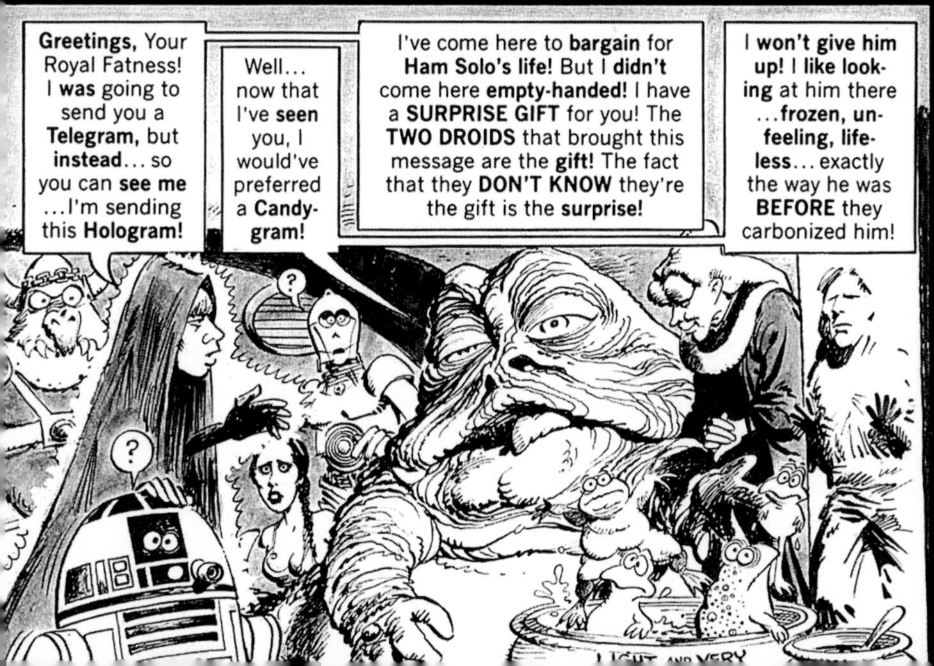
Greetings, Your Royal Fatness! I was going to send you a Telegram, but instead... so you can see me ...I'm sending this Hologram!
Well... now that I've seen you, I would've preferred a Candy-gram!
I've come here to bargain for Ham Solo's life! But I didn't come here empty-handed! I have a SURPRISE GIFT for you! The TWO DROIDS that brought this message are the gift! The fact that they DON'T KNOW they're the gift is the surprise!
I won't give him up! I like looking at him there ...frozen, unfeeling, lifeless... exactly the way he was BEFORE they carbonized him!
?
?

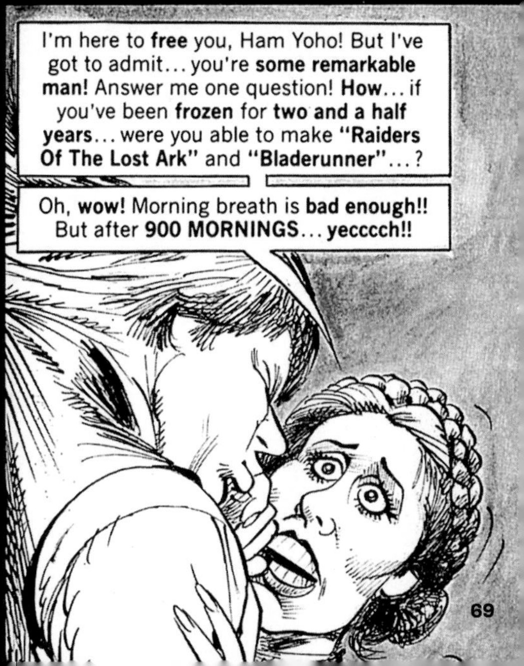
I'm here to free you, Ham Yoho! But I've got to admit... you're some remarkable man! Answer me one question! How... if you've been frozen for two and a half years... were you able to make "Raiders Of The Lost Ark" and "Bladerunner"...?
Oh, wow! Morning breath is bad enough!! But after 900 MORNINGS... yecccch!!

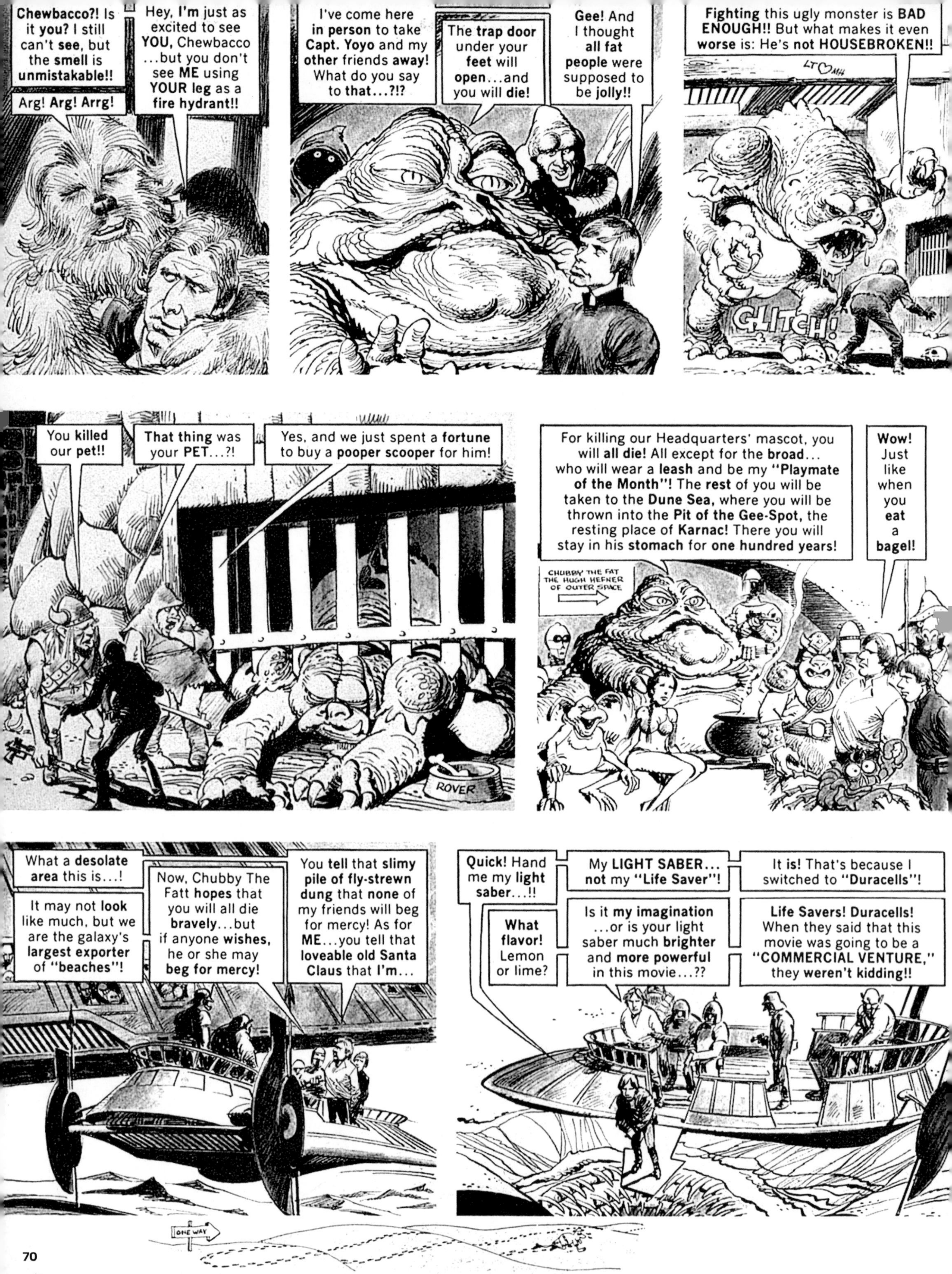
Chewbacco?! Is it you? I still can't see, but the smell is unmistakable!!
Arg! Arg! Arrg!
Hey, I'm just as excited to see YOU, Chewbacco ...but you don't see ME using YOUR leg as a fire hydrant!!
I've come here in person to take Capt. Yoyo and my other friends away! What do you say to that...?!?
The trap door under your feet will open...and you will die!
Gee! And I thought all fat people were supposed to be jolly!!
Fighting this ugly monster is BAD ENOUGH!! But what makes it even worse is: He's not HOUSEBROKEN!!
GLITCH!
You killed our pet!!
That thing was your PET...?!
Yes, and we just spent a fortune to buy a pooper scooper for him!
ROVER
For killing our Headquarters' mascot, you will all die! All except for the broad... who will wear a leash and be my "Playmate of the Month"! The rest of you will be taken to the Dune Sea, where you will be thrown into the Pit of the Gee-Spot, the resting place of Karnac! There you will stay in his stomach for one hundred years!
Wow! Just like when you eat a bagel!
CHUBBY THE FAT THE HUGH HEFNER OF OUTER SPACE
What a desolate area this is...!
It may not look like much, but we are the galaxy's largest exporter of "beaches"!
Now, Chubby The Fatt hopes that you will all die bravely...but if anyone wishes, he or she may beg for mercy!
You tell that slimy pile of fly-strewn dung that none of my friends will beg for mercy! As for ME...you tell that loveable old Santa Claus that I'm...
Quick! Hand me my light saber...!!
What flavor! Lemon or lime?
My LIGHT SABER... not my "Life Saver"!
Is it my imagination ...or is your light saber much brighter and more powerful in this movie...??
It is! That's because I switched to "Duracells"!
Life Savers! Duracells! When they said that this movie was going to be a "COMMERCIAL VENTURE," they weren't kidding!!
ONE WAY

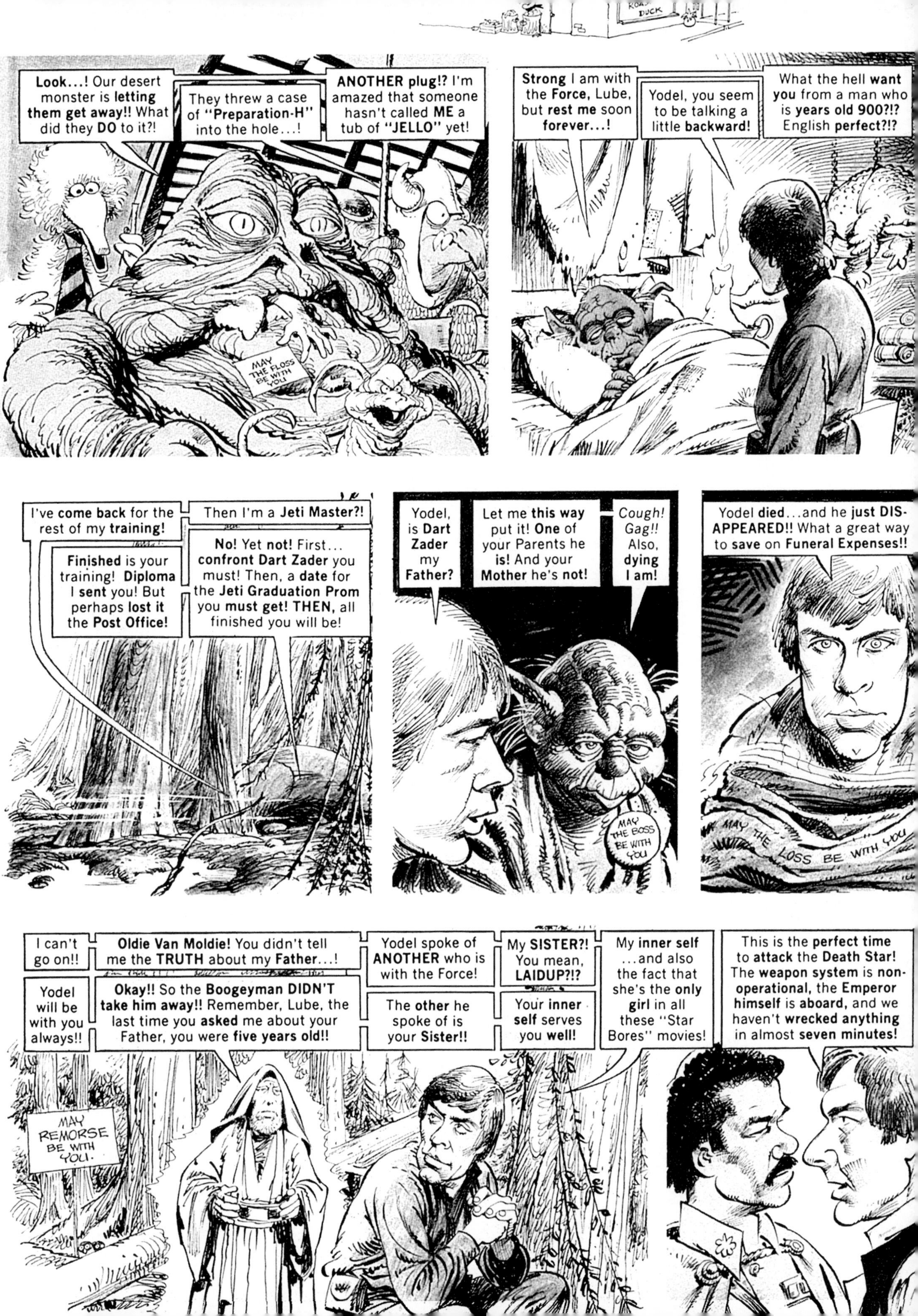
Look...! Our desert monster is letting them get away!! What did they DO to it?!
They threw a case of "Preparation-H" into the hole...!
ANOTHER plug!? I'm amazed that someone hasn't called ME a tub of "JELLO" yet!
MAY THE FLOSS BE WITH YOU
Strong I am with the Force, Lube, but rest me soon forever...!
Yodel, you seem to be talking a little backward!
What the hell want you from a man who is years old 900?!? English perfect?!?
I've come back for the rest of my training!
Then I'm a Jeti Master?!
Finished is your training! Diploma I sent you! But perhaps lost it the Post Office!
No! Yet not! First... confront Dart Zader you must! Then, a date for the Jeti Graduation Prom you must get! THEN, all finished you will be!
Yodel, is Dart Zader my Father?
Let me this way put it! One of your Parents he is! And your Mother he's not!
Cough! Gag!! Also, dying I am!
MAY THE BOSS BE WITH YOU
Yodel died...and he just DIS-APPEARED!! What a great way to save on Funeral Expenses!!
MAY THE LOSS BE WITH YOU
I can't go on!!
Oldie Van Moldie! You didn't tell me the TRUTH about my Father...!
Yodel will be with you always!!
Okay!! So the Boogeyman DIDN'T take him away!! Remember, Lube, the last time you asked me about your Father, you were five years old!!
MAY REMORSE BE WITH YOU.
Yodel spoke of ANOTHER who is with the Force!
The other he spoke of is your Sister!!
My SISTER?! You mean, LAIDUP?!?
Your inner self serves you well!
My inner self ...and also the fact that she's the only girl in all these "Star Bores" movies!
This is the perfect time to attack the Death Star! The weapon system is non-operational, the Emperor himself is aboard, and we haven't wrecked anything in almost seven minutes!

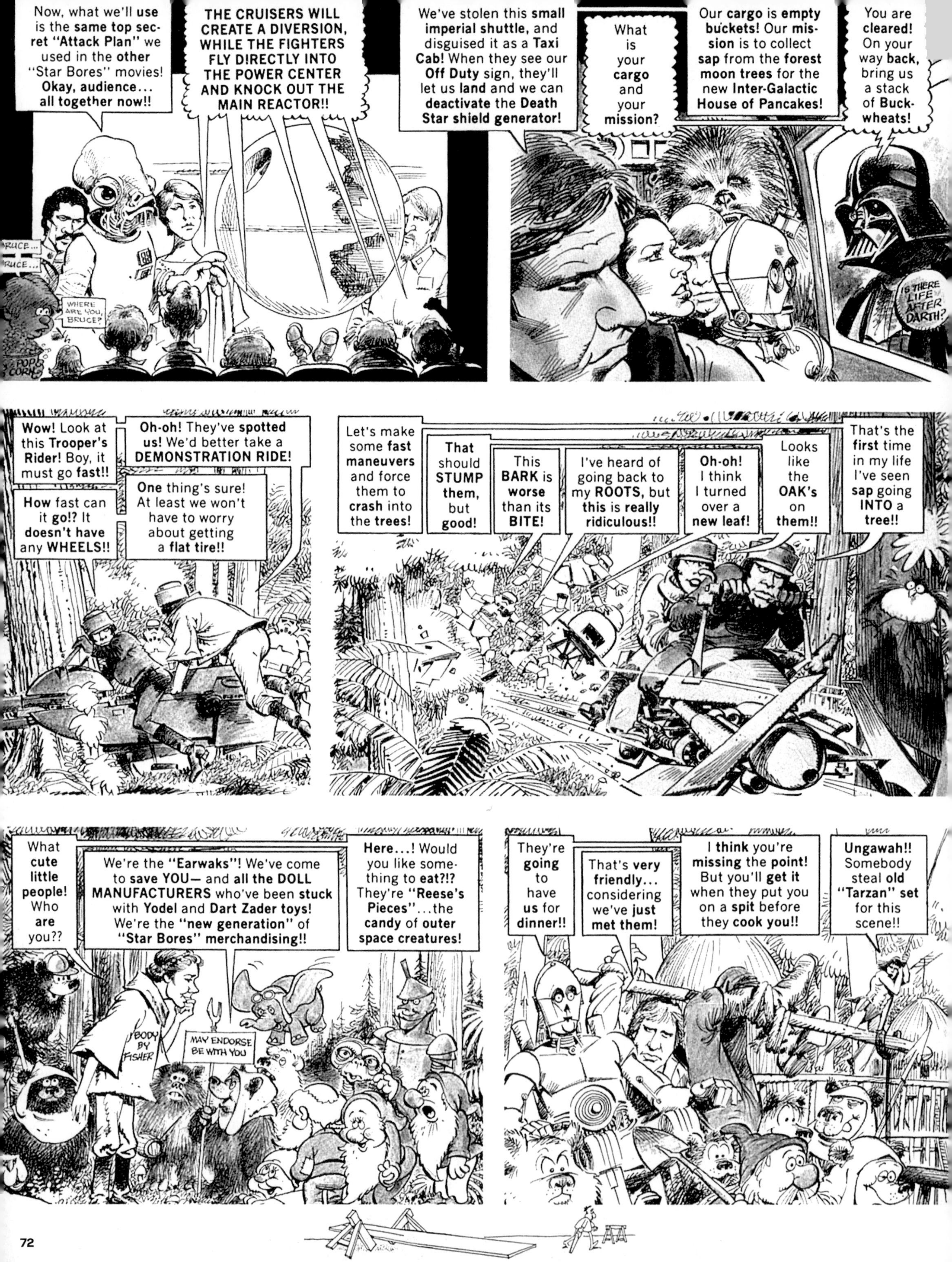

Now, what we'll use is the same top secret "Attack Plan" we used in the other "Star Bores" movies! Okay, audience... all together now!!
THE CRUISERS WILL CREATE A DIVERSION, WHILE THE FIGHTERS FLY DIRECTLY INTO THE POWER CENTER AND KNOCK OUT THE MAIN REACTOR!!
RUCE...
RUCE...
WHERE ARE YOU, BRUCE?
POP CORN
We've stolen this small imperial shuttle, and disguised it as a Taxi Cab! When they see our Off Duty sign, they'll let us land and we can deactivate the Death Star shield generator!
What is your cargo and your mission?
Our cargo is empty buckets! Our mission is to collect sap from the forest moon trees for the new Inter-Galactic House of Pancakes!
You are cleared! On your way back, bring us a stack of Buckwheats!
IS THERE LIFE AFTER DARTH?
Wow! Look at this Trooper's Rider! Boy, it must go fast!!
Oh-oh! They've spotted us! We'd better take a DEMONSTRATION RIDE!
How fast can it go!? It doesn't have any WHEELS!!
One thing's sure! At least we won't have to worry about getting a flat tire!!
Let's make some fast maneuvers and force them to crash into the trees!
That should STUMP them, but good!
This BARK is worse than its BITE!
I've heard of going back to my ROOTS, but this is really ridiculous!!
Oh-oh! I think I turned over a new leaf!
Looks like the OAK's on them!!
That's the first time in my life I've seen sap going INTO a tree!!
What cute little people! Who are you??
We're the "Earwaks"! We've come to save YOU— and all the DOLL MANUFACTURERS who've been stuck with Yodel and Dart Zader toys! We're the "new generation" of "Star Bores" merchandising!!
Here...! Would you like something to eat?!? They're "Reese's Pieces"...the candy of outer space creatures!
BODY BY FISHER
MAY ENDORSE BE WITH YOU
They're going to have us for dinner!!
That's very friendly... considering we've just met them!
I think you're missing the point! But you'll get it when they put you on a spit before they cook you!!
Ungawah!! Somebody steal old "Tarzan" set for this scene!!

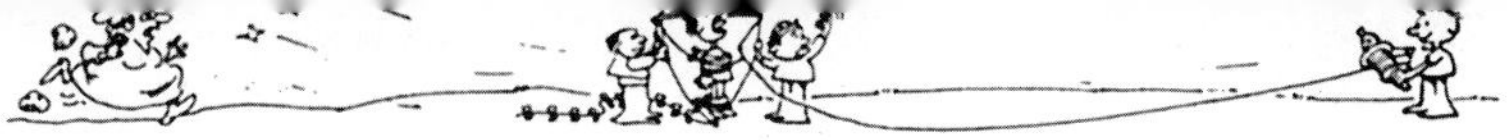

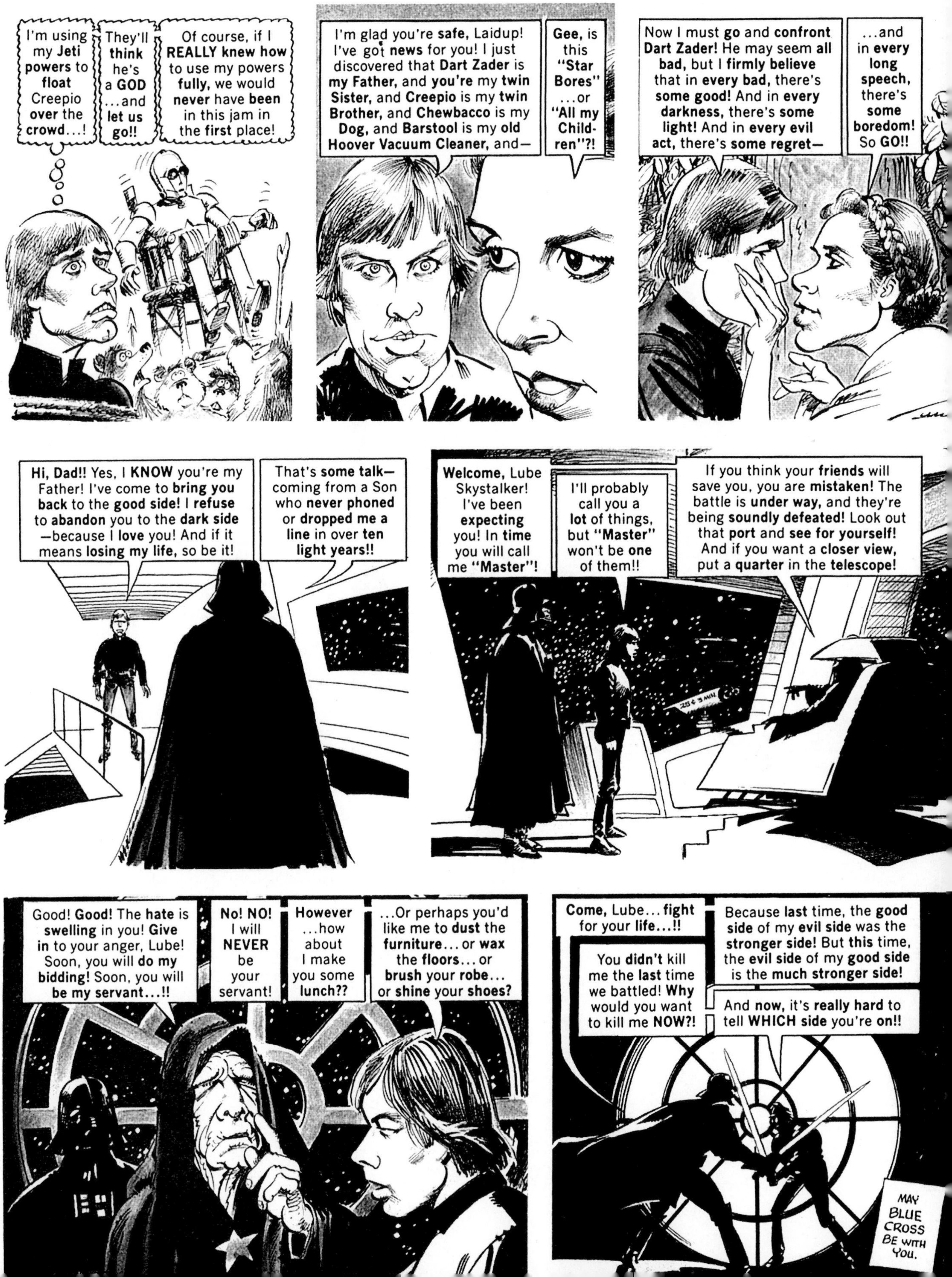
I'm using my Jeti powers to float Creepio over the crowd...!
They'll think he's a GOD ...and let us go!!
Of course, if I REALLY knew how to use my powers fully, we would never have been in this jam in the first place!
I'm glad you're safe, Laidup! I've got news for you! I just discovered that Dart Zader is my Father, and you're my twin Sister, and Creepio is my twin Brother, and Chewbacco is my Dog, and Barstool is my old Hoover Vacuum Cleaner, and—
Gee, is this "Star Bores" ...or "All my Children"?!
Now I must go and confront Dart Zader! He may seem all bad, but I firmly believe that in every bad, there's some good! And in every darkness, there's some light! And in every evil act, there's some regret—
...and in every long speech, there's some boredom! So GO!!
Hi, Dad!! Yes, I KNOW you're my Father! I've come to bring you back to the good side! I refuse to abandon you to the dark side —because I love you! And if it means losing my life, so be it!
That's some talk— coming from a Son who never phoned or dropped me a line in over ten light years!!
Welcome, Lube Skystalker! I've been expecting you! In time you will call me "Master"!
I'll probably call you a lot of things, but "Master" won't be one of them!!
If you think your friends will save you, you are mistaken! The battle is under way, and they're being soundly defeated! Look out that port and see for yourself! And if you want a closer view, put a quarter in the telescope!
Good! Good! The hate is swelling in you! Give in to your anger, Lube! Soon, you will do my bidding! Soon, you will be my servant...!!
No! NO! I will NEVER be your servant!
However ...how about I make you some lunch??
...Or perhaps you'd like me to dust the furniture... or wax the floors... or brush your robe... or shine your shoes?
Come, Lube... fight for your life...!!
You didn't kill me the last time we battled! Why would you want to kill me NOW?!
Because last time, the good side of my evil side was the stronger side! But this time, the evil side of my good side is the much stronger side!
And now, it's really hard to tell WHICH side you're on!!
MAY BLUE CROSS BE WITH YOU.

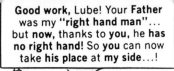
Good work, Lube! Your **Father** was my "**right hand man**"... but **now**, thanks to **you**, he has **no right hand!** So **you** can now take **his** place at my side...!

I would rather **DIE first!!**

Normally I **don't DO** requests, but okay!

Help! **HELP! OWW! OOH!!**

I'm giving you a **billion volts**, Lube, And if **this** doesn't kill you, your **electric bill WILL!!**

You **saved** my life, Father! You threw the **Emperor** down the **shaft!** Is that because of your **GOOD SIDE?!?**

No, Lube, that's because of my **BAD EYESIGHT!** I **thought** I was throwing **YOU** down the shaft!

A LONG VADER GO

Boy, I sure am glad we found this **secret entrance** to the **shield generator** bunker!

SECRET ENTRANCE TO SHIELD GENERATOR BUNKER

ADMISSION

ADULTS $5.00   CHILDREN $2.00   REBELS $25.00

SECRET ENTRANCE T-SHIRTS $7.00   SECRET ENTRANCE POST CARDS 50¢

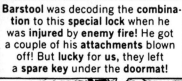
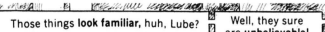

Barstool was decoding the **combination** to this **special lock** when he was **injured** by **enemy fire!** He got a couple of his **attachments** blown off! But **lucky** for **us**, they left a spare key under the doormat!

Those things **look familiar**, huh, Lube?

They **should!** Remember the four-legged machines in "**The Empire Strikes Back**"? They were **cut in half** for **this** movie!

Well, they sure are **unbelievable!**

Because they're so—so **AWESOME?**

No, because they're **two million dollars** of **high technology** that can be **tripped up** and **destroyed** with a **few heavy logs!!**

CLOSED USE NEXT DOOR

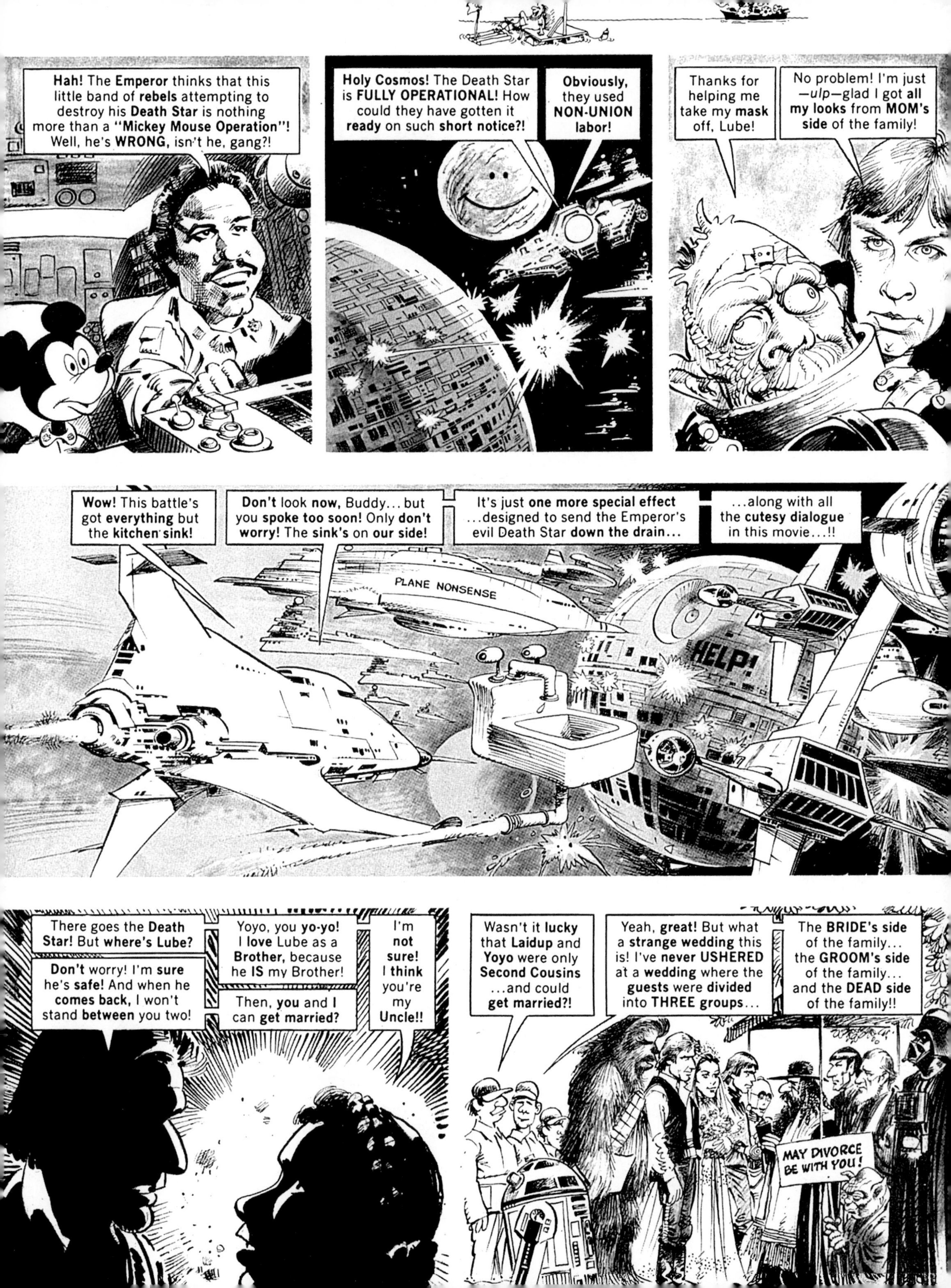

Hah! The Emperor thinks that this little band of rebels attempting to destroy his Death Star is nothing more than a "Mickey Mouse Operation"! Well, he's WRONG, isn't he, gang?!
Holy Cosmos! The Death Star is FULLY OPERATIONAL! How could they have gotten it ready on such short notice?!
Obviously, they used NON-UNION labor!
Thanks for helping me take my mask off, Lube!
No problem! I'm just —ulp—glad I got all my looks from MOM's side of the family!
Wow! This battle's got everything but the kitchen sink!
Don't look now, Buddy... but you spoke too soon! Only don't worry! The sink's on our side!
It's just one more special effect ...designed to send the Emperor's evil Death Star down the drain...
...along with all the cutesy dialogue in this movie...!!
PLANE NONSENSE
HELP!
There goes the Death Star! But where's Lube?
Don't worry! I'm sure he's safe! And when he comes back, I won't stand between you two!
Yoyo, you yo-yo! I love Lube as a Brother, because he IS my Brother!
Then, you and I can get married?
I'm not sure! I think you're my Uncle!!
Wasn't it lucky that Laidup and Yoyo were only Second Cousins ...and could get married?!
Yeah, great! But what a strange wedding this is! I've never USHERED at a wedding where the guests were divided into THREE groups...
The BRIDE's side of the family... the GROOM's side of the family... and the DEAD side of the family!!
MAY DIVORCE BE WITH YOU!

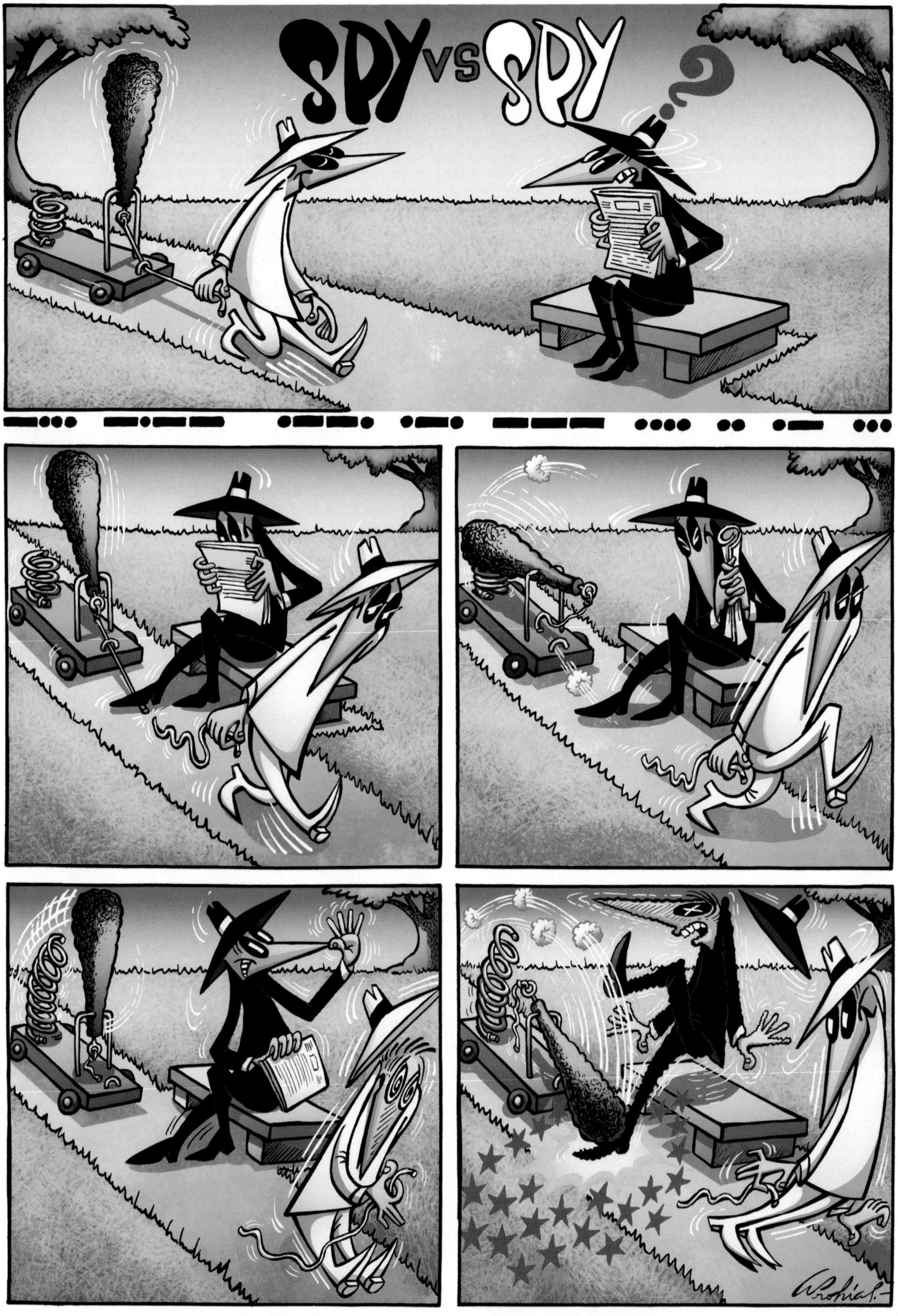
SPY vs SPY
Prohias.

WRITER AND ARTIST: ANTONIO PROHIAS COLORIST: CARRIE STRACHAN

Sergio Aragonés Presents A MAD Look at Cats

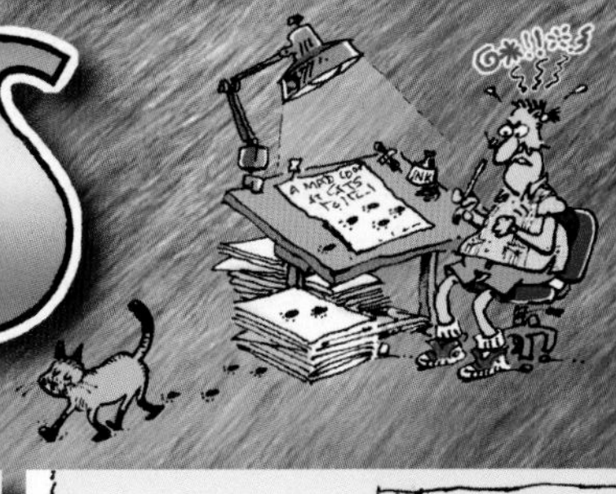

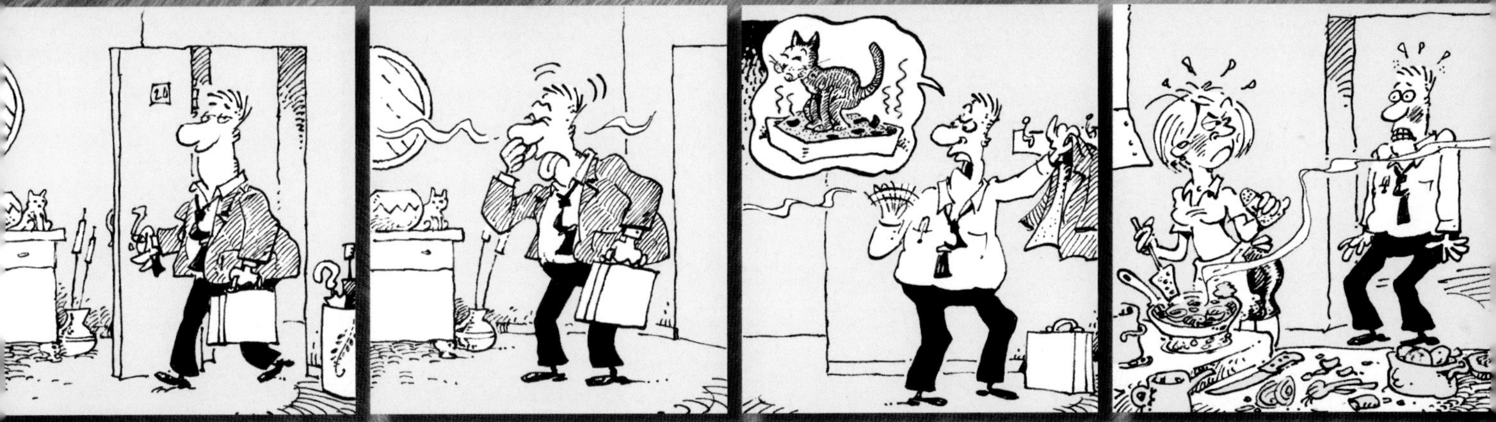

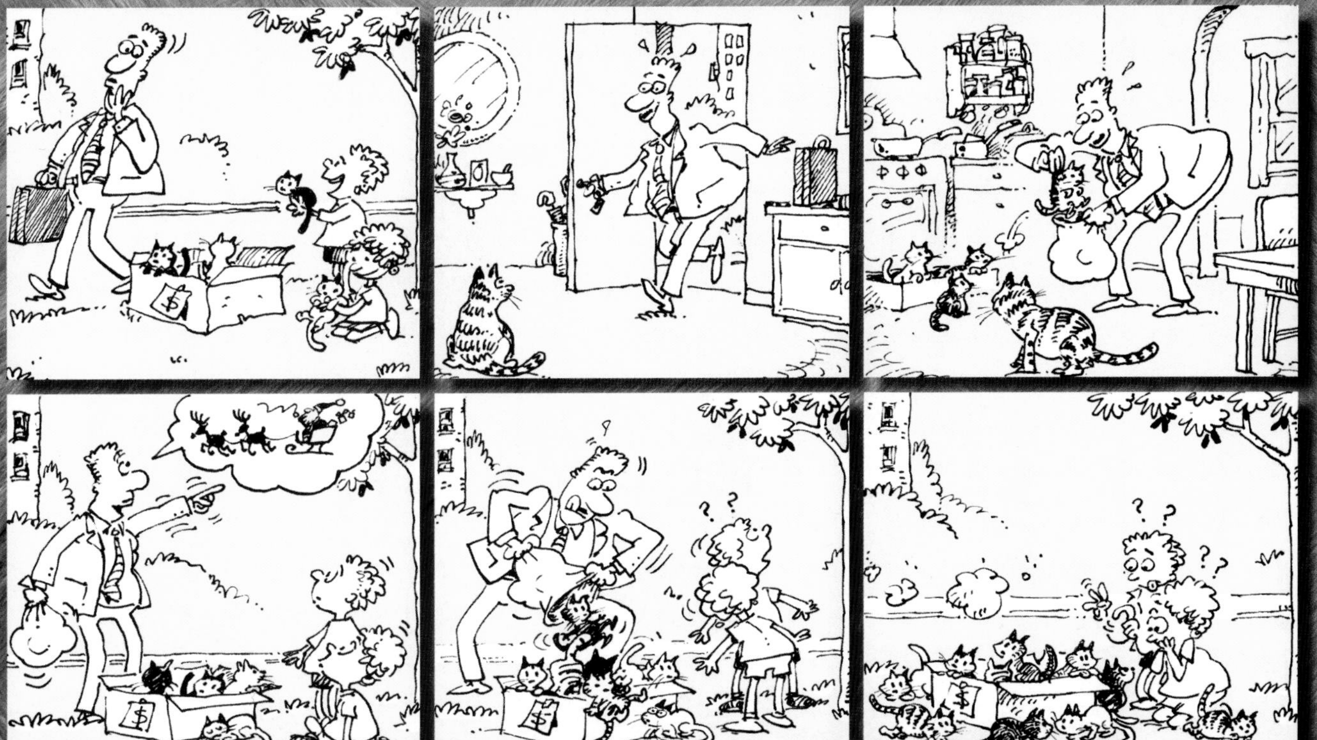

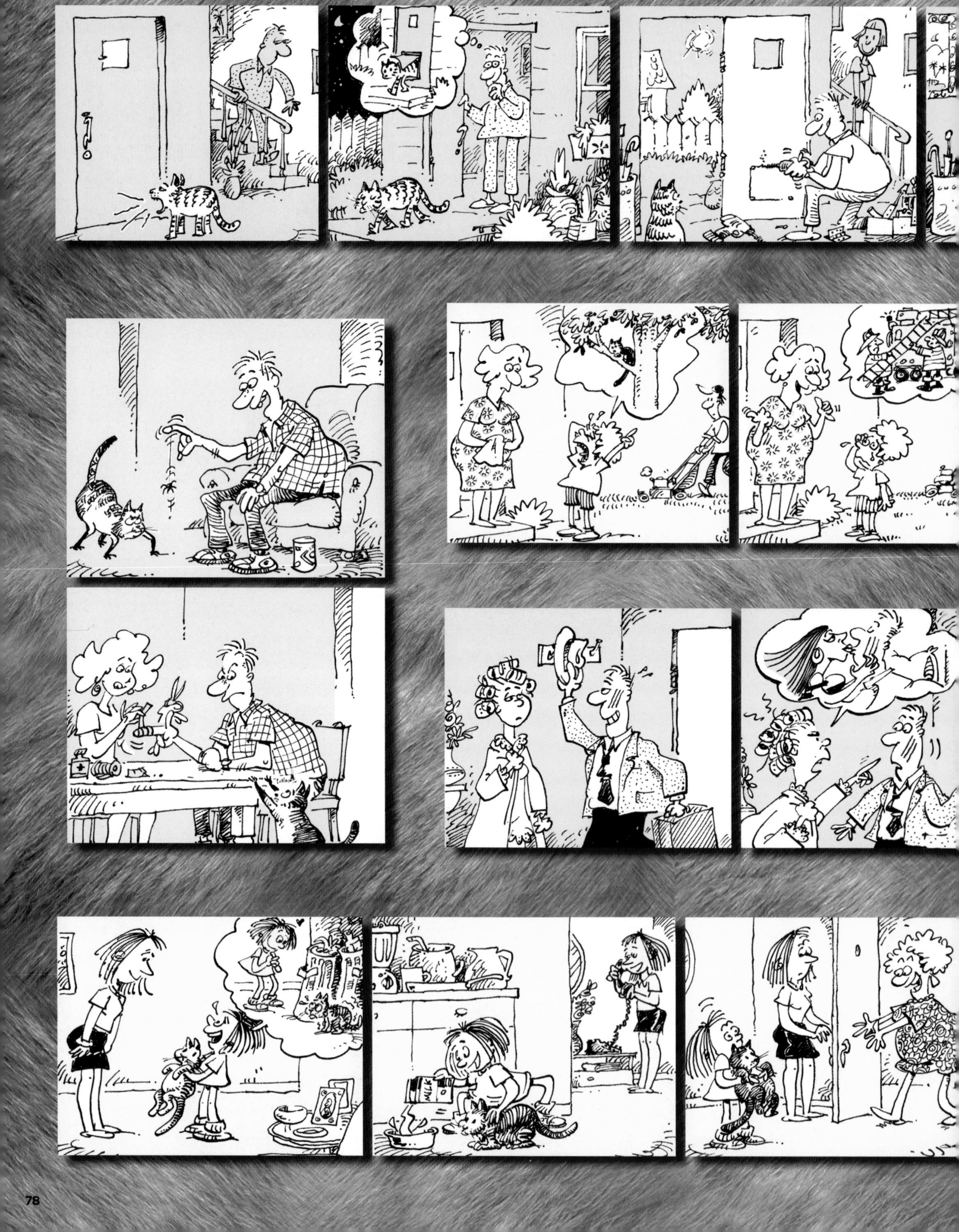
MILK

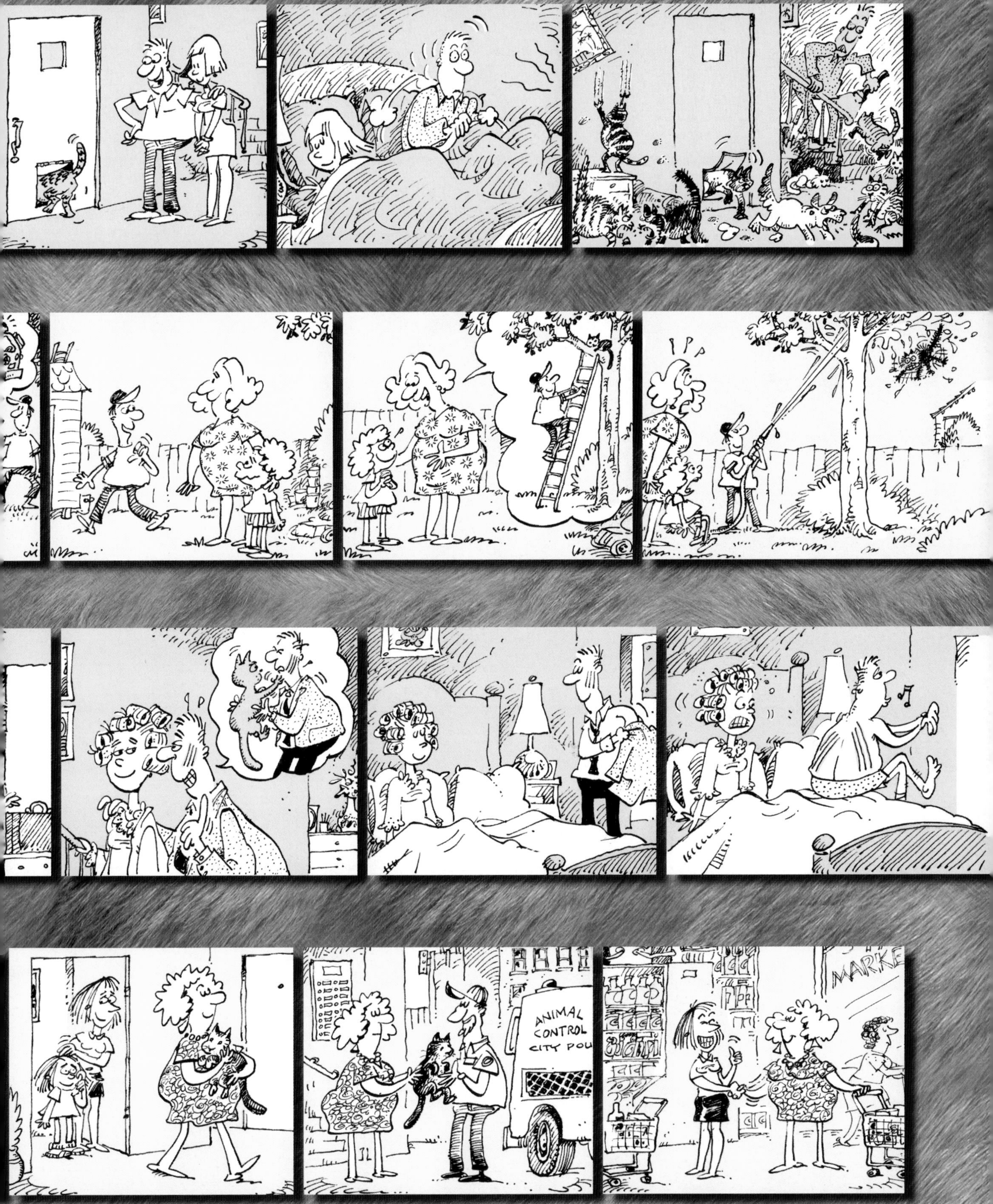
ANIMAL
CONTROL
CITY POU
MARKE

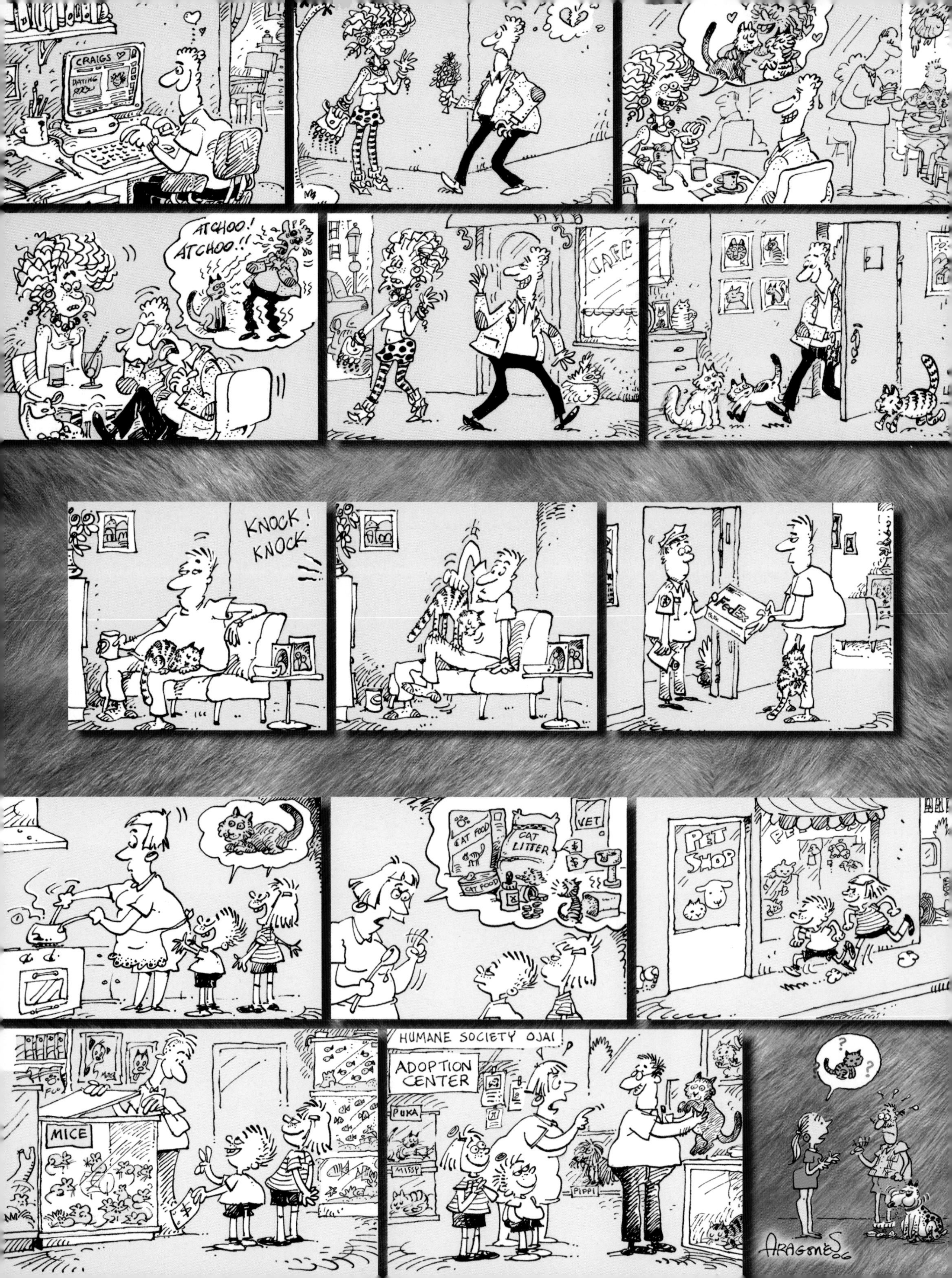

CRAIGS
DATING
ATCHOO!
ATCHOO!!
CAFE
KNOCK!
KNOCK
FedEx
CAT FOOD
CAT LITTER
VET
CAT FOOD
PET SHOP
MICE
HUMANE SOCIETY OJAI
ADOPTION CENTER
PUKA
MISSY
PIPPI
ARAGONÉS 06

MAD WILL RETURN AFTER THIS COMMERCIAL MESSAGE

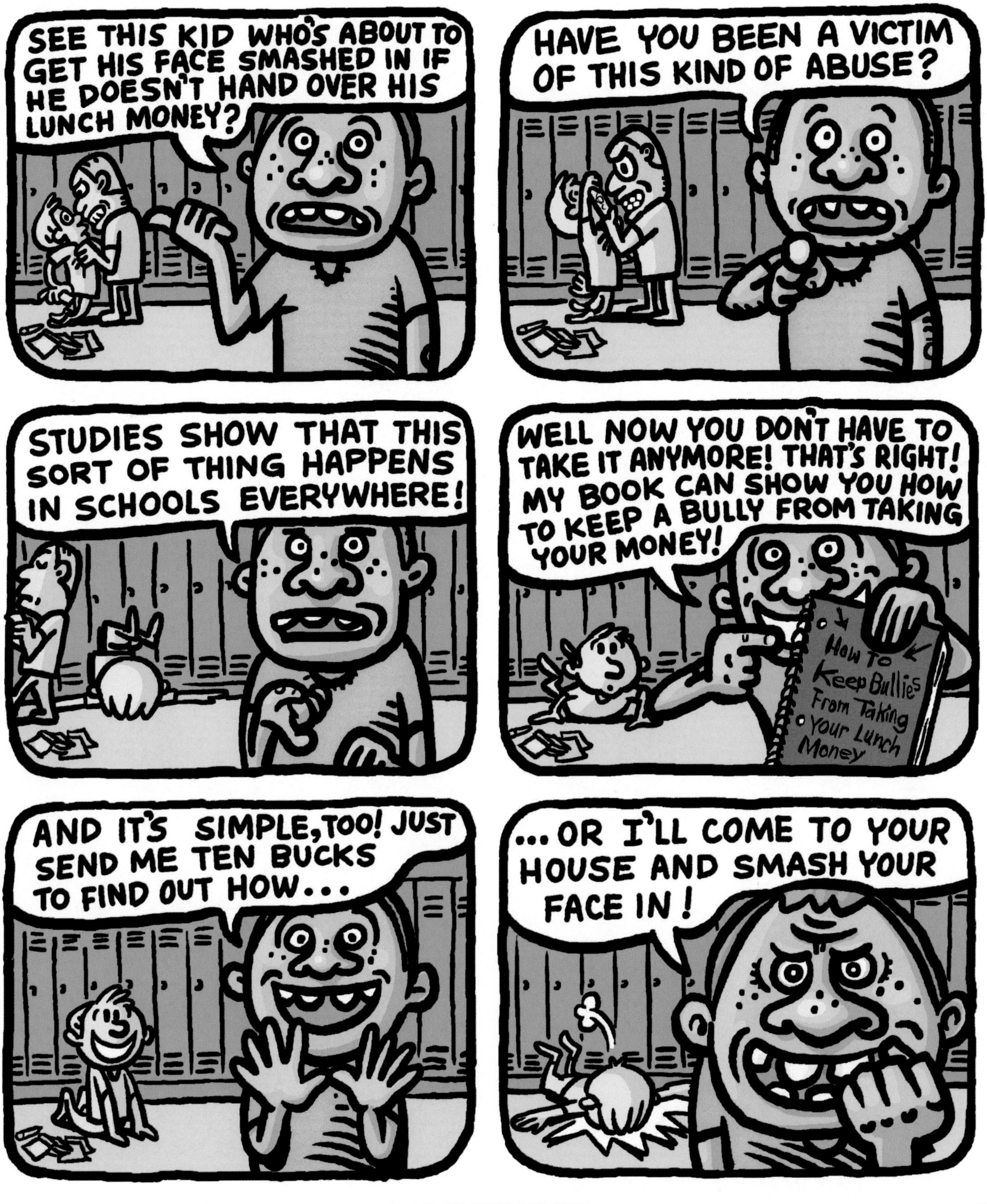
SEE THIS KID WHO'S ABOUT TO GET HIS FACE SMASHED IN IF HE DOESN'T HAND OVER HIS LUNCH MONEY?
HAVE YOU BEEN A VICTIM OF THIS KIND OF ABUSE?
STUDIES SHOW THAT THIS SORT OF THING HAPPENS IN SCHOOLS EVERYWHERE!
WELL NOW YOU DON'T HAVE TO TAKE IT ANYMORE! THAT'S RIGHT! MY BOOK CAN SHOW YOU HOW TO KEEP A BULLY FROM TAKING YOUR MONEY!
How To Keep Bullies From Taking Your Lunch Money
AND IT'S SIMPLE, TOO! JUST SEND ME TEN BUCKS TO FIND OUT HOW...
...OR I'LL COME TO YOUR HOUSE AND SMASH YOUR FACE IN!

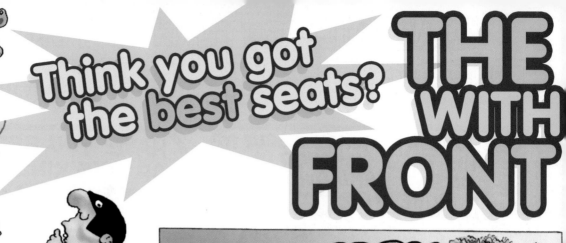

Think you got the best seats? THE WITH FRONT

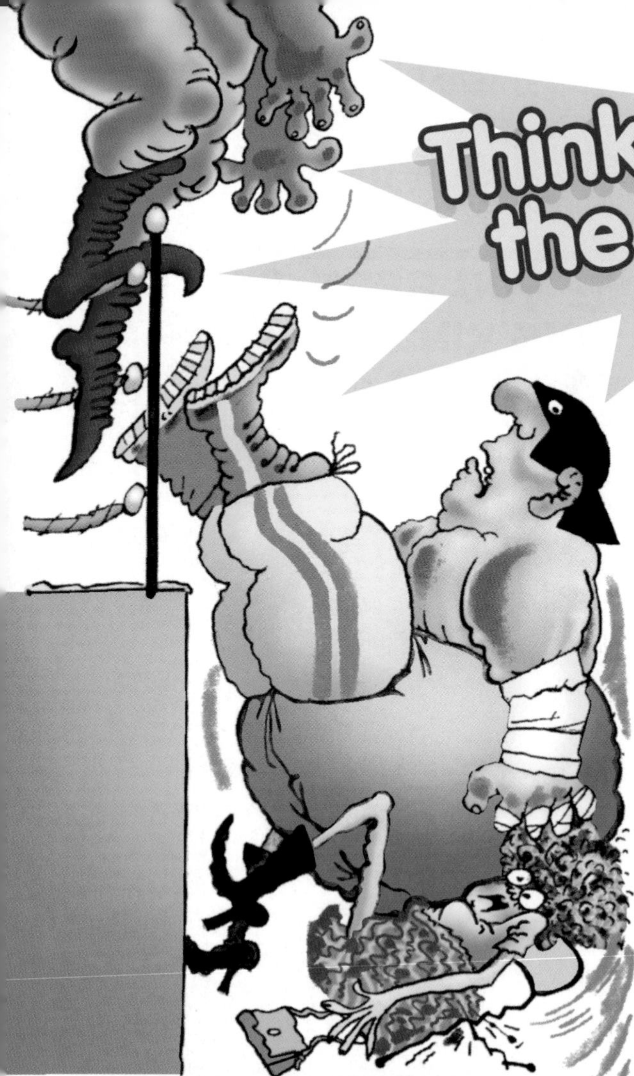

FRONT ROW CENTER AT THE WRESTLING MATCH

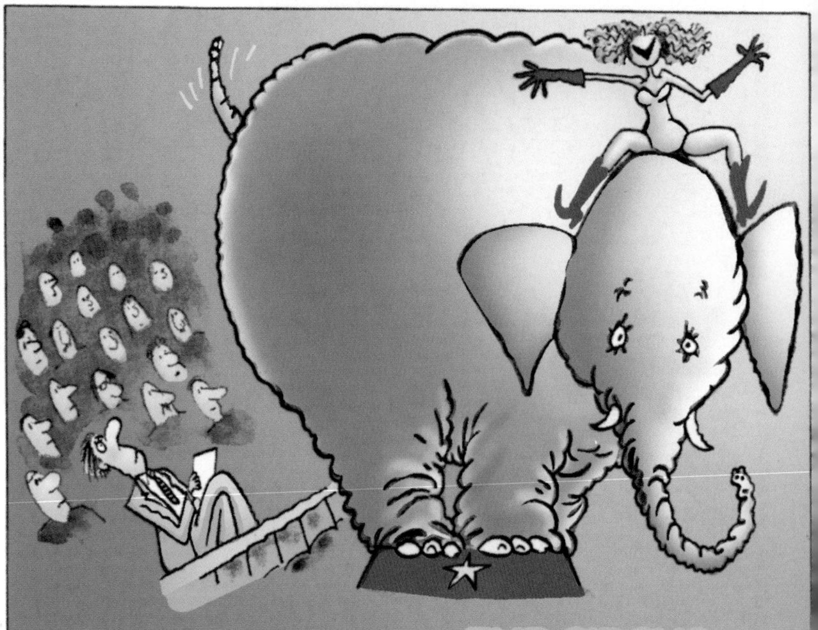

FRONT ROW CENTER AT THE CIRCUS

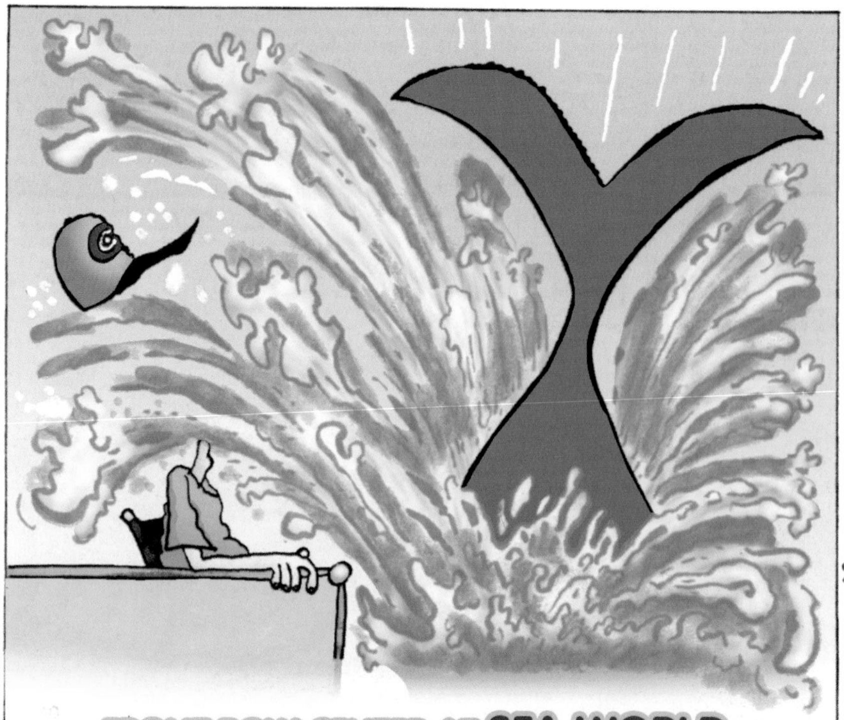

FRONT ROW CENTER AT SEA WORLD

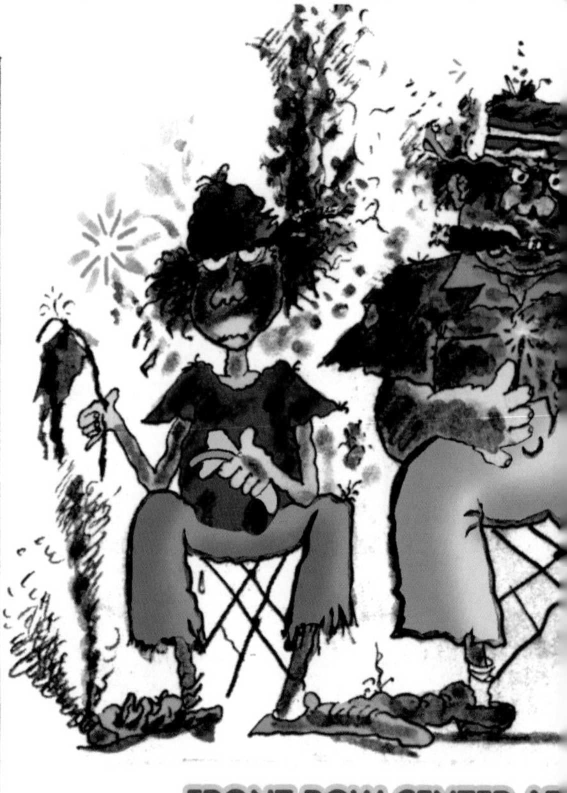

FRONT ROW CENTER AT

PROBLEMS SITTING ROW CENTER

WRITER AND ARTIST:
PAUL PETER PORGES

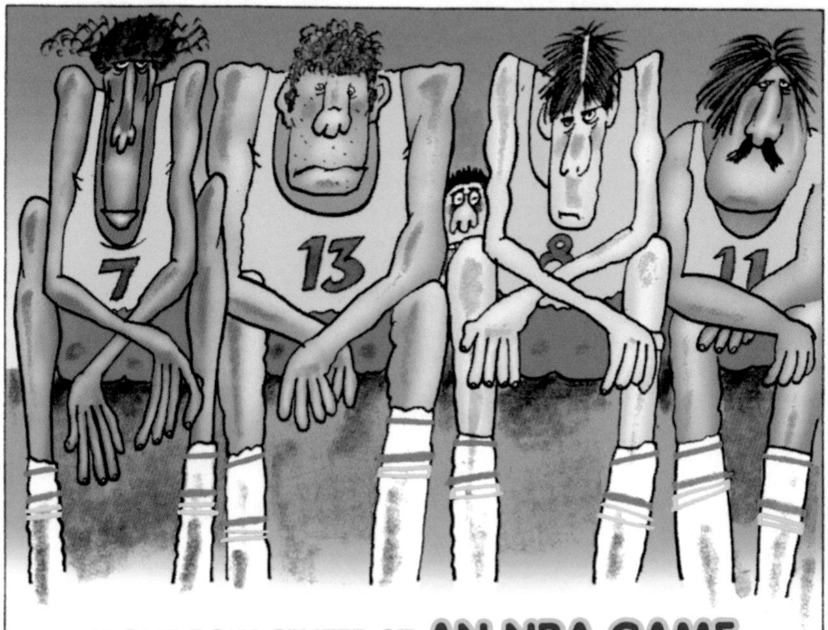
7
13
8
11

FRONT ROW CENTER AT **AN NBA GAME**

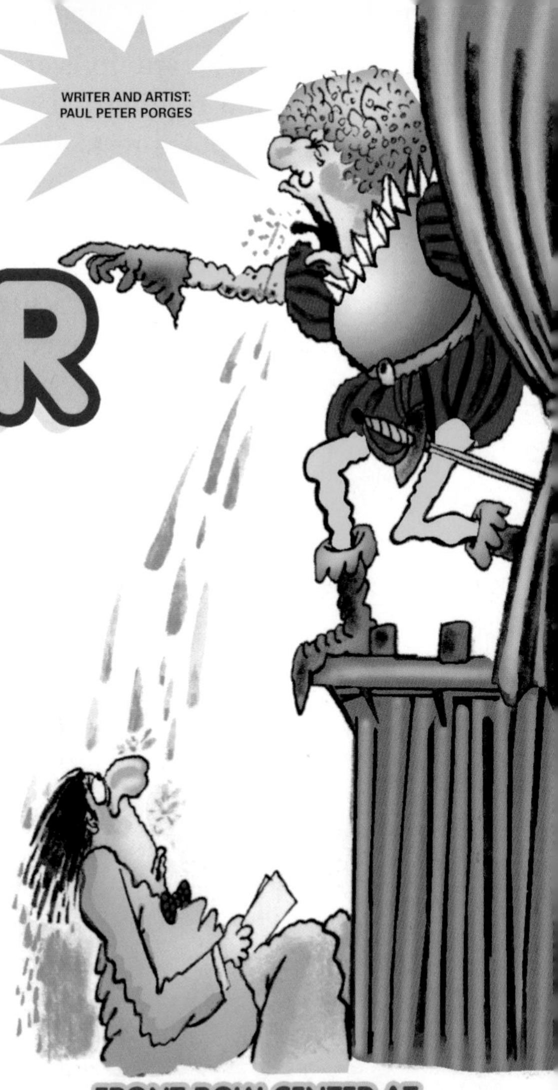

FRONT ROW CENTER AT
A SHAKESPEARE FESTIVAL

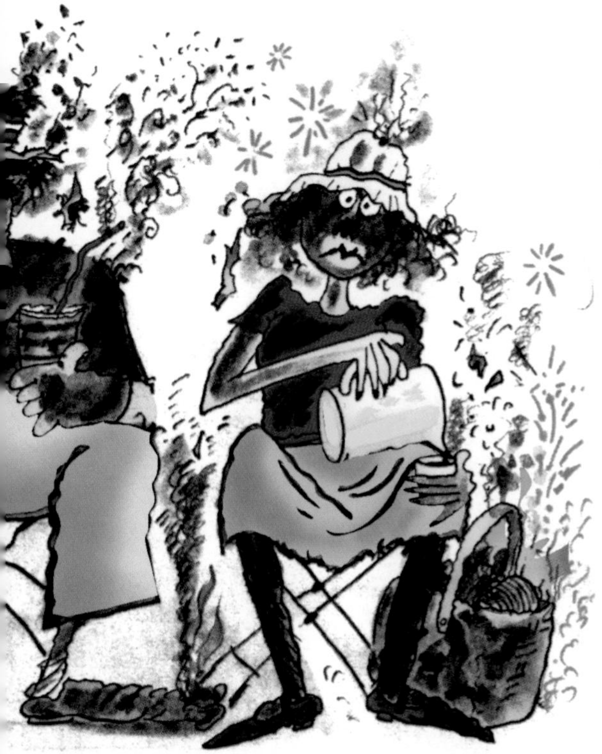

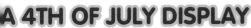

A 4TH OF JULY DISPLAY

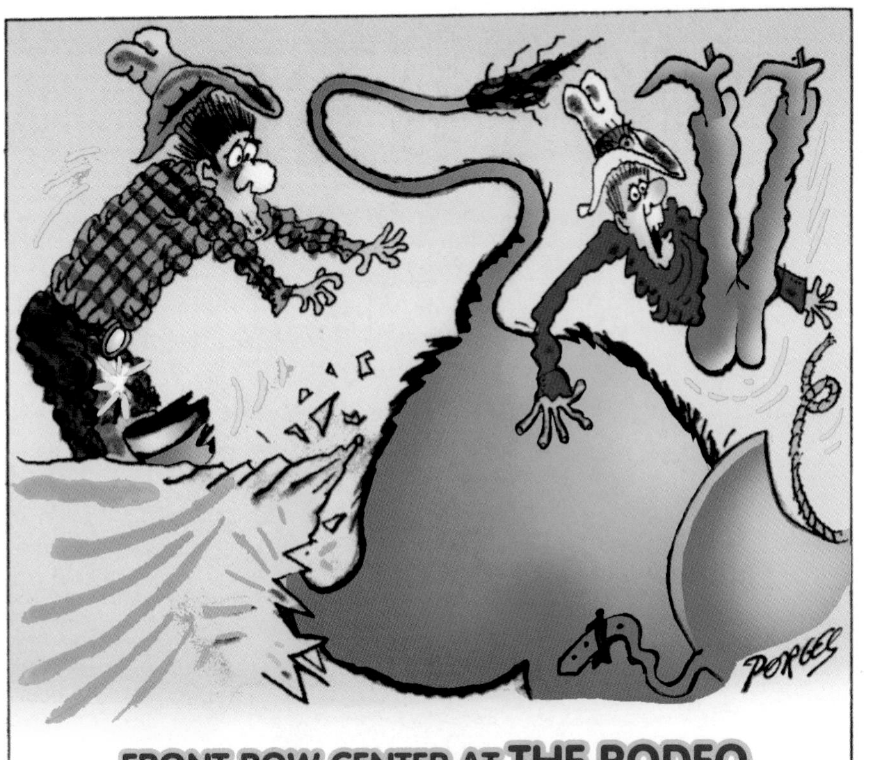
PORGES

FRONT ROW CENTER AT **THE RODEO**

FROM THE SUB-RHYME TO THE RIDICULOUS DEPT.

Parents and teachers are forever screaming about what kids are reading today. They say that children are exposed to too much "trash" such as Comic Books and Horror Stories and MAD! But for some strange reason, they never point their fingers at the worst Children's Literature of all—"Mother Goose." Just pick up any collection of Nursery Rhymes and you will quickly see how horribly written, badly rhymed and poorly metered they are. The whole trouble with Nursery Rhymes is that the folks who wrote them were "amateurs"! Obviously, the "professional touch" was sorely needed. So let's take a look at what we'd have...

IF FAMOUS POETS HAD WRITTEN "MOTHER GOOSE"

If RUDYARD KIPLING had written

JACK AND JILL

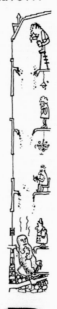

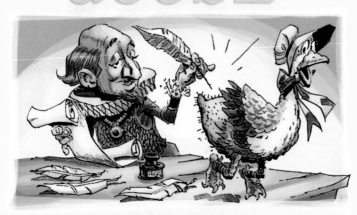

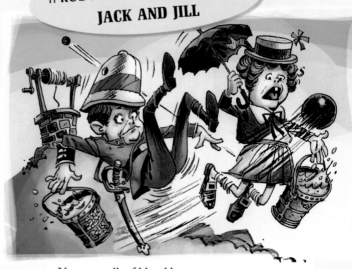

You can talk of blood 'n gore
When you're in a shootin' war
And the enemy is chargin' for the kill—
But if you're likin' slaughter
Then you oughta haul some water
Like that brave and fearless couple, Jack and Jill.

Well, they had a pail to fill
When they climbed that craggy hill
And they never thought that soon they
would be dead;
But Jack he took a fall
And he bounced just like a ball
Till he landed in a gulley on his head.

He hollered, "Jill, Jill, Jill!
I'm a-lyin' at the bottom of the hill!"
But poor Jill had plunged as well,
And they died right where they fell.
You've a lot more guts than I have, Jack and Jill.

If OGDEN NASH had written

THE OLD WOMAN WHO LIVED IN A SHOE

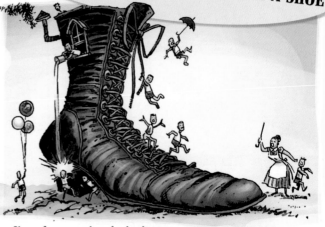

I've often wondered whether we
Should allow an old woman to raise a lot of children in a
shoe under conditions which can only be described as
leathery.

WRITER: FRANK JACOBS
ARTIST: JACK RICKARD COLORIST: CARRIE STRACHAN

If HENRY WADSWORTH LONGFELLOW had written LITTLE MISS MUFFET

By the house of Mother Hubbard,
Near the fabled Pumpkin Eater,
Sat the hungry one, Miss Muffet,
On her tuffet sat Miss Muffet,
Eating curds and whey for supper;
(She was tired of eating chicken
And could not afford a pot-roast.)
But behind her loomed a creature,
Not the cat who plays the fiddle,
Not the three blind mice a-running,
Not the sheep Bo Peep lost track of,
But a single icky spider
Who sat down beside Miss Muffet,
Though he had no invitation.

"Eek! A spider!" cried Miss Muffet,
When she saw the icky spider,
And she jumped up from the tuffet
And ran down the dirt road screaming
Past the house of Mother Hubbard,
Past the fabled Pumpkin Eater,
Never ever looking backward
At the single icky spider
Who remained there on the tuffet
Where the curds and whey were sitting,
And who tasted them, despised them,
Found them lacking in nutrition,
Then departed from the tuffet
While the curds and whey just sat there,
Turning sour in the sunshine,
Smelling awful in the sunshine,
Looking ecchy in the sunshine,
While the neighbors held their noses,
And I really am not certain
That this poem is an improvement.

If EDGAR ALLAN POE had written OLD KING COLE

Hear the call of Old King Cole—
    Old King Cole!
What a frantic, fearful craving fills his morbid soul!
    Hear him moaning, moaning, moaning
        For his pipe and for his bowl,
    Like the dreaded, deadly groaning
    Of some ghoul that is intoning
        From its ghostly, graveyard hole!
    Hear him plea, plea, plea
    As he calls his fiddlers three!
Ah, what horrifying hunger fills the terror-troubled soul
    Of King Cole, Cole, Cole, Cole,
        Cole, Cole, Cole—
Of the bleak and blackened soul of Old King Cole!

If WALT WHITMAN had written HUMPTY DUMPTY

O Humpty! O Dumpty! You've had a fearful spill,
You've tumbled from the stony height,
    you're lying cold and still;
Your shell is cracked, your yolk runs out,
    your breath is faint and wheezy;
You landed as a scrambled egg, instead of over easy;
    The king has sent his steeds and men
        To mend you if they can;
        I pray that they did not forget
            To bring a frying pan.

If ROBERT W. SERVICE had written LITTLE BOY BLUE

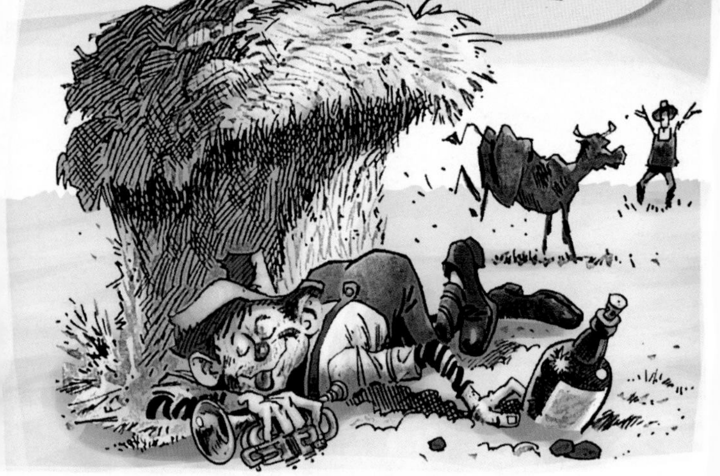

A bunch of the cows were mooing it up
in the cornfield, so they tell;
And down in the meadow a big flock of sheep
were raising a bit of hell;
There wasn't a way on that God-awful day
of stopping that crop-wrecking crew—
'Cause under a haystack, flopped out on his back,
lay that gold-bricking Little Boy Blue!

The folks from the farm, they all cried with alarm
on that sad but sunny morn;
Each one of them knew he could save all their crops
if he'd only blow his horn;
But none of them dared or especially cared
to waken him from his snooze;
'Cause Little Boy Blue was as drunk as a skunk
from a bottle of two-dollar booze!

If WILLIAM BLAKE had written LITTLE JACK HORNER

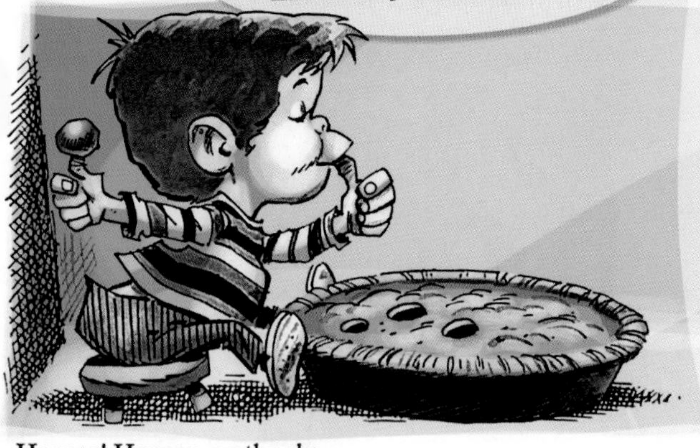

Horner! Horner, on the sly,
In thy corner, eating pie!
What immortal, gastric force
Makes thee hungry as a horse?

Horner! Horner, greedy bum,
Sticking in thy grimy thumb!
What cheap, greasy luncheonette
Taught thee such bad etiquette?

Horner! Horner, full of crumbs,
Always eating pies with plums!
Why not pumpkin, peach or mince—
Or, better still, a cherry blintz?

If JOYCE KILMER had written JACK SPRAT

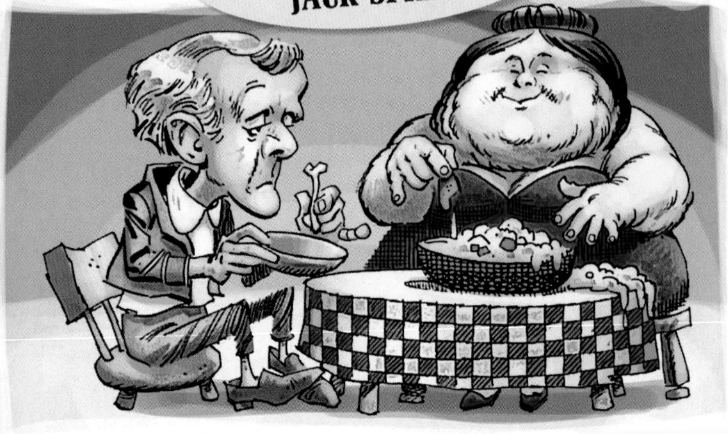

I think that I have never seen
A platter that was licked so clean
As that one licked with fork and knife
By Jack Sprat and his hungry wife;
Betwixt the two, they've made a deal
That puts an end to beef and veal;
Lean is shunned by Mrs. Sprat,
But only Jack can eat no fat.

If CARL SANDBURG had written TOM, TOM, THE PIPER'S SON

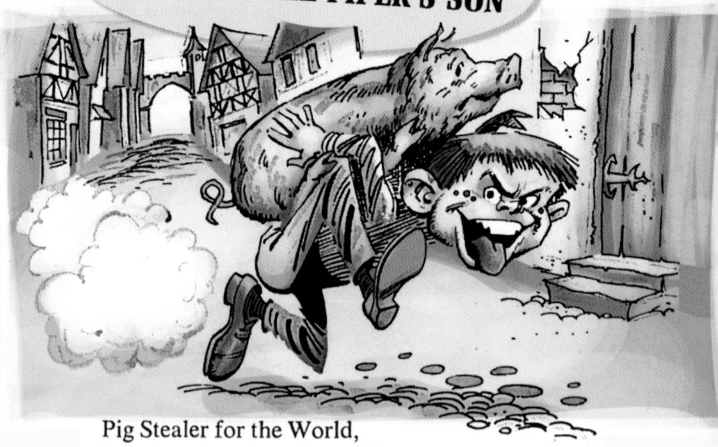

Pig Stealer for the World,
Law Breaker, Snatcher of Hogs,
Son of a Piper and the Nation's Swine Handler;
Sneaky, rotten, under-age,
Big Shot of the Pork Grabbers:
They tell me you are wicked, and I believe them,
for I have seen you seize a pig and go
running down the street.
And they tell me you are crooked, and I answer:
Yes, I have seen you eat a pig and then
go free to eat again.
And having answered, I have to ask myself:
Why do I waste my time writing a poem
glorifying a Pig Stealer, Law Breaker,
Snatcher of Hogs, Son of a Piper, and
the Swine Handler of the Nation?

ONE DAY AT MOUNT RUSHMORE

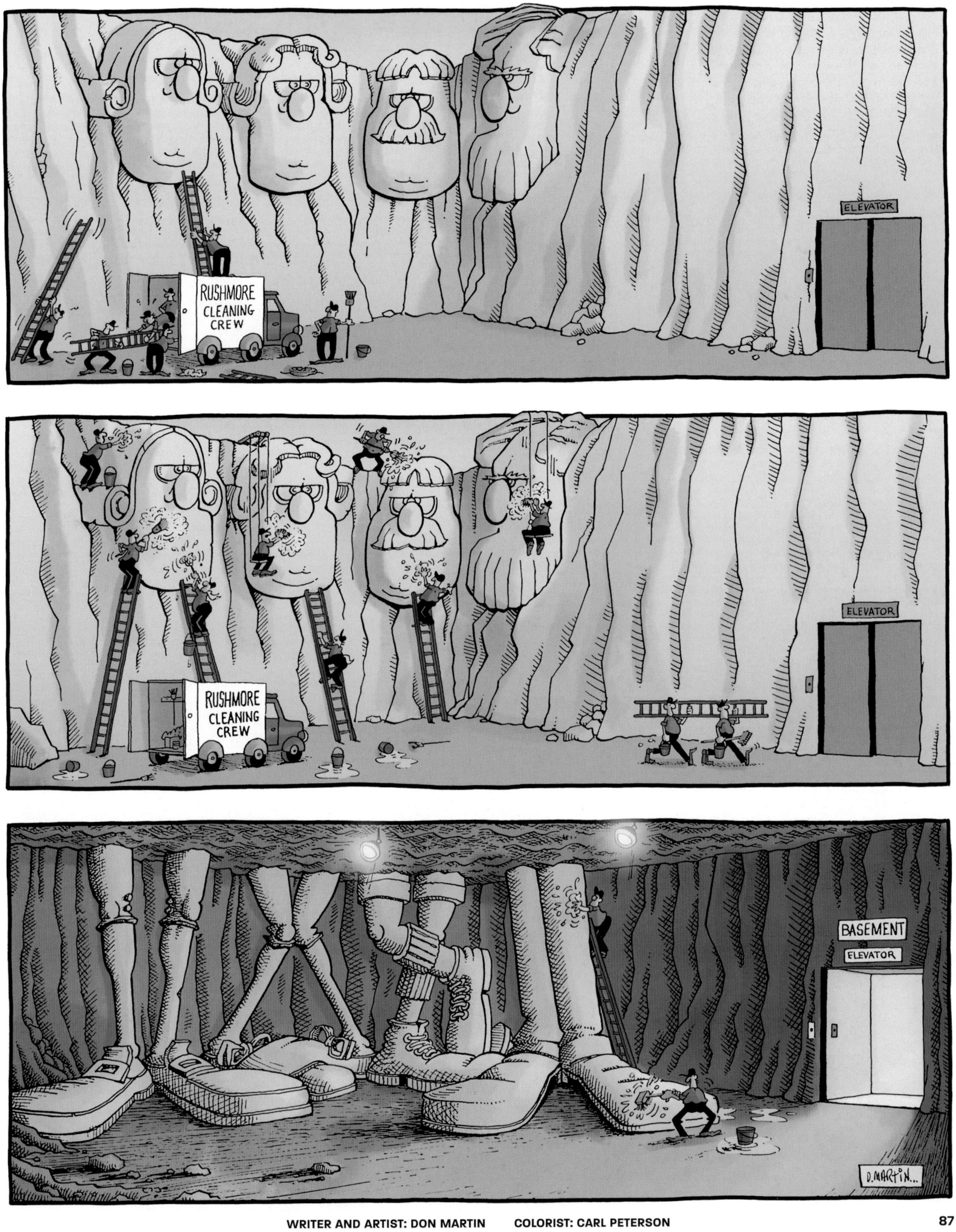

RUSHMORE CLEANING CREW
ELEVATOR
RUSHMORE CLEANING CREW
ELEVATOR
BASEMENT
ELEVATOR
D.MARTIN...

WRITER AND ARTIST: DON MARTIN COLORIST: CARL PETERSON

KEVIN CAN WAIT DEPT.

By now, everyone's familiar with "Six Degrees Of Kevin Bacon," the game where you begin with the name of any movie actor and move through a chain of associations until, in six steps or less, you end up at the star of *Footloose*. But we were thinking: who needs actors? Who needs six degrees? And for that matter, who needs Kevin? That's how we came up with the new lean, mean game we call...

FIVE DEGREES

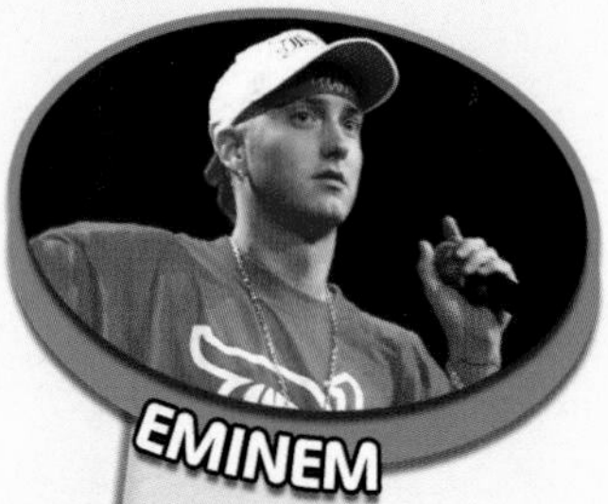

EMINEM

is a white rapper, as was...

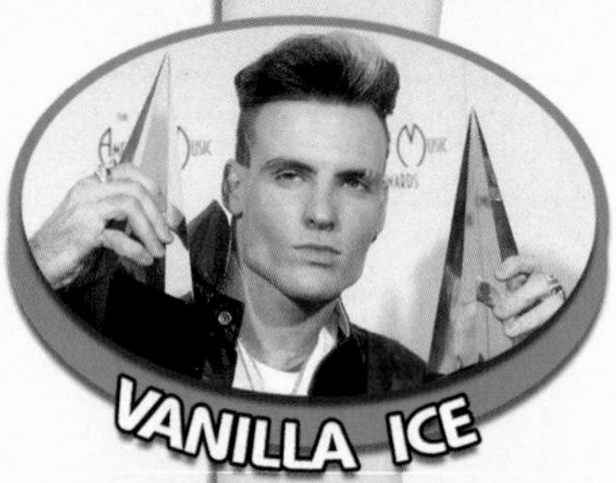

VANILLA ICE

who shares part of his name with the sport of...

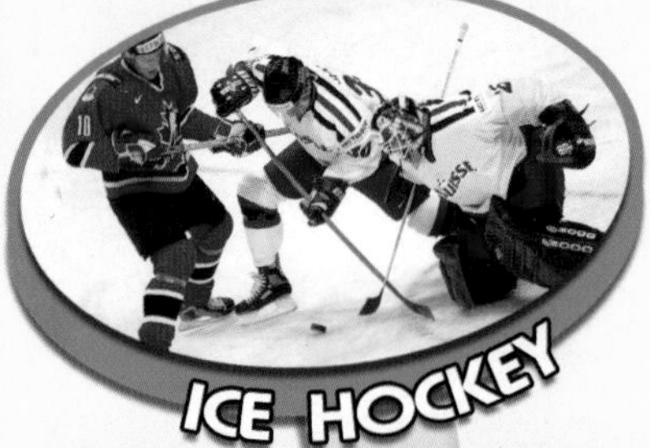

ICE HOCKEY

which is the national pastime of...

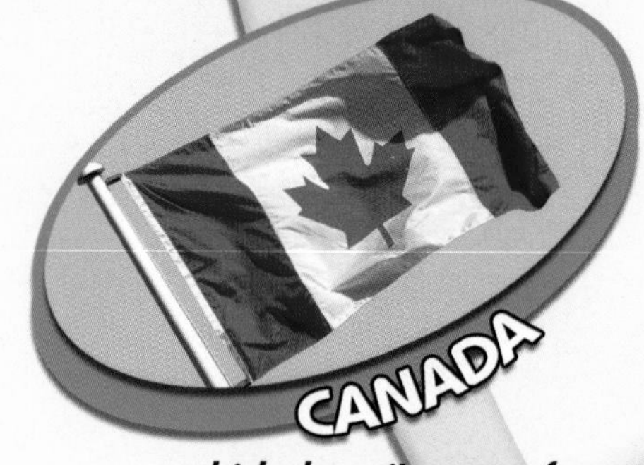

CANADA

which has its own famous style of...

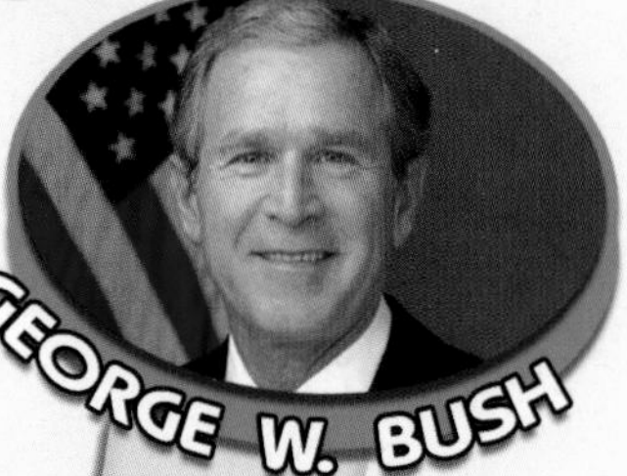

GEORGE W. BUSH

runs the country with...

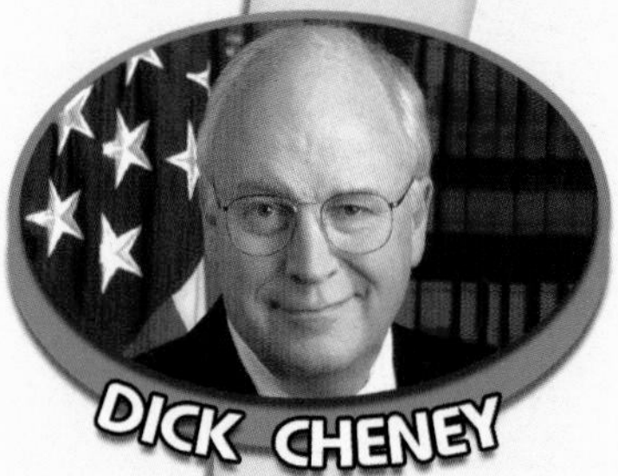

DICK CHENEY

who has had several...

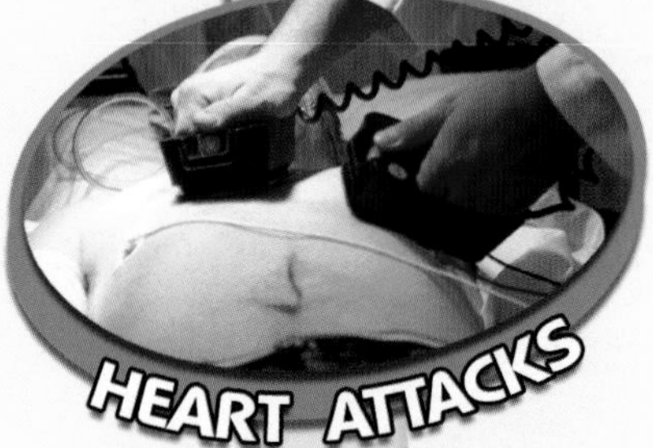

HEART ATTACKS

which are the result of...

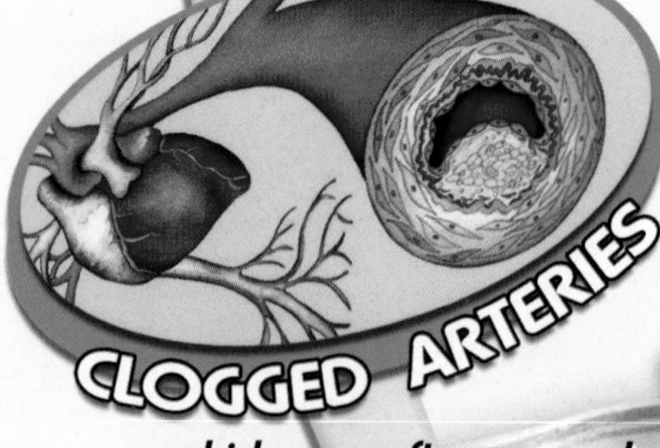

CLOGGED ARTERIES

which are often caused by consuming too much...

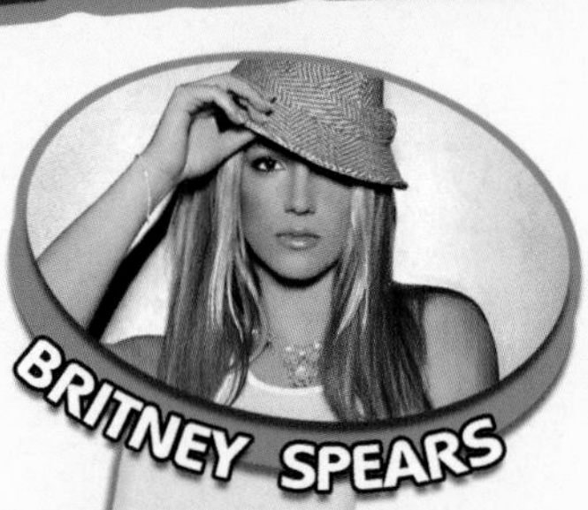

BRITNEY SPEARS

was married for about five minutes to a guy named...

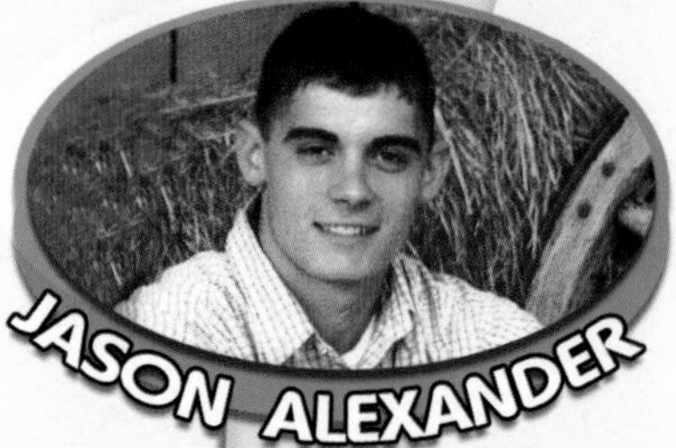

JASON ALEXANDER

which is also the name of the Seinfeld star who did commercials for...

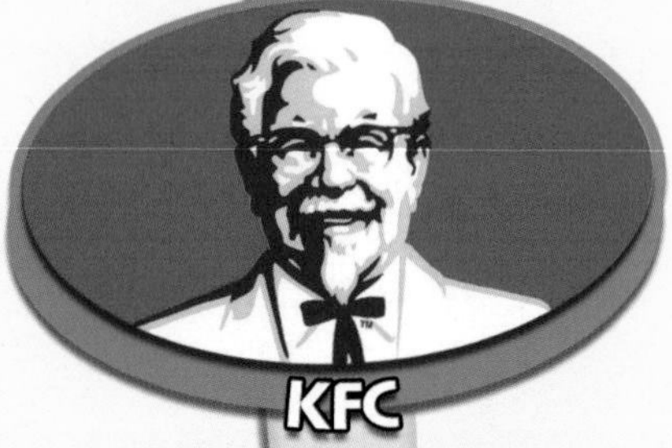

KFC

where you can order your chicken...

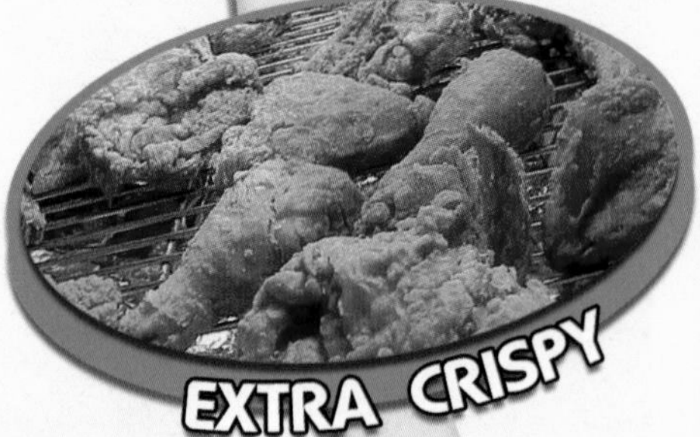

EXTRA CRISPY

which is also how many people like their...

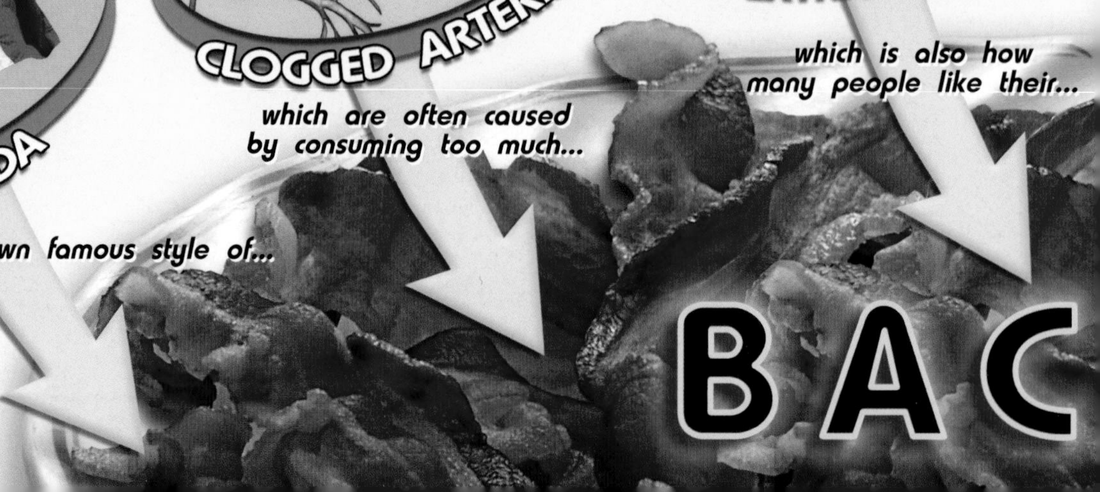

BAC

WRITER: MICHAEL RODMAN

BACON/CLUB SANDWICH PHOTOS: IRVING SCHILD

PHOTOS: AP/WIDE WORLD PHOTOS • CORBIS • IMAGE SOURCE • PHOTODISC • RUBBER BALL

OF BACON

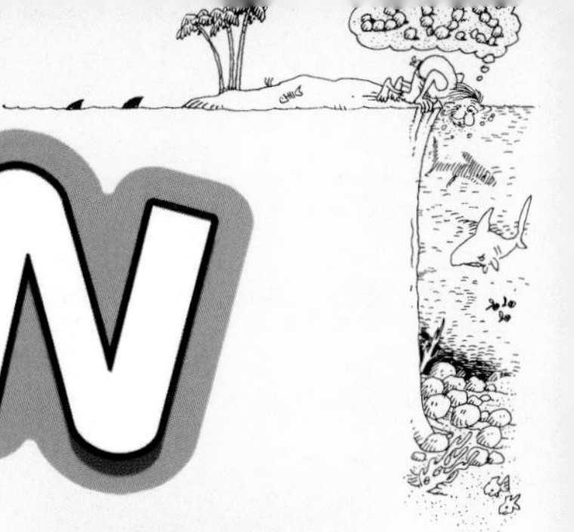

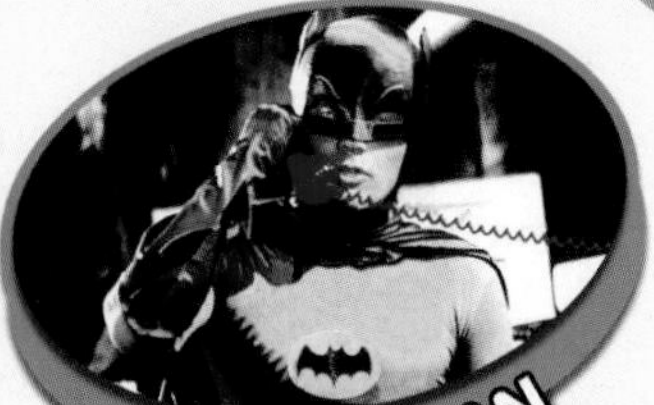

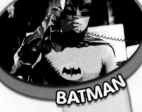

BATMAN

has a sidekick named...

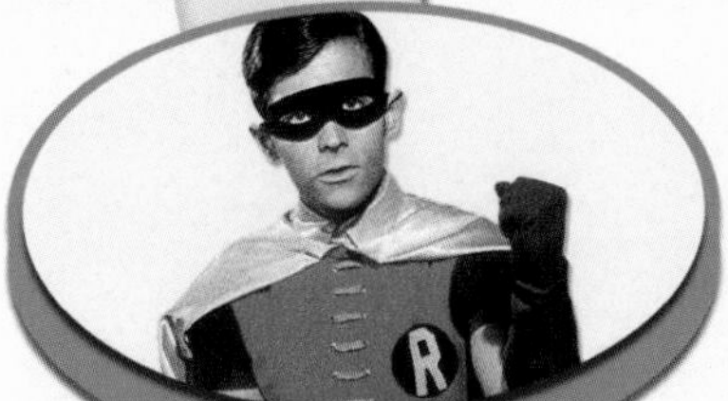

ROBIN

as does...

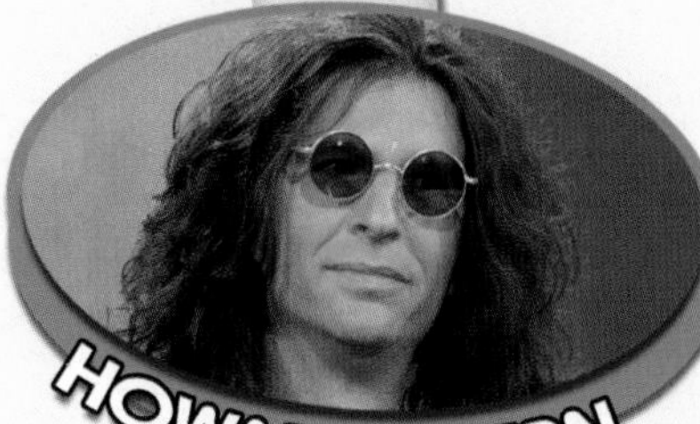

HOWARD STERN

who frequently encourages his guests to...

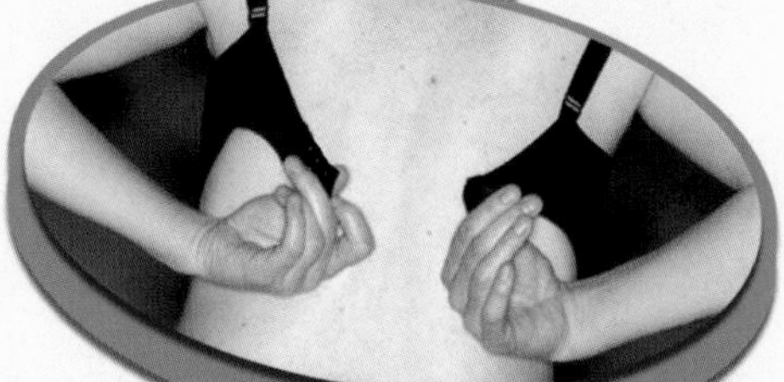

STRIP

which is what you call a serving of...

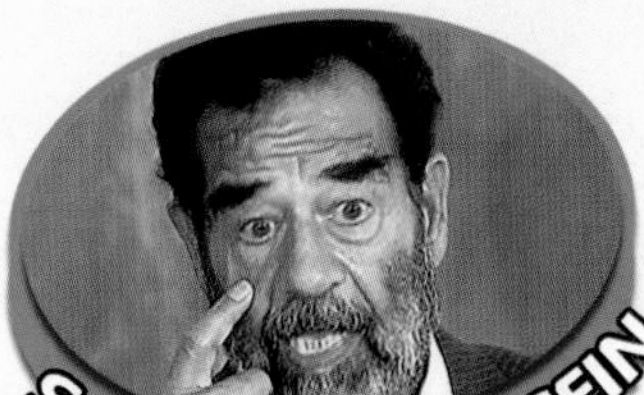

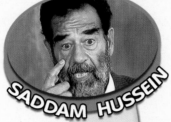

SADDAM HUSSEIN

is the former leader of...

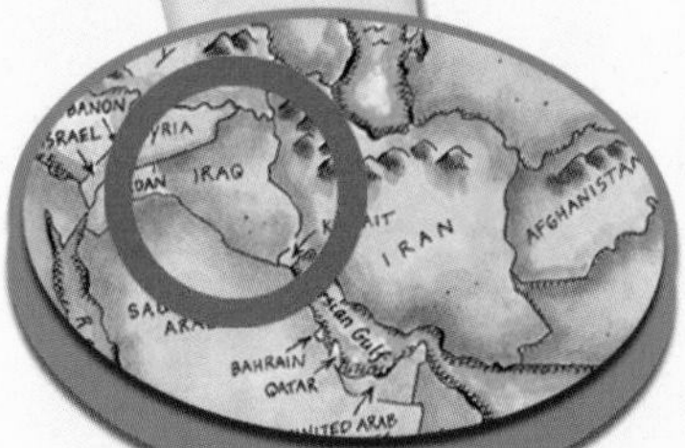
IRAQ
IRAN
AFGHANISTAN
BAHRAIN
QATAR

IRAQ

which is a country that borders...

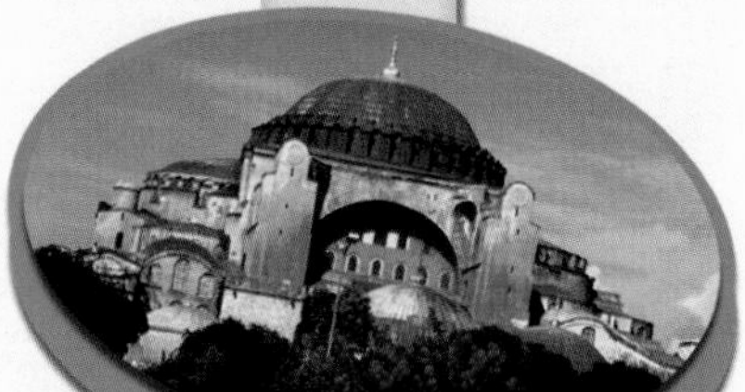

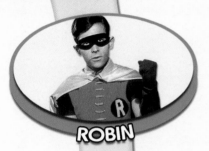

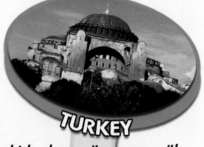

TURKEY

which shares its name with a key ingredient of a...

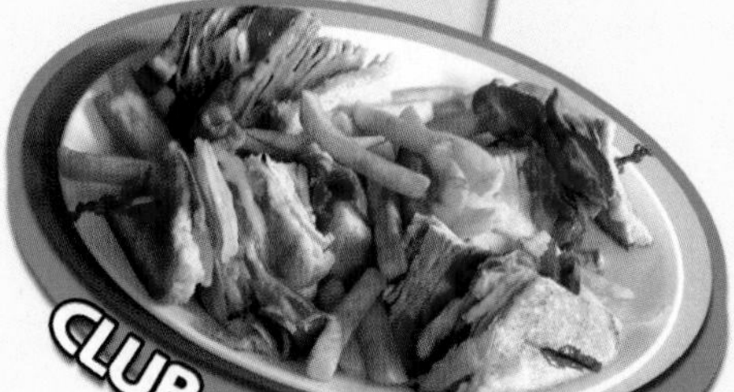

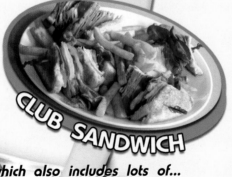

CLUB SANDWICH

which also includes lots of...

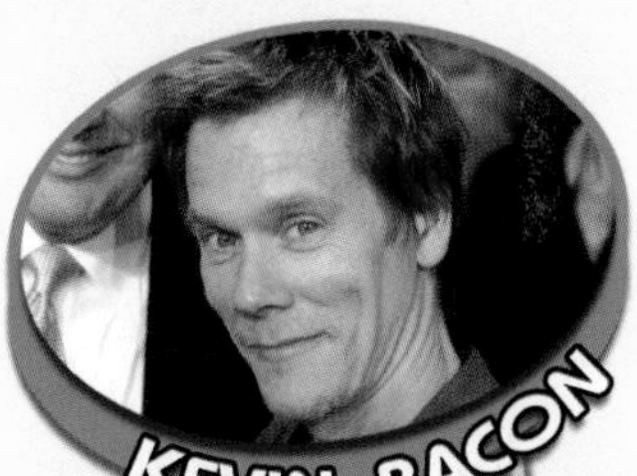

KEVIN BACON

appears in Mystic River with...

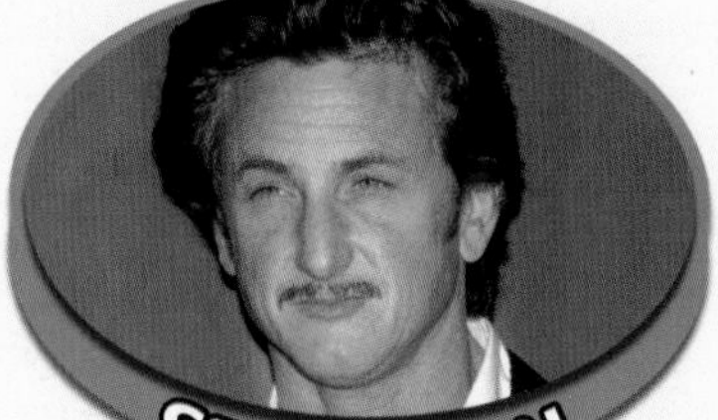

SEAN PENN

who was in The Thin Red Line with...

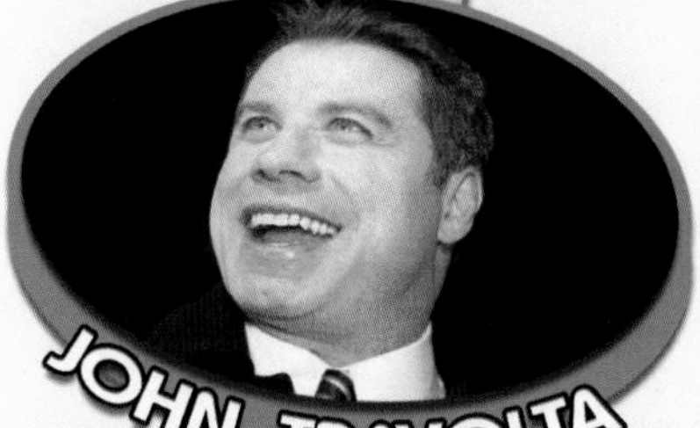

JOHN TRAVOLTA

who was the star of...

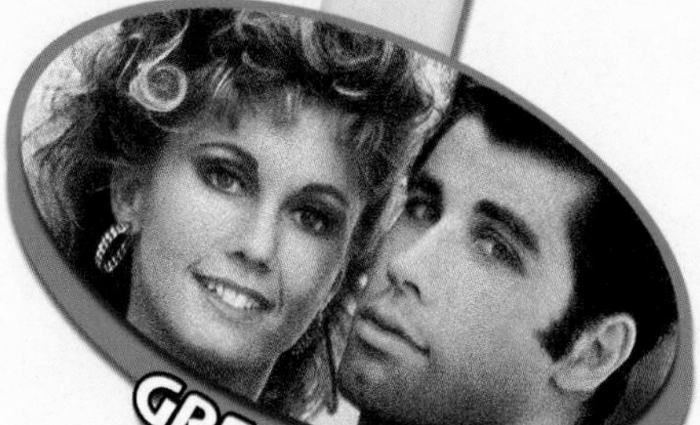

GREASE

which is what's left in the pan after you fry up some...

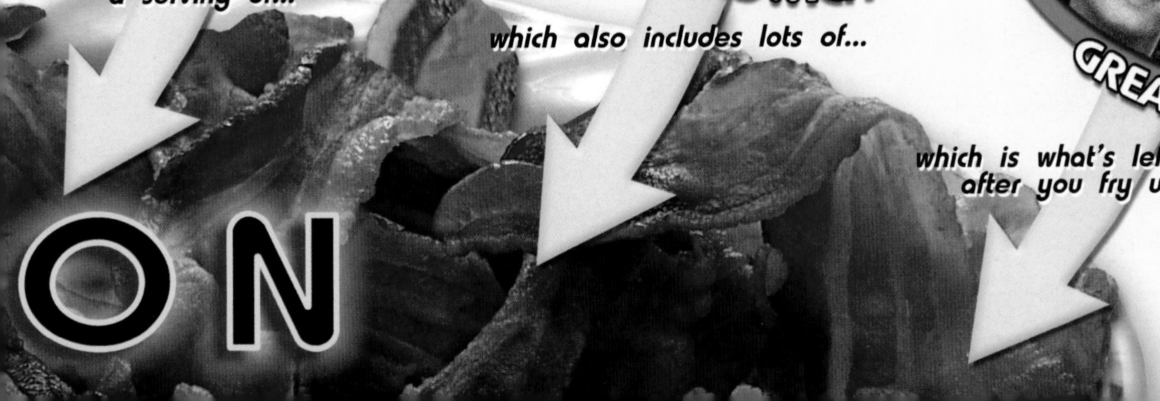

ON

MAD thanks the Bacon Council for its invaluable assistance in preparing this article.

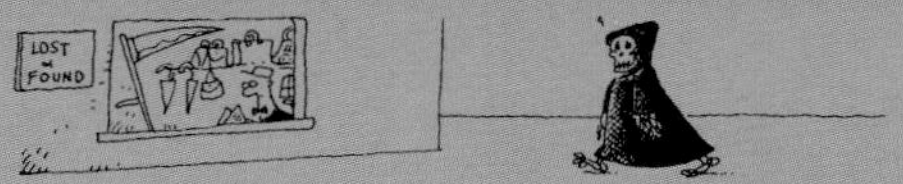
LOST & FOUND

Planet TAD!!!!!

http://www.galaxyo'blogs.com/planettad

Search

Planet TAD!!!!!

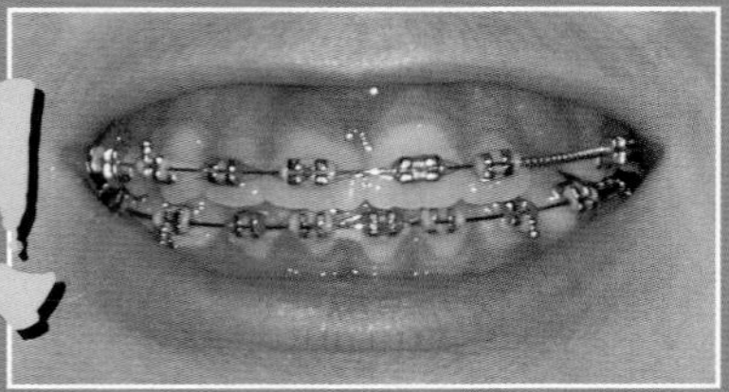

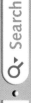

[**About Me**]

[**Name**|Tad]
[**Grade**|9]
[**Favorite aircraft**|Flying squirrel]

[21 May|**10:37am**]

[**mood**| dizzy]

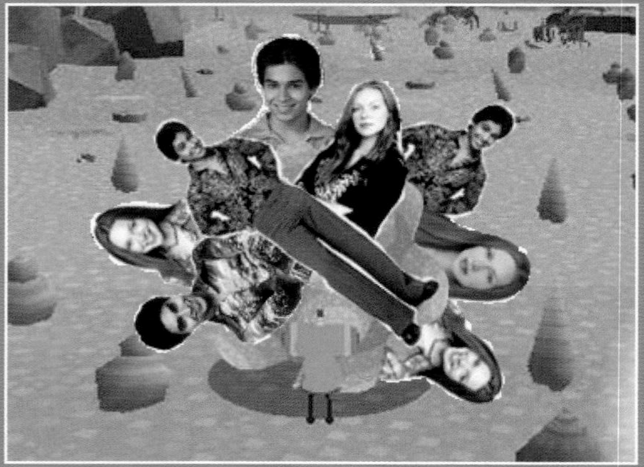

Ugh. I don't feel so good. I spent five hours yesterday at Evan's house, switching between playing We Love Katamari and watching That '70s Show reruns on FX. Then I came home and spent the whole night dreaming that I was rolling up a lot of little Wilmer Valderramas and Laura Prepons into a giant ball.

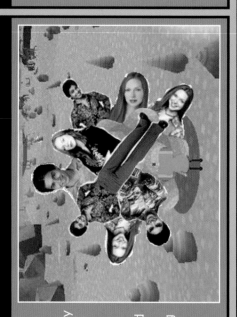

[22 May|**02:58pm**]

[**mood**| irked]

Attention, friends of Tad!

If you go onto MySpace and find this profile with my name on it, please be aware that IT IS NOT my profile! It is a fake profile that my friend Chet put up. He thought it would be funny. But if I had a MySpace profile, I wouldn't list my interests as "nose-picking, butt-scratching, playing classical banjo and dressing up like a girl." I don't even like the banjo.

However, rest assured that this profile of Chet is the real one. Honestly, I'm as surprised as anyone to find out that Chet cried at the end of Titanic and still wets the bed, but if that's what his profile says, then it must be true.

[23 May|**08:03pm**]

[**mood**| pseudo-sad]

Oh, man. So I came down to breakfast this morning, and my mom looked really sad, and my dad said: "Your great-aunt Sophie died yesterday." And I said, "Which one was she?" And my dad said, "She was your mother's father's sister." And I said, "The one with the bright-red hair?" And my mom said, "No. That's your great-aunt Katie. Sophie's the one with the cane." And I said, "Oh! You mean the mean one who always picked her terrier up by the neck? Wasn't she dead already?" And my dad gave me a look that told me that that was the wrong thing to say.

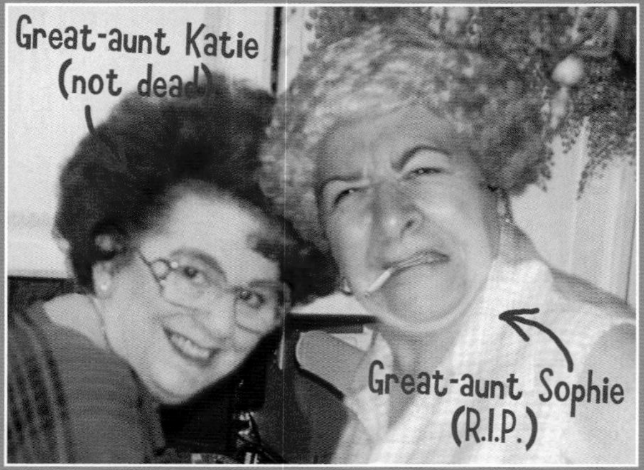
Great-aunt Katie (not dead)
Great-aunt Sophie (R.I.P.)

My little sister Sophie's pretty upset — she was named for our great-aunt Sophie. She came into my room tonight and said, "Where do you think aunt Sophie went?" And I gave her the same answer my parents gave me when our golden retriever died: Great-aunt Sophie was taken to a farm where she gets to spend all day chasing rabbits and playing with other great aunts.

That seemed to make her happy.

[24 May|**05:26pm**]

I wonder how it is that the X-Men all got their names. Like, did they get to pick their own? I'm sure that Storm wasn't named "Storm" by her parents, and, coincidentally, wound up being able to control the weather. I bet there was some time for all of them where they tried out different names to see if they would fit. Like, for a couple of weeks, Cyclops had everyone calling him "Shades", and Wolverine went around practicing signing his name as "Slicey-Hands", just to see if that seemed like a good fit for him.

[25 May|**04:33pm**]

[**mood**| slightly irregular]

After school today, Mom took me to the outlet mall to buy a new suit for great-aunt Sophie's funeral, because I outgrew my last one. Mom always takes me to the outlet mall to get clothes. One day, when I'm older, I want to wear clothes whose labels don't have the words "SLIGHTLY IRREGULAR" stamped on them. I wanted to get a bright red suit, like Jack White wears, but Mom wouldn't let me — she got me a really boring dark-grey one instead. When I got it home and showed my dad, he said, "Are you leaning over to your left?" And I said, "No." That's when we realized that the right arm was a lot shorter than the left one. Stupid irregular suit. Now I'm going to have to spend all day Saturday leaning slightly to the right, to compensate.

[25 May|**07:12pm**]

[**mood**| puzzled]

Do Chinese people have Scrabble?

[26 May|**03:50pm**]

Today in history class we learned about the Donner Party, which is nowhere near as much fun as the word "party" makes it sound. I guess they were a group of pioneers who were going across the country and ran out of food, so they wound up eating each other. I think there was more to the story, but I spent the rest of the period distracted by trying to figure out how that worked — like, did they cook the people they ate? Or eat them raw? How did they decide who'd get eaten and who'd be doing the eating? Did they just start with the fat guys? Or what? I looked through my textbook for more information, but they didn't have anything — not even a recipe. I hate textbooks. They always leave out the most important parts.

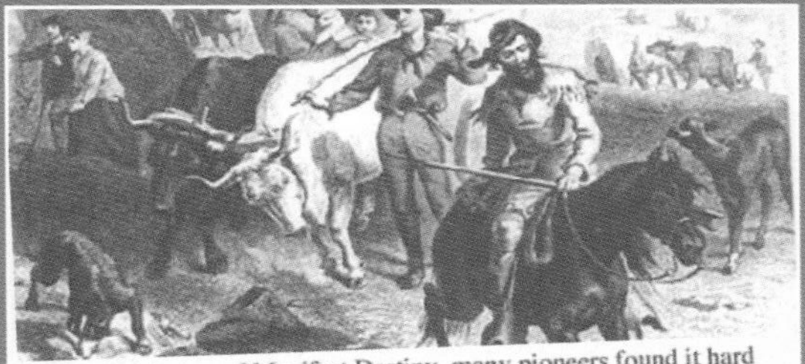

During the era of Manifest Destiny, many pioneers found it hard going on the plains. The notorious Donner Party found itself stranded for a winter, leading them to turn to cannibalism.

I also think that the Donner Party's situation would have made for the best episode of Little House on the Prairie ever.

[27 May|**03:02pm**]

[**mood**| relieved]

Well, today was the funeral. Everyone said nice things about great-aunt Sophie, but the truth is, she smoked nonstop and hit her terrier with her cane and was super-mean. She wasn't a nice lady. But I guess you can't say that at a funeral. So everyone pretended to be really sad. Except for her terrier. He looked happier than I'd ever seen him. He spent the whole funeral licking his 'nads non-stop. We all pretended not to notice.

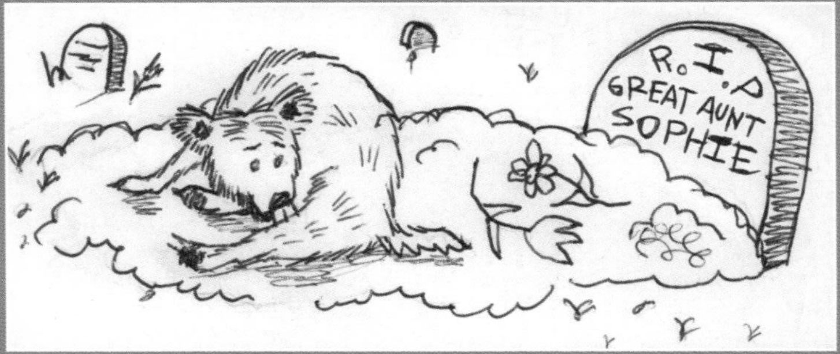
R.I.P
GREAT AUNT
SOPHIE

WRITER: TIM CARVELL ARTIST: BRIAN DURNIAK

One Fine Morning In the Windy City

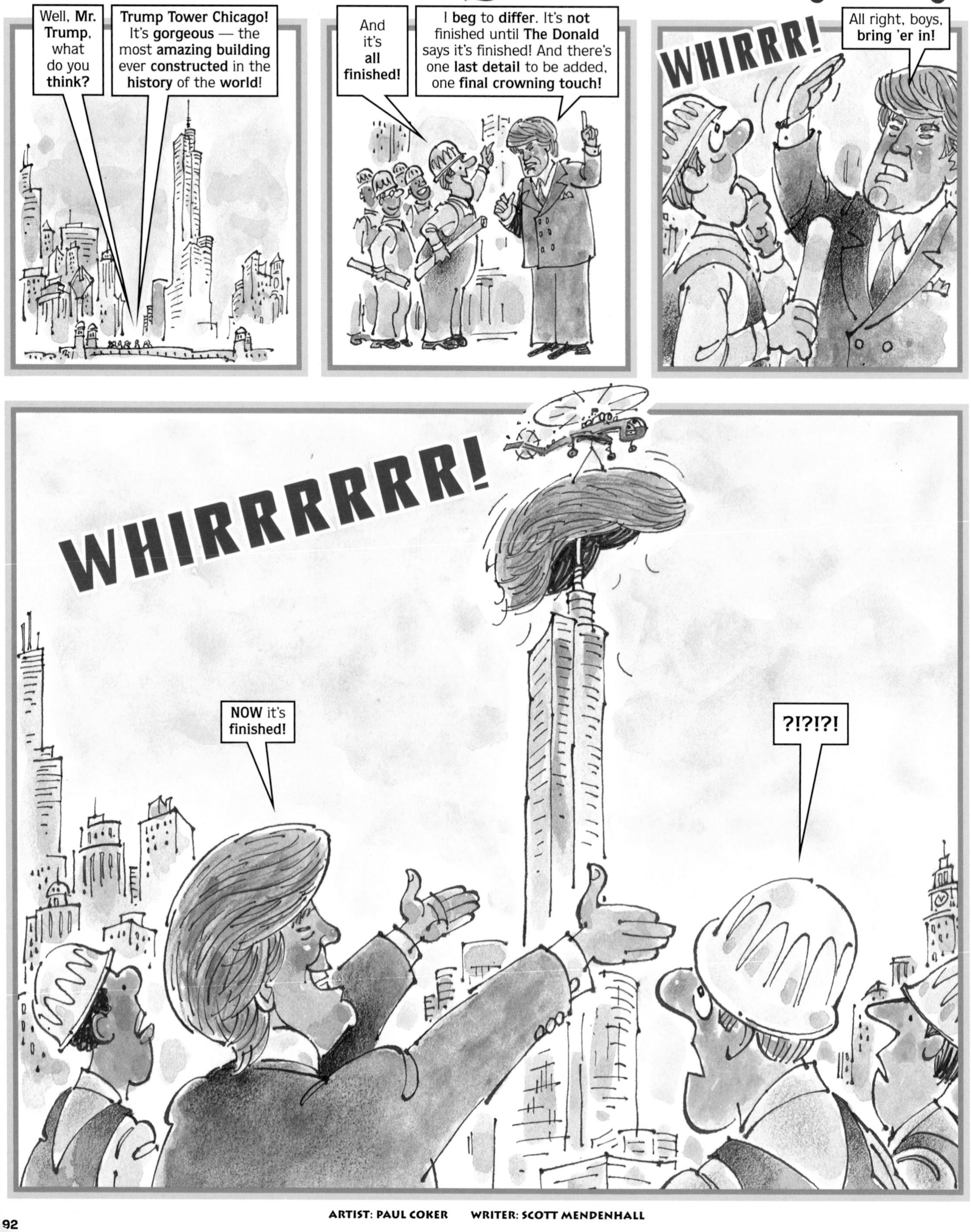
Well, Mr. Trump, what do you think?
Trump Tower Chicago! It's gorgeous — the most amazing building ever constructed in the history of the world!
And it's all finished!
I beg to differ. It's not finished until The Donald says it's finished! And there's one last detail to be added, one final crowning touch!
WHIRRR!
All right, boys, bring 'er in!
WHIRRRRRRR!
NOW it's finished!
?!?!?!

ARTIST: PAUL COKER WRITER: SCOTT MENDENHALL

PEN AND STINK DEPT.

The Comic Club

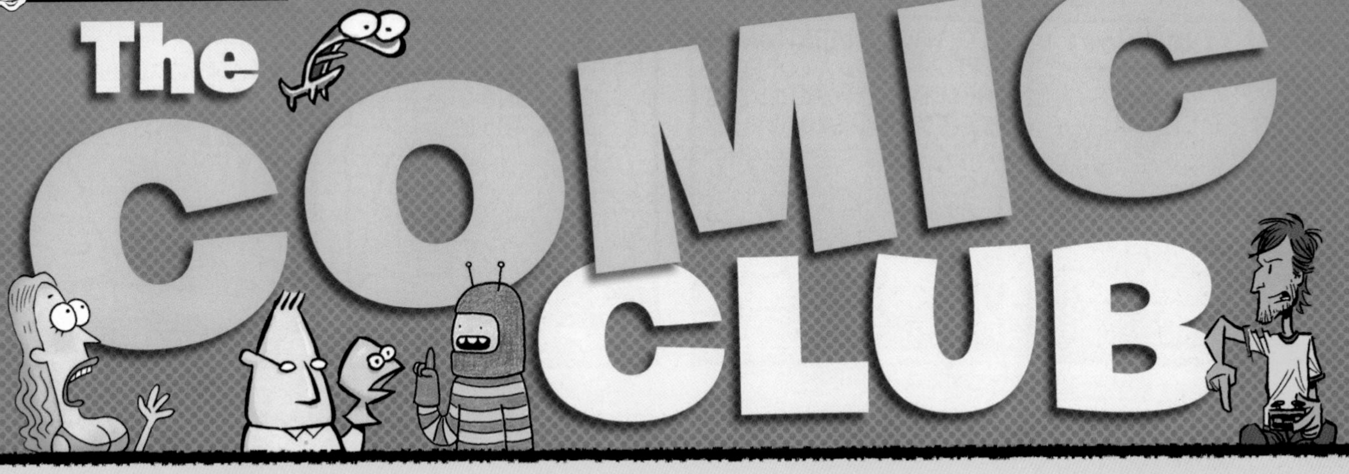

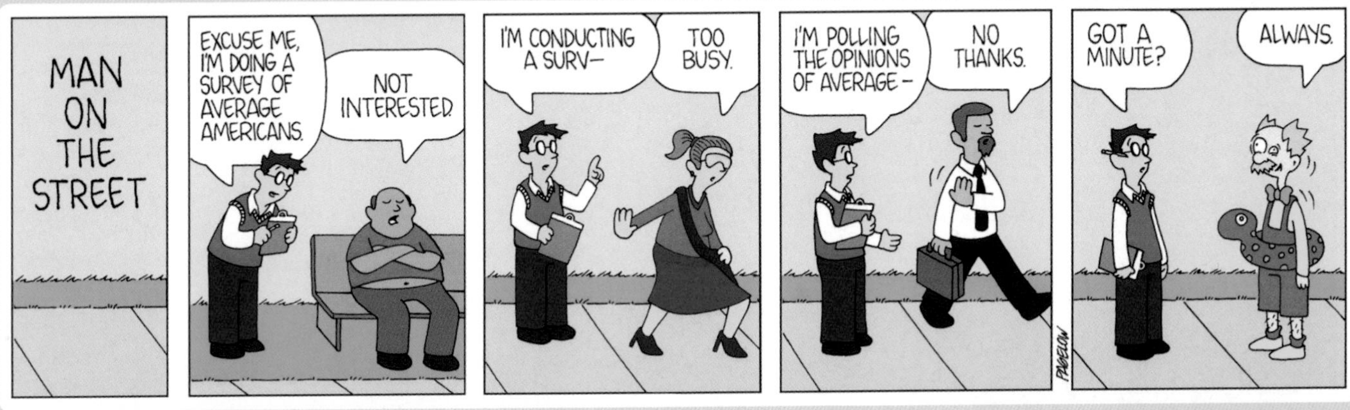

MAN ON THE STREET
EXCUSE ME, I'M DOING A SURVEY OF AVERAGE AMERICANS.
NOT INTERESTED.
I'M CONDUCTING A SURV—
TOO BUSY.
I'M POLLING THE OPINIONS OF AVERAGE—
NO THANKS.
GOT A MINUTE?
ALWAYS.
PAGELOW

RYAN PAGELOW

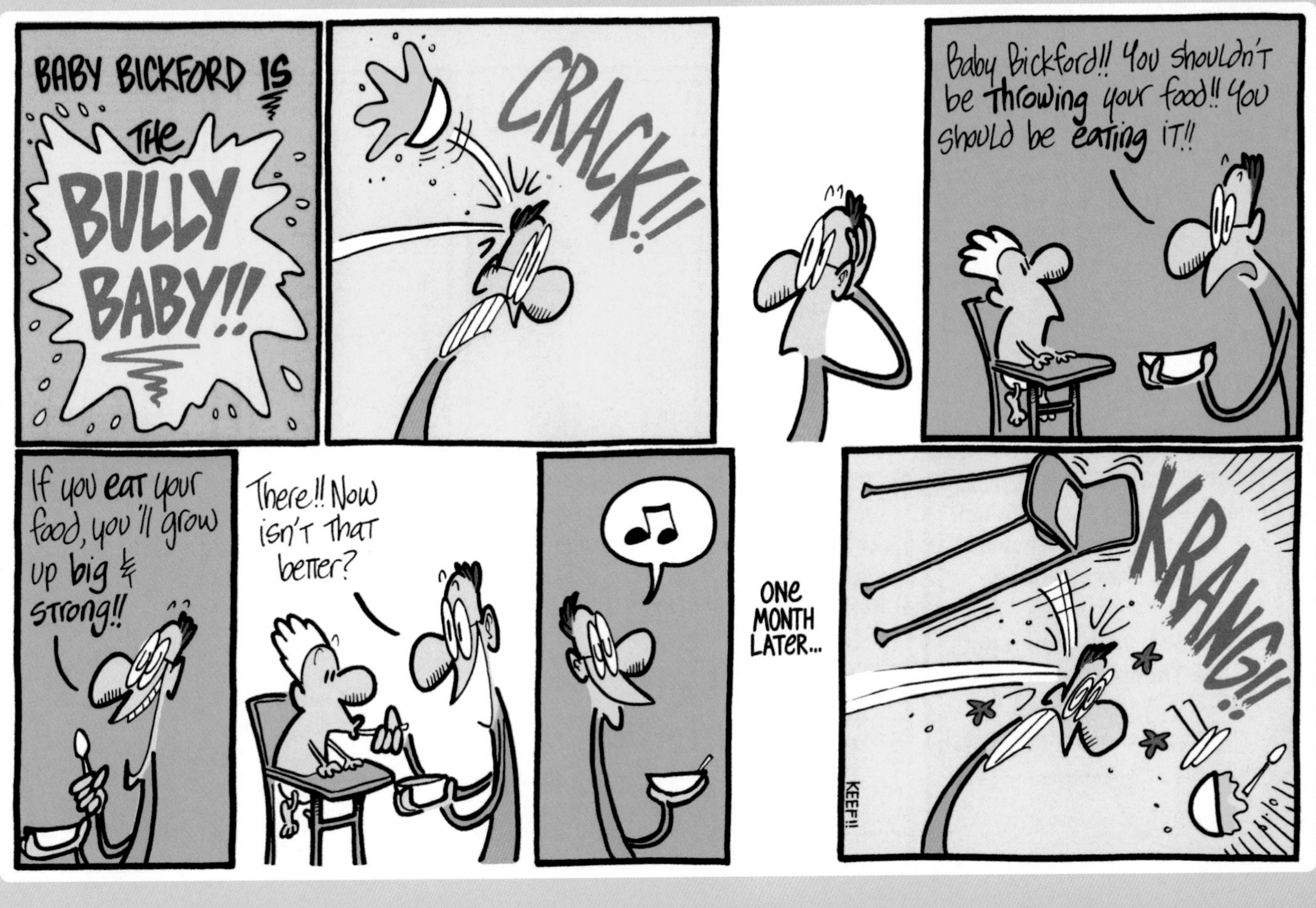

BABY BICKFORD IS THE BULLY BABY!!
CRACK!!
Baby Bickford!! You shouldn't be throwing your food!! You should be eating it!!
If you eat your food, you'll grow up big & strong!!
There!! Now isn't that better?
ONE MONTH LATER...
KRANG!!
KEEF!!

KEITH KNIGHT

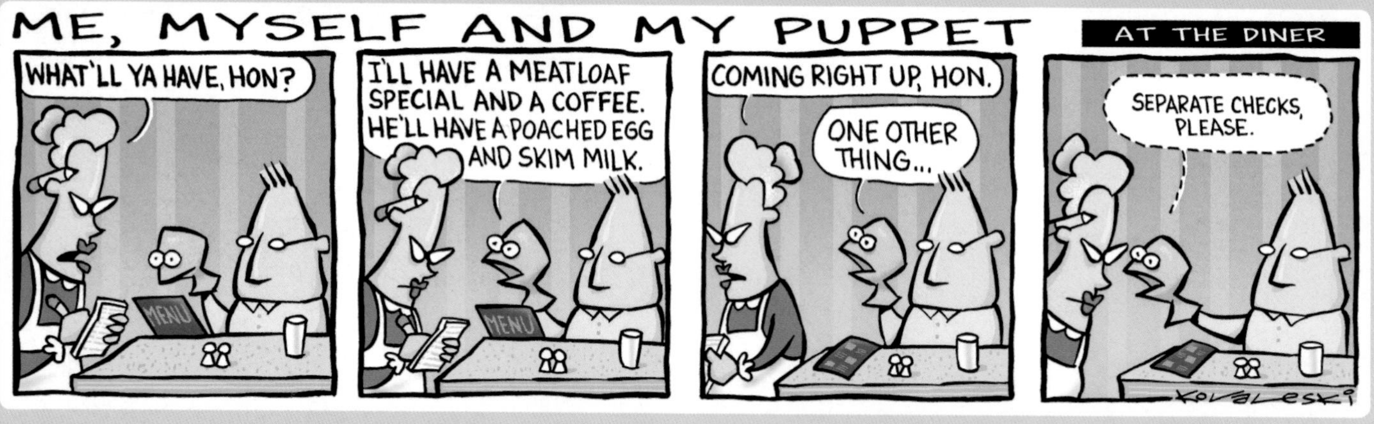
ME, MYSELF AND MY PUPPET
AT THE DINER
WHAT'LL YA HAVE, HON?
MENU
I'LL HAVE A MEATLOAF SPECIAL AND A COFFEE. HE'LL HAVE A POACHED EGG AND SKIM MILK.
MENU
COMING RIGHT UP, HON.
ONE OTHER THING...
SEPARATE CHECKS, PLEASE.
KOVALESKI

JOHN KOVALESKI

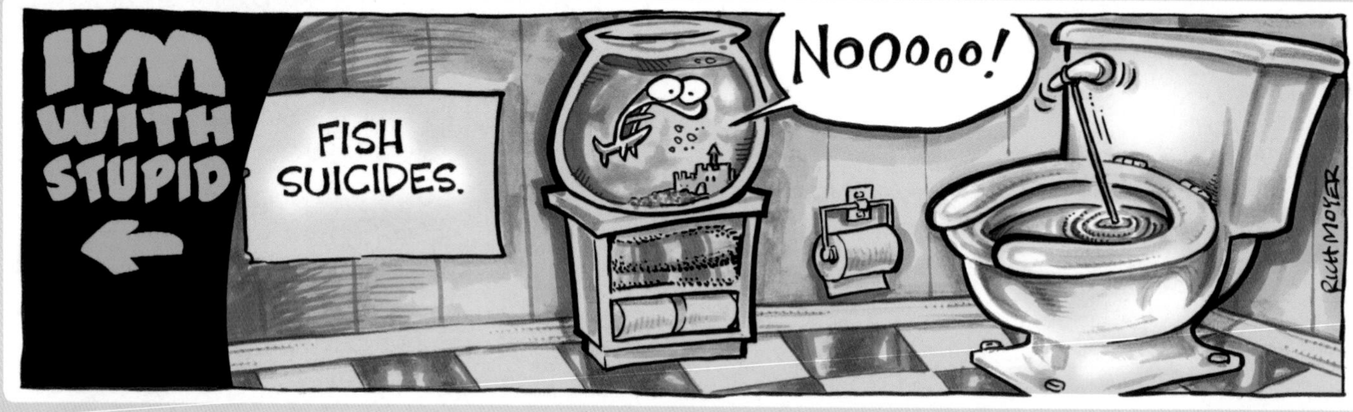
I'M WITH STUPID
FISH SUICIDES.
Nooooo!
RICH MOYER

RICH MOYER

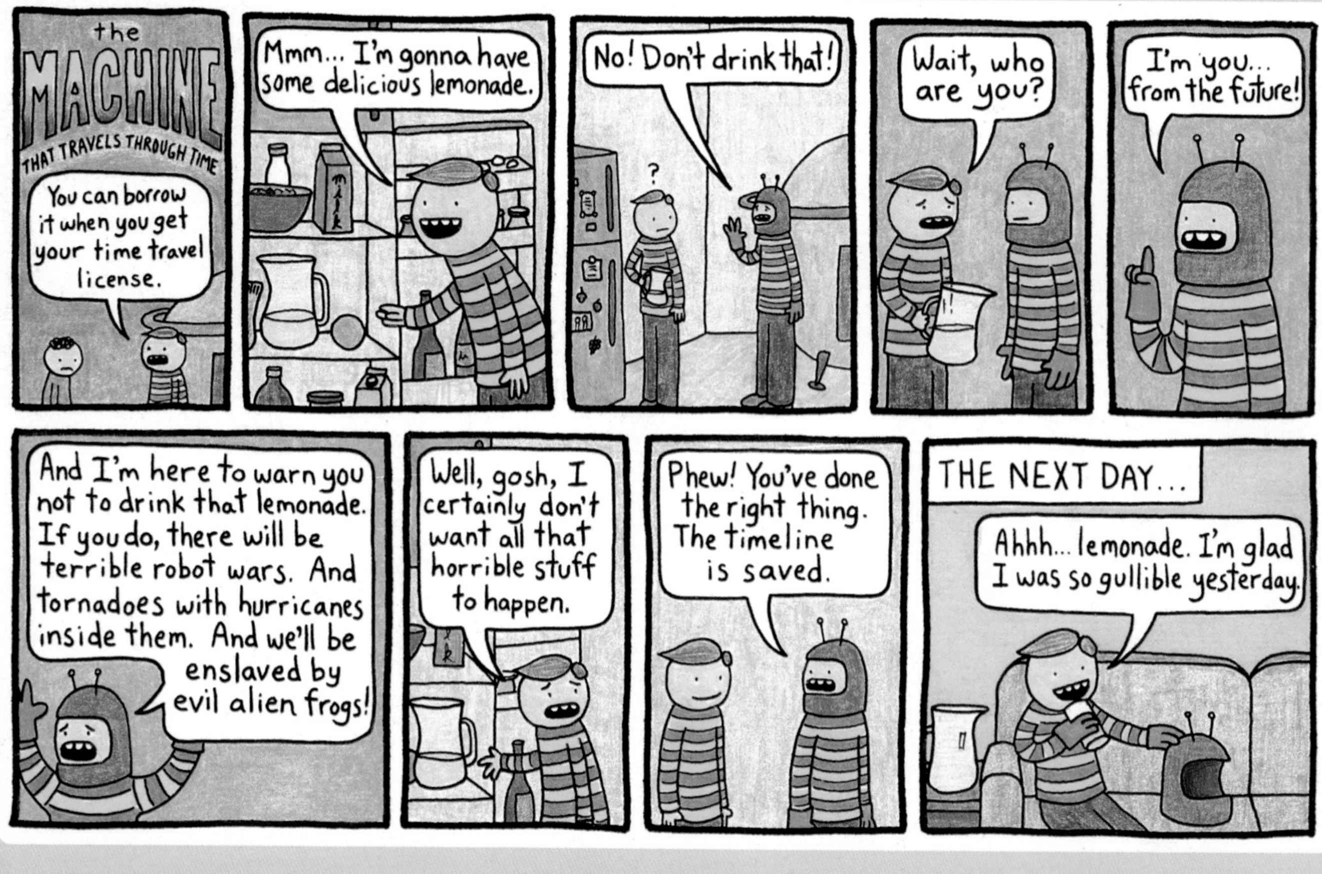
the MACHINE THAT TRAVELS THROUGH TIME
You can borrow it when you get your time travel license.
Mmm... I'm gonna have some delicious lemonade.
MILK
No! Don't drink that!
?
Wait, who are you?
I'm you... from the future!
And I'm here to warn you not to drink that lemonade. If you do, there will be terrible robot wars. And tornadoes with hurricanes inside them. And we'll be enslaved by evil alien frogs!
Well, gosh, I certainly don't want all that horrible stuff to happen.
Phew! You've done the right thing. The timeline is saved.
THE NEXT DAY...
Ahhh... lemonade. I'm glad I was so gullible yesterday.

JOEY ALISON SAYERS

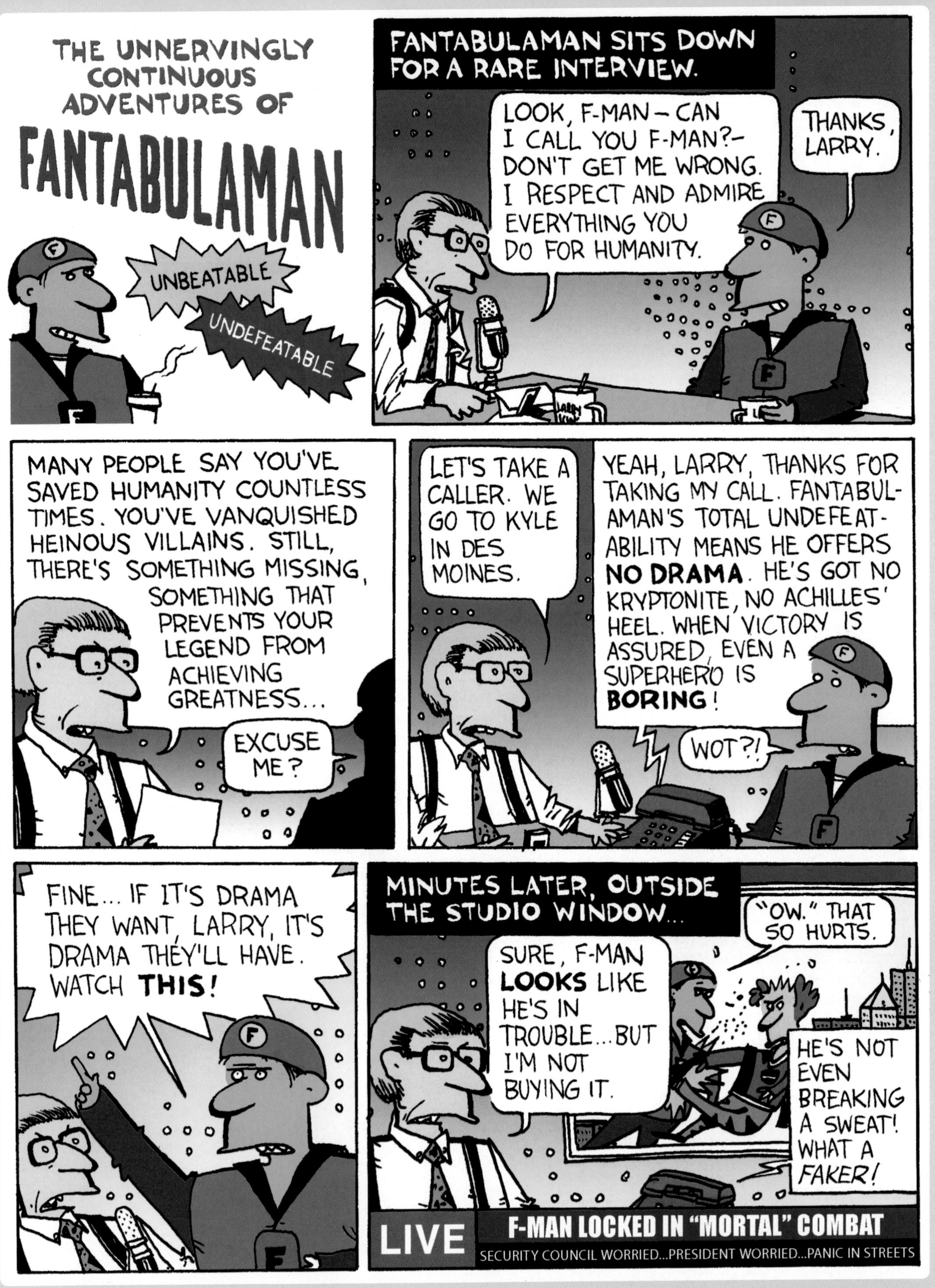
THE UNNERVINGLY CONTINUOUS ADVENTURES OF
FANTABULAMAN
UNBEATABLE
UNDEFEATABLE
FANTABULAMAN SITS DOWN FOR A RARE INTERVIEW.
LOOK, F-MAN – CAN I CALL YOU F-MAN?– DON'T GET ME WRONG. I RESPECT AND ADMIRE EVERYTHING YOU DO FOR HUMANITY.
THANKS, LARRY.
MANY PEOPLE SAY YOU'VE SAVED HUMANITY COUNTLESS TIMES. YOU'VE VANQUISHED HEINOUS VILLAINS. STILL, THERE'S SOMETHING MISSING, SOMETHING THAT PREVENTS YOUR LEGEND FROM ACHIEVING GREATNESS...
EXCUSE ME?
LET'S TAKE A CALLER. WE GO TO KYLE IN DES MOINES.
YEAH, LARRY, THANKS FOR TAKING MY CALL. FANTABULAMAN'S TOTAL UNDEFEATABILITY MEANS HE OFFERS **NO DRAMA**. HE'S GOT NO KRYPTONITE, NO ACHILLES' HEEL. WHEN VICTORY IS ASSURED, EVEN A SUPERHERO IS **BORING**!
WOT?!
FINE... IF IT'S DRAMA THEY WANT, LARRY, IT'S DRAMA THEY'LL HAVE. WATCH **THIS**!
MINUTES LATER, OUTSIDE THE STUDIO WINDOW...
SURE, F-MAN **LOOKS** LIKE HE'S IN TROUBLE...BUT I'M NOT BUYING IT.
"OW." THAT SO HURTS.
HE'S NOT EVEN BREAKING A SWEAT! WHAT A *FAKER*!
LIVE
F-MAN LOCKED IN "MORTAL" COMBAT
SECURITY COUNCIL WORRIED...PRESIDENT WORRIED...PANIC IN STREETS
TED RALL

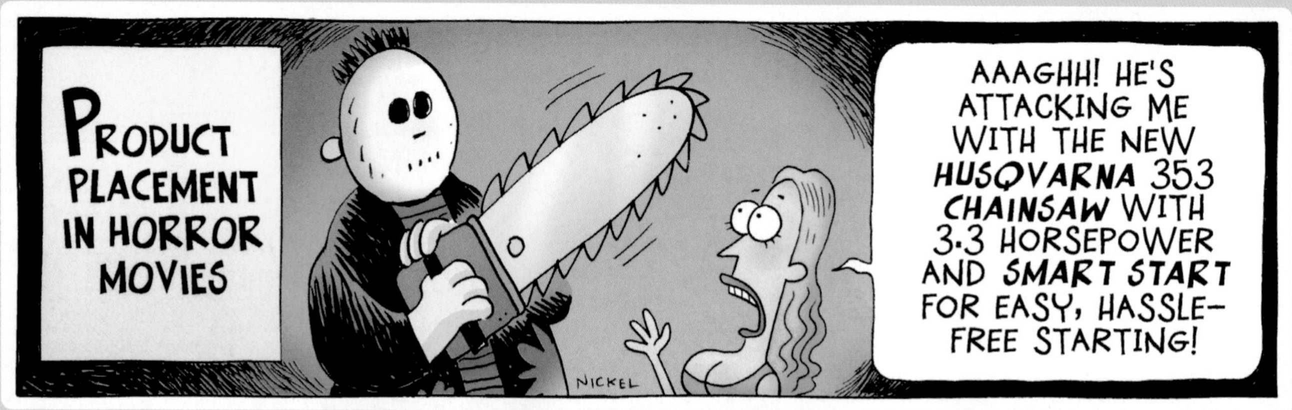
PRODUCT PLACEMENT IN HORROR MOVIES
AAAGHH! HE'S ATTACKING ME WITH THE NEW HUSQVARNA 353 CHAINSAW WITH 3.3 HORSEPOWER AND SMART START FOR EASY, HASSLE-FREE STARTING!
NICKEL

SCOTT NICKEL

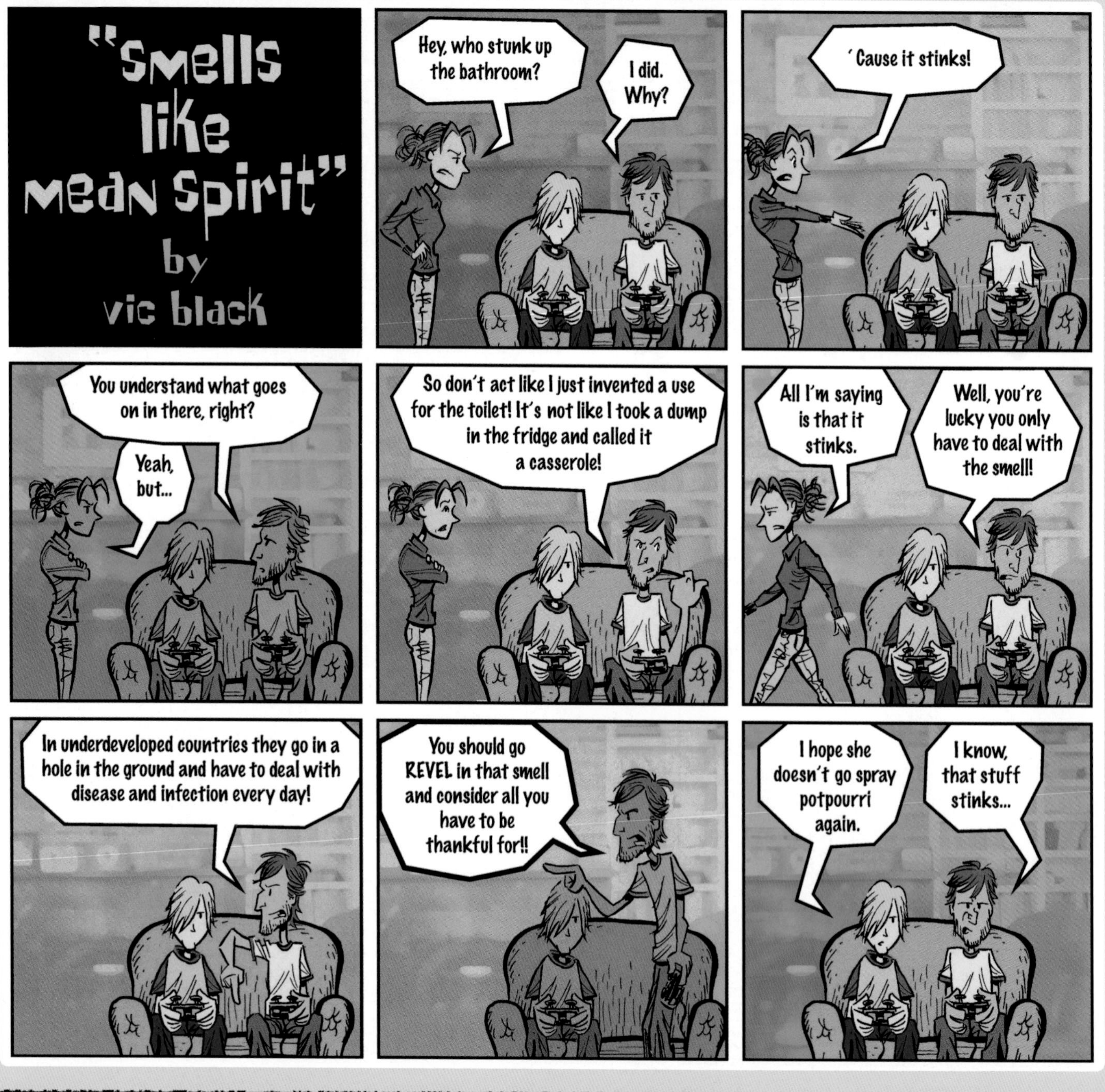
"Smells like mean spirit" by vic black
Hey, who stunk up the bathroom?
I did. Why?
'Cause it stinks!
You understand what goes on in there, right?
Yeah, but...
So don't act like I just invented a use for the toilet! It's not like I took a dump in the fridge and called it a casserole!
All I'm saying is that it stinks.
Well, you're lucky you only have to deal with the smell!
In underdeveloped countries they go in a hole in the ground and have to deal with disease and infection every day!
You should go REVEL in that smell and consider all you have to be thankful for!!
I hope she doesn't go spray potpourri again.
I know, that stuff stinks...

VIC BLACK

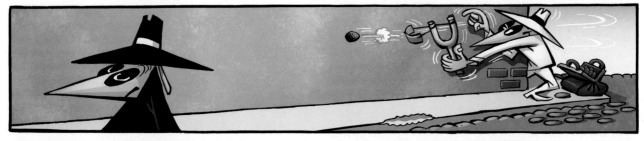

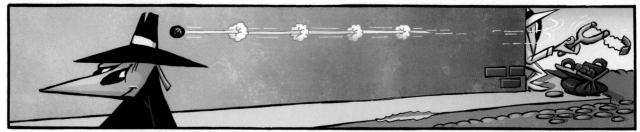

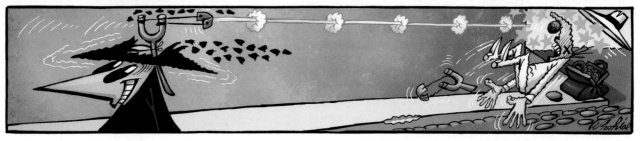

WRITER AND ARTIST: ANTONIO PROHIAS   COLORIST: CARRIE STRACHAN

In the last few years, it seems like everything around us has become sponsored by corporations. There's nothing as exciting as going to the Staples Center box office to pick up tickets for the Jeep Music Festival, unless you're taking in a ball game at Tropicana Field! Pretty soon, we won't be able to go anywhere that doesn't have a corporate handle! For that fateful day, here's MAD's handy guide to let you know...

WHEN CORPORATE OUT OF

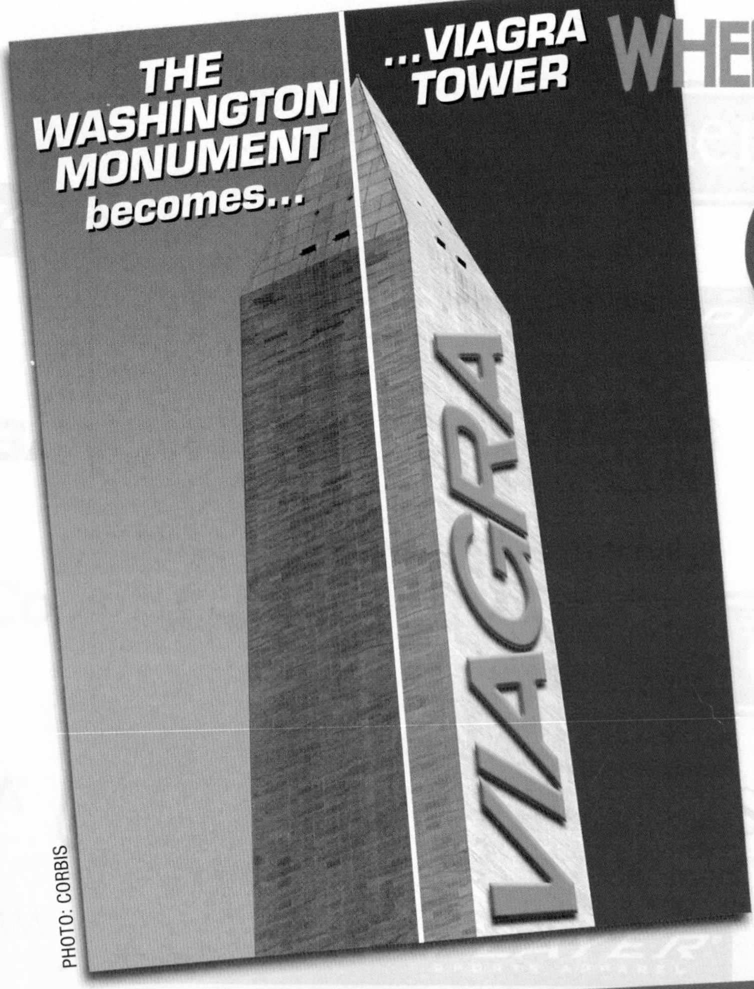
THE WASHINGTON MONUMENT becomes...
...VIAGRA TOWER
VIAGRA
PHOTO: CORBIS

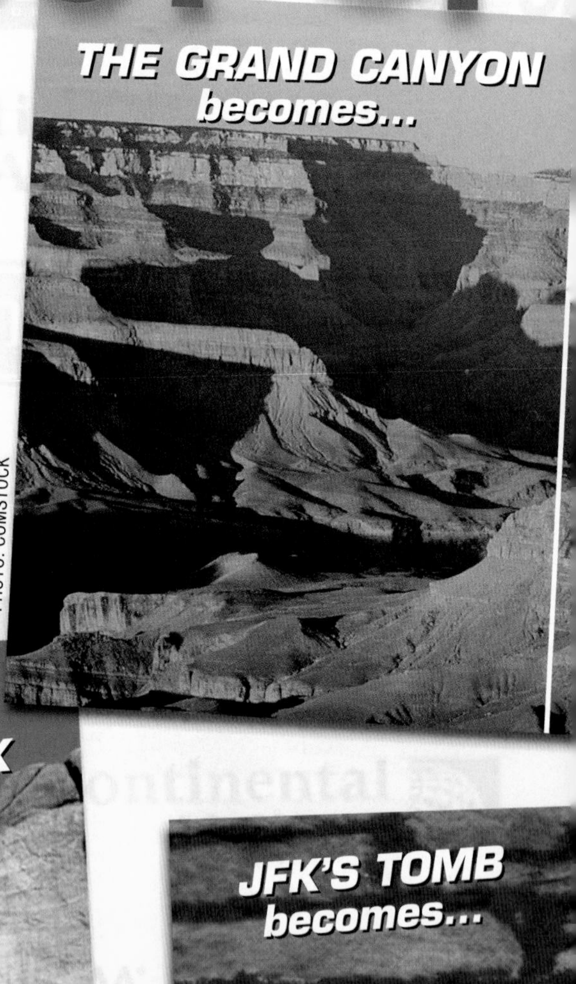
THE GRAND CANYON becomes...
PHOTO: COMSTOCK

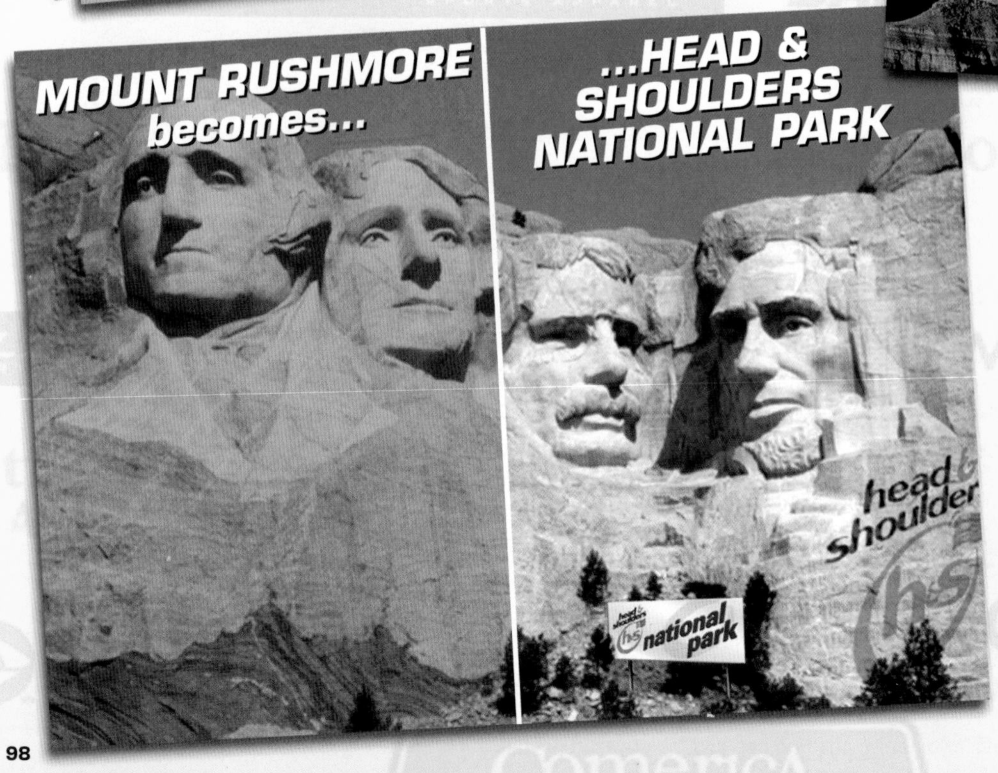
MOUNT RUSHMORE becomes...
...HEAD & SHOULDERS NATIONAL PARK
head & shoulders
national park

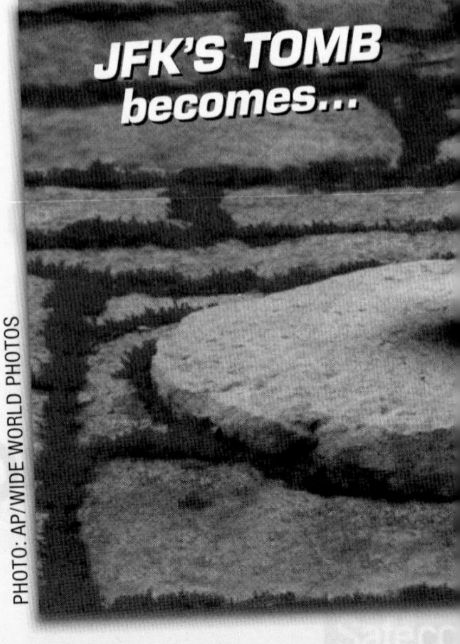
JFK'S TOMB becomes...
PHOTO: AP/WIDE WORLD PHOTOS

NAMING GETS CONTROL

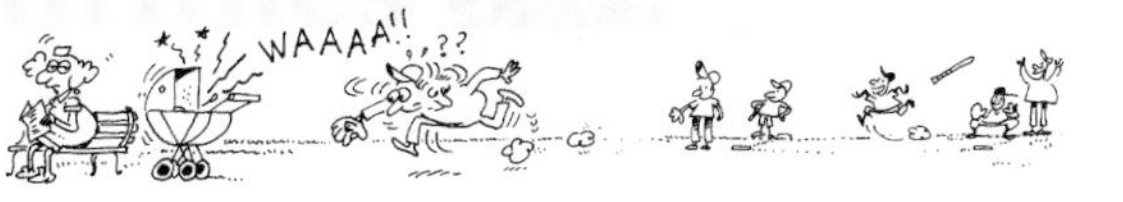
WAAAA!!
??

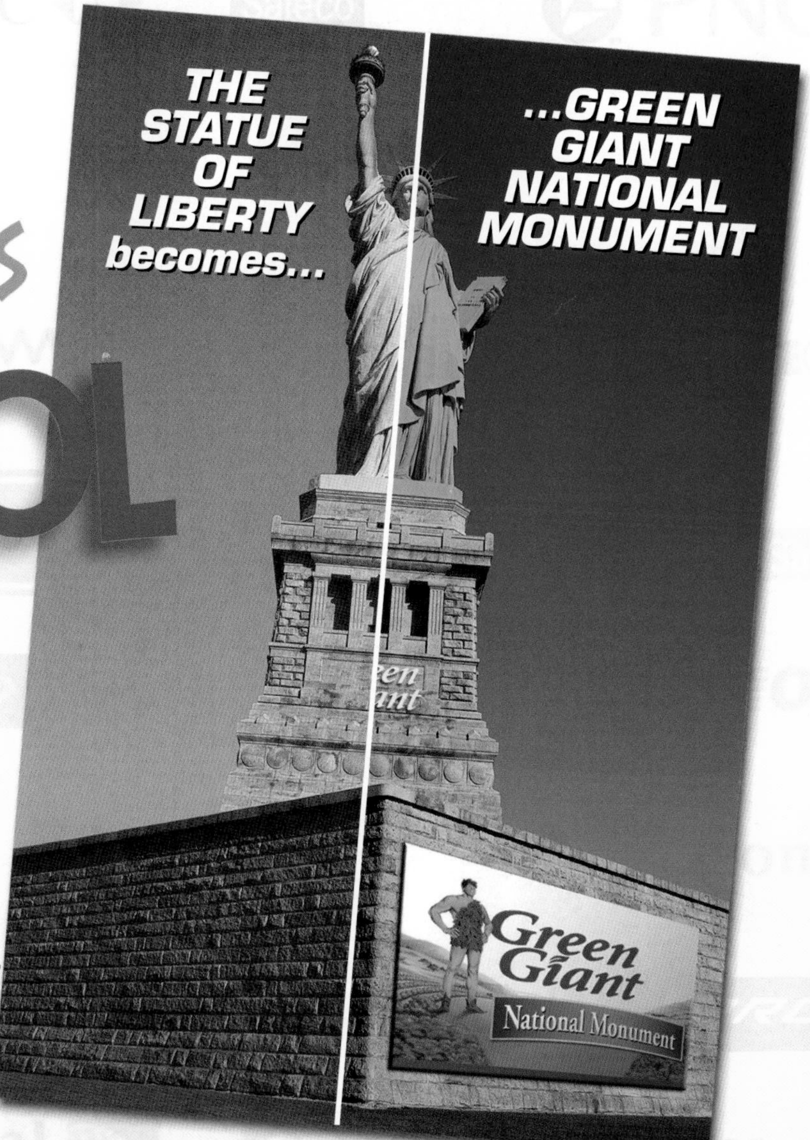
THE STATUE OF LIBERTY becomes...
...GREEN GIANT NATIONAL MONUMENT
Green Giant
National Monument

PHOTO: CORBIS

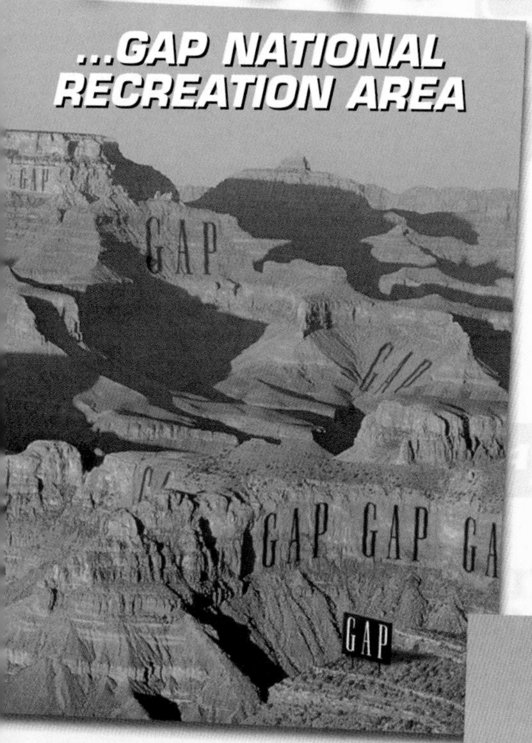
...GAP NATIONAL RECREATION AREA
GAP
GAP GAP
GAP

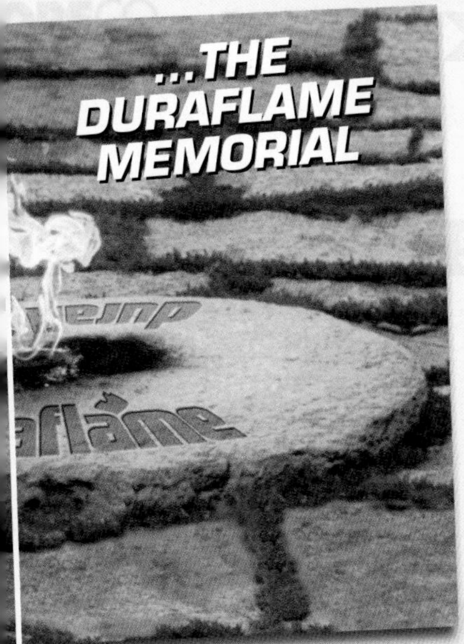
...THE DURAFLAME MEMORIAL

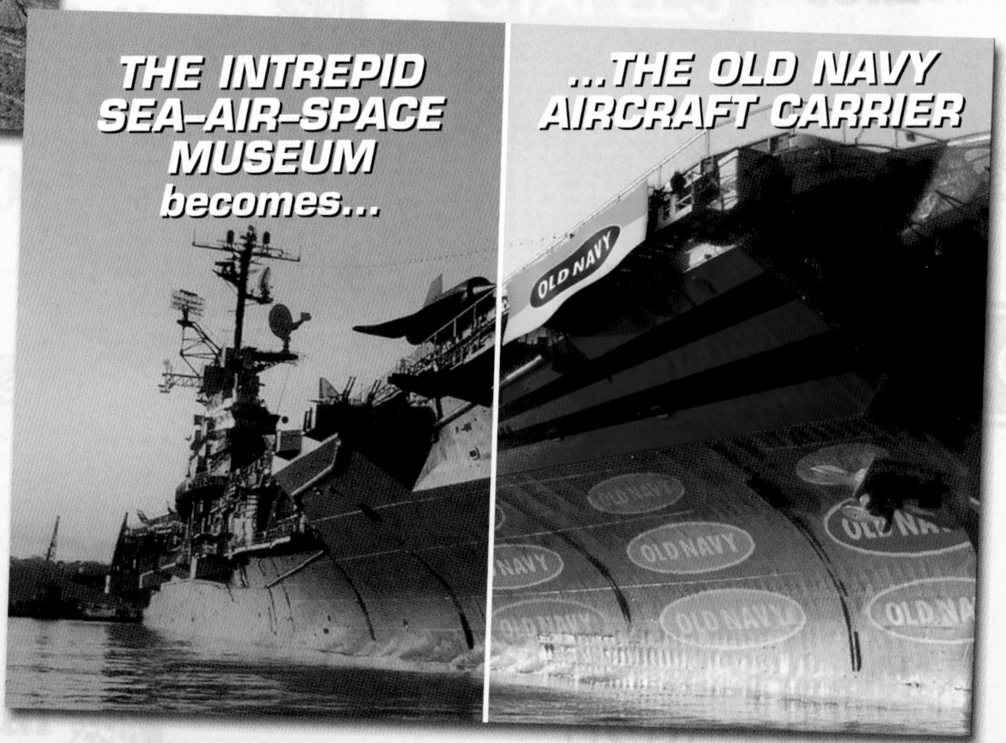
THE INTREPID SEA-AIR-SPACE MUSEUM becomes...
...THE OLD NAVY AIRCRAFT CARRIER
OLD NAVY
OLD NAVY
OLD NAVY

WRITER: JACOB LAMBERT

ONE DAY AT THE BULLFIGHTS

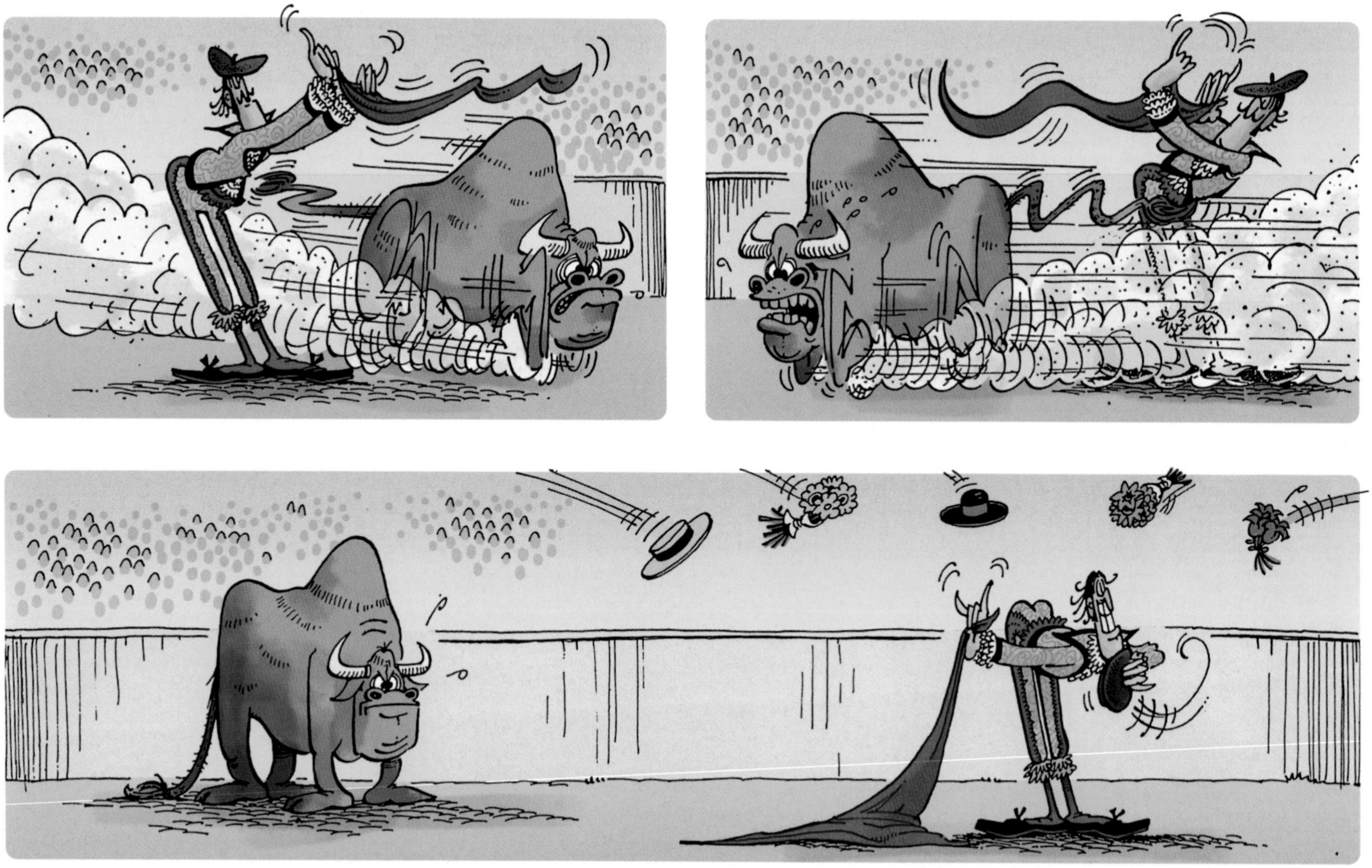

WRITER AND ARTIST: DON MARTIN   COLORIST: CARL PETERSON

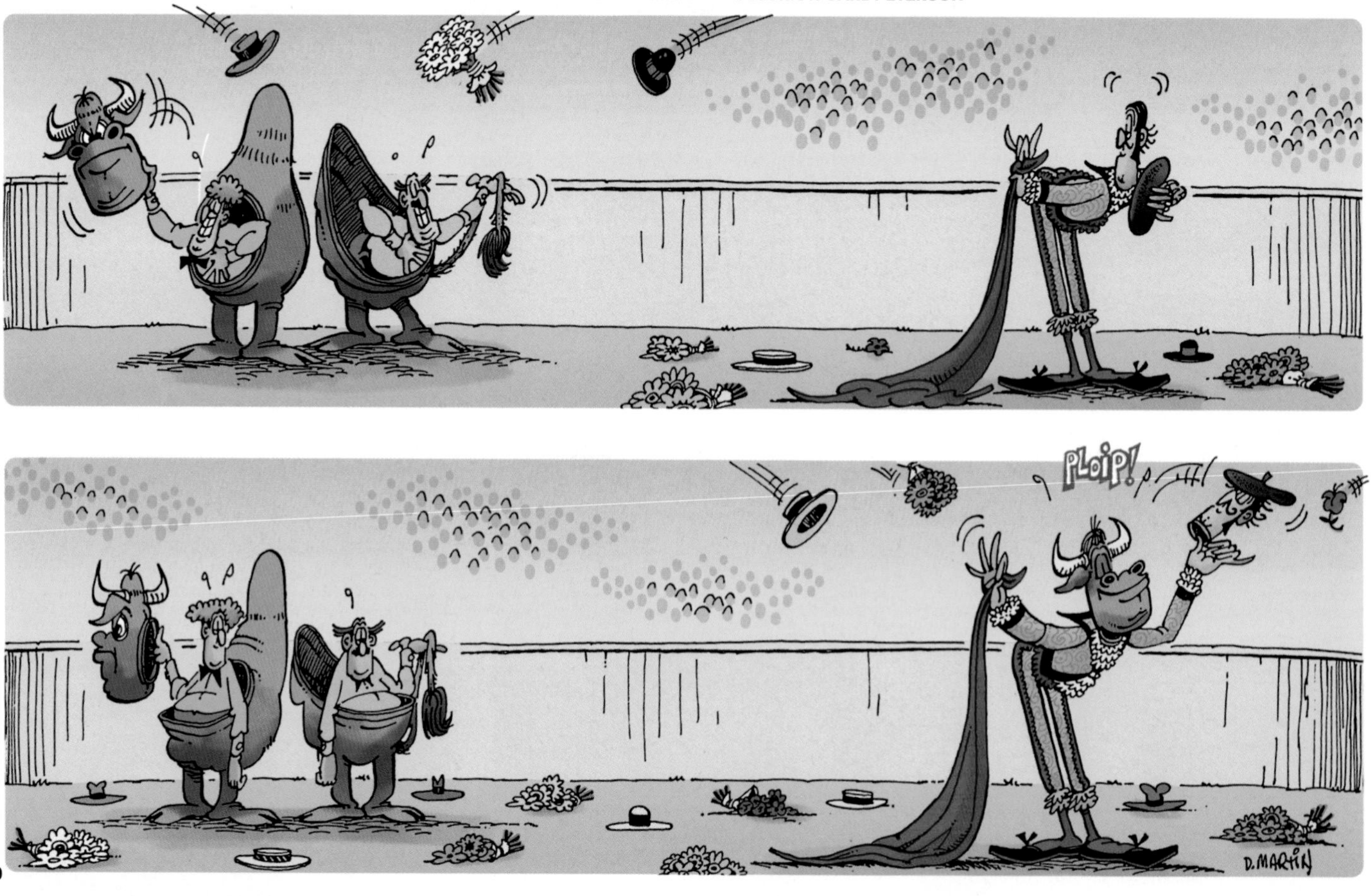
PLOIP!
D. MARTIN

R2-D2-STEP DEPT.

Let's face it, *Dancing with the Stars* is hurting real bad for quality contestants. (Kyle Massey, anyone?) If they want to save their sorry show, they should partner with a popular movie franchise — like *Star Wars* — and get some REAL characters on there! Actually, George Lucas will put the *Star Wars* name on pretty much ANYTHING, so chances are we'll actually get to see:

dancing with the STAR WARS

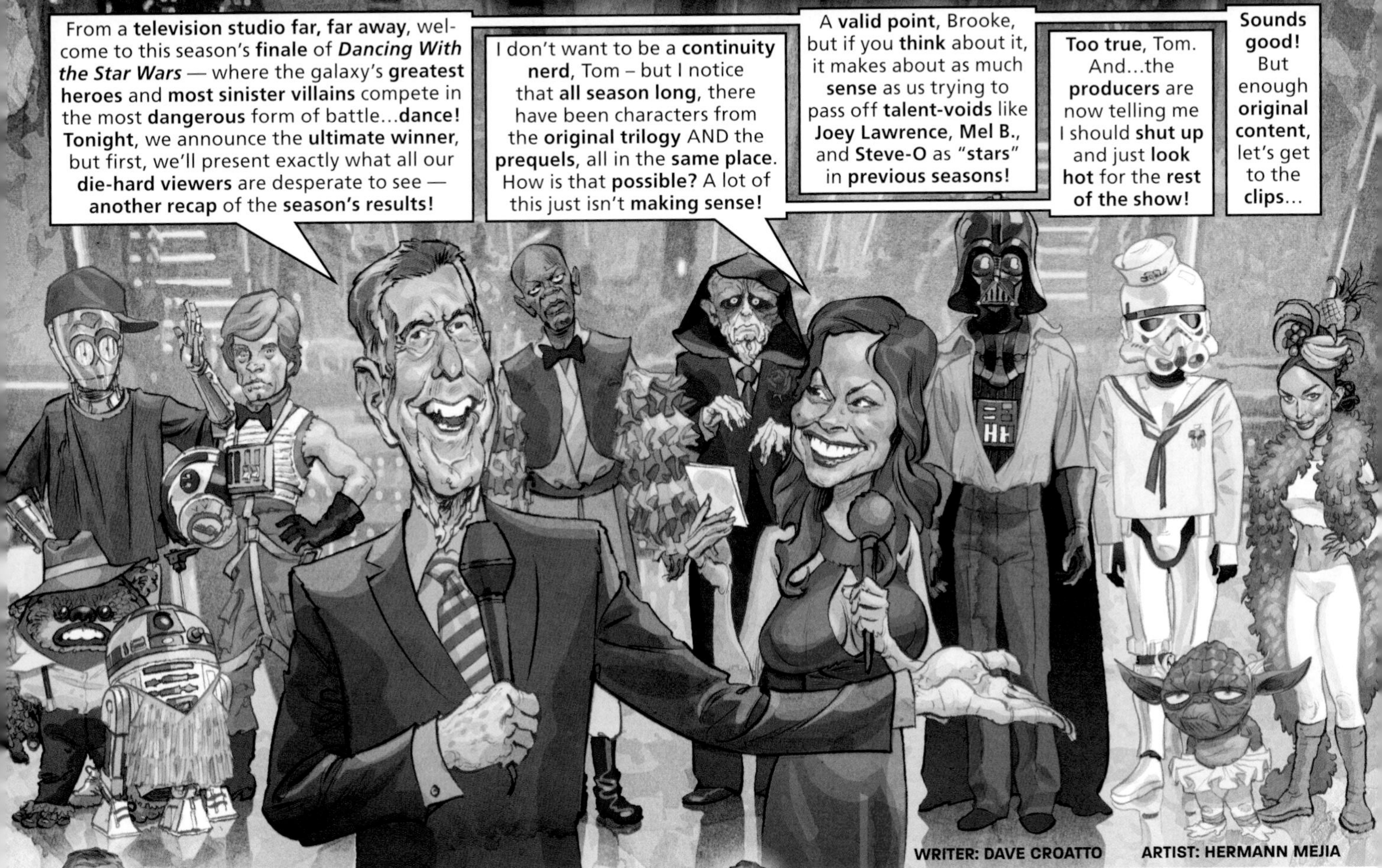
From a **television studio far, far away**, welcome to this season's **finale** of ***Dancing With the Star Wars*** — where the galaxy's **greatest heroes** and **most sinister villains** compete in the most **dangerous** form of battle...**dance! Tonight**, we announce the **ultimate winner**, but first, we'll present exactly what all our **die-hard viewers** are desperate to see — **another recap** of the **season's results!**
I don't want to be a **continuity nerd**, Tom – but I notice that **all season long**, there have been characters from the **original trilogy** AND the **prequels**, all in the **same place**. How is that **possible?** A lot of this just isn't **making sense!**
A **valid point**, Brooke, but if you **think** about it, it makes about as much **sense** as us trying to pass off **talent-voids** like **Joey Lawrence, Mel B.,** and **Steve-O** as **"stars"** in **previous seasons!**
Too true, Tom. And...the **producers** are now telling me I should **shut up** and just **look hot** for the **rest of the show!**
Sounds good! But enough **original content,** let's get to the **clips**...
WRITER: DAVE CROATTO ARTIST: HERMANN MEJIA

*It's been an **exciting season** of **amazing dancing**, complete with **unexpected twists**, both **onstage** and **OFF!** As we saw firsthand, during **Darth Vader's backstage flare-up**...*

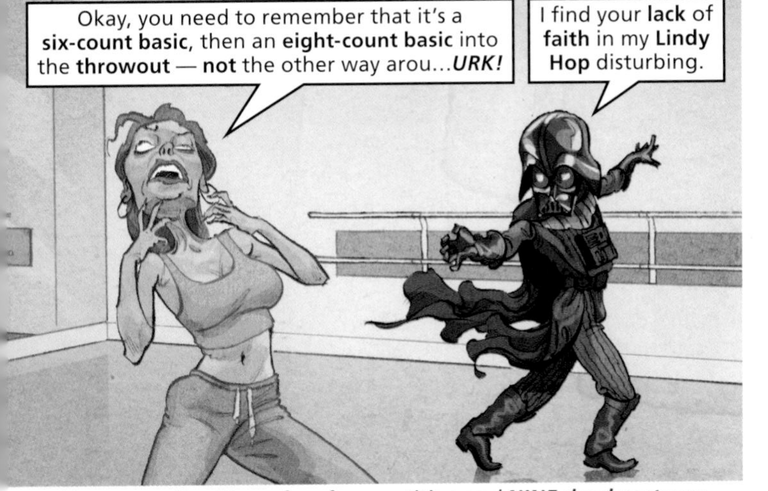
Okay, you need to remember that it's a **six-count basic**, then an **eight-count basic** into the **throwout** — **not** the other way arou...***URK!***
I find your **lack** of **faith** in my **Lindy Hop** disturbing.

*However, after **10 weeks** of competition and **NINE dead partners**, **Darth Vader** was finally **sent home**.*

*And there were even MORE **unexpected turns!** The competition was **fierce** — and as we all know, the game can **change** in a moment's notice — as **Stormtrooper #156** learned during his and Chelsie Hightower's **hip-hop routine**...*

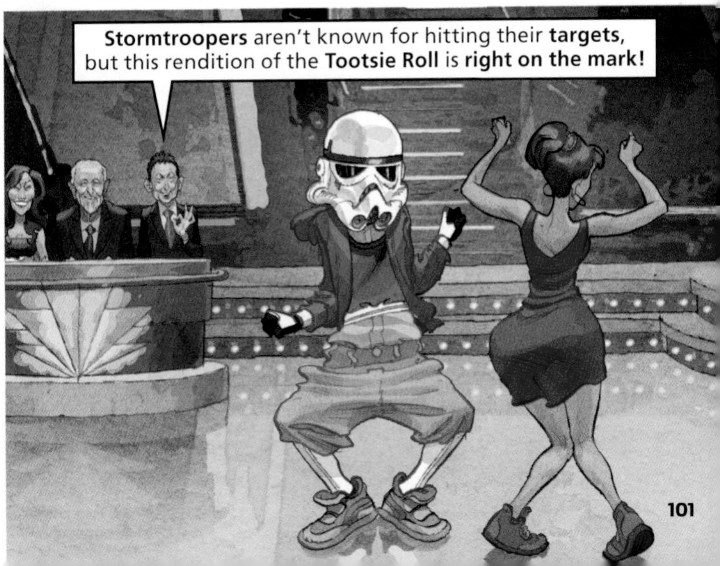
Stormtroopers aren't known for hitting their **targets**, but this rendition of the **Tootsie Roll** is **right on the mark!**

...And in a *surprise maneuver*, **Wicket** advanced past his **Storm-trooper competition**, and moved ahead to an **unexpected lead!**

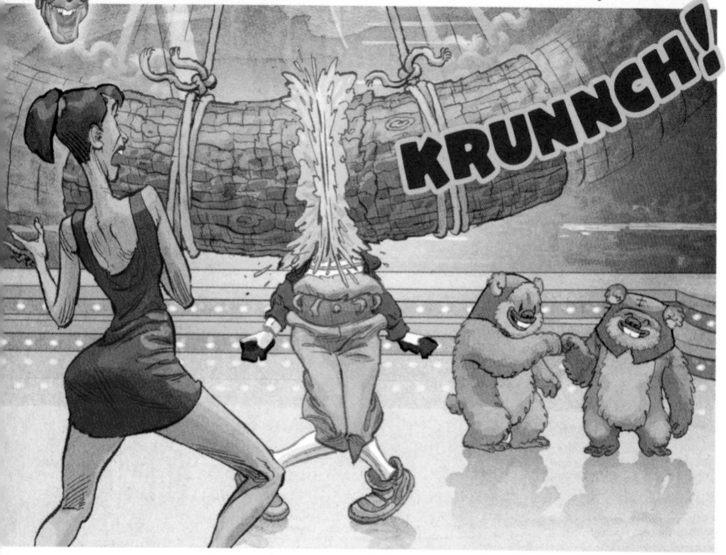

KRUNNCH!

There were moments that were truly ***inspiring*** and ***energizing***, such as **Jabba the Hutt's** *amazing* ***lift*** as he and **Lacey Schwimmer** danced to ***"The Time of My Life"*** from the film **Dirty Dancing.**

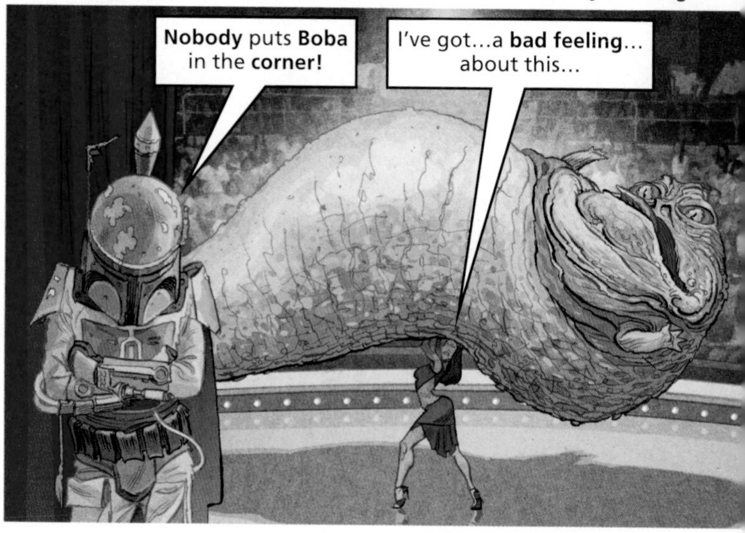

Nobody puts **Boba** in the **corner!**
I've got…a **bad feeling**… about this…

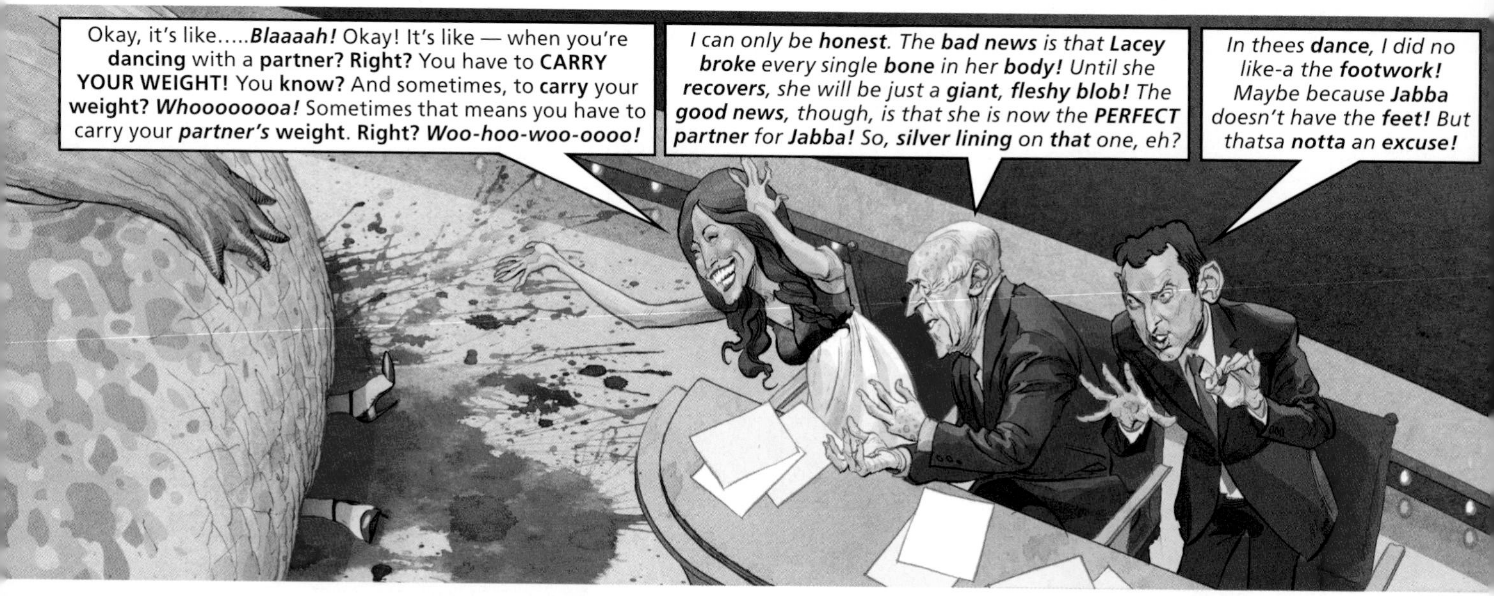

Okay, it's like…..***Blaaaah!*** Okay! It's like — when you're **dancing** with a **partner? Right?** You have to **CARRY YOUR WEIGHT!** You **know?** And sometimes, to **carry** your **weight? *Whoooooooa!*** Sometimes that means you have to carry your ***partner's*** **weight. Right? *Woo-hoo-woo-oooo!***
*I can only be **honest**. The **bad news** is that **Lacey broke** every single **bone** in her **body!** Until she **recovers**, she will be just a **giant**, **fleshy blob!** The **good news**, though, is that she is now the **PERFECT partner** for **Jabba!** So, **silver lining** on **that** one, eh?*
*In thees **dance**, I did no like-a the **footwork!** Maybe because **Jabba** doesn't have the **feet!** But thatsa **notta** an **excuse!***

Sadly, *that would **not** be the season's only **tragedy**. Happily, however, there's **nothing** this show loves more than a **disastrous accident** that we can **revisit** over and over again. And **again!** No one will be able to look back on this season without recalling **Darth Maul's** heart-breaking **elimination** during **"Swing Night"**…*

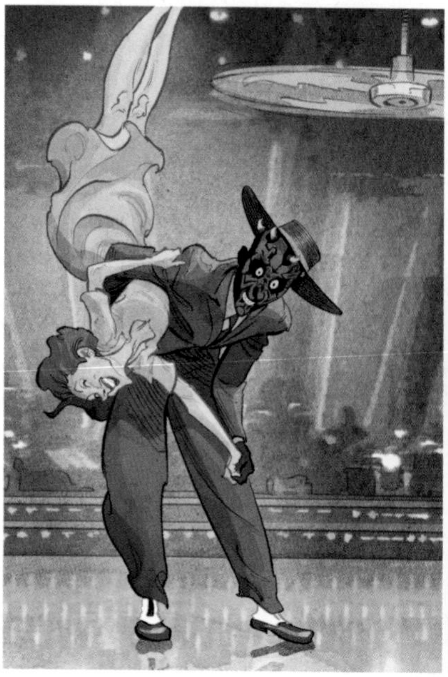

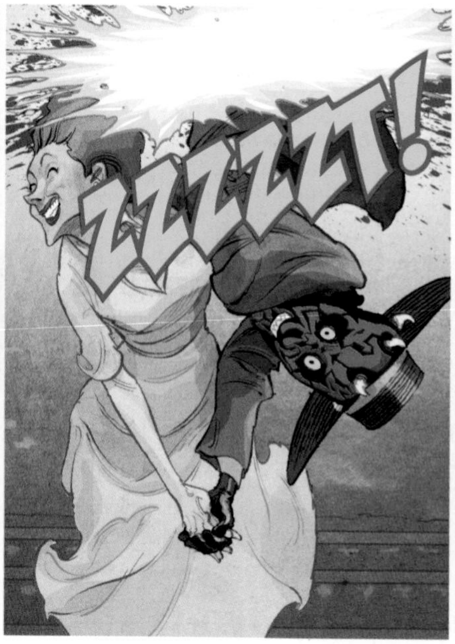

ZZZZZT!

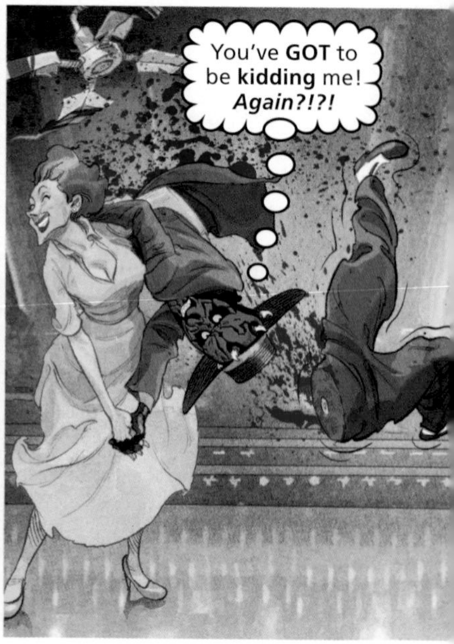

You've **GOT** to be **kidding** me! ***Again?!?!***

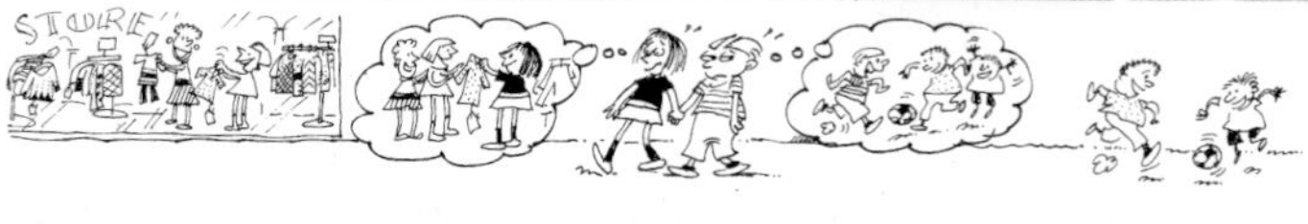

*And no one will forget the **controversy** after **Greedo** and **Han Solo's face-off!** After a **particularly close competition,** the **contestants** all **eagerly waited** for the **results** to be **announced**...*

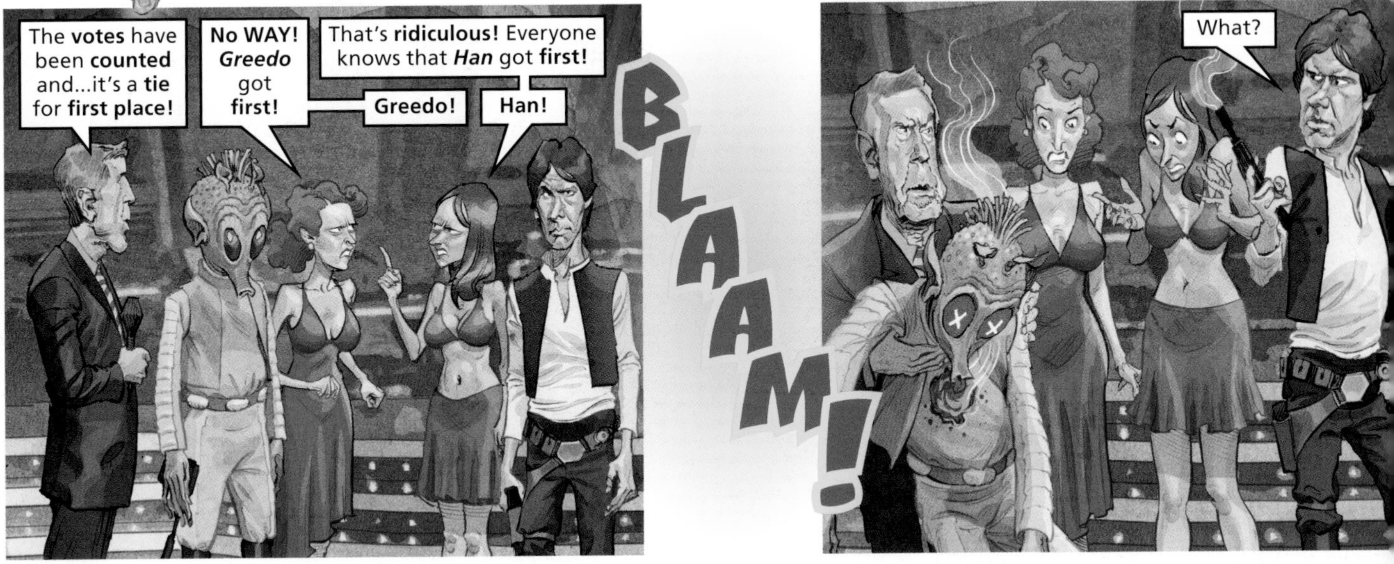

The **votes** have been **counted** and...it's a **tie** for **first place!**
No WAY! ***Greedo*** got **first!**
That's **ridiculous!** Everyone knows that ***Han*** got **first!**
Greedo!
Han!
BLAAM!
What?

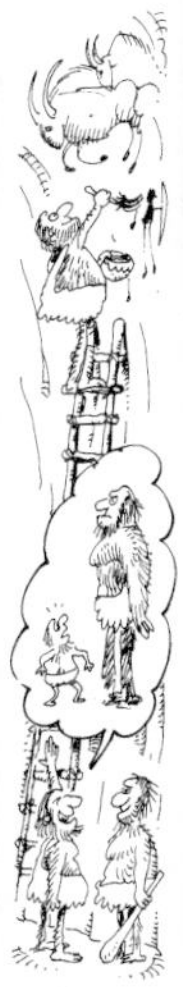

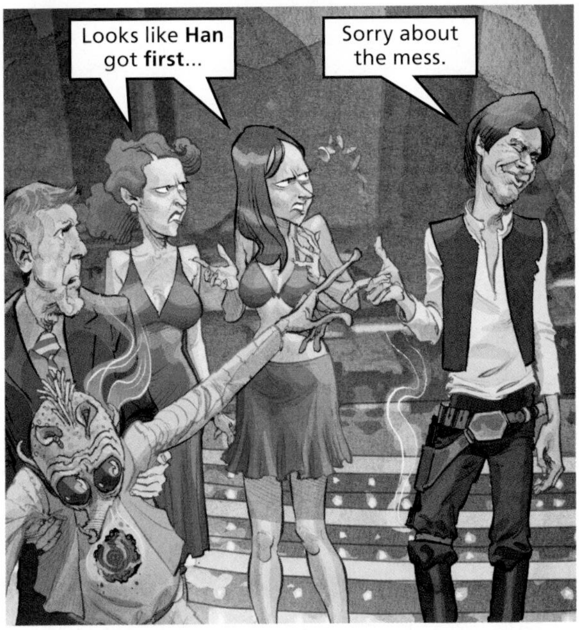

Looks like **Han** got **first**...
Sorry about the mess.

*But the past season has also provided some **unforgettable triumphs** — like **General Grievous'** performance on **"Broadway Night"...***

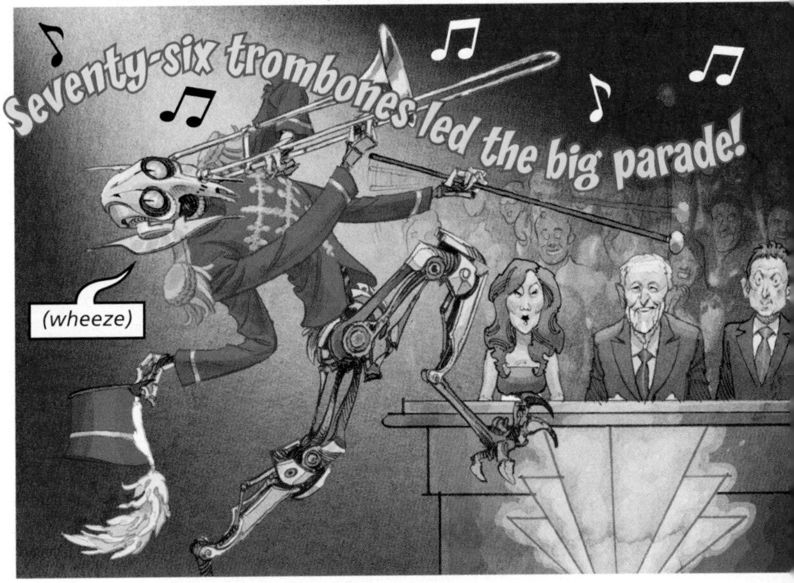

Seventy-six trombones led the big parade!
(wheeze)

*And, of course, **no season** would be **complete** without some **special visits** from competitors who were **eliminated** earlier in the season!*

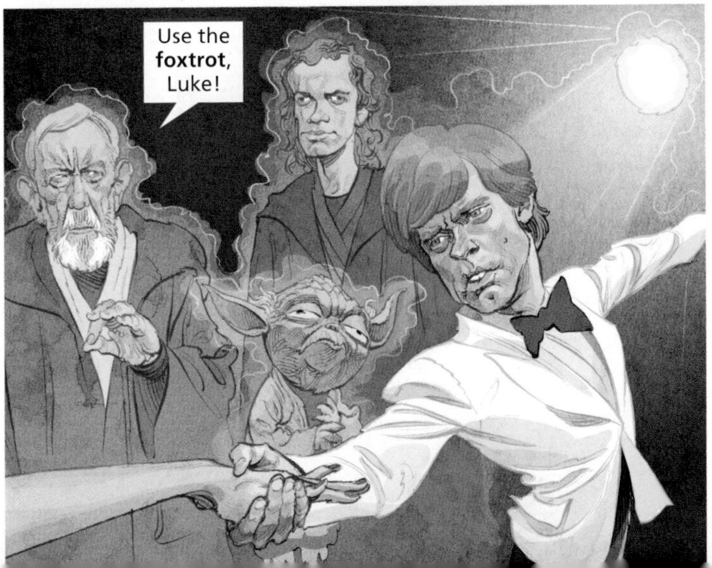

Use the **foxtrot**, Luke!

*And we even had a **special guest dance performance** from the stars of* **Tatooine's Best Dance Crew**...***Jawa-wockeez!***

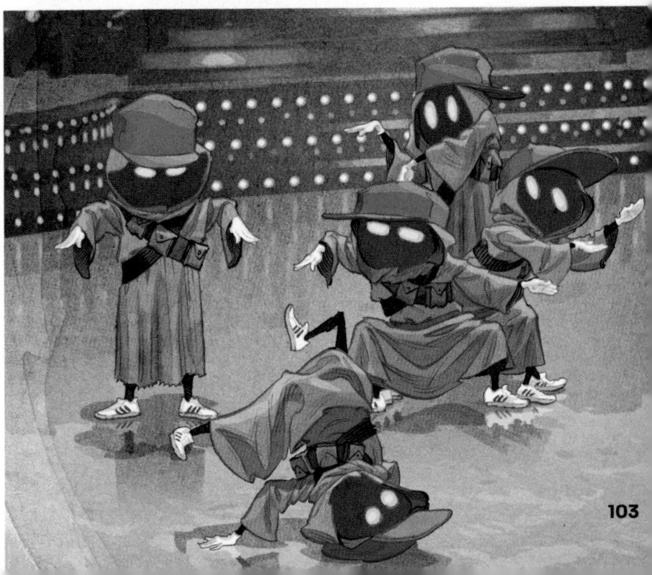

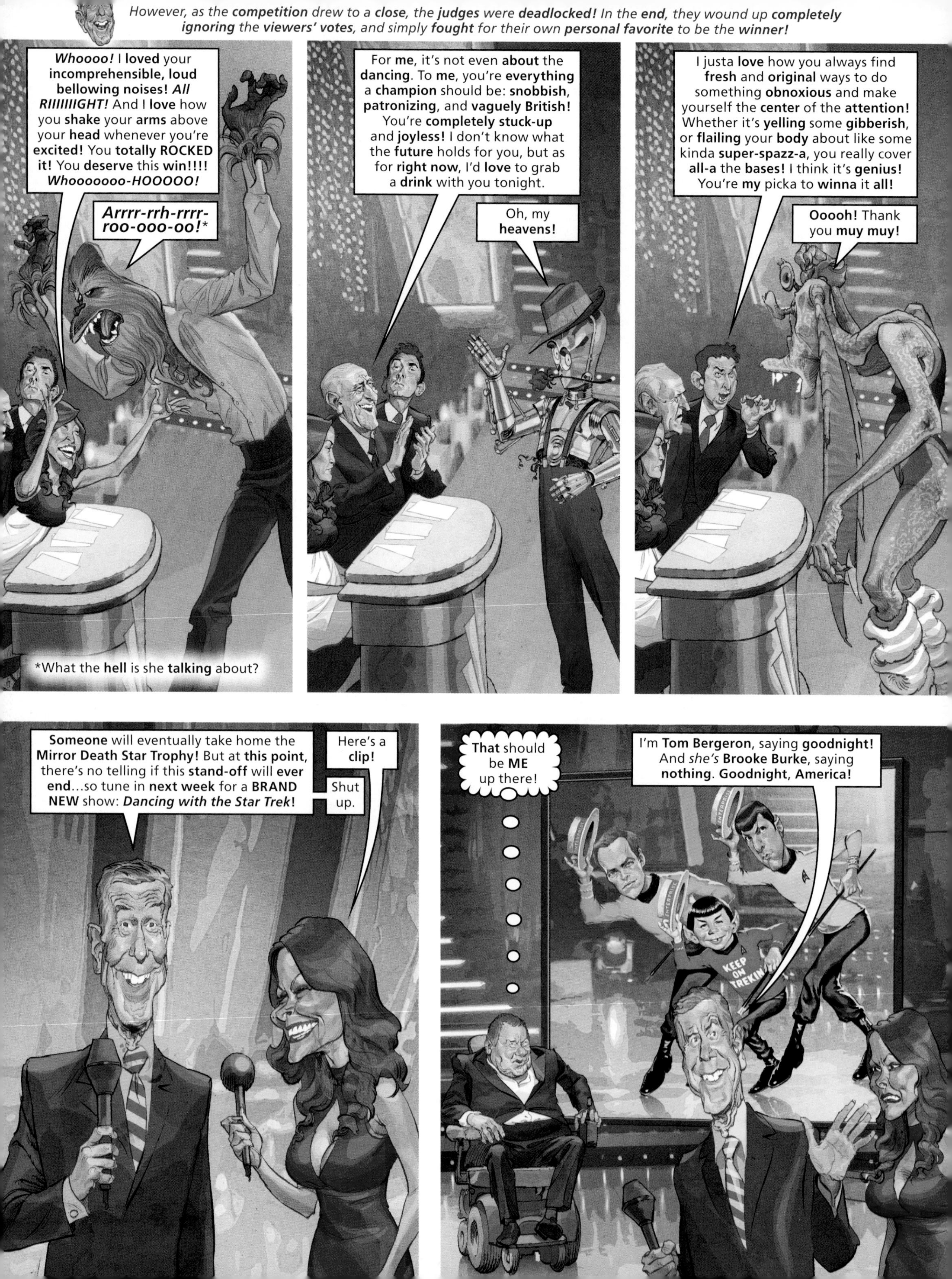
However, as the competition drew to a close, the judges were deadlocked! In the end, they wound up completely ignoring the viewers' votes, and simply fought for their own personal favorite to be the winner!
Whoooo! I loved your incomprehensible, loud bellowing noises! All RIIIIIIGHT! And I love how you shake your arms above your head whenever you're excited! You totally ROCKED it! You deserve this win!!!! Whooooooo-HOOOOO!
Arrrr-rrh-rrrr-roo-ooo-oo!*
*What the hell is she talking about?
For me, it's not even about the dancing. To me, you're everything a champion should be: snobbish, patronizing, and vaguely British! You're completely stuck-up and joyless! I don't know what the future holds for you, but as for right now, I'd love to grab a drink with you tonight.
Oh, my heavens!
I justa love how you always find fresh and original ways to do something obnoxious and make yourself the center of the attention! Whether it's yelling some gibberish, or flailing your body about like some kinda super-spazz-a, you really cover all-a the bases! I think it's genius! You're my picka to winna it all!
Ooooh! Thank you muy muy!
Someone will eventually take home the Mirror Death Star Trophy! But at this point, there's no telling if this stand-off will ever end…so tune in next week for a BRAND NEW show: Dancing with the Star Trek!
Here's a clip!
Shut up.
That should be ME up there!
I'm Tom Bergeron, saying goodnight! And she's Brooke Burke, saying nothing. Goodnight, America!
KEEP ON TREKIN

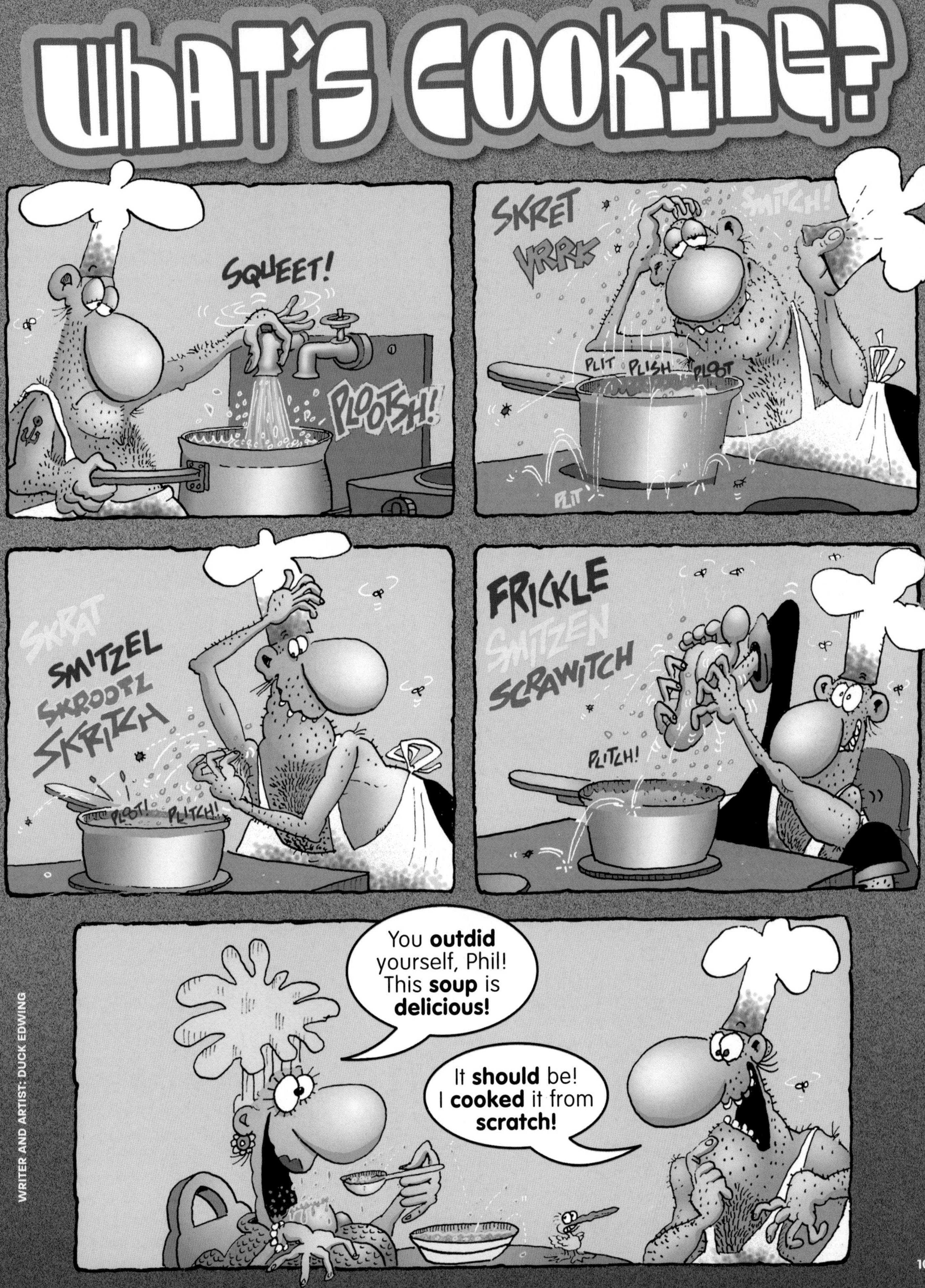

WHAT'S COOKING?
SQUEET!
PLOOTSH!
SKRET
VRRK
SMITCH!
PLIT
PLISH
PLOOT
PLIT
SKRAT
SMITZEL
SKROOTZ
SKRITCH
PLOOT!
PLITCH!
FRICKLE
SMITZEN
SCRAWITCH
PLITCH!
You **outdid** yourself, Phil! This **soup** is **delicious!**
It **should** be! I **cooked** it from **scratch!**
WRITER AND ARTIST: DUCK EDWING

DONALD YUCK DEPT.

MAD's TRUMPED-UP SCENES FROM THE APPRENTICE

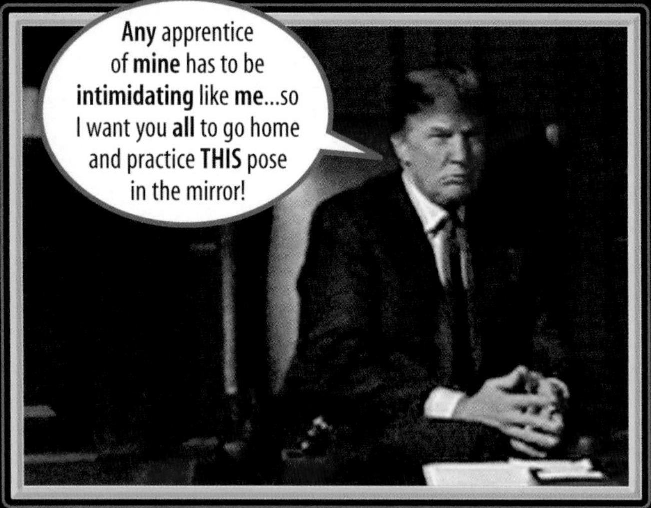
Any apprentice of **mine** has to be **intimidating** like **me**...so I want you **all** to go home and practice **THIS** pose in the mirror!

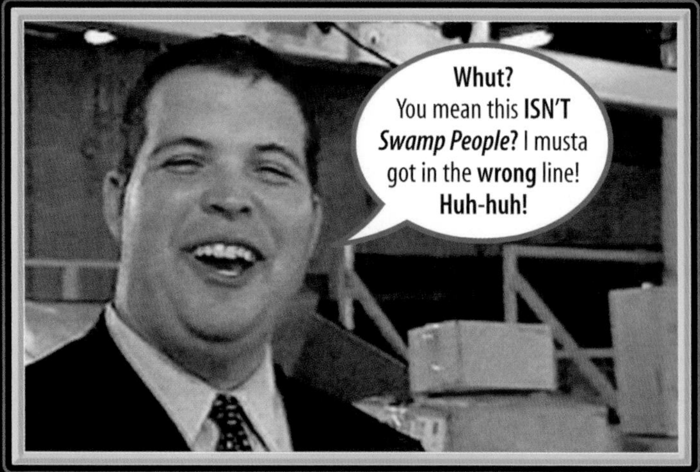
Whut? You mean this **ISN'T** ***Swamp People*?** I musta got in the **wrong** line! **Huh-huh!**

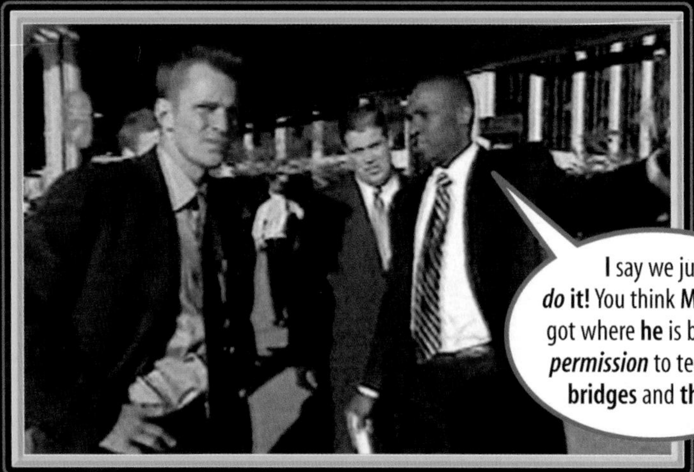
I say we just ***do* it!** You think **Mr. Trump** got where **he** is by asking ***permission*** to tear down **bridges** and **things**?

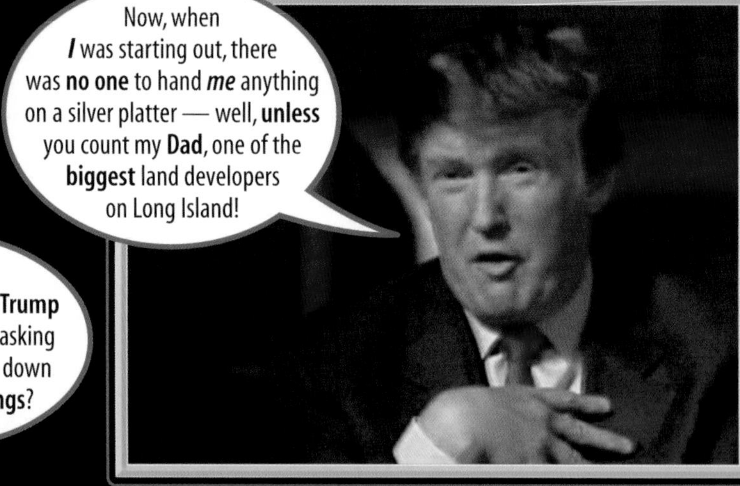
Now, when ***I*** was starting out, there was **no one** to hand ***me*** anything on a silver platter — well, **unless** you count my **Dad**, one of the **biggest** land developers on Long Island!

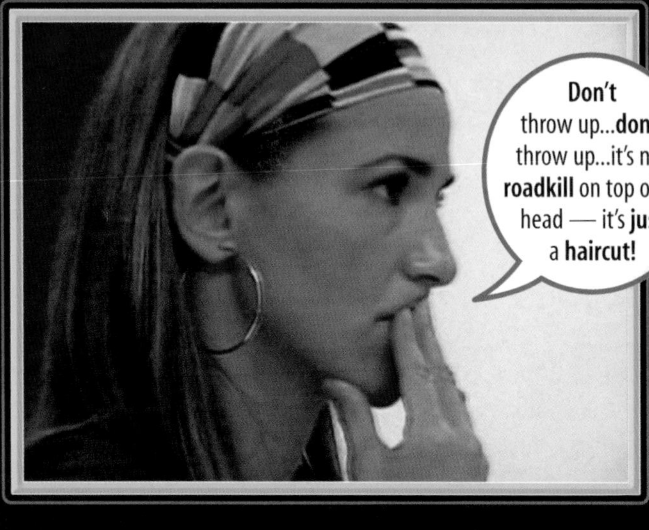
Don't throw up...**don't** throw up...it's not **roadkill** on top of his head — it's **just** a **haircut!**

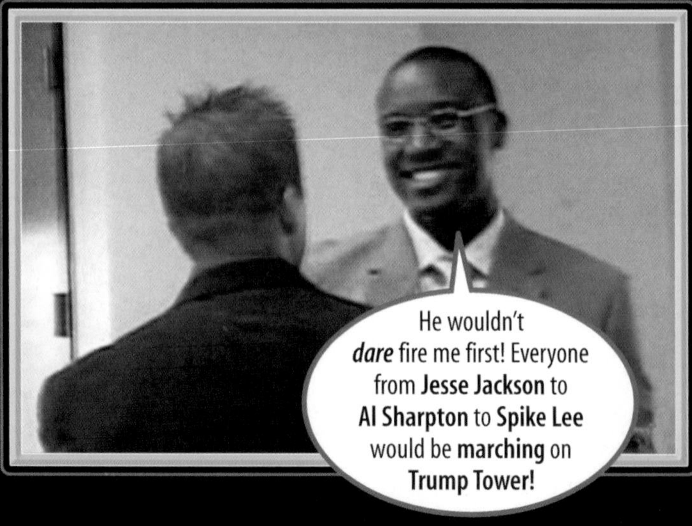
He wouldn't ***dare*** fire me first! Everyone from **Jesse Jackson** to **Al Sharpton** to **Spike Lee** would be **marching** on **Trump Tower!**

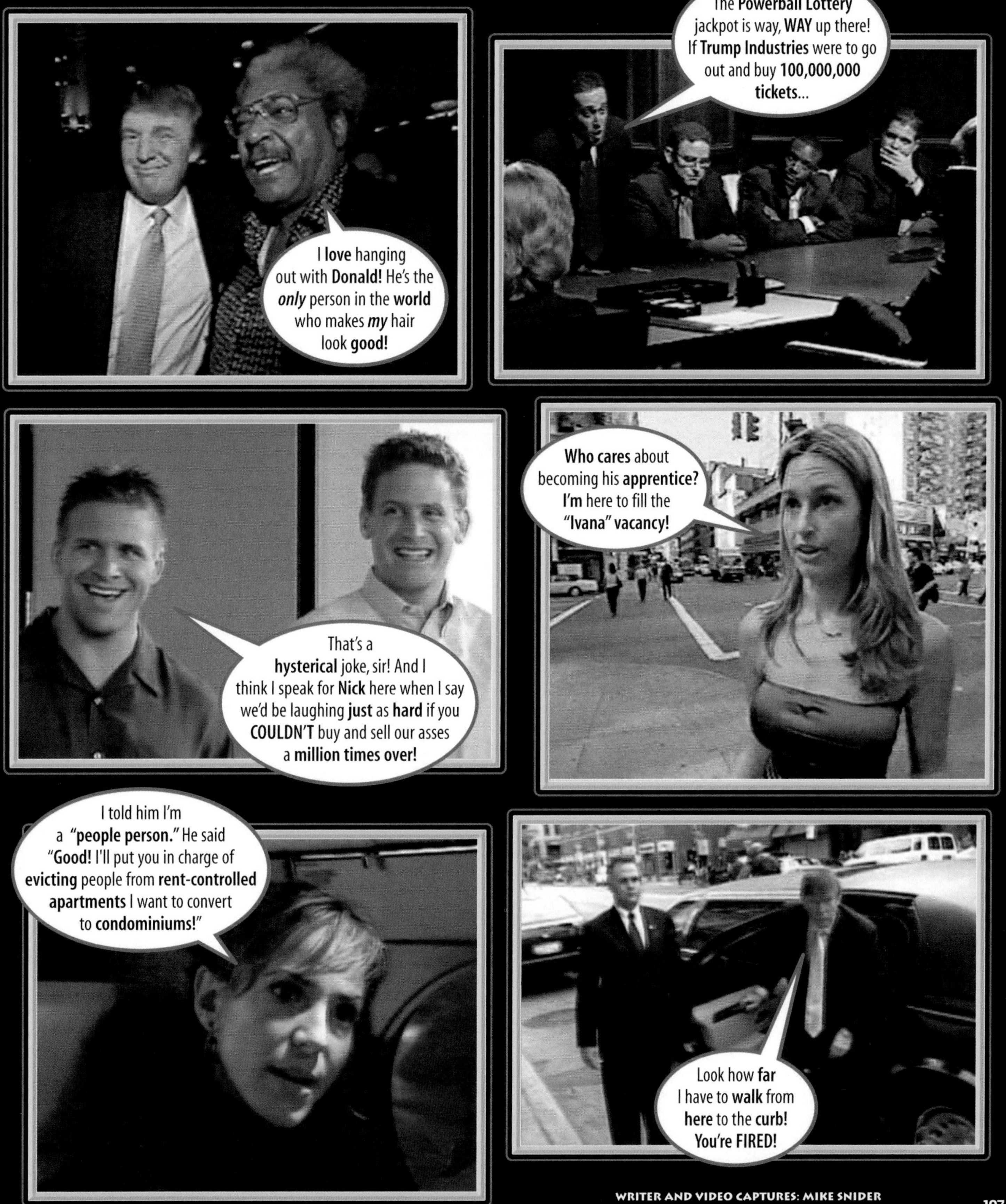
I **love** hanging out with **Donald!** He's the *only* person in the **world** who makes *my* hair look **good!**
The **Powerball Lottery** jackpot is way, **WAY** up there! If **Trump Industries** were to go out and buy **100,000,000 tickets**...
That's a **hysterical** joke, sir! And I think I speak for **Nick** here when I say we'd be laughing **just** as **hard** if you **COULDN'T** buy and sell our asses a **million times over!**
Who cares about becoming his **apprentice? I'm** here to fill the **"Ivana" vacancy!**
I told him I'm a **"people person."** He said "**Good!** I'll put you in charge of **evicting** people from **rent-controlled apartments** I want to convert to **condominiums!**"
Look how **far** I have to **walk** from **here** to the **curb! You're FIRED!**

WRITER AND VIDEO CAPTURES: MIKE SNIDER

Each year, *The Sporting News* names "The 100 Most Powerful People in Sports." The list usually includes the likes of George Steinbrenner, Phil Knight, Paul Tagliabue and even a few actual athletes. But have you ever wondered about those dedicated, sports-loving people who work just as hard but toil in obscurity, albeit well-deserved obscurity? Of course you haven't. But that won't stop us from presenting…

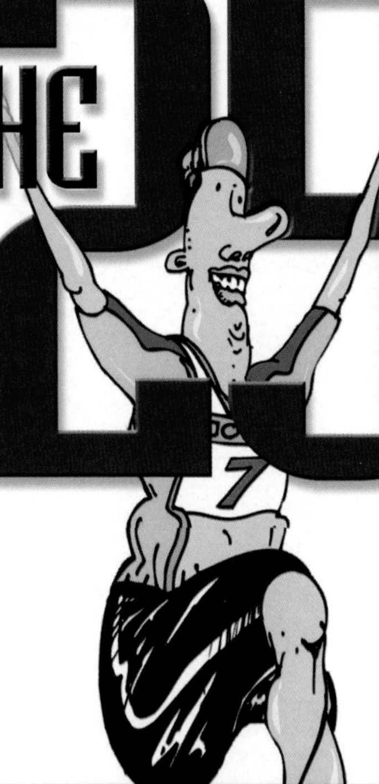

THE 25 LEAST POWERFUL PEOPLE IN SPORTS

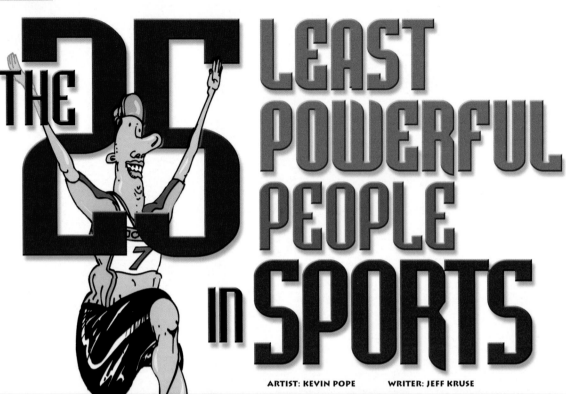

ARTIST: KEVIN POPE WRITER: JEFF KRUSE

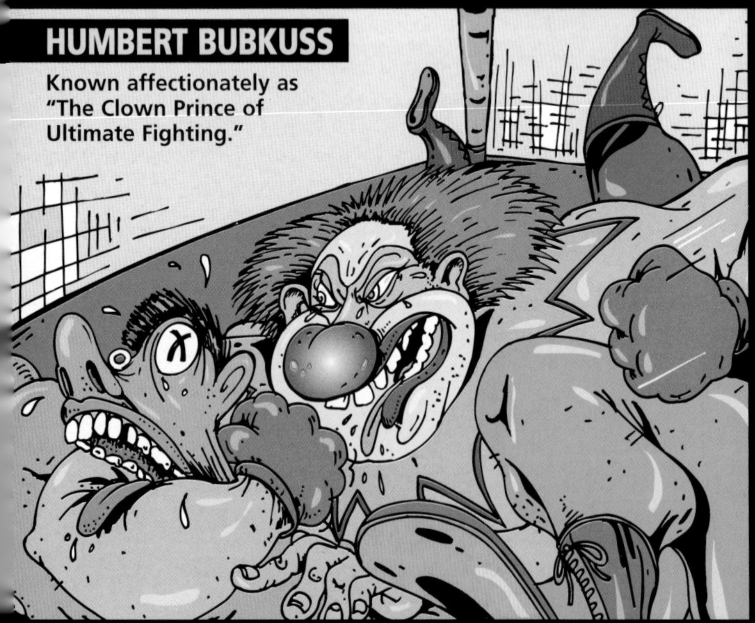

HUMBERT BUBKUSS

Known affectionately as "The Clown Prince of Ultimate Fighting."

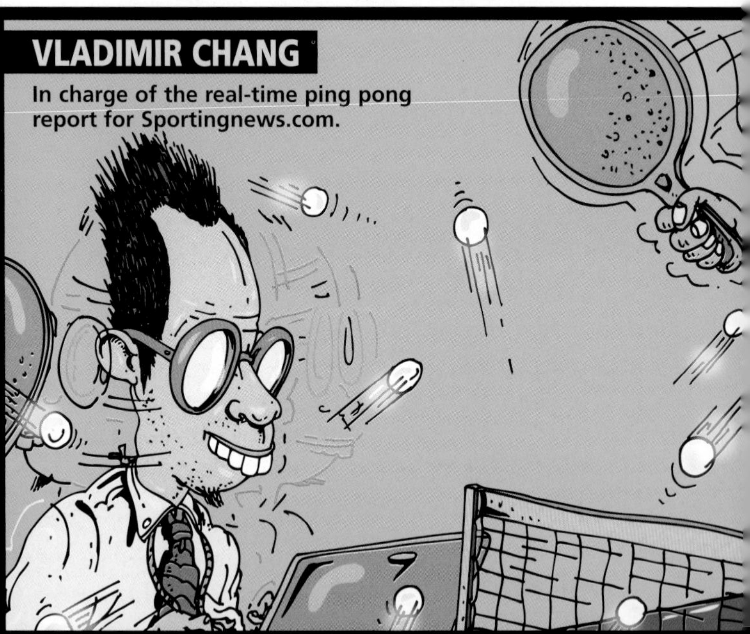

VLADIMIR CHANG

In charge of the real-time ping pong report for Sportingnews.com.

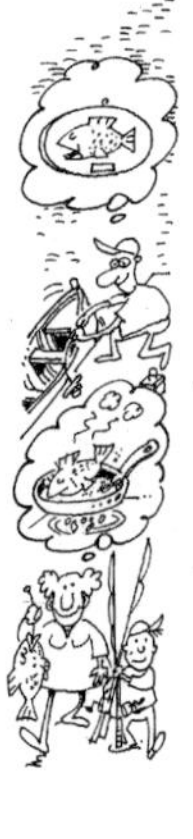

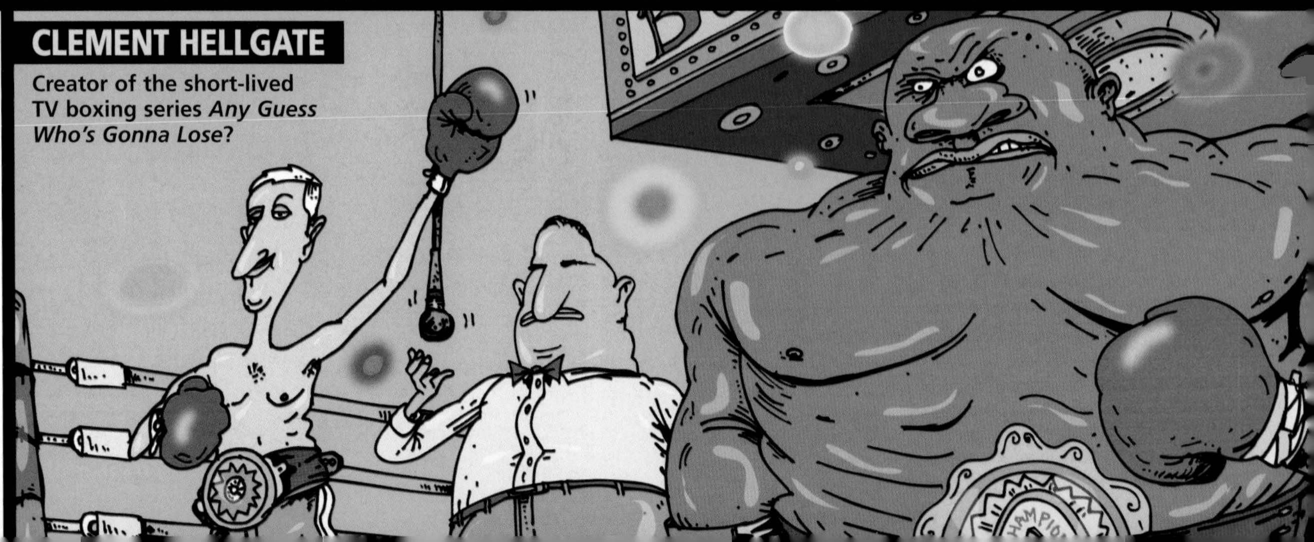

CLEMENT HELLGATE

Creator of the short-lived TV boxing series *Any Guess Who's Gonna Lose*?

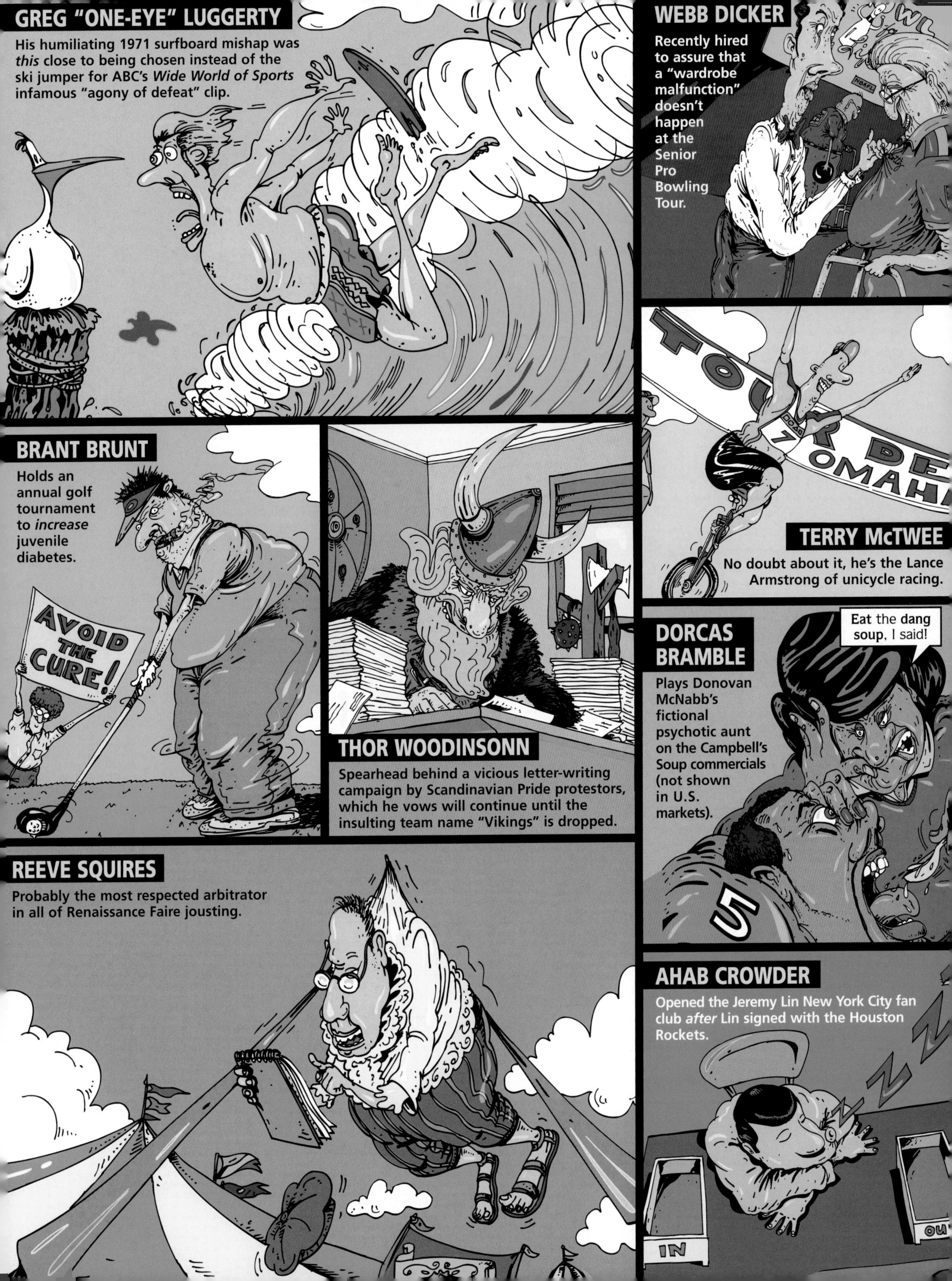
GREG "ONE-EYE" LUGGERTY
His humiliating 1971 surfboard mishap was *this* close to being chosen instead of the ski jumper for ABC's *Wide World of Sports* infamous "agony of defeat" clip.
WEBB DICKER
Recently hired to assure that a "wardrobe malfunction" doesn't happen at the Senior Pro Bowling Tour.
TERRY McTWEE
No doubt about it, he's the Lance Armstrong of unicycle racing.
BRANT BRUNT
Holds an annual golf tournament to *increase* juvenile diabetes.
AVOID THE CURE!
THOR WOODINSONN
Spearhead behind a vicious letter-writing campaign by Scandinavian Pride protestors, which he vows will continue until the insulting team name "Vikings" is dropped.
DORCAS BRAMBLE
Plays Donovan McNabb's fictional psychotic aunt on the Campbell's Soup commercials (not shown in U.S. markets).
Eat the dang soup, I said!
5
REEVE SQUIRES
Probably the most respected arbitrator in all of Renaissance Faire jousting.
AHAB CROWDER
Opened the Jeremy Lin New York City fan club *after* Lin signed with the Houston Rockets.
IN

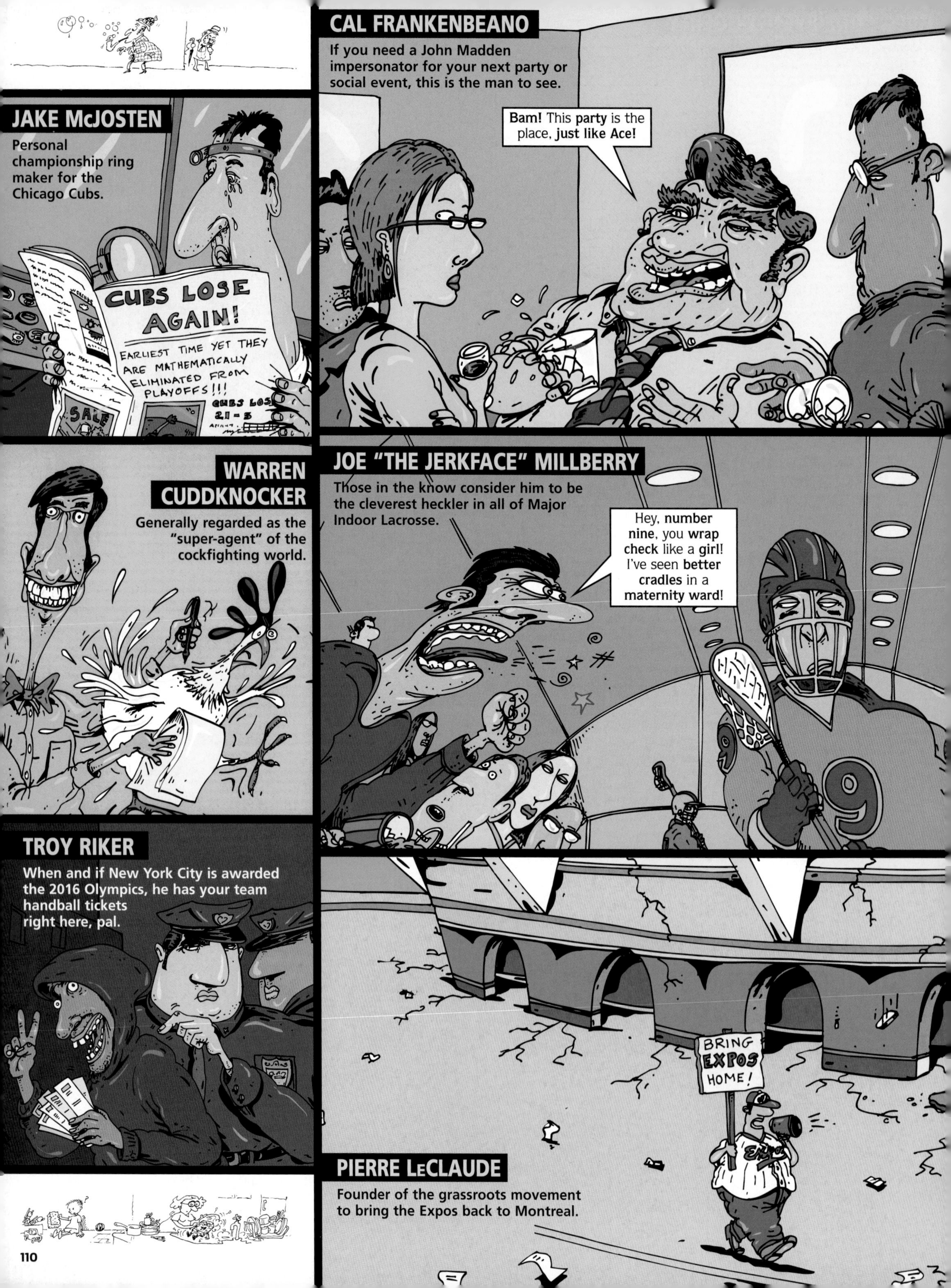

CAL FRANKENBEANO
If you need a John Madden impersonator for your next party or social event, this is the man to see.
Bam! This party is the place, just like Ace!
JAKE McJOSTEN
Personal championship ring maker for the Chicago Cubs.
CUBS LOSE AGAIN!
EARLIEST TIME YET THEY ARE MATHEMATICALLY ELIMINATED FROM PLAYOFFS!!!
CUBS LOSE 21-3
SALE
WARREN CUDDKNOCKER
Generally regarded as the "super-agent" of the cockfighting world.
JOE "THE JERKFACE" MILLBERRY
Those in the know consider him to be the cleverest heckler in all of Major Indoor Lacrosse.
Hey, number nine, you wrap check like a girl! I've seen better cradles in a maternity ward!
9
TROY RIKER
When and if New York City is awarded the 2016 Olympics, he has your team handball tickets right here, pal.
BRING EXPOS HOME!
PIERRE LeCLAUDE
Founder of the grassroots movement to bring the Expos back to Montreal.

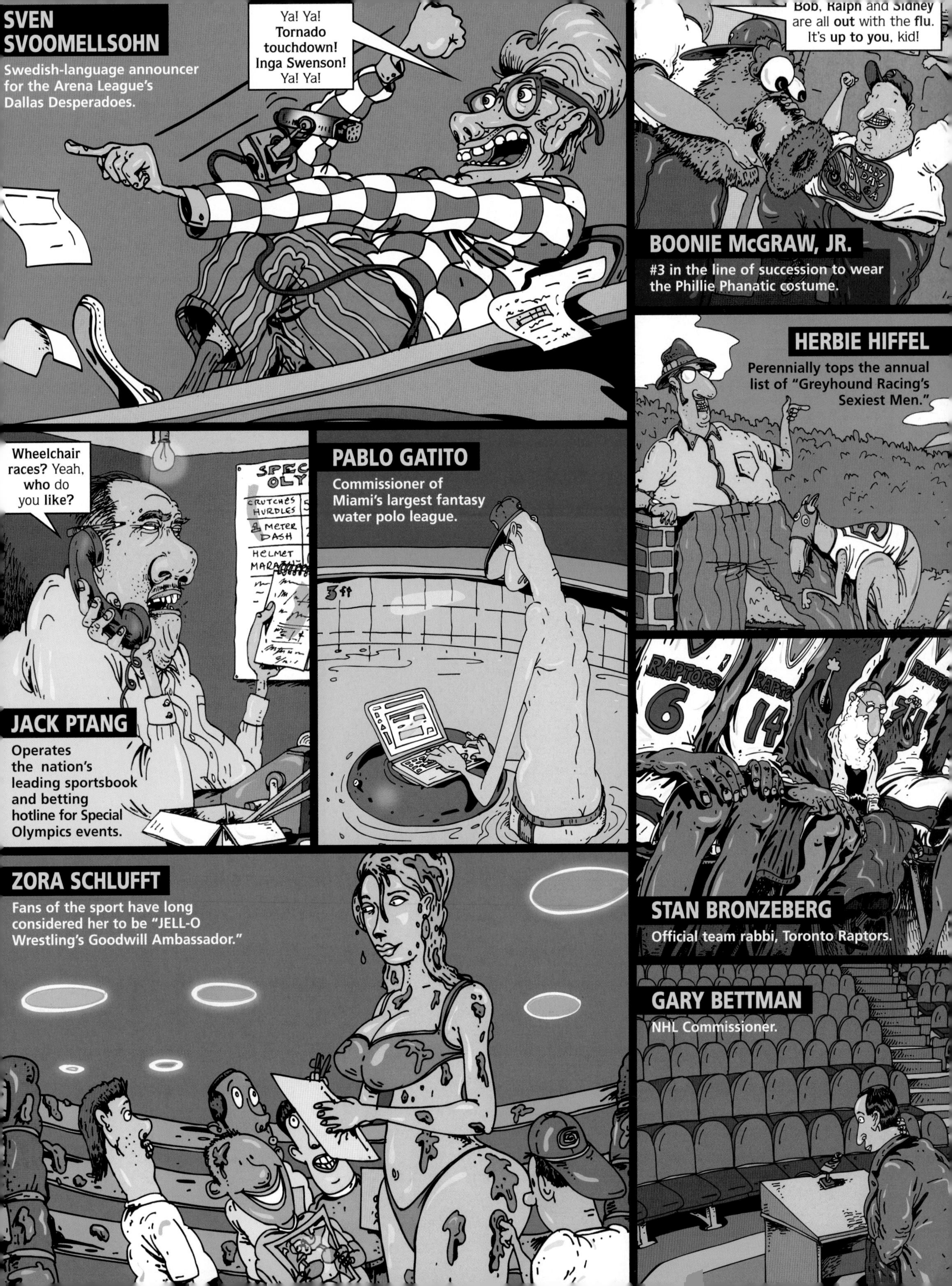
SVEN SVOOMELLSOHN
Swedish-language announcer for the Arena League's Dallas Desperadoes.
Ya! Ya! Tornado touchdown! Inga Swenson! Ya! Ya!
Bob, Ralph and Sidney are all out with the flu. It's up to you, kid!
BOONIE McGRAW, JR.
#3 in the line of succession to wear the Phillie Phanatic costume.
Wheelchair races? Yeah, who do you like?
SPEC OLY
CRUTCHES HURDLES
1 METER DASH
HELMET MARA
JACK PTANG
Operates the nation's leading sportsbook and betting hotline for Special Olympics events.
PABLO GATITO
Commissioner of Miami's largest fantasy water polo league.
3 ft
HERBIE HIFFEL
Perennially tops the annual list of "Greyhound Racing's Sexiest Men."
RAPTORS
6
14
STAN BRONZEBERG
Official team rabbi, Toronto Raptors.
ZORA SCHLUFFT
Fans of the sport have long considered her to be "JELL-O Wrestling's Goodwill Ambassador."
GARY BETTMAN
NHL Commissioner.

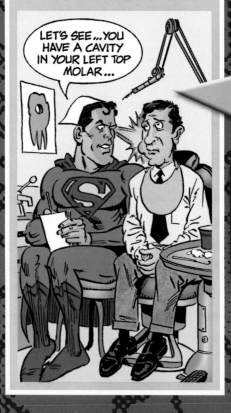

IF SUPER HEROES NEEDED EXTRA MONEY

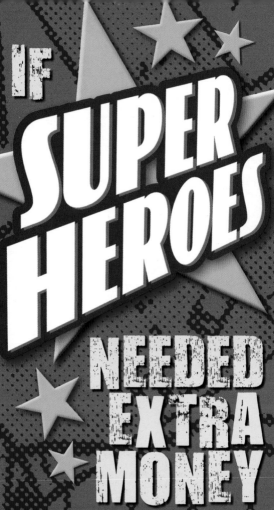

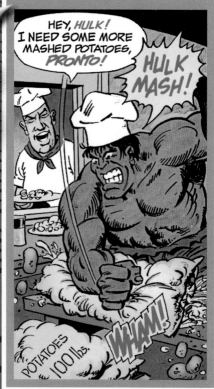

WRITER: BOB SUPINA ARTIST: ANGELO TORRES

SUPERMAN COULD BE AN X-RAY TECHNICIAN...

LET'S SEE...YOU HAVE A CAVITY IN YOUR LEFT TOP MOLAR...

THE HULK COULD WORK FOR A CHEF...

HEY, HULK! I NEED SOME MORE MASHED POTATOES, PRONTO!
HULK MASH!
WHAM!
POTATOES 100 lbs.

SPIDER-MAN COULD BE A WINDOW WASHER...

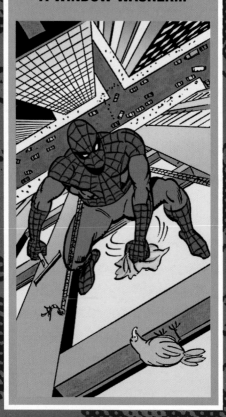

THE HUMAN TORCH COULD WORK AT A SUMMER CAMP...

FLAME ON!
CAMP
CAMP

THE FLASH COULD DELIVER PIZZAS...

WOW! I JUST FINISHED ORDERING IT!
THAT'LL BE $13.50, SIR!
Pizza
torres

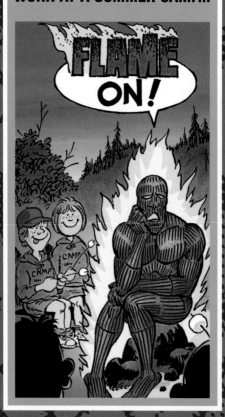

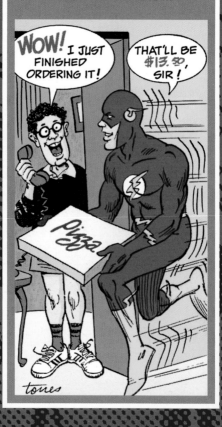

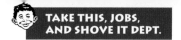

TAKE THIS, JOBS, AND SHOVE IT DEPT.

One of the most over-hyped, overrated and over-heated movies of the season is Pixar Studio's *Cars*. You've probably heard about it or read about it in newspapers and on websites. But, as usual, the true inside scoop can only be found here, in America's most respected chronicler of the seamy side of Tinseltown. Here's...

LITTLE KNOWN FACTS, RUMORS AND TOTAL FABRICATIONS ABOUT *Cars*

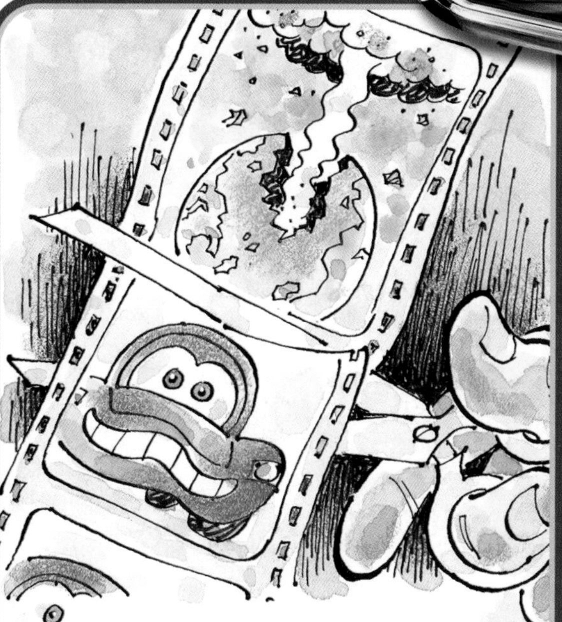

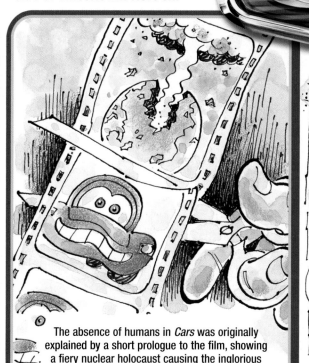

The absence of humans in *Cars* was originally explained by a short prologue to the film, showing a fiery nuclear holocaust causing the inglorious end to mankind. But with it, the movie ran too long and so the two-minute sequence was snipped.

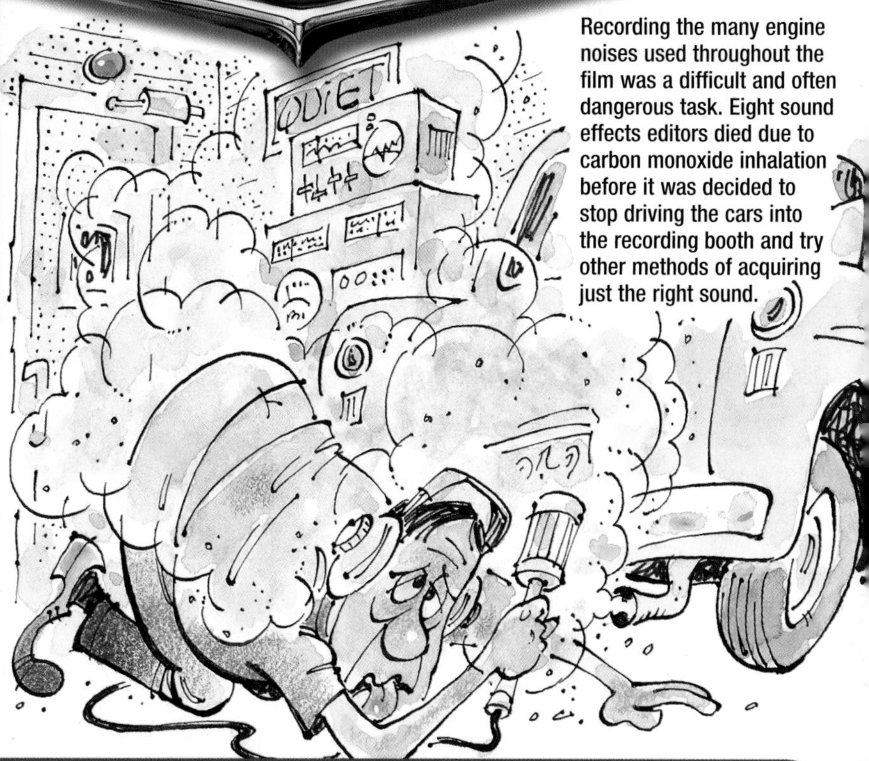
QUIET

Recording the many engine noises used throughout the film was a difficult and often dangerous task. Eight sound effects editors died due to carbon monoxide inhalation before it was decided to stop driving the cars into the recording booth and try other methods of acquiring just the right sound.

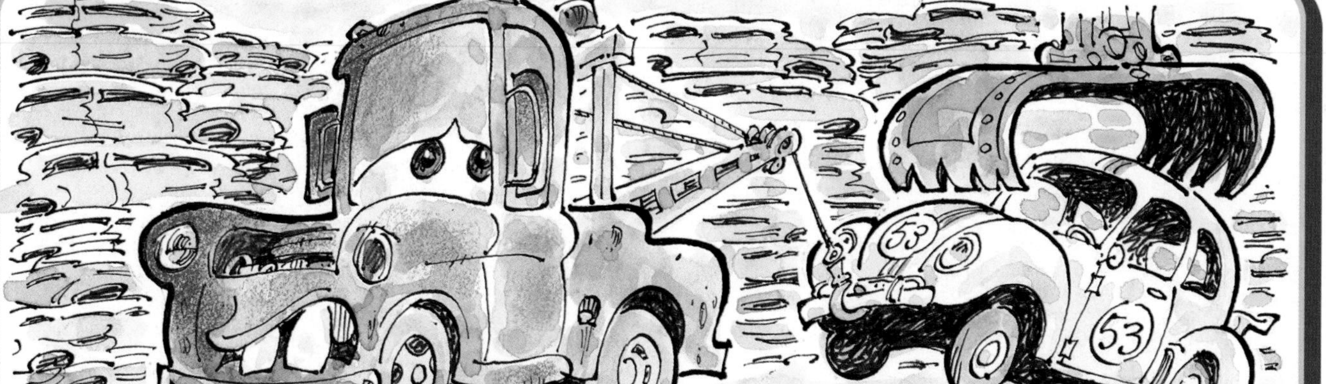
53
53

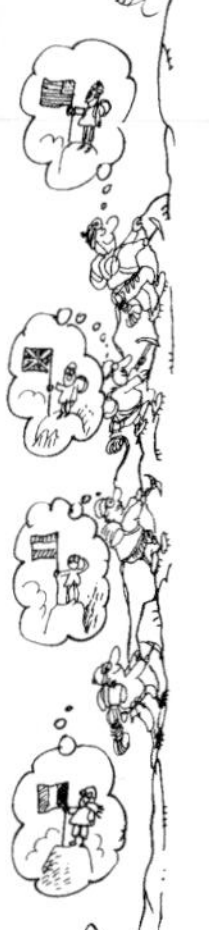

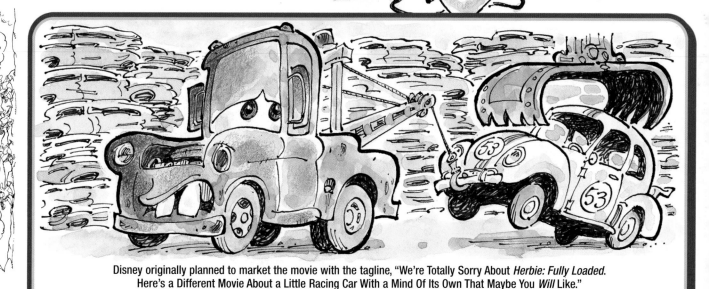

Disney originally planned to market the movie with the tagline, "We're Totally Sorry About *Herbie: Fully Loaded.* Here's a Different Movie About a Little Racing Car With a Mind Of Its Own That Maybe You *Will* Like." But this left little room on the poster for any kind of illustration.

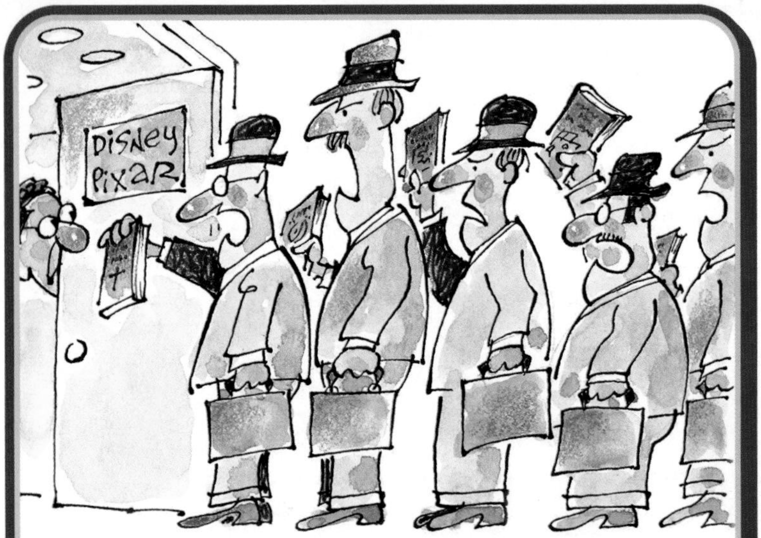
DISNEY
PIXAR
Authors of the 1982 non-fiction book *The Holy Blood and the Holy Grail* have claimed that the screenplay for *Cars* borrows heavily from their book and have sought an injunction to bar the film's release. Law experts doubt they will succeed, but this has not stopped others, including the publishers of the *Kelley Blue Book* and *Chilton's Guide to Small Engine Repair*, from filing similar lawsuits.

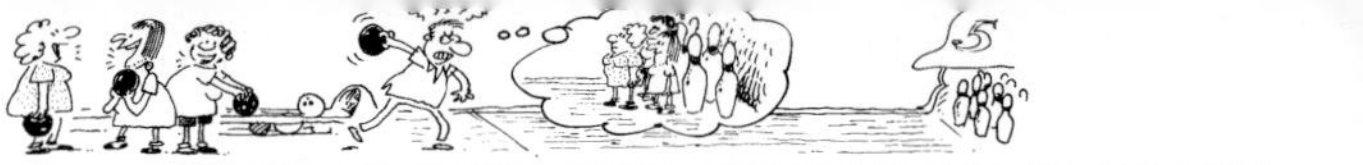

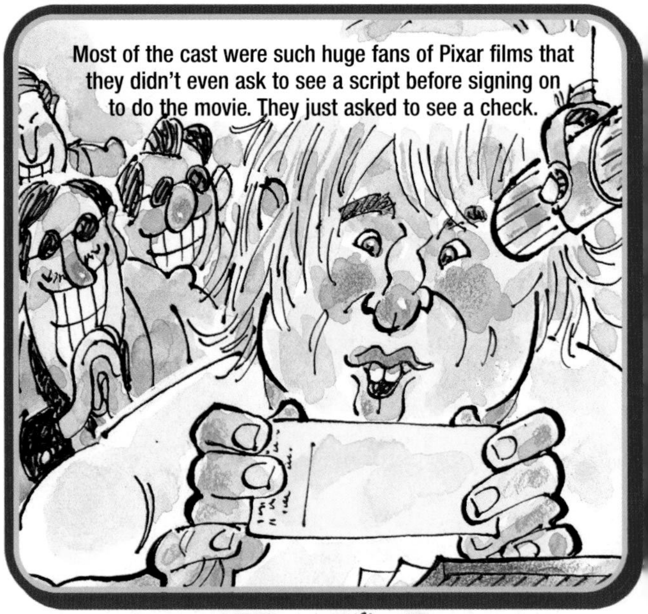
Most of the cast were such huge fans of Pixar films that they didn't even ask to see a script before signing on to do the movie. They just asked to see a check.

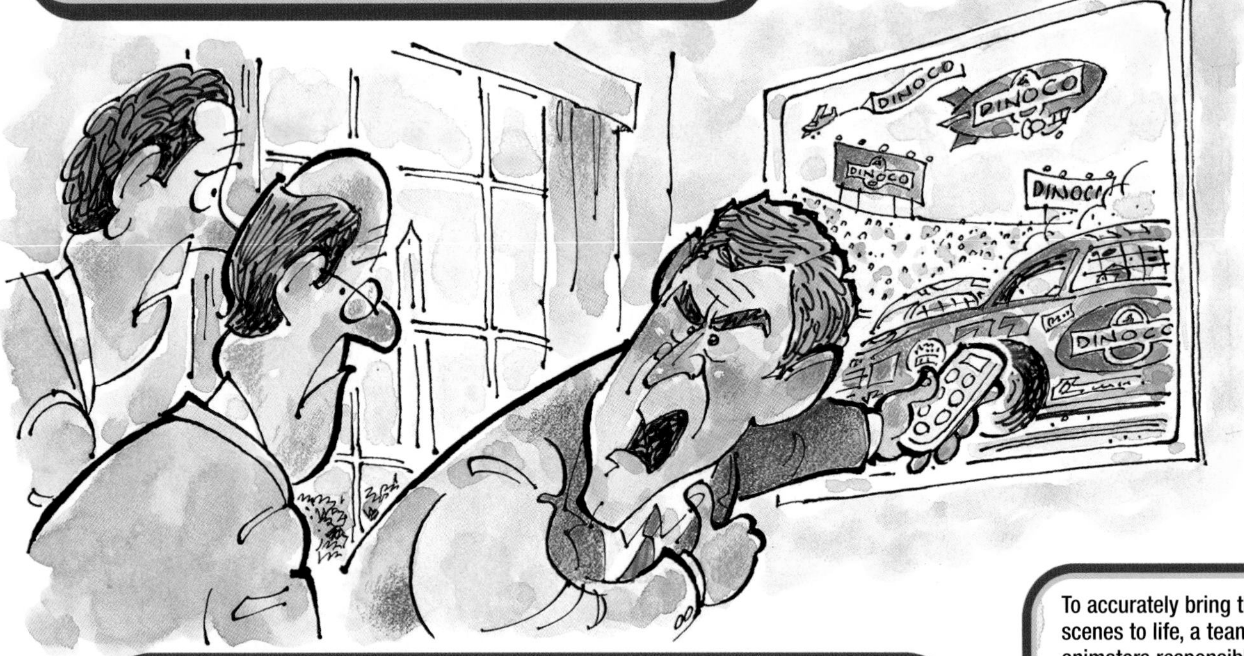
DINOCO
DINOCO
DINOCO
DINOCO
DINOCO
Following a special advance screening of *Cars* at the White House, an angry President Bush immediately held a meeting with his advisors, demanding to know how such an enormous gas company as Dinoco could exist without him having financial ties to it.

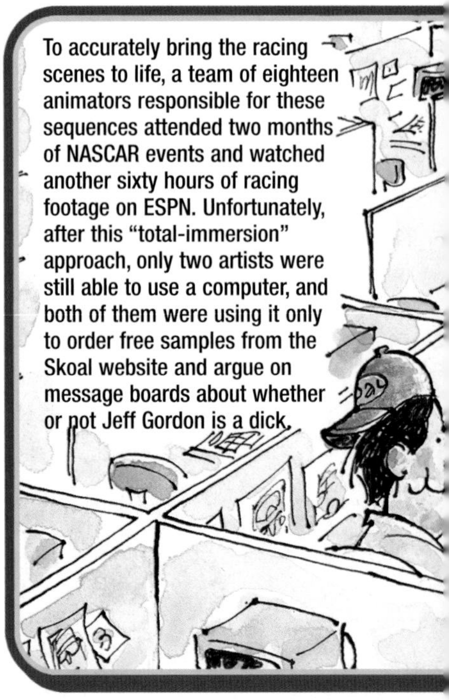
To accurately bring the racing scenes to life, a team of eighteen animators responsible for these sequences attended two months of NASCAR events and watched another sixty hours of racing footage on ESPN. Unfortunately, after this "total-immersion" approach, only two artists were still able to use a computer, and both of them were using it only to order free samples from the Skoal website and argue on message boards about whether or not Jeff Gordon is a dick.

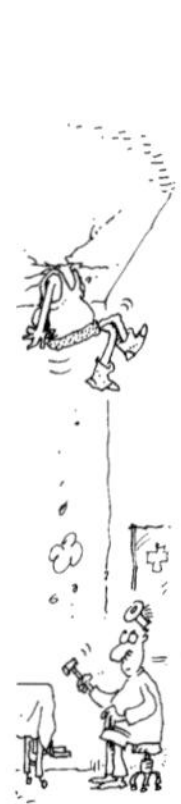

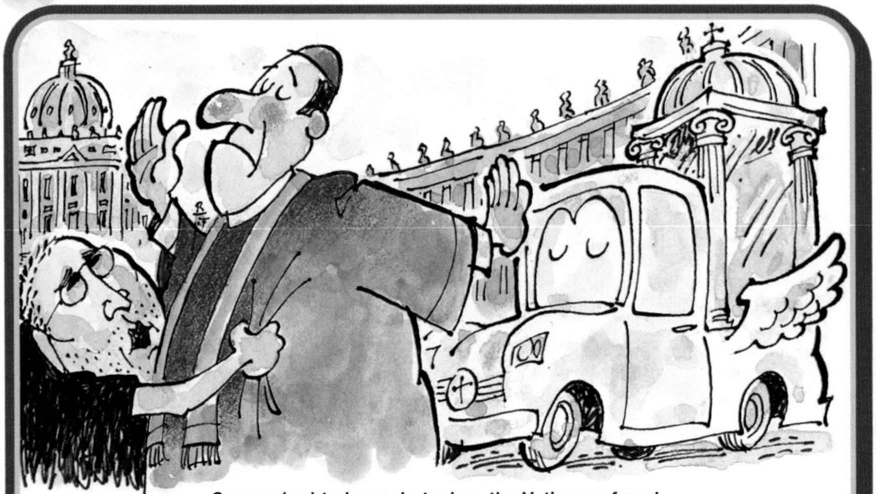
Scenes had to be reshot when the Vatican refused to license the Popemobile for use in the film.

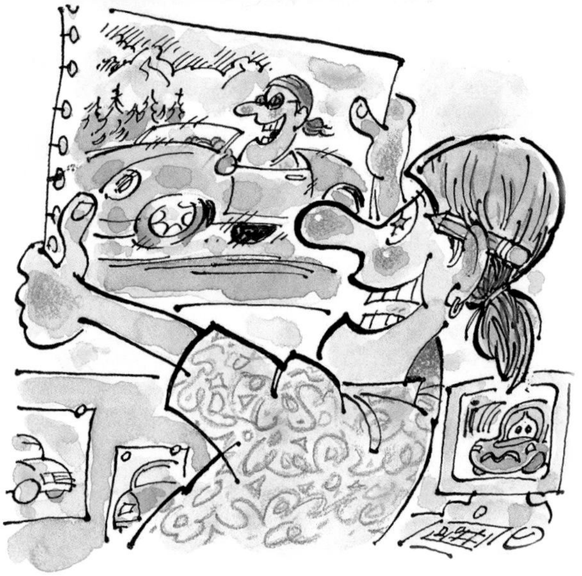

The film's animators sketched over 43,000 designs of vehicles; mostly of the dream cars they planned on purchasing once Disney's $7.4 billion buy-out of Pixar is finalized.

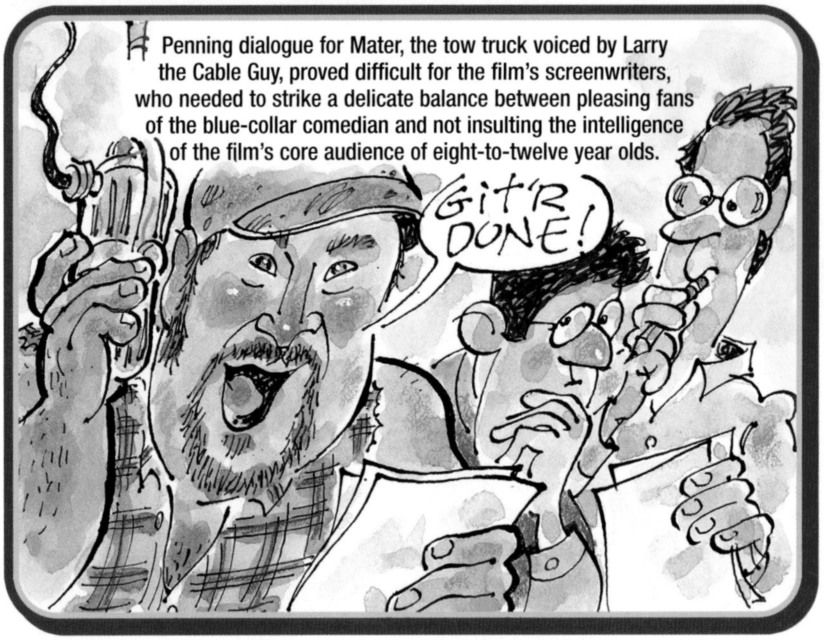
GIT'R DONE!

Penning dialogue for Mater, the tow truck voiced by Larry the Cable Guy, proved difficult for the film's screenwriters, who needed to strike a delicate balance between pleasing fans of the blue-collar comedian and not insulting the intelligence of the film's core audience of eight-to-twelve year olds.

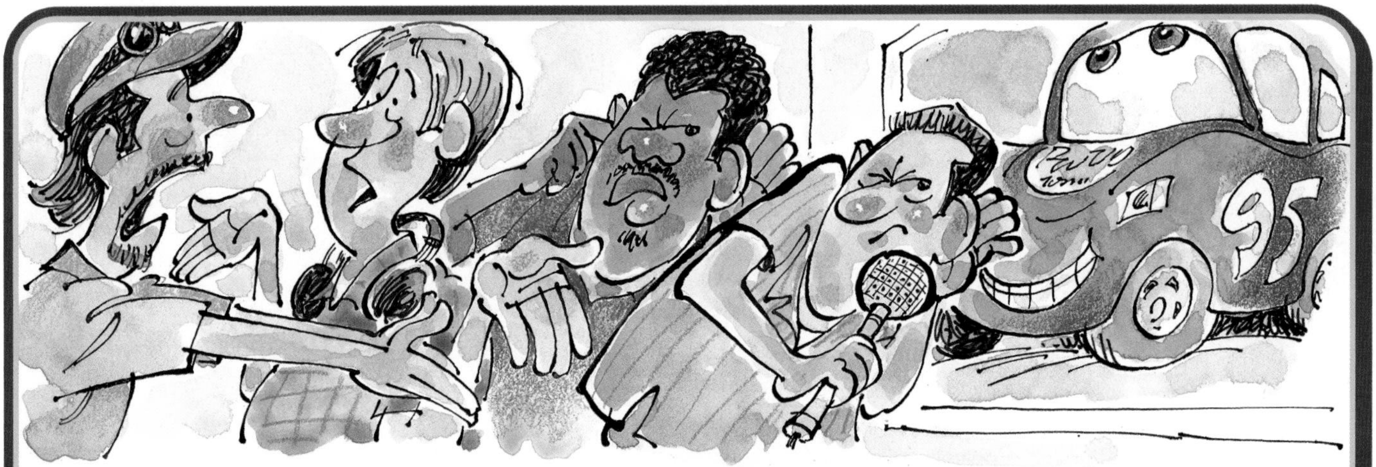
95

The film was set to be released back in November of 2005, but was pushed back after a strange knocking sound was heard on the soundtrack that would, of course, disappear as soon as sound technicians were brought in to find out what was wrong.

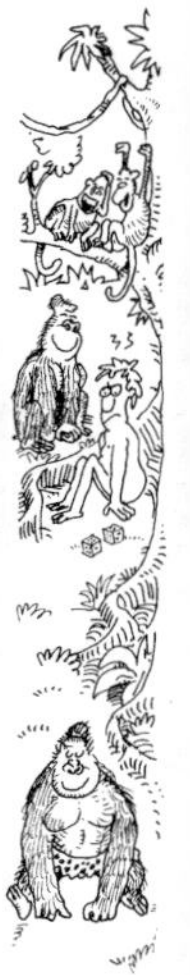

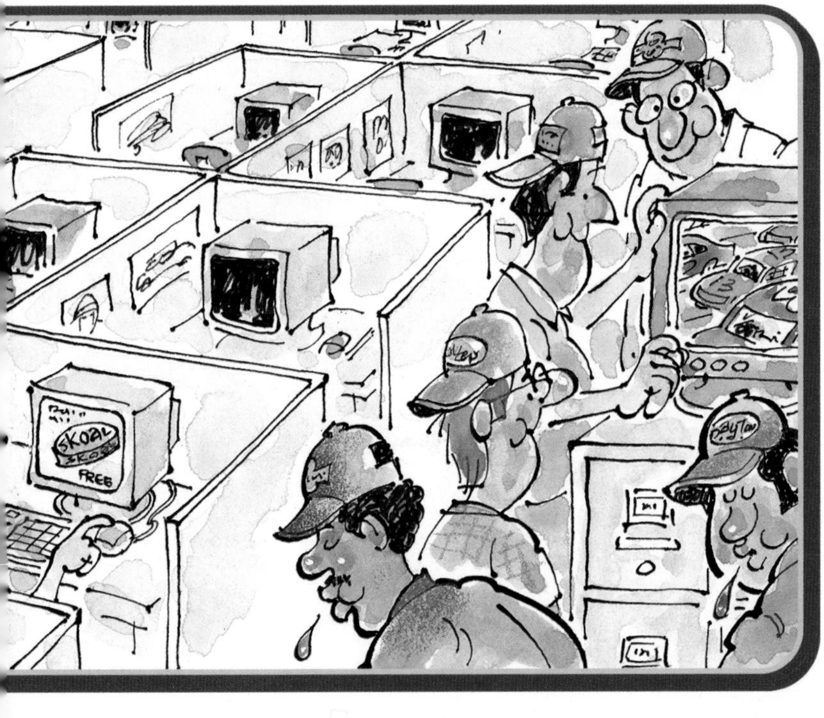
SKOAL
FREE

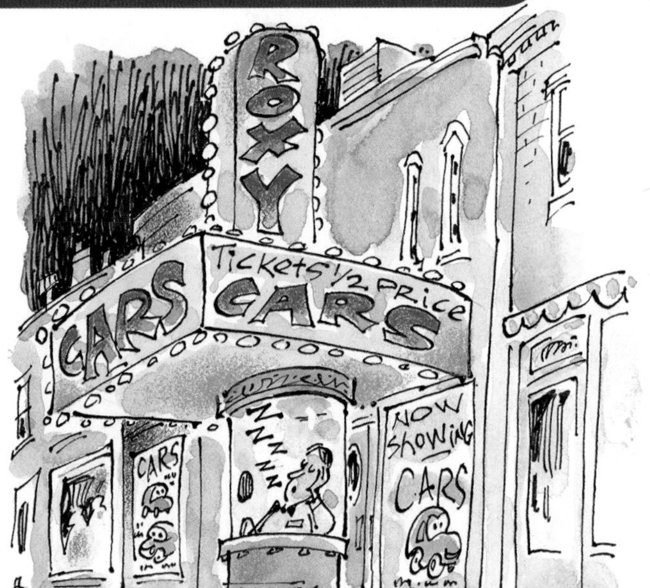
ROXY
Tickets 1/2 Price
CARS
CARS
NOW SHOWING
CARS
CARS
ZZZZ

It's estimated that *Cars* cost over $125 million to produce, however, once the final print was driven off the Pixar lot, its value immediately depreciated by 50%.

The Con

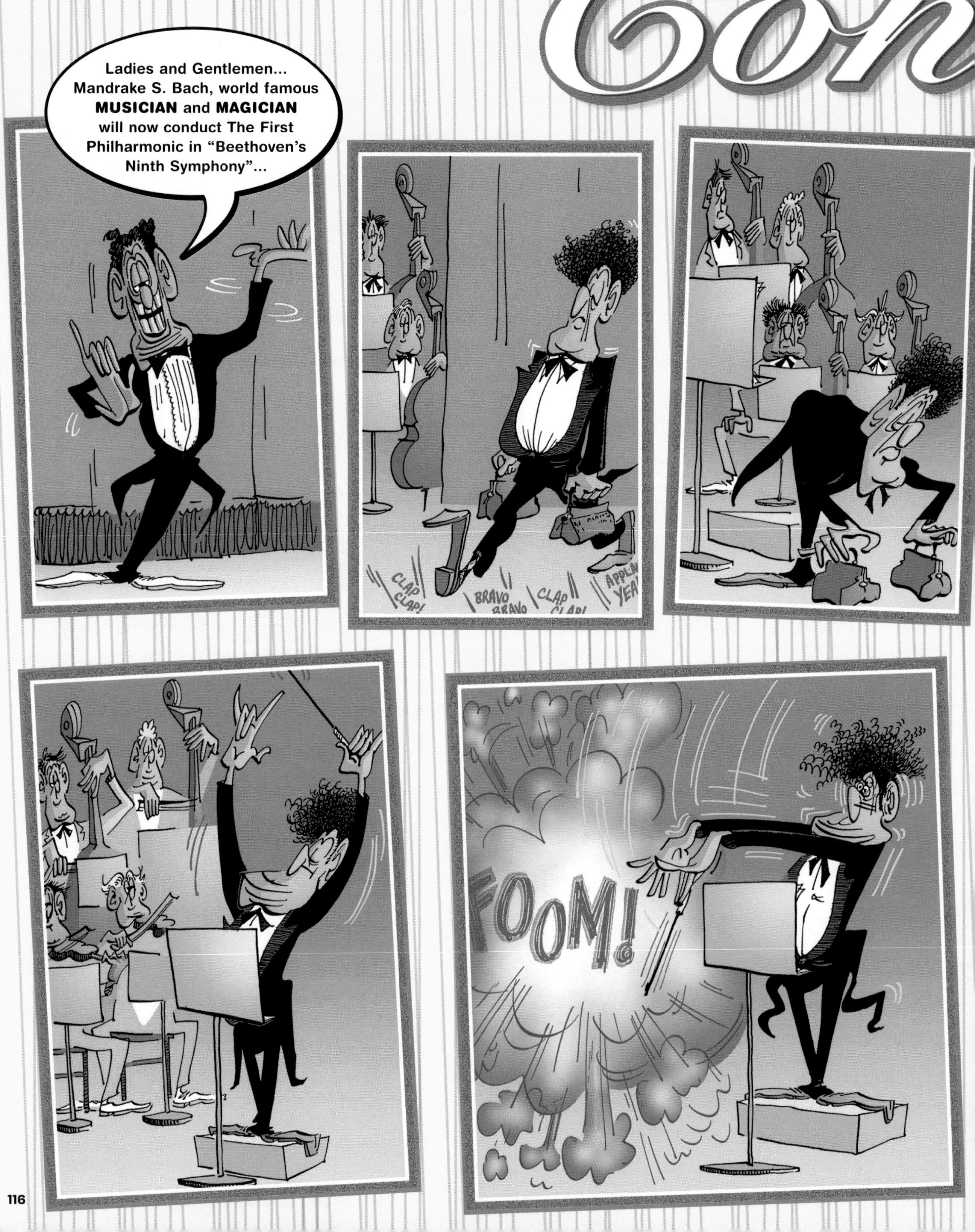

Ladies and Gentlemen... Mandrake S. Bach, world famous **MUSICIAN** and **MAGICIAN** will now conduct The First Philharmonic in "Beethoven's Ninth Symphony"...
CLAP CLAP!
BRAVO
CLAP
FOOM!

cert

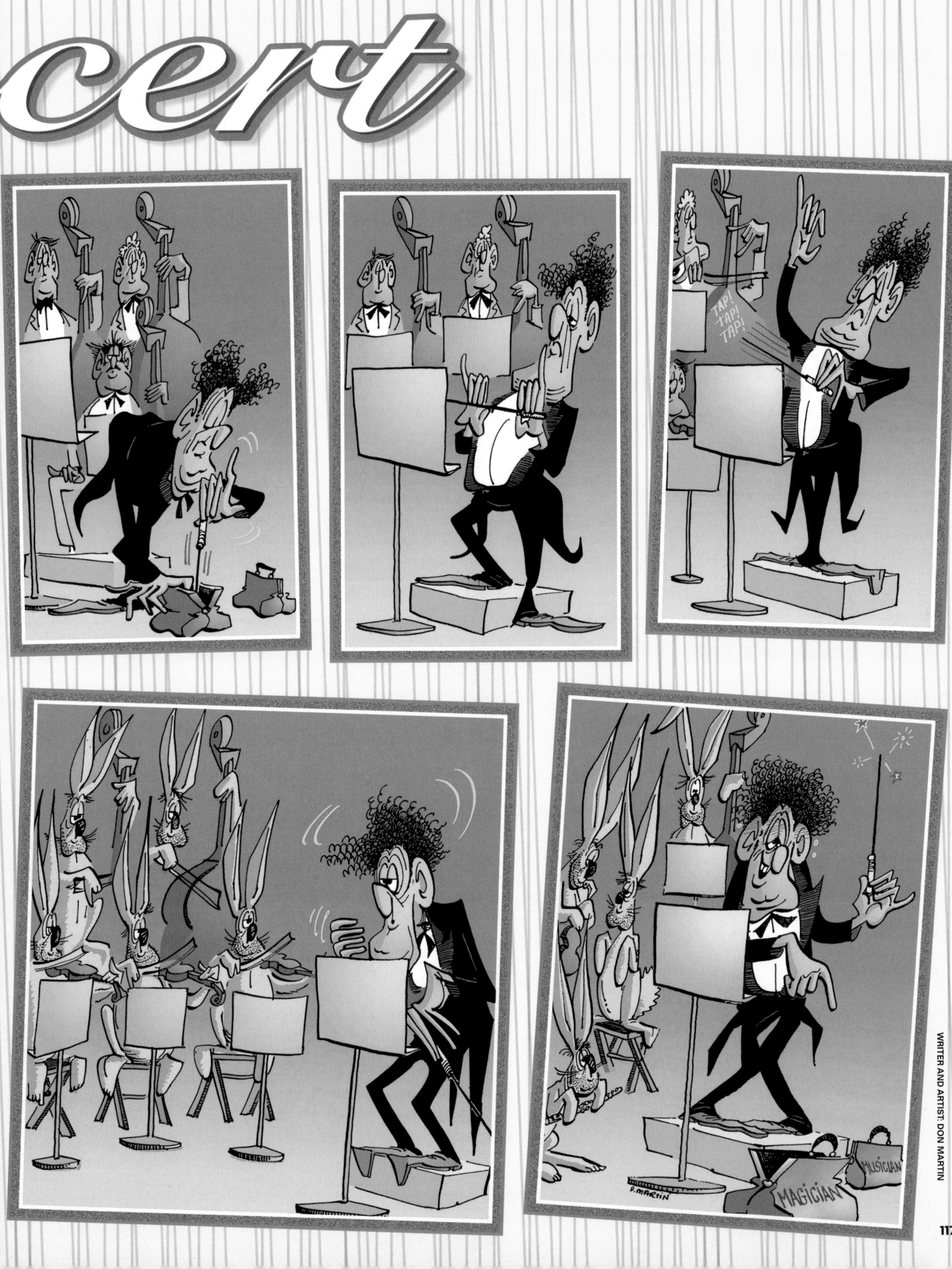
TAP!
TAP!
TAP!
D. MARTIN
MUSICIAN
MAGICIAN

WRITER AND ARTIST: DON MARTIN

ONE DAY ON THE SNOWY PLAINS OF HOTH

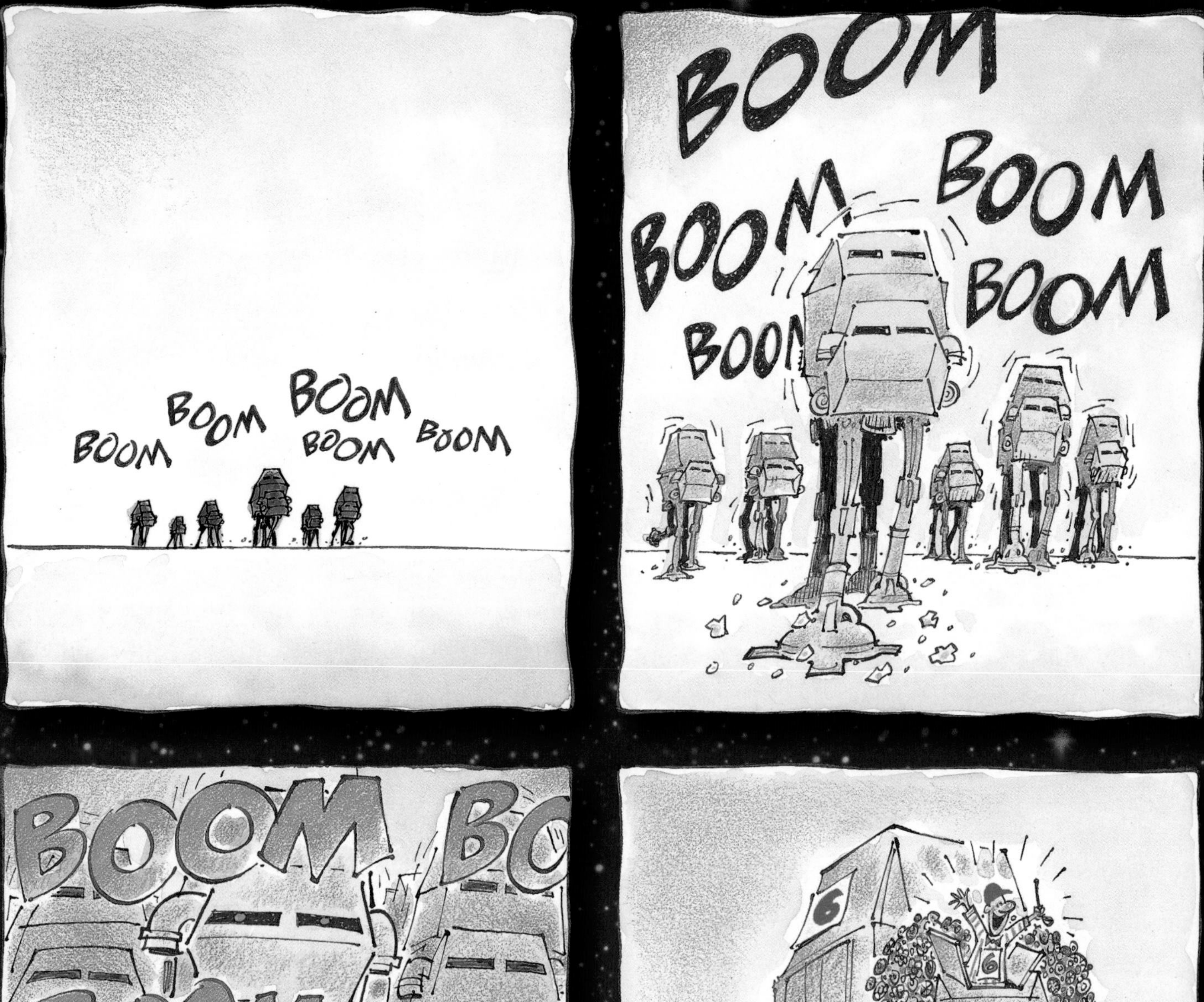
BOOM
BOOM
BOOM
BOOM
BOOM
BOOM
BOOM
BOOM
BOOM
BOOM
BOOM
BOOM
BO
BOOM
BOOM
BOO
WINNER

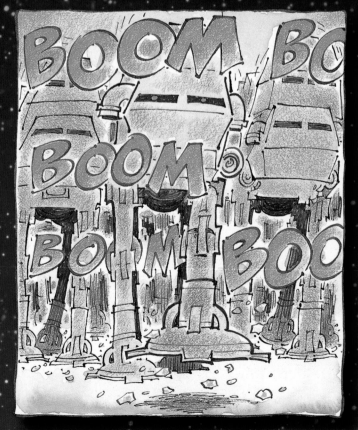

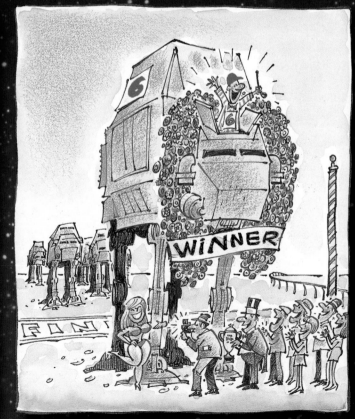

WRITER: DUCK EDWING ARTIST: PAUL COKER

If you like **THIS BOOK**, be sure to check out our **OTHER PUBLICATIONS** shown on the following pages!

Don't be afraid to ask for them by name!

Thank You!

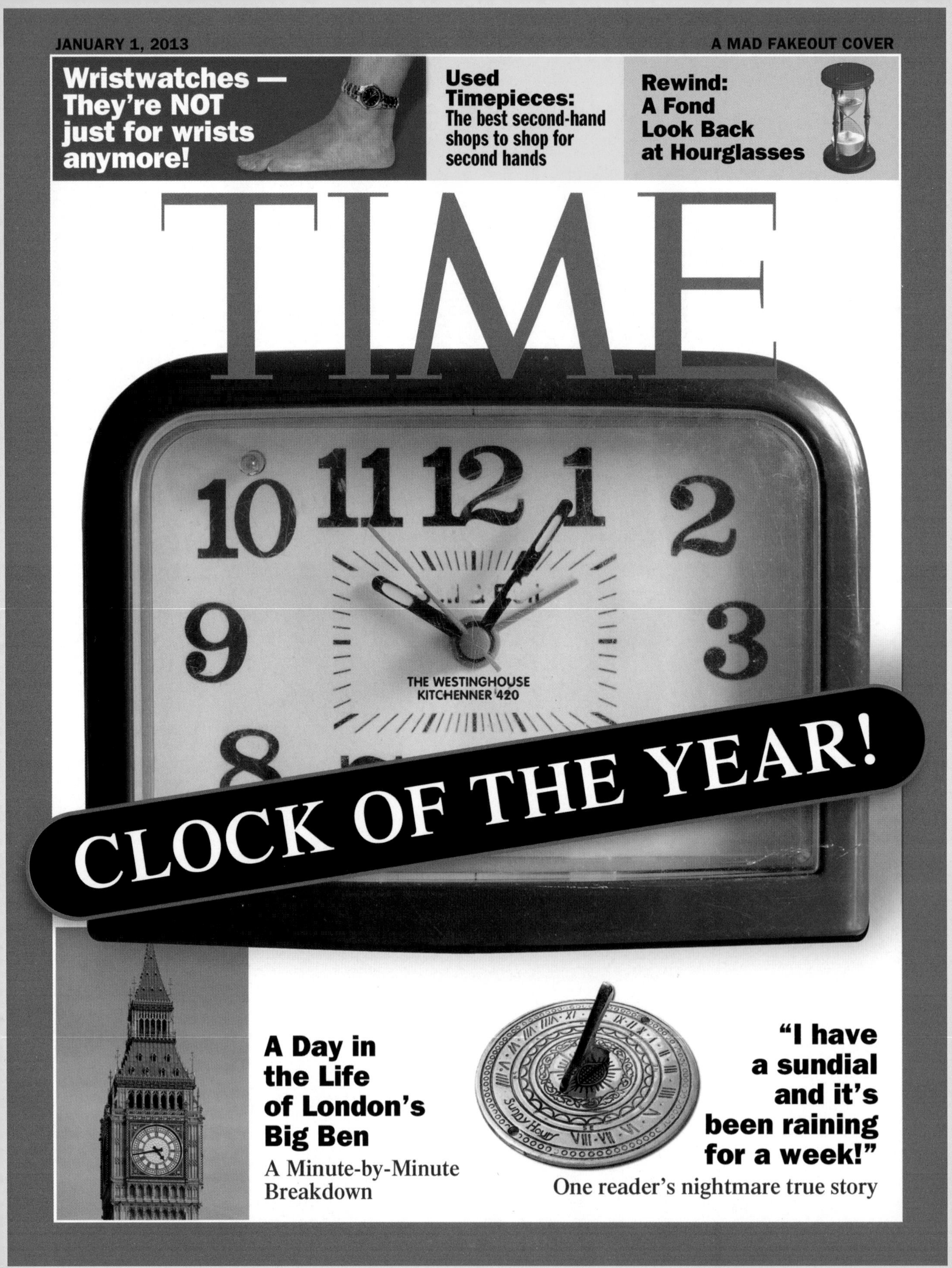
JANUARY 1, 2013
A MAD FAKEOUT COVER
Wristwatches — They're NOT just for wrists anymore!
Used Timepieces: The best second-hand shops to shop for second hands
Rewind: A Fond Look Back at Hourglasses
TIME
THE WESTINGHOUSE KITCHENNER 420
CLOCK OF THE YEAR!
A Day in the Life of London's Big Ben
A Minute-by-Minute Breakdown
"I have a sundial and it's been raining for a week!"
One reader's nightmare true story

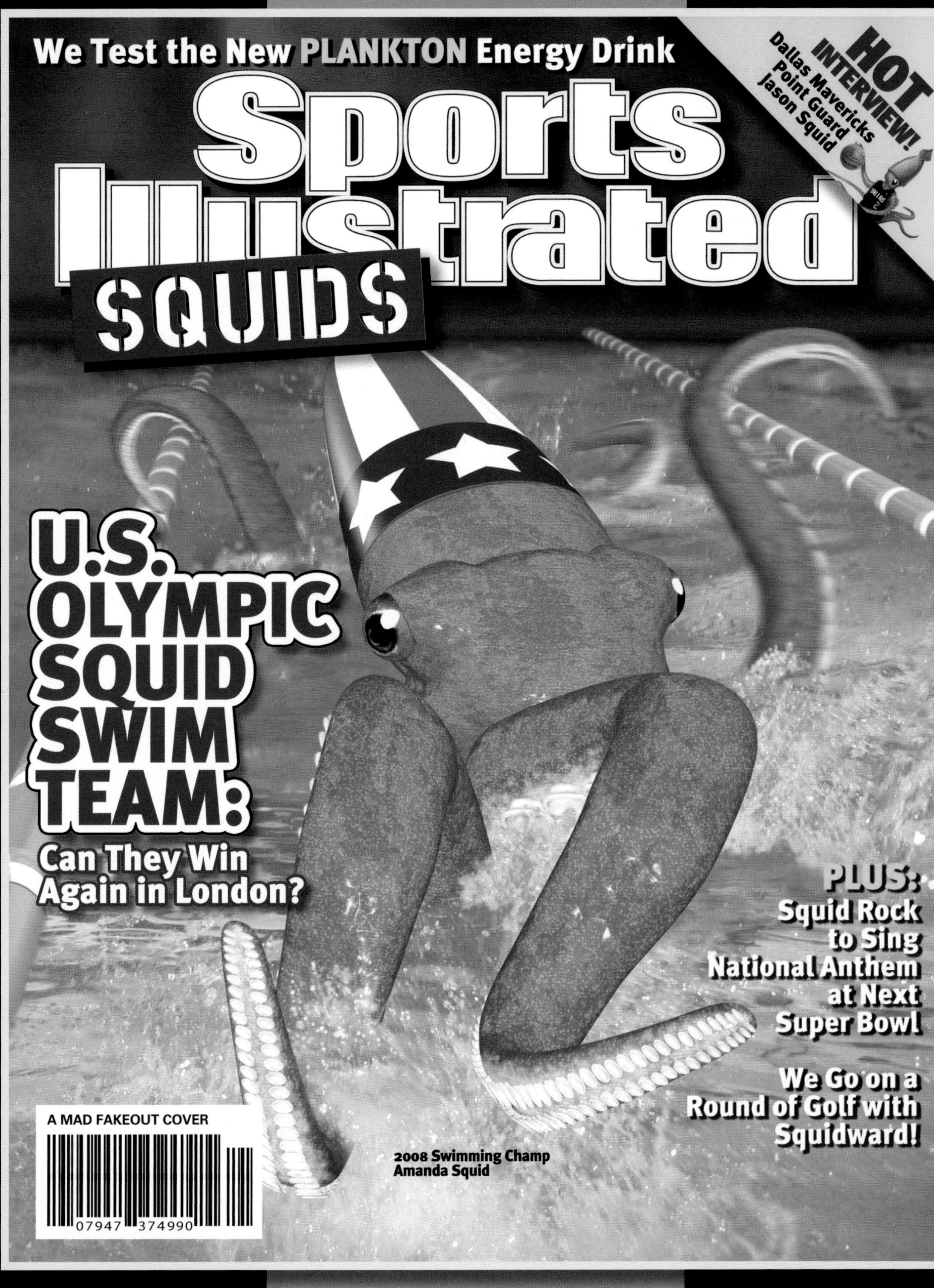
We Test the New PLANKTON Energy Drink
HOT INTERVIEW!
Dallas Mavericks Point Guard Jason Squid
Sports Illustrated
SQUIDS
U.S. OLYMPIC SQUID SWIM TEAM:
Can They Win Again in London?
PLUS:
Squid Rock to Sing National Anthem at Next Super Bowl
We Go on a Round of Golf with Squidward!
2008 Swimming Champ
Amanda Squid
A MAD FAKEOUT COVER
07947 374990

JOKE AND DAGGER DEPT.

SPY VS SPY VS SPY

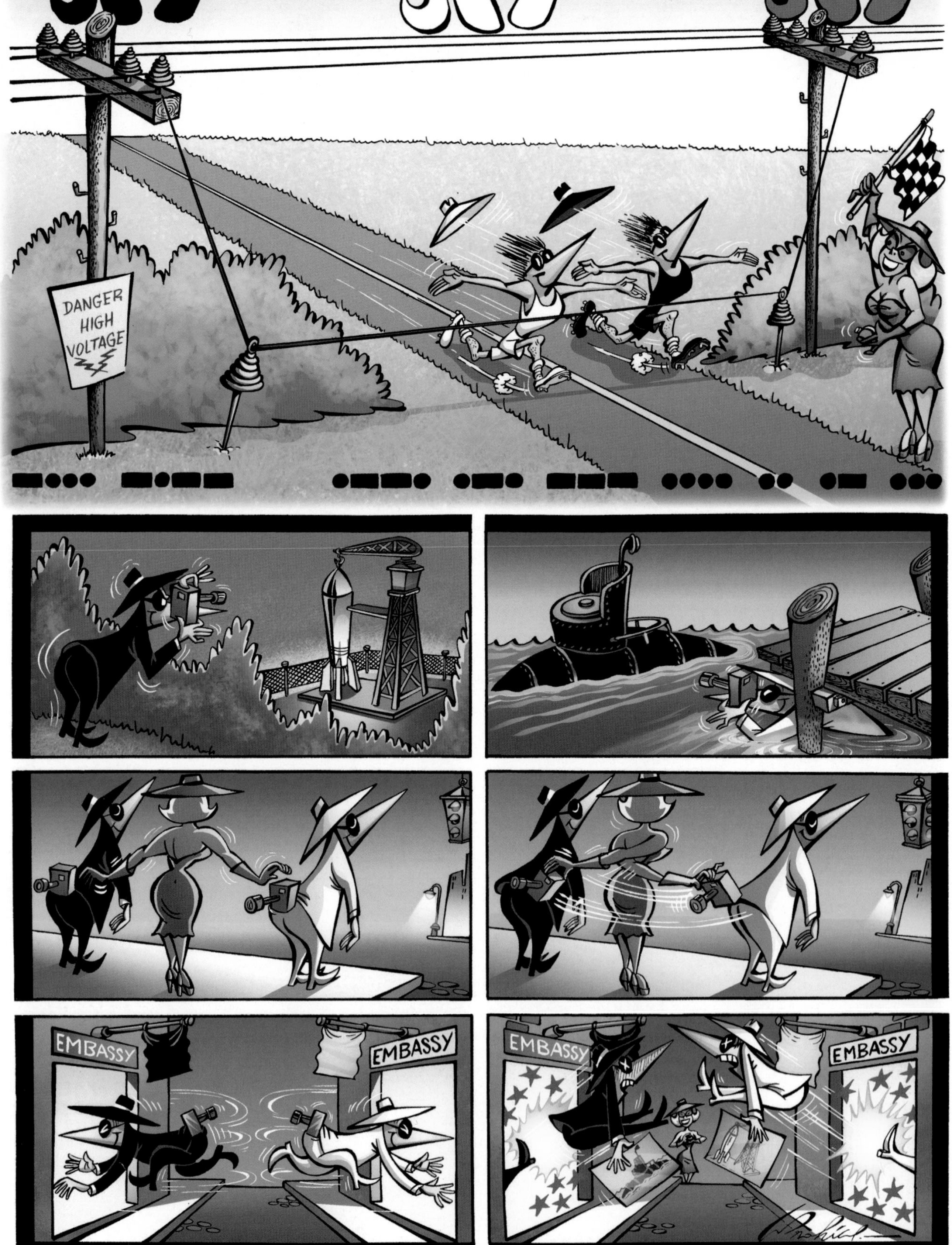
DANGER
HIGH
VOLTAGE
EMBASSY
EMBASSY
EMBASSY
EMBASSY

WRITER AND ARTIST: ANTONIO PROHIAS COLORIST: CARRIE STRACHAN

IF THE STAR WARS GALAXY HAD CLASSIFIED ADS

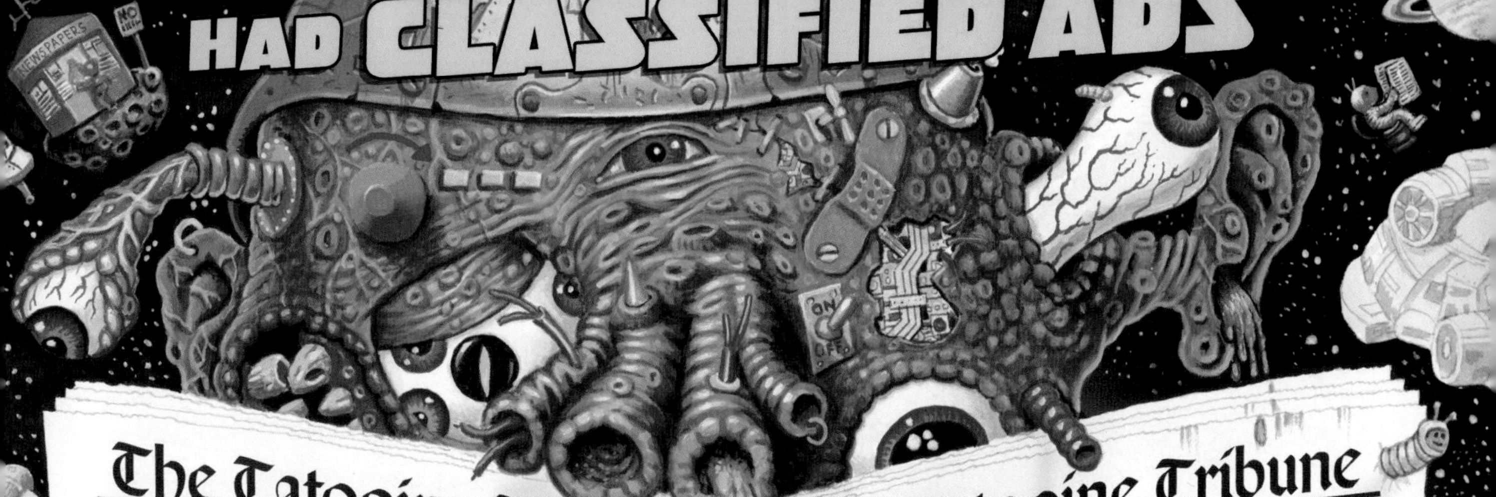
NEWSPAPERS
NO
ON
OFF

The Tatooine Tribune

PERSONALS

Male Seeking Female

YOU were the gal wearing a sexy slave bikini around Jabba's palace. I was the fella who looks like a blue elephant playing the piano. I felt a disturbance in the Force when I saw you. Call me. (Comlink Channel 4) Max Rebo

MESA WANSA BE HAVIN' A GOOD TIME!

Yousa lookin' for de fun? Mesa too! Mesa gooood-lookin' maxi big boss from Naboo. Yousa come to mesa pad so we be havin' a gooood time! Thisa how mesa talk when mesa no workin'!

Contact Supreme Chancellor Palpatine Comlink Channel 8839

Female Seeking Male

HELP ME, OBI-WAN KENOBI, YOU'RE MY ONLY HOPE!

General Kenobi, years ago you served my father in the Clone Wars. Now he begs you to help him in his struggle against the Empire. I regret that I am unable to present my father's request to you in person, but my ship has fallen under attack and I'm afraid my mission to bring you to Alderaan has failed. I have placed information vital to the survival of the Rebellion into the memory systems of this R2 unit. My father will know how to retrieve it. You must see this droid safely delivered to him on Alderaan. This is our most desperate hour. Help me, Obi-Wan Kenobi, you're my only hope. Call me – Leia – Comlink Channel 7008392

Droid Seeking Droid

ARE YOU THE DROID I'M LOOKING FOR?

Single, golden, protocol droid tired of human-cyborg relations, seeks short, dome-headed R2 unit on which to lavish loving abuse and motor oil. "Goldenrod," Comlink 1138

Droid Seeking Droid

BLOOP BLEEP BLOOT BEEP?

Boop Boop Beep Deet Blat! Dirp Weeeee Ding Bweeee Blop? Be-doo, Bwip, Bop, Bloot, Candlelit dinners. Boop Beep Bop Ding Whoop Blot. R2-D2, Comlink Channel 8675309

Misc.

SWC (Single White Clone) seeks same Comlink Channel 8923

SWC (Single White Clone) seeks same Comlink Channel 8924

SWC (Single White Clone) seeks same Comlink Channel 8925

SWC (Single White Clone) seeks same Comlink Channel 8926

You were the astromech droid in the speeder. I was the Jawa with lights in his eyes (literally). We passed at 774th floor of the Big Blue Building in Coruscant. Was there a spark? Or was that your restraining bolt? Let's find out. Comlink Channel 20939

LOST AND FOUND

LOST LIGHTSABER

Standard Jedi issue, blue blade. Still has my severed hand attached from when my dad "accidentally" chopped it off. Last seen falling down Cloud City exhaust shaft. If found, please call L. Skywalker (Comlink 72929)

REWARD!

HAVE YOU SEEN MY TAUNTAUN?

Missing since last Thursday on snowy plains of Hoth. Long snout. Lots of drool. House-broken, with Rebel saddle. Answers to the name "Barry."

REWARD!

Wedge Antilles, Comlink 293002

MERCHANDISE FOR SALE

Vehicles – New and Used

Why WALK the forest when you can ZIP through it? New SPEEDERBIKES at CLOSEOUT PRICES! FREE "Tree Dodging" Seminar w/every purchase ALL NAME BRANDS: Imperial, Rebel, Kawasaki

ENDOR SPEEDERBIKE LEASING AND SALES

Endor Freeway, just opposite Ewok Village

Misc.

HELMETS, HELMETS, HELMETS

Want to strike fear into the hearts of Rebel Scum? Worried your Imperial Wardrobe is missing that certain "something"? Well, we've got just what you need — helmets! That's right! STORMTROOPER HELMETS! CLONE TROOPER HELMETS! BOBA FETT! JANGO FETT! GAMORREAN GUARDS! IMPERIAL GUARDS! TIE FIGHTER PILOTS and DEATH STAR GUNNERS! Even a couple of helmets custom-made for Vader himself! So come on down! We can custom color match your new helmet with your existing armor! Mention this ad!

THE IMPERIAL HELMET STATION

Comlink Channel 83936

BANTHAS, BANTHAS, BANTHAS

My bantha just gave birth to a litter of eight bantha pups and we are giving them away — free! Who wouldn't want these cuddly, 8-foot-tall horned omnivores? Their tendency to eat everything in sight makes them natural garbage disposals. The copious amounts of poodoo make great garden fertilizer, and the frequent scent-marking keeps pesky nunas away. Come by anytime. (Please!)

T. Usken Raider Comlink Channel 288309

The Tatooine Tribune

EDUCATION

ALWAYS FALLING FOR THE JEDI MIND TRICK?

This is the mind training course you are looking for. You will send 50,000 credits to: Jedi Mind Tricks 837 Greedo Way Coruscant X82-87

LEARN THE WAYS OF THE FORCE – DARK & LIGHT

* Levitation * Mind Control * Object Throwing * Choking People Without Touching Them * Foreseeing the Future * Shooting Laser Bolts From Your Fingers *

IMPRESS YOUR FRIENDS! IMPRESS YOUR DATES! GREAT PARTY TRICKS!

For an application: www.ForceAcademy.emp

YOUSA NO SPEAK SO GOOD? SPEAK WELL, YOU DO NOT?

Whether yousa speaksa de Gungun or talk like Yoda you do, we can help you speak better!

EMPIRE SPEECH INSTITUTE Comlink Channel 3648

"Speak or speak not — there is no try!"

EMPLOYMENT

Job Opportunities

TIE FIGHTER PILOTS NEEDED

To fly around space station, get shot at by X-wing Fighters. IMMEDIATE OPENINGS Contact: Grand Moff Tarkin c/o Death Star

X-WING FIGHTER PILOTS NEEDED

To fly around space station, get shot at by TIE Fighters. IMMEDIATE OPENINGS Contact: Gold Leader, Rebel Forces

Job Opportunities

BOUNTY HUNTERS NEEDED

Short-term, part-time, long-term. Must be comfortable with both scum AND villainy. No long hair. Contact: Admiral Piett, c/o Imperial Star Destroyer Executor

APPRENTICES WANTED

Interested in the Dark Side of the Force? Looking for an internship that'll get you college credit? Prominent Sith Lord is looking for a few dedicated students. Benefits include black cloaks, red lightsabers, and the name "Darth." Contact: ~~Supreme Chancellor Palpatine~~ Darth Sidious

HOUSING

Sales

Slimy!? Mudhole!? My home this is! (But yours it can be!) For over 900 years have I lived in this spacious 2BR hut complete with:

- Wood-burning stove
- Roomy 2 1/2' Ceilings
- Swamp-side views
- 800,000 Credits or Best Offer

CONTACT: Dagobah Realty Ask for Yoda

You truly belong among the clouds . . . and now you can be!

CLOUD CITY CONDOMINIUMS

Every apartment features:

- Dining room with killer views
- Living room with killer views
- Imperial torture chamber with killer electro-rack

AVAILABLE NOW

500,000 credits and up! Lando Calrissian Real Estate www.Calrissian.emp

MUSICIANS

CANTINA BAND

3 Piece Cover Band Knows Your Favorite Hits: "Lapti Nek," "Imperial March," "In Da Club," "Chicken Dance" * Weddings * Wookiee Life Day Celebrations * No Bar Mitzvahs * Comlink 399272

JOB TRAINING

LEARN TO TEND BAR

Earn extra $$ while working in exotic locations: Tatooine Cantina Downtown Coruscant Jabba's Sail Barge

* 1- or 2-week training
* Creatures with 6 or more arms a plus!

IMPERIAL BARTENDING INSTITUTE

MEDICAL SERVICES

PSYCHOLOGICAL COUNSELING

Is your father trying to kill you? Does your Wookiee always roar when you ask him to do the simplest tasks? Did that princess you fooled around with turn out to be your sister?

* Individuals * Couples * * Families * Children * Droids *

Dr. R7-D5, Licensed Intergalactic Clinical Therapist Empire Medical Plan Accepted Comlink 239823

HAND REPLACEMENT

I specialize in post-lightsaber injuries – whether it's hands or entire arms, lower bodies, legs, torsos, even heads! Dr. 2-1B, Medical Droid Comlink 227756

MIDI-CHLORIAN SCREENING

Precise midi-chlorian count reveals just how powerful you are with the Force. Find out if you're a Jedi Knight . . . or a Jedi Nobody. Fast, 24-hour turnaround — **CONFIDENTIAL!** www.MidichlorianClinic.jed

TOM BUNK

ARTIST: TOM BUNK

WRITER: DAVID SHAYNE

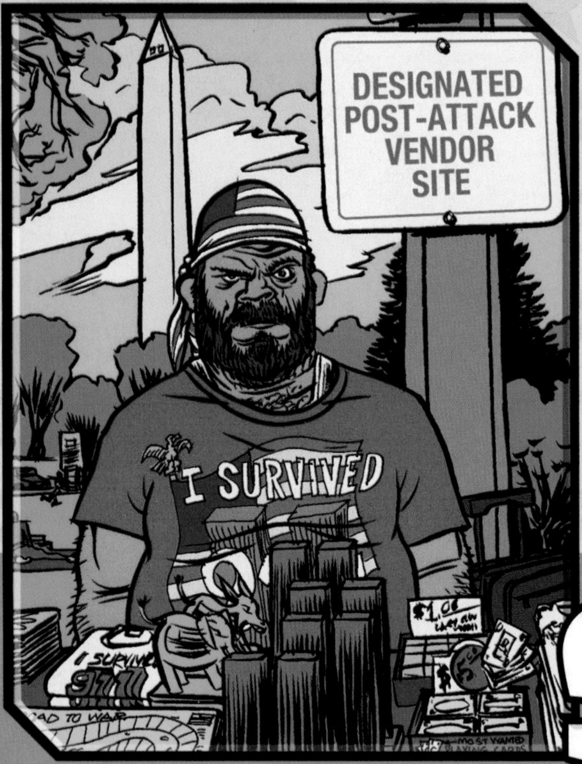
DESIGNATED POST-ATTACK VENDOR SITE
I SURVIVED

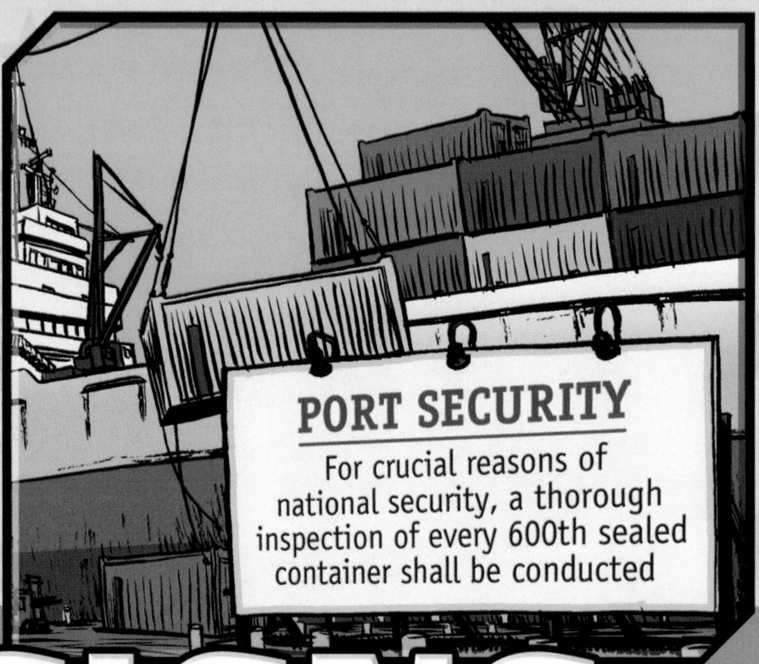
PORT SECURITY
For crucial reasons of national security, a thorough inspection of every 600th sealed container shall be conducted

SIGNS WE NEED IN

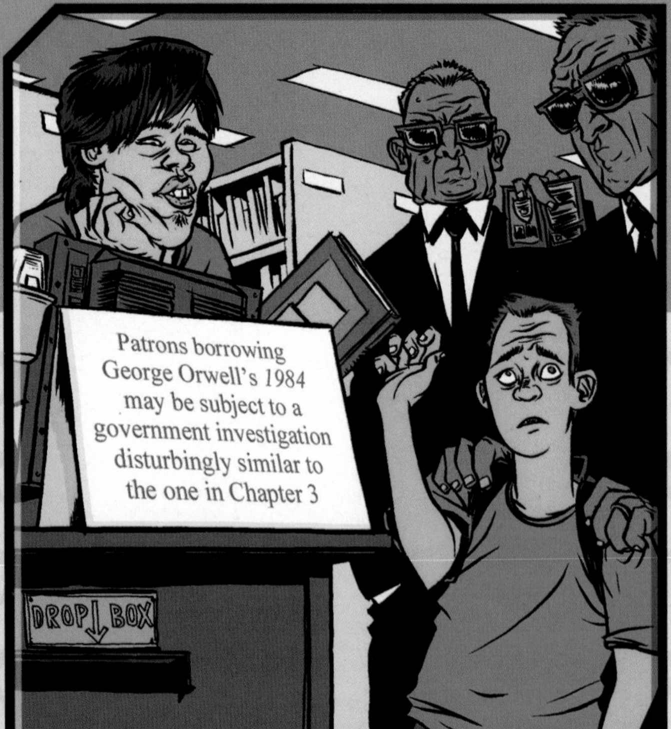
Patrons borrowing George Orwell's *1984* may be subject to a government investigation disturbingly similar to the one in Chapter 3
DROP BOX

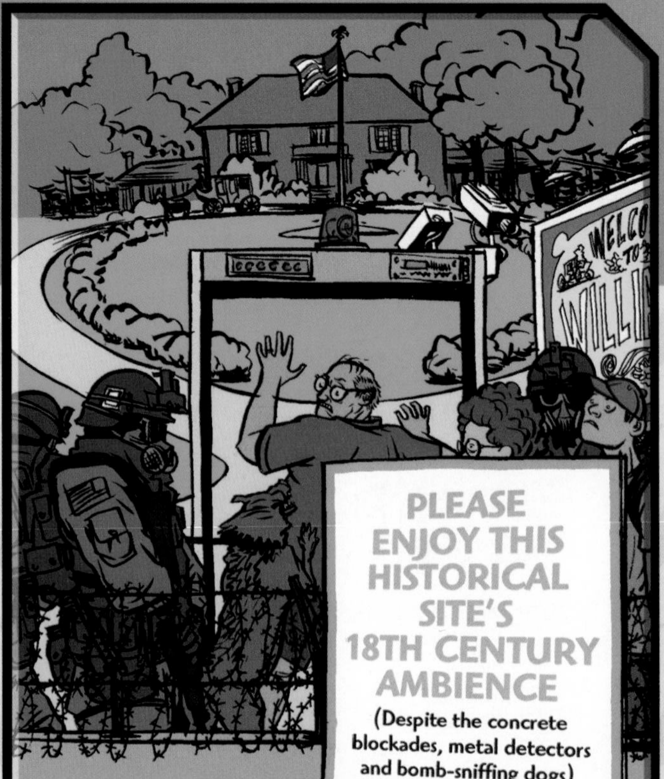
PLEASE ENJOY THIS HISTORICAL SITE'S 18TH CENTURY AMBIENCE
(Despite the concrete blockades, metal detectors and bomb-sniffing dogs)

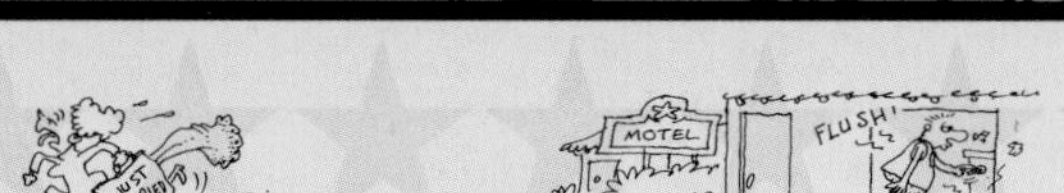
JUST MARRIED
MOTEL
FLUSH!

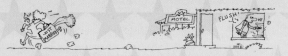

ARTIST: NATHAN FOX WRITER: JACOB LAMBERT

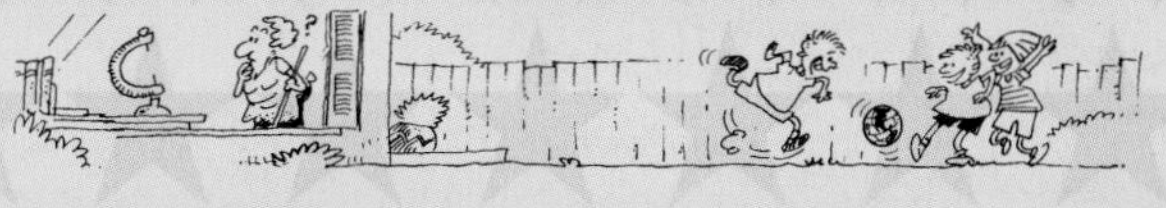

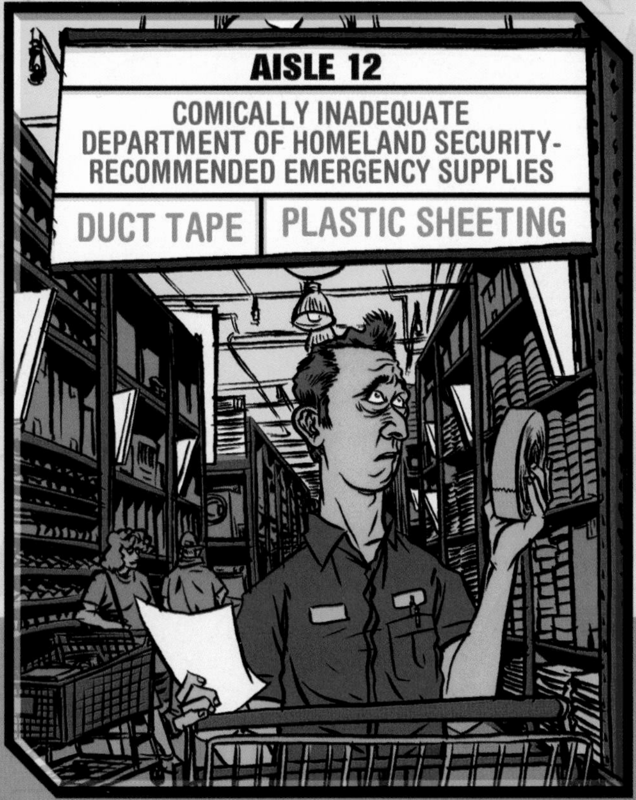
AISLE 12
COMICALLY INADEQUATE DEPARTMENT OF HOMELAND SECURITY-RECOMMENDED EMERGENCY SUPPLIES
DUCT TAPE
PLASTIC SHEETING

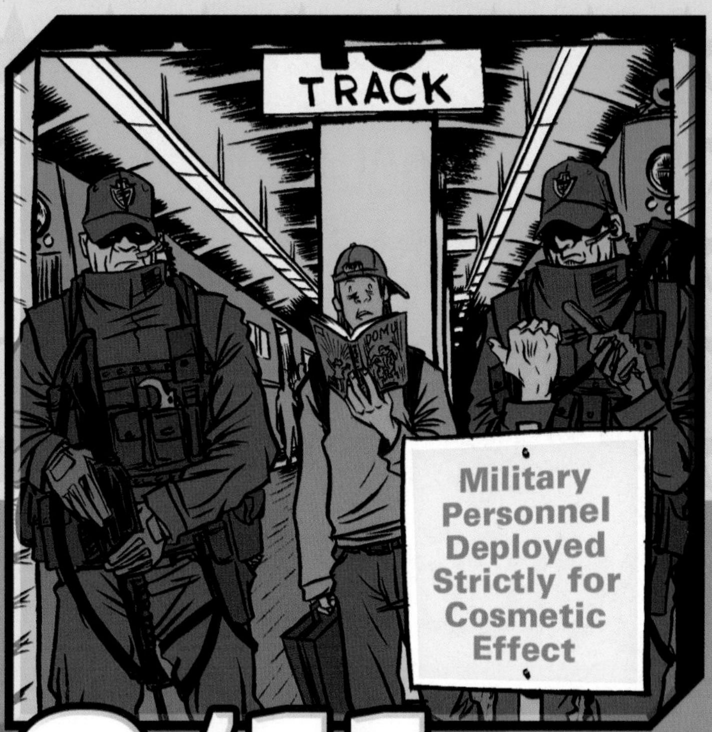
TRACK
Military Personnel Deployed Strictly for Cosmetic Effect

POST 9/11 AMERICA

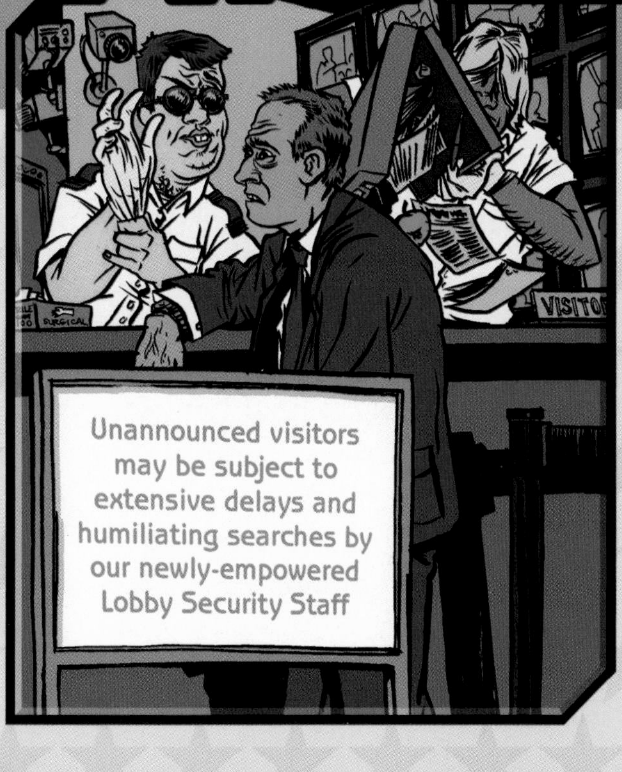
VISITO
Unannounced visitors may be subject to extensive delays and humiliating searches by our newly-empowered Lobby Security Staff

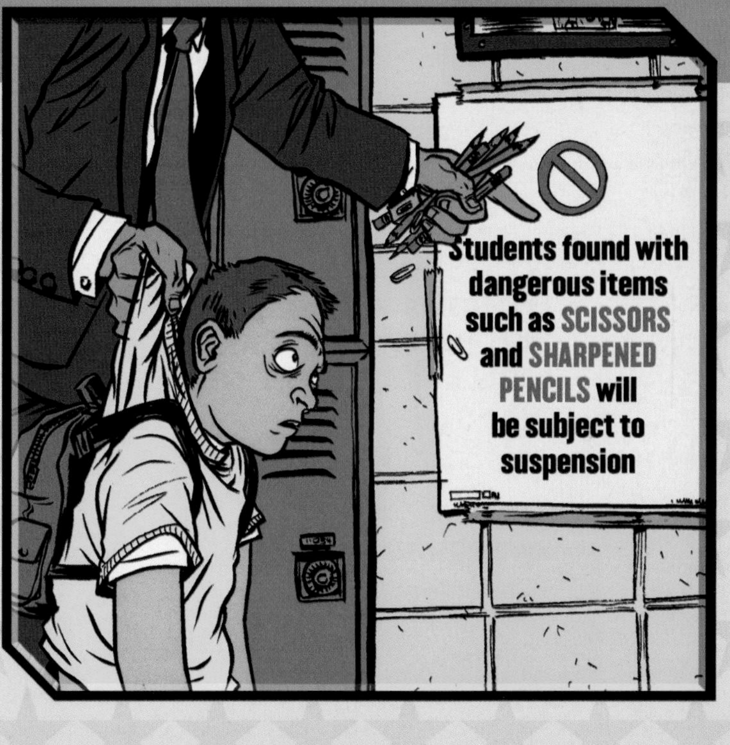
Students found with dangerous items such as SCISSORS and SHARPENED PENCILS will be subject to suspension

Since the dawn of mankind, class clowns have waged the relentless battle against classroom boredom. But being a class clown is harder than it looks — and watching a bad one is more excruciating than actually sitting through that boring lecture about wombat mating rituals! So, before you start cracking jokes, be sure to study:

JOHN CALDWELL'S

BACK-TO-SCHOOL LOOK AT THE COMMON MISCUES, FLUBS & SCREW-UPS OF THE NOVICE CLASS CLOWN

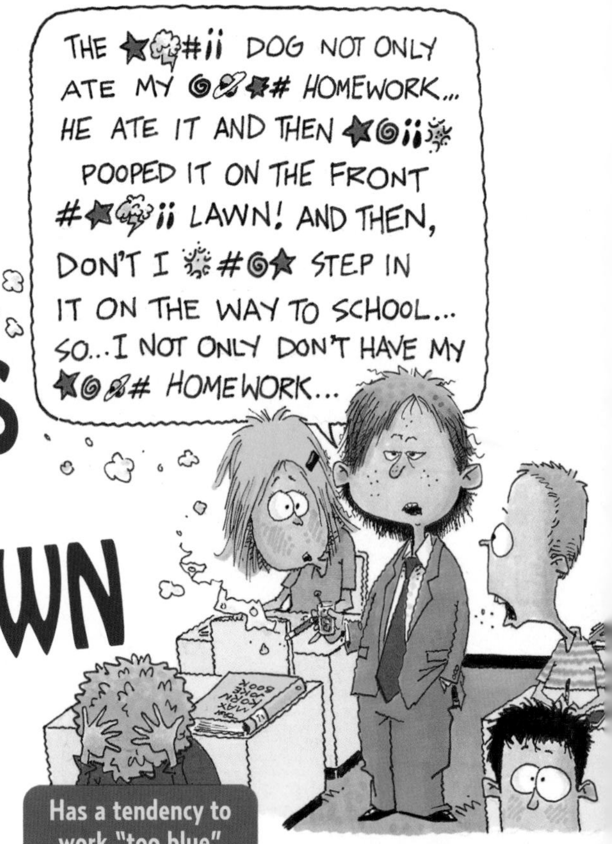
THE ★#ii DOG NOT ONLY ATE MY @# HOMEWORK... HE ATE IT AND THEN ★@ii POOPED IT ON THE FRONT #★ii LAWN! AND THEN, DON'T I #@★ STEP IN IT ON THE WAY TO SCHOOL... SO...I NOT ONLY DON'T HAVE MY ★@# HOMEWORK...

Has a tendency to work "too blue"

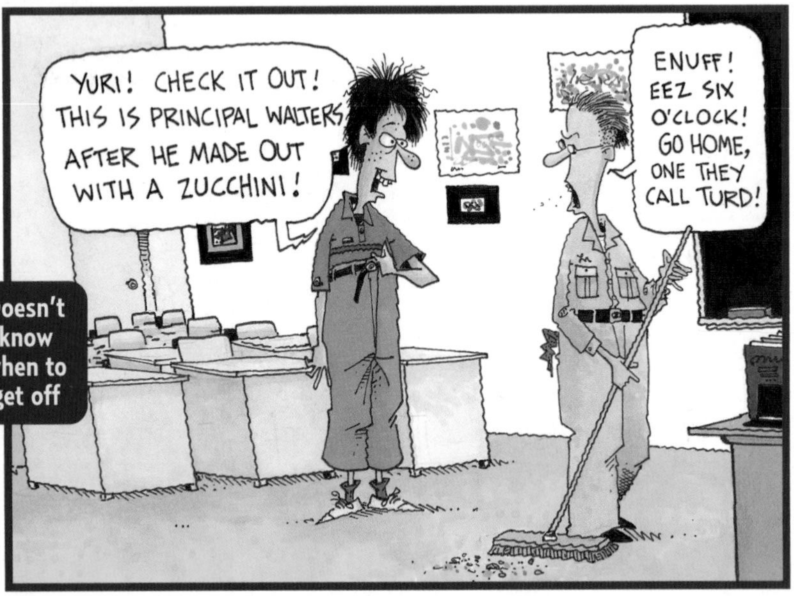
YURI! CHECK IT OUT! THIS IS PRINCIPAL WALTERS AFTER HE MADE OUT WITH A ZUCCHINI!
ENUFF! EEZ SIX O'CLOCK! GO HOME, ONE THEY CALL TURD!

Doesn't know when to get off

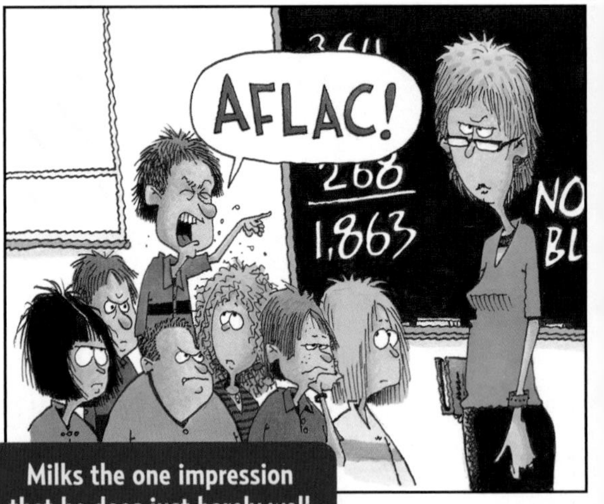
AFLAC!
268
1,863

Milks the one impression that he does just barely well enough to be recognizable

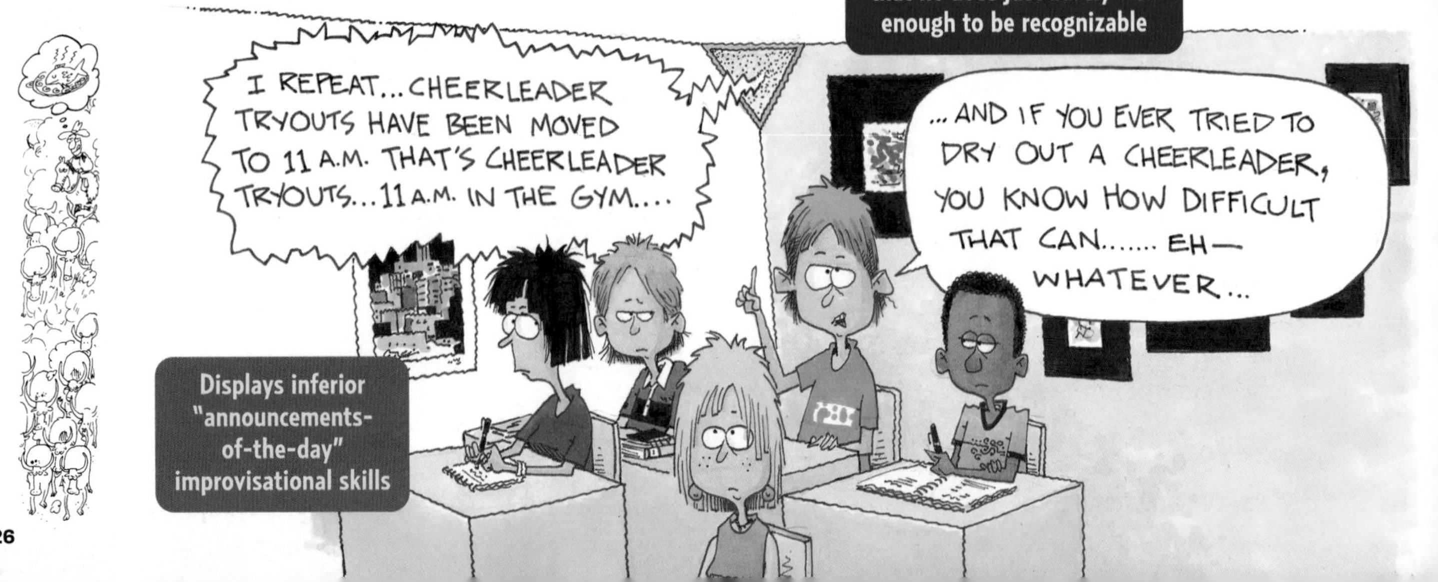
I REPEAT... CHEERLEADER TRYOUTS HAVE BEEN MOVED TO 11 A.M. THAT'S CHEERLEADER TRYOUTS... 11 A.M. IN THE GYM....
...AND IF YOU EVER TRIED TO DRY OUT A CHEERLEADER, YOU KNOW HOW DIFFICULT THAT CAN....... EH— WHATEVER...

Displays inferior "announcements-of-the-day" improvisational skills

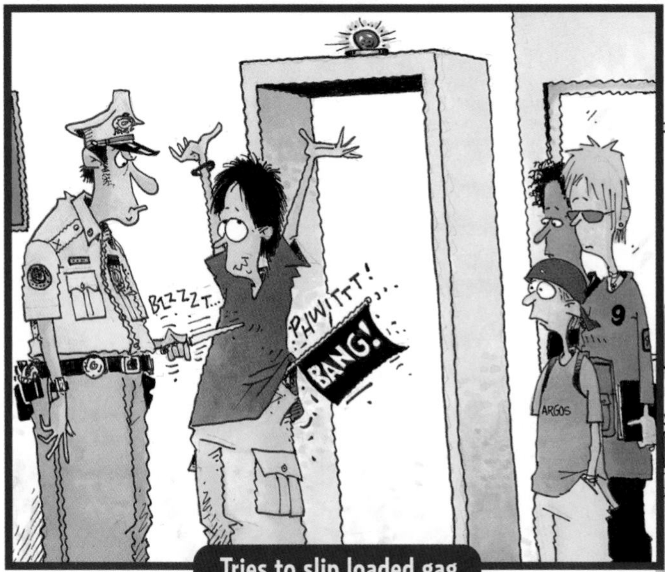
BIZZZT...
PHWITTT!
BANG!
ARGOS
9

Tries to slip loaded gag weapons past security

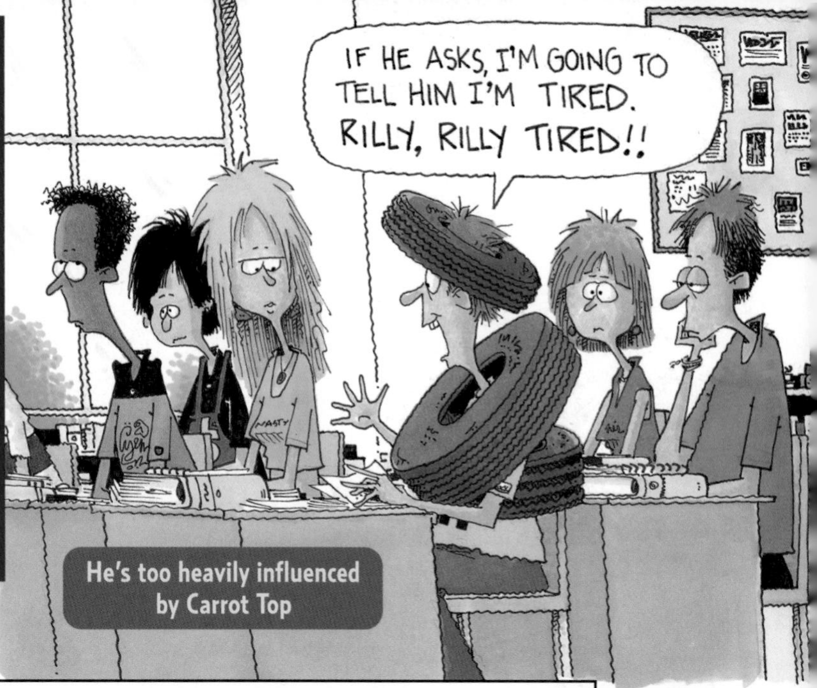
IF HE ASKS, I'M GOING TO TELL HIM I'M TIRED. RILLY, RILLY TIRED!!
NASTY

He's too heavily influenced by Carrot Top

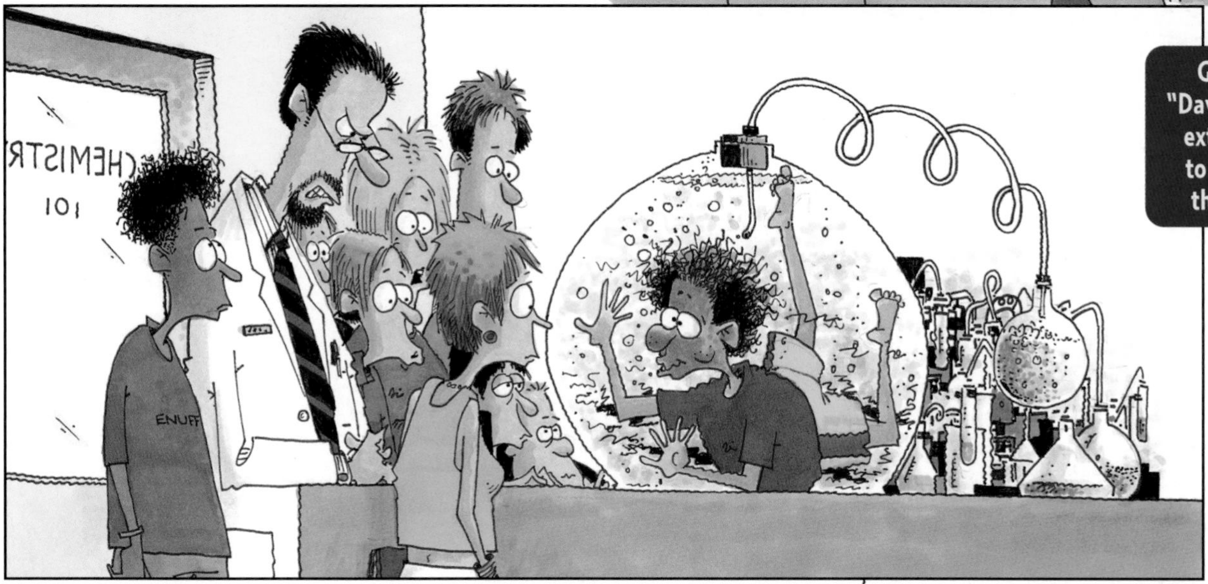
101
ENUFF

Goes to "David Blaine extremes" to disrupt the class

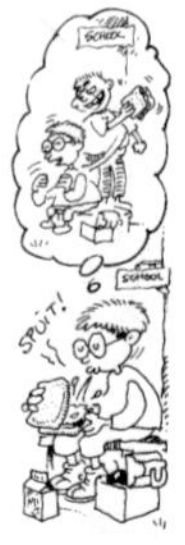

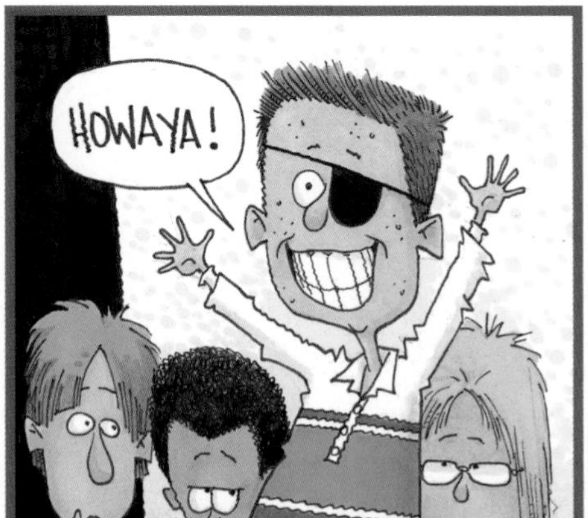
HOWAYA!

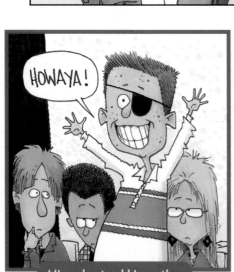

Misunderstood his mother and thinks it's *always* funny when somebody puts out an eye

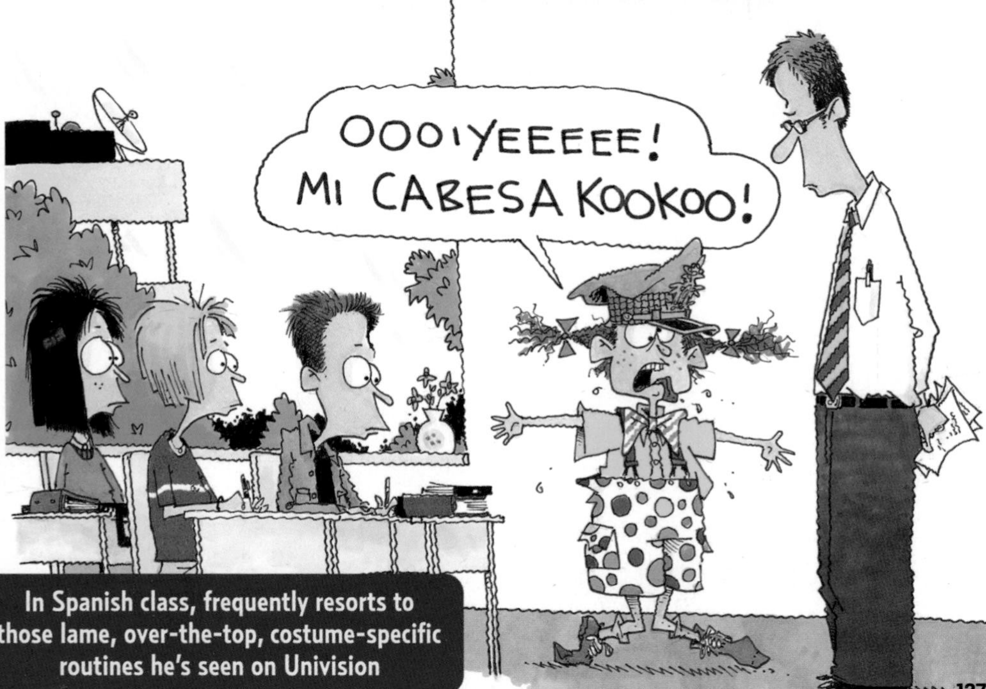
OOOIYEEEEE! MI CABESA KOOKOO!

In Spanish class, frequently resorts to those lame, over-the-top, costume-specific routines he's seen on Univision

Subscribe to MAD!

You'll Never Miss An Issue... and Neither Will Your Bird!

6 Issues
for only $19.⁹⁹
(Cheep! Cheep! Cheep!)

Flock to madmagazine.com
or call 1-800-4 MAD MAG
6 2 3   6 2 4

Mon-Fri 6 a.m.-8 p.m.   Sat 7 a.m.-4 p.m.   Sun 8 a.m.-4 p.m.   Eastern Time
$19.99 offer valid for U.S. and Canada orders only! Foreign orders please add $10.

If under 18,
please be sure
to get your
parrot's
permission!